Preaching that Grabs the Heart

A Rhetorical-Stylistic Study of the Chichewa Revival Sermons of Shadrack Wame

Ernst R. Wendland

with a foreword by Dr. Kenneth R. Ross

A Kachere Monograph

CLAIM

Copyright 2000 Ernst R. Wendland

All rights reserved. No part of this publication may be reproduced, stored in a retrieval system, or transmitted in any form or by any means, electronic, mechanical, photocopying, recording or otherwise, without prior permission from the publishers.

Published by the
Christian Literature Association in Malawi (CLAIM),
P.O. Box 503, Blantyre, Malawi
ISBN 9990816298

ISSN 1025-0956

Cover illustration: Shadrack Wame in Zomba by Amy Elizabeth Jones
Layout and editorial assistance: Amy Elizabeth Jones
Index: Mercy Mpaso

Printed in Malawi by Assemblies of God Press, P.O. Box 5749, Limbe

Preaching that Grabs the Heart

A Rhetorical-Stylistic Study of the Chichewa Revival Sermons of Shadrack Wame

Ernst R. Wendland

with a foreword by Dr. Kenneth R. Ross

Kachere Monograph no. 11

CLAIM
Christian Literature Association in Malawi
Blantyre

2000

Kachere Series,
P.O. Box 1037, Zomba, Malawi
Email: kachere@sdnp.org.mw

This book is part of the Kachere Series, a range of books on theology and religion in Malawi. Other Kachere Monographs published so far are:

Andrew C. Ross, *Blantyre Mission and the Making of Modern Malawi*

Harry Langworthy, *"Africa for the African": The Life of Joseph Booth*

Isabel Apawo Phiri, *Women, Presbyterianism and Patriarchy: Religious Experience of Chewa Women in Central Malawi*

Matthew Schoffeleers, *Religion and the Dramatization of Life: Spirit Beliefs and Spirit Possession in Central and Southern Malawi*

J.C. Chakanza, *Voices of Preachers in Protest: The Ministry of Two Malawian Prophets: Elliot Kamwana and Wilfred Gudu*

Kenneth R. Ross (ed.), *God, People and Power in Malawi: Democratization in Theological Perspective*

Klaus Fiedler, *Christianity and African Culture. Conservative German Protestant Missionaries in Tanzania 1900-1940*

Other Kachere title by the same author:

Buku Loyera – An Introduction to the New Chichewa Bible Translation

The Kachere Series is the publications arm of the Department of Theology and Religious Studies of the University of Malawi.

Series Editors: J.C. Chakanza, F.L. Chingota, Klaus Fiedler, P.A. Kalilombe, Hilary Mijoga, Fulata L. Moyo, Martin Ott, Isabel Apawo Phiri

IN APPRECIATION

To my Father, Prof. E.H. Wendland:
One of the best preachers and teachers
whom I have had the privilege ($\chi\alpha\rho\iota\varsigma$) of learning from.

*Koma ife timalalika Khristu
amene adapachikidwa pa mtanda.
Kwa Ayuda mau amenewa ndi okhumudwitsa,
pamene kwa anthu a mitundu ina mauwa ndi opusa.
Koma amene Mulungu adawaitana,
kaya ndi Ayuda kaya ndi Agriki,
onsewo amazindikira
kuti Khristu ndi mphamvu ya Mulungu ndiponso nzeru ya Mulungu.*
(1 Akorinto 1:23-24, *Buku Loyera*)

---

*Pamaso pa Mulungu ndi pamaso pa Khristu Yesu,
amene adzaweruza anthu onse, amoyo ndi akufa omwe,
ndipo potamanda kubwera kwake ndi ufumu wake wa Khristuyo
ndikukulamula ndithu kuti uzilalika mau a Mulungu molimbikira,
pa nthawi imene anthu akuwafuna, ngakhalenso pamene sakuwafuna.
Uziwalozera zolakwa zao, uziwadzudzula, uziwalimbitsa mtima,
osalephera kuwaphunzitsa moleza mtima kwenikweni.*
(2 Timoteo 4:1-2, *Buku Loyera*)

Contents

	Foreword by Dr. K.R. Ross	8
	Series Editors' Preface	10
	Preface	12
1.	Preaching in Chichewa	17
	What Do the Revival Preachers Preach About?	17
	On the Power and Prominence of *Pathos* and *Pronunciatio*	26
2.	The Inductive Art of Participatory Preaching	37
	A Chewa Tale: Konza kapansi kuti kam'mwamba katsike	37
	The Indigenous Model of Oral Tradition	39
	Induction versus Deduction: What's the Difference?	44
	Seven Prominent Inductive Devices	52
	Application of the Inductive Method	62
	Summary: Five Basic Homiletical Steps	76
3.	Ten Verbal Power Tactics for Rhetorical Proclamation in Chichewa Preaching	81
	Introduction: The Word at Work	81
	Narrative Preference	83
	Personal Exemplification	88
	Traditional Allusion	93
	Dramatic Delivery	98
	Affective Appeal	104
	Evocative Description	109
	Strategic Reiteration	116
	Verbal Intensification	121
	Idiomatic Figuration	124
	Audience Involvement	129
	The Rhetoric of Inductive Discourse Organization	140
4.	Induction in Detail: Wame in Action	149
	Introduction to the Annotation	149

	"No Shortcuts to Heaven: Building Your House on Christ, the Rock!" (SW5)	151
	"Are You Ready to Go? Preparing for the Trip to Heaven" (SW37)	166
	"Christian Offerings – Storing up Treasures in Heaven" (SW40)	184
5.	Summary and Assessment: Induction – Some Pros and Cons	224
	Strong on Contextual Exemplification, Weak on Textual Exposition	224
	Conclusion: Five Proposals	231
6.	Appendix: "My Testimony" by Shadrack Jonas Wame	239
	Further Comments by aWame on Preaching	246
	Appendix B	252
	Palibe Chidule Kupita Kumwamba (SW5)	252
	Kukonzekera Ulendo Wopita Kumwamba (SW37)	262
	Undido wa Mkhristu (SW 40)	271
Bibliography		295
Index		301

Foreword

No scholar engaged with the African situation today could fail to take account of the extraordinary impact of Christian faith at all levels of society. Where many do fall down, however, is in taking African Christianity as a "given" and pushing on quickly to consider its social, political, economic or ecological implications. They thus dodge the more fundamental scholarly challenge of coming to terms with the nature and character of African Christian faith. Until we are more fully aware of how the faith is understood at the popular level and how it functions in personal, domestic and communal life, our efforts to explain the influence of Christianity in Africa today are likely to remain superficial. When we do approach this task, we find that the Christian faith is expressed in many ways. Song, dance, service and discipline invite exploration. Yet none are more central to the Christian movement in Africa today than preaching. If one had to choose a single figure to represent African experience in the 20th century, the impassioned preacher would certainly be a contender. This study of preaching offered by Ernst Wendland is therefore a most welcome addition to the literature on Christianity in Malawi.

All the more so, since Wendland has ventured to consider a Christian movement which has received little attention compared to the "mainline" churches which have produced their own scholars or the African Instituted Churches which attracted the anthropologist and sociologist. Since the 1970s, "revival" meetings or crusades have been a regular and popular feature of urban life in Malawi. Often organised on a "para-church" basis, such events have been instrumental in bringing a gripping presentation of the Christian message to large sections of the urban population. The revival movements have built up their own *genre* which is very well illustrated by the sermons of Shadrack Wame on which this book is based. A love for this distinctive brand of Christian faith has sometimes led its followers to form new churches in which its evangelical tones are given constant emphasis. More often, those influenced and inspired by crusades have remained in their existing churches but have brought fresh devotion and new enthusiasm to their Christian life and witness. Wendland's study of Wame's sermons gives us the opportunity to glimpse into the heart of this significant contemporary Christian movement.

As well as providing a valuable case study of a contemporary Malawian evangelist, this book will be particularly useful for anyone concerned with teaching or learning homiletics and seeking to earth their study in the African context. Wendland offers illuminating lines of analysis which lead to a mature appreciation of what is involved in the event of the preaching and reception of such sermons. The rigour with which the analytical enquiry is pursued does not take away, however, from the sympathetic portrayal of the preacher himself. Many are the African historians who have wished that they had access to better accounts of the life and work of the teachers and evangelists who were on the frontline of Christian advance in the late 19th and early 20th centuries. Many, both in the present and in the future, will have reason to be thankful to Ernst Wendland for not only introducing us to a remarkable evangelist of the late 20th century but also enabling us to critically consider the style and content of his preaching.

Kenneth R. Ross
General Secretary, Church of Scotland Board of World Mission (formerly Professor of Theology, Chancellor College, University of Malawi)

Series Editors' Preface

The Kachere Series is an initiative of the Department of Theology and Religious Studies at the University of Malawi. It aims to promote the emergence of a body of literature which will enable students and others to engage critically with religion in Malawi, its social impact and the theological questions which it raises. An important starting point lies with the publication of essays and theses which until now have been inaccessible to all but the most dedicated specialist. It is also hoped, however, that the development of theological scholarship in Malawi will stimulate the writing of many new books. General works with popular appeal can be published as *Kachere Books*, with Mambo Press in Gweru. Documents and essays, which are of value as sources for the study of religion in Malawi, can be published as *Kachere Texts*, with CLAIM in Blantyre. It is in the third branch of the series, known as *Kachere Monographs*, that full-length academic treatises are published. Only the fruits of sound primary research which meet rigorous academic standards will be accepted for publication in this prestigious branch of the Series. The Editors intend the Monographs to contribute substantially to the growth of a body of knowledge in the area of theology and religious studies in Malawi. As important resources for study related to this field, we are confident that they will come to be prized not only within Malawi but in every academic centre concerned with religion and society in Africa.

The Bible, preaching and conversion are in the very centre of the church in Malawi, and not only there. As Kachere editors we therefore welcome this study of popular and evangelistic preaching, centred on the person of Shadrack Wame, not a trained theologian, but one of the best known evangelistic speakers in the country, whose preaching changed many a heart. Though it would surely not be wise to imitate Shadrack Wame's style and personality, any student of preaching – or public speaking for that – may do well to learn from Shadrack Wame's preaching that grabs the heart. It is therefore a book for those who prepare themselves to be preachers, and for all who want to study popular preaching in Malawi.

It may be incidental or not that this book on preaching comes after Dr Wendland's book on the Bible, introducing the Buku Loyera, the new meaning oriented Chichewa Bible Translation, its history, settings and principles to the public in Malawi and wherever Chinyanja (Chichewa) is spoken. The Bible and preaching are twins, and it may not be possible to decide who of the two is the first-born. Just as the two belong together, we hope that both readers of the Bible and students of preaching can profit from both books. We thank Mr Shadrack Wame for writing his Testimony and contributing the "Four Characteristics of a Good Gospel Preacher", and we express our appreciation to Amy Jones, Presbyterian Missionary from Pittsburgh and teacher at Domasi Mission for making the text into a print ready book.

Kachere Series Editors

Zomba, November 1999

Preface

Since the late 1980s, I have been engaged in an intermittent study of the compositional style and rhetoric of popular Chewa preachers from Malawi.[1] My research has been regretfully indirect in the sense that I have normally not been able to *personally* participate in any of the worship services at which their sermons have been presented.[2] Rather, I have had to base my studies upon recordings broadcast weekly via TransWorld Radio (49 m band, short wave) on a programme called *Nthawi ya chisomo – Tisanthule m'Mau* ('A time of good fortune – Let us search in the Word'; all text translations from the Chichewa are my own). My ongoing cassette collection consists of over one hundred and twenty five Chewa sermons, ranging in length from just under fifteen minutes to well over an hour (the average being about thirty five to forty minutes), most of which have been roughly transcribed and topically analyzed.[3]

Despite the absence of a full reproduction and description of the interpersonal dynamic between a given preacher and his congregation (except for their various vocal responses picked up on the tape recording), my corpus has a certain advantage in that it contains a select set of examples. In other words, these are sermons which have been presented by some of the best, mainline Protestant preachers (unfortunately, limited in this denominational respect) currently ministering in Malawi, about twelve

---

[1] The 'Chewa' (the people, *Achewa*; the language, *Chichewa*) are a major matrilineal and matrilocal (but patriarchal) Bantu speaking people living primarily in central and southern Malawi, but also in the near cross-border areas of Zambia and Mozambique. Traditionally the Achewa are agriculturists in the main, with considerable numbers engaged also in hunting, fishing, and herding as local conditions allow. Chichewa is spoken as a first or second language by well over ten million people in south-central Africa, making it one of the most important languages of the entire region.

[2] On 10-11 April 1998, I was able to attend and videotape two revival worship services that featured the sermons of Evangelist Wame. These took place at the Kamwala Reformed Church in Lusaka, Zambia.

[3] I wish to acknowledge the able assistance of my seminary students in both the transcription and, to a much lesser extent, also the translation of these Chewa sermon texts. Obviously, a complete analysis of such public oral proclamations would require also a careful video recording of the event, especially to document the close verbal and psychological interaction of the preacher with his audience/congregation, including all significant gestures and facial expressions that complement the message. I also wish to acknowledge the excellent editorial assistance of Ms Amy Jones of the Kachere staff who put in a great deal of voluntary work on this project in order to get the text ready for publication. Many thanks indeed!

in all, including several women. Most of these sermons have also been preached outside the normal framework of a Sunday worship service, that is, at some special revivalistic gathering or a distinct occasion of Christian celebration and commemoration. For this reason, the preachers may have felt freer to present messages that were more open, flexible, or innovative in terms of form and/or content. This observation has been confirmed by my personal attendance at many, more traditional worship services in Zambia and also by the firsthand reports of other knowledgeable Chewa speakers (i.e., Malawian students at the seminary where I teach).[4]

The main purpose of my research has been to investigate, in some detail, the principal stylistic resources and rhetorical strategies of these popular preachers. What is it from the point of view of language that grabs the hearts of their audiences?[5] This description is carried out in relation to their primary goal of stimulating or encouraging a spiritual renewal (revival) and religious reinforcement among the specific audience which they happen to be addressing on a particular occasion. This monograph presents an initial report of my findings. It is intended to elicit comments and criticisms from all who are interested in the theological discipline of homiletics, particularly from a rhetorical and stylistic perspective and within the logical framework of an inductive method of composition. Perhaps a little network or working group can be formed that will be able to serve as a resource centre, point of contact and promotional agency for similar studies of this nature, with respect to Chichewa as well as the other Bantu languages of south central Africa.

In my analysis of the corpus at hand, I have identified ten principal stylistic features, pertaining to the rhetorical strategy of *elocutio*,[6] that appear to be common to the repertory of most of the men (they are not as prominent in the women's texts). There are, of course, significant individual differences

---

[4] I have lived in Zambia since 1962 where I have taught as a seminary instructor (Lutheran) since 1968 and later also as a Bible translation consultant (United Bible Societies). Conversely, I have also been taught much by my many classes of 'students' and national colleagues during these same years.
[5] The Chichewa idiom *kulalikira kogwira [or: kokoka] mtima* ('preaching that grabs [or pulls] the heart') serves as a title for the present monograph since it characterizes the rhetorical nature of the sermons that are being described. In other words, these are persuasive spiritual messages conveyed by language that features 'salty Chewa' (*chichewa chamchere*)!
[6] B.L. Mack, *Rhetoric and the New Testament* (Guides to Biblical Scholarship), Minneapolis: Fortress Press, 1990, p. 33.

with regard to both the proportion, or selection, and also the manner of usage of these compositional devices, but, by and large, the basic inventory remains intact in terms of both form and function. However, it turned out that they are manifested with the greatest overall concentration, distribution, diversity and creativity in the sermons of a Chewa lay evangelist by the name of Shadrack Wame, who will be the focus of our attention in this introductory study.[7]

Indeed, Mr Shadrack Jonas Wame (aged fifty eight), who comes from Salima, on the lakeshores of Lake Malawi, appears to be one of the most popular of the contemporary corps of Chewa evangelistic preachers. He regularly preaches at revivals and crusades all over Malawi and in neighbouring countries as well, particularly at Presbyterian (CCAP) and related denominational gatherings. The amazing thing is that Mr Wame has had no formal theological training and ended his secular, government education after Standard Four. According to his own admission,[8] he does not know very much English and therefore preaches only in Chichewa. Until 1980, Mr Wame worked as a government gardener, but he currently supports himself and his wife as a local farmer and grocer in the Salima area. The couple have six children.[9]

The ten outstanding oratorical techniques referred to above may be summarised as follows: narrative preference, dramatic delivery, personal exemplification, affective appeal, traditional allusion, strategic reiteration, verbal intensification, idiomatic figuration, evocative description and audience involvement. To the extent possible, special attention is given also to the crucial phonological dimension of these features and the key pragmatic role that this plays in the dramatic interaction of the preacher with his audience via the religious message thereby proclaimed.[10] Naturally,

---

[7] This is essentially a personal opinion, based on my doctoral research project (Ernst R. Wendland, "Stylistic Form and Communicative Function in the Nyanja Radio Narratives of Julius Chongo", PhD, University of Wisconsin, 1980), subsequent studies in this field and also the various opinions expressed by national collaborators and colleagues.

[8] From a taped interview broadcast on TransWorld Radio.

[9] Further biographical details and comments by Mr Wame will be found in the Appendix.

[10] The rhetorical power of persuasion as it is manifested in the Wame corpus appears to be concentrated in three major and three minor general pragmatic (communicative) intentions, namely: warning, encouragement, reproof; instruction, reminding, comfort, respectively. These are posited in relation to the preacher's primary, public audience – not necessarily the diverse and dispersed, secondary radio audience, who are in a sense eavesdroppers on the original live performance-event.

the individual items tend to overlap formally in certain respects, so these categories are posited merely as one possible way of examining and evaluating the current collection of sermonic materials. These stylistic-rhetorical devices will be described and illustrated in my text almost exclusively with reference to the sermons of Shadrack Wame. This deliberate restriction is due firstly to limitations of available publication space, but, more importantly, so that a more extensive and systematic treatment of a single, gifted preacher-rhetor can be made available as a basis for future comparative and critical analyses.

I begin (ch 1) with a brief topical overview of the Chewa sermon corpus and by roughly situating the ten critical stylistic features within a broad classical (Greco-Roman) framework of rhetoric, which has proved to be more helpful for a general descriptive analysis of Chewa sermonody than many modern developments of rhetorical theory. This is followed in chapter 2 by an introduction to the inductive approach to literary composition in comparison with a deductive method as this concerns basic homiletical composition. My selective, paradigmatic description of the ten stylistic (form oriented) and rhetorical (function oriented) devices constitutes a major portion of the present monograph (ch 3). This includes some initial observations on the non-analytical and iterative, inductive-relational manner of organizing the typical Chewa revival sermon as a complete discourse unit. The preceding synchronic study is then illustrated diachronically (ch 4) and extensively with reference to three complete sermons by Shadrack Wame (presented in English translation, supplemented by key expressions from the original Chichewa transcription). In the final chapter (5), this dynamic (south central) African homiletical style, which has many features in common with its more famous Afro-American counterpart, will be briefly evaluated from a somewhat wider functional perspective with regard to its overall communicative effectiveness and also in comparison with a traditional Western, deductive homiletical model. My presentation ends with a few comments concerning the significance of this and related studies that seek to elucidate the nature of the rhetorical potency of preaching in the context of a contemporary African society and setting.[11]

[1111] Ross notes in this regard. "The origins of the Presbyterian, Anglican and Roman Catholic churches in Malawi have been subject to a good deal of scholarly attention. By contrast, their contemporary life and impact seems to have attracted little in the way of systematic study" (Kenneth R. Ross, "Preaching in Mainstream Christian Churches in Malawi: A Survey and Analysis", in *Gospel Ferment in Malawi:*

I have included an appendix which presents the biographical testimony of Evangelist Wame in terms of his personal life history and religious pilgrimage. Here, Mr Wame reveals, in his own words, some of the dramatic visions that accompanied his initial conversion and guided him into his current itinerant evangelistic preaching ministry. This document, written by Mr Wame in English, is supplemented by some of his pertinent comments on the nature and purpose of preaching the Christian gospel in south central Africa today.[12]

Theological Essays, Gweru, Zimbabwe: Mambo Press, p. 81). John Mbiti, too, observes that "we have extremely little written information on how and to what extent the Bible is used [in African sermonizing]. We know that the Whole Bible is used for preaching, but we do not know the content of that preaching" (John S. Mbiti, *Bible and Theology in African Christianity*, Nairobi: Oxford University Press, 1986 p. 52). I am aware of several book length studies on this subject that were completed several decades ago (none of which were available to me, but which Mbiti summarizes), and one of more recent origin (E. Forslund, *The Word of God in Ethiopian Tongues: Rhetorical Features in the Preaching of the Ethiopian Evangelical Church Mekane Yesus*, Uppsala: International Tryck, 1993). I have copies of only two, similarly dated essays, i.e. Shorter (A. Shorter, "Form and Content in the African Sermon: An Experiment", AFER?, 1969 (?), pp. 265-279) and Burkle (H. Burkle, "Patterns of Sermons from Various Parts of Africa", in D.B. Barrett (ed.), *African Initiatives in Religion*, Nairobi: East African Publishing House, 1971, pp. 222-231), plus one current article of rather indirect reference (G. Kings, "Proverbial, Intrinsic, and Dynamic Authorities: A Case Study on Scripture and Mission in the Dioceses of Mount Kenya East and Kirinyaga", *Missiology* XXIV:4, 1996, pp. 491-501). I have recently come to know of some important research being done in Malawi by Professor Hilary Mijoga on the preaching being done in the African Instituted Churches (forthcoming, to appear in this same Kachere Series). I would indeed be grateful for any other relevant bibliographical information on the rhetorical dimension of African [especially Bantu] vernacular preaching (and teaching). Please direct this along with any other comments and criticisms of the present study to: Dr Ernst Wendland, Lutheran Seminary, P.O. Box 310091, Lusaka, Zambia (*wendland@zamnet.zm*).

[12] These notes have been selected and translated from the original Chichewa tape recording that I made during an interview with Mr Wame in Lusaka on 13 April 1998.

Preaching in Chichewa

What do the Revival Preachers Preach About?

Mr. Shadrack Wame

Before we enter upon a discussion of a selection of some of the more useful concepts and categories of so called Classical (Greco-Roman) rhetoric in relation to Chewa sermonizing, it may be helpful to establish at least a partial setting and framework for our analysis by presenting an overview of the major theological and ethical subjects that the popular evangelistic preachers tend to favour in their homiletical compositions.[13] This constitutes the raw material, so to speak, from which they construct a persuasive (consequential, attractive, convincing and motivating) discourse through the application of the various rhetorical strategies and stylistic techniques at their disposal, that is, in keeping with the ancient, widely practised verbal genre known as 'public Christian proclamation,' or simply, 'preaching.'[14]

---

[13] These preachers are popular in two senses: (a) they direct their messages to the general public, the common man; and (b) they are widely acclaimed and well-liked. The aspect of choice of appropriate subject matter is to a large degree (though not completely) covered by the Classical canon termed 'invention' (or *inventio*), which involves "gathering information and constructing arguments" that were based on a collection of traditional topics (*topoi*), i.e., "headings or lines of questioning that suggested materials from which arguments for the case at hand could be constructed" (N.C. Murphy, *Reasoning and Rhetoric in Religion*, Valley Forge, PA: Trinity Press International, 1994, pp. 63f). The primary source of such topics for the purpose of Christian preaching is (or should be) the word of God – the Bible or Holy Scriptures.

[14] In this connection it may be observed that "in general, Africa does not know the kind of monologue implied by the term 'preaching.' Africans always interact with the speaker during a sermon" (Joseph Donders, cited in J. Healey and D. Sybertz, *Towards and African Narrative Theology*, Nairobi: Paulines Publications Africa, 1996, p. 336). Thus preaching in (central) Africa is manifested more along the lines of an implicit or explicit dialogue that features the preacher in communicative interaction, to a greater or lesser extent depending on the situation, with his/her audience or congregation. Albrecht too stresses the dialogic nature of the typical African sermon in his study of evangelical preaching in the Lutheran Church of Tanzania, entitled (a translation from the original German), "A Drum Alone Sings No Song: Preaching as Dialogical Event in an Oral Culture" (R. Albrecht, *Eine Trommel allein singt kein Lied: Predigt als dialogisches Geschehen in einer Kultur der Oralitaet. Untersuchung zu Inhalt und Struktur evangelischer Predigt in Nordwest-Tanzania*, Erlangen: Verlag der Ev.-Luth. Mission, 1996).

To begin at the heart of this matter, it should be noted that a great many, perhaps the majority, of the sermons broadcast on TransWorld Radio (which, we recall, are actually *recordings* of publicly preached sermons) deal with some form of spiritual power encounter with the diverse forces of evil which surround the ordinary Christian on every side. Oftentimes such forces are viewed, much as in a traditional Western theological context, as arising from within an individual – the product of humanity's inherited sinfulness (though the latter notion does not receive a great deal of emphasis in most sermons). These give rise to sinful passions such as greed, pride, lust, envy, anger, hatred and so forth, which lead in turn to corresponding wicked behaviours like lying, stealing, drunkenness, sexual promiscuity, malicious gossip and physical violence. The results of my investigation would tend to support the conclusions of Kenneth R. Ross in his study of contemporary "preaching in mainstream Christian churches in Malawi".

> It is apparent that it is the subjective rather than the objective pole of the Christian faith which predominates in the preaching. ... Christianity appears to be presented as primarily a matter of personal faith and personal conduct. [15]

In terms of topic then, sermons of this sort would be quite familiar also to a typical European evangelical-type congregation, except for the rather surprising limitation of having "relatively little emphasis on Christ himself."[16] Just as often, however, the powers of evil – always personalized – are considered more from a traditional African point of view. Accordingly, they are viewed as being constituted by, or originating from, malevolent and malicious forces that operate outside the individual and affect also the larger social group of which that person forms a part. In this

---

[15] Ross, "Preaching in Maistream Christian Churches in Malawi", p. 84.

[16] Ibid., p. 85. The person (nature) and especially the works of Christ do receive considerable emphasis in the sermons of my corpus, much more so than the corresponding attributive features of God the Father or the Holy Spirit. The revivalist preachers definitely promote a strongly Christocentric theology. This is apparently true also of Black American sermons: "The sermons in the black church are predominantly christocentric" (B.K. Blount, *Cultural Interpretation: Reorienting New Testament Criticism*, Minneapolis: Fortress Press, 1995, p. 76), which issues from a strong Reformation tradition, as expressed by Martin Luther (in Latin): *Nihil nisi Christus predicantur*, "Nothing except Christ is [to be] preached" (F.W. Meusner, *Luther the Preacher*, Minneapolis: Augsburg Publishing House, 1983, p. 16). This African-American focus on Christ apparently goes back to the time of the slave preachers, who saw in Jesus Christ both a model for suffering and a deliverer from oppression (D.L. Jones, "The Sermon as 'Art' of Resistance: A Comparative Analysis of the Rhetorics [sic] of the African-American Slave Preacher and the Preacher to the Hebrews", *Semeia* 79 (1997), p. 15).

respect, we appear to have a rather significant divergence from Ross' results.

> Little attention is devoted either to family life or to society as a whole. ... Given the profound engagement of Christian faith and African culture which is basic to the life of the church, it is striking that the research assistants found only 8 sermons out of 587 in which the preacher called for a response in terms of relating to the African tradition, ... [in particular] three issues of great importance in traditional Africa understanding: witchcraft, the ancestors, and disease, health and healing .[17]

Thus, while it may appear "that Christian faith and the experience of witchcraft coexist in separate compartments in the minds of believers and that there is little if any interaction between the two"[18], the more popular Chewa preachers certainly do not seem to hold such a dichotomous attitude. On the contrary, a confrontational and concerted dealing with these vital indigenous religious issues as they impinge upon the Christian faith is frequently found in their sermons.[19] In this effort to achieve a greater, more relevant level of message contextualization, the local religious belief system may or may not be modified in favour of a biblical perspective. That is to say, Satan and his demonic forces may (or may not) be set forth as constituting the motivating cause behind the usual traditional anthropocentric explanation for the various evils and wicked powers that people encounter in this world, namely, witchcraft (*ufiti*), sorcery (*zanyanga*), malevolent magic (*mankhwala oipa*) or antagonistic ancestral spirits (*ziwanda*).[20] In any case, as far as these preachers are concerned,

---

[17] Ross, "Preaching in Mainstream Christian Churches in Malawi", pp. 91f. He suggests that "there is much tension and ambivalence in this area which may help to explain why it is an area that receives relatively little attention in preaching despite its great importance" (Ibid., p. 91). An interaction with traditional religious beliefs does not appear to play a major role in Forslund's extensive corpus of Ethiopian sermons either (E. Forslund, *The Word of God in Ethiopian Tongues*, pp. 124f, 144-149, 165f). I should add that it may well be the physical context or setting of the message that might have at least some bearing on its content. In other words, when confined within the formal framework a Western-style church service, the preachers are more reluctant to discuss traditional religious topics than if they are presenting a sermon in the psychologically and socially less restrictive atmosphere of a large revivalistic gathering for worship, repentance, renewal, healing, personal testimony, and praise.

[18] Ross, "Preaching in Mainstream Chirstian Churches in Malawi", p. 93.

[19] For example, one well-known Malawian evangelist, Naise Nachiye, devoted two entire (over half-hour) sermons to the subject of the indigenous Chewa occult at a gathering for revival (*chitsitsimutso*).

[20] For an anthropological attempt to distinguish between witchcraft and sorcery as manifested in a Chewa sociocultural setting, see Ernst R. Wendland, "*Ufiti* - Foundation of an Indigenous Philosophy of Misfortune: The Socioreligious Implications of Witchcraft and Sorcery in a Central African Setting", in

there is little if any doubt "as to how the church's message should be related to [the] central features of African consciousness",[21] or, we might add, their everyday experience in life. The evil powers that continually wage war against the individual Christian and the Church at large are vigorously confronted in a dynamic mode of verbal discourse that is designed to equip the saints both to defend themselves spiritually and also to take the offensive in this ongoing battle of light against darkness (to cite a common homiletical metaphor from the Chewa corpus, e.g., SW5; cf. 2Cor 6:14; 1John 1:5-7) – for Christ and against Satan (Mt 16:17, 23; Eph 6:10-17).[22]

We move now to a more general report of the preferred topics that occurred in our corpus of over one hundred Chewa sermons. Two trained, seminary research assistants (Daison Phiri and Solomon Njovu) were assigned the task of recording and tabulating the various subjects that were dealt with in a given text according to the following etic index:[23]

1. the Holy Scriptures (inspiration, attributes)
2. natural knowledge of God and his law

M.L. Lynn and D.O. Moberg (eds.), *Research in the Social Scientific Study of Religion* Vol. 4 (1992), Greenwich, CT: JAI Press, pp. 209-243. For a more detailed description of these and other subjects related to the study of traditional religion in Malawi, see the essays in Matthew Schoffeleers, *Religion and the Dramatisation of Life: Spirit Beliefs and Rituals in Southern and Central Malawi*, Blantyre: CLAIM, 1997.

[21] Ross, "Preaching in Mainstream Christian Churches in Malawi", p. 96.

[22] Sermons referred to from the Wame corpus of forty texts are designated by a number preceded by SW. This life-death conflict with Satan and his forces of darkness was also keenly felt by Martin Luther: "He preached as if the sermon were not a classroom, but instead a battleground! Every sermon was a battle for the souls of the people....[and aimed to] hurl the power and victory of Christ against the power of evil" (Meusner, *Luther the Preacher*, pp. 25f).

[23] An 'etic' grid, format or framework is one that is constructed according to an external or universal perspective. This will accordingly be more – or less – relevant diagnostically or descriptively in relation to a particular world culture or ethic group. The etic contrasts with an 'emic' point of view, which is a categorization or classification that is based strictly upon indigenous data, making use of local terminology (whether in original or translated form). Thus, "etic and emic are but two views of the same data: general with respect to all other cultures and specific with respect to the principles of one culture" (R. D. Shaw, *Transculturation: The Cultural Factor in Translation and Other Communication Tasks*, Pasadena: William Carey Library, 1988, pp. 26f). For the present study, an etic index was used in order to highlight the gaps and special concentrations that occur in comparison with any other corpus, in this case including topics that would normally appear in a Western (Lutheran?) systematic theological inventory. The topical listing above may be compared with that used by Ross (Ross, "Preaching in Mainstream Christian Churches in Malawi", pp. 84f), which was developed independently of my own. On the basis of my results, I would modify my index in future to more adequately cater for some of the principal topic areas and issues of concern that were revealed in the present study, e.g., category 22, "sickness, death, and other trials," where a more specific breakdown might be instructive.

3. the nature (essence and attributes) of God (Trinity)
4. creation and preservation of the world
5. good angels (attributes and mission)
6. Satan and the evil angels/demons (nature, activities, judgement)
7. the fall of humanity into sin and human sinful nature
8. God's revealed law – its nature and purpose
9. actual sins (and temptations):
    a) idolatry (including worldliness and materialism)
    b) sins against God's name – cursing, swearing, etc.
    c) sins against the Lord's day
    d) sins against parents and authorities
    e) hatred and murder
    f) evil lust and sexual sins (especially adultery and prostitution)
    g) stealing and cheating
    h) false witness, lying, slander, etc.
    i) coveting, jealousy, envy, selfishness
    j) drunkenness and other sins against one's physical body
    k) pride and self-righteousness
    l) magic, witchcraft, sorcery
    m) spiritism – good or evil spirits (including possession)
    n) other unbiblical customs (cleansing, *nyau* cult, *mdulo*)
10. the divine nature and attributes of Christ
11. the human nature and attributes of Christ
12. the sacrificial work of redemption
13. justification by grace through faith
14. the nature and work of the Holy Spirit
15. the nature and purpose of prayer
16. the nature and results of conversion
17. the nature and purpose of baptism
18. the nature and purpose of the Lord's Supper
19. the nature and function of the church/Holy Christian Church
20. the nature, purpose and practice of church discipline
21. the local church in relation to the government and politics
22. sickness, death and other trials
23. the second coming of Christ, last days and final judgment

24. the nature of life after death and heaven
25. the nature of hell and damnation
26. fruit/gifts of the Holy Spirit
27. marriage and family life/responsibilities (the issue of polygamy)
28. crucial social problems and the responsibility of the church
29. stewardship – offering personal/corporate gifts and service to Christ
30. the need for personal/corporate witness and evangelism
31. the oneness and fellowship of the Church
32. [any other topic – to be specified]

Before taking up this classificatory exercise, my student assistants had previously transcribed all of the sermon texts being examined and had also prepared written summaries of their contents in addition to listing the different Scripture passages that were cited (see below). They were therefore quite familiar with the subject matter of these sermons, the Wame corpus in particular, which they also double checked for accuracy. Nevertheless, this categorization of topics was subject to their own individual interpretation plus any personal analytical limitations or perceptual biases. However, since my purpose was only to give a rough overview of the data, it was deemed sufficient to let their results stand as recorded simply as part of the general comparative background for a more detailed examination of the Wame material.[24] Forty sermons by Shadrack Wame and sixty sermons by other revivalist preachers (for a total of one hundred) were examined in detail. The results are as follows in terms of the listing of topics given above:

---

[24] Ross offers the pertinent remark that "preaching is not a field which lends itself very readily to empirical research. ... What is intended, however, is simply a profile which may highlight some broad trends and thus suggest areas which merit further investigation" (Ibid., p. 83). As more studies of this nature become available and can be compared or contrasted, our observations and conclusions regarding this phenomenon will become more reliable. In his survey of Malawian mainstream Christian preaching (i.e., Presbyterian, Roman Catholic, and Anglican), Ross found the following pair of "themes" to be clearly predominant: "Need for personal conversion" and "Duties of the Christian life" (Ibid., p. 84). Similarly, personal interviews revealed that parishioners perceived that their preachers stressed Christian "warning and duty" (72%) much more than "celebration and joy" (28%) (Ibid., p. 88). Black American sermons tend to be much more "sociopolitical" in nature than those in the Malawian corpus, despite the fact that the reason adduced for this is true also in the latter context: "The black preacher readily includes sociopolitical issues in sermonic material because there is no dichotomy between sacred and secular realms in the black experience" (Blount, *Cultural Interpretation*, pp. 73f; cf. Ross, "Preaching in Mainstream Christian Churches in Malawi", pp. 84f).

Wame: #1 – magic, witchcraft, sorcery (9l) = 16 times (as a major topic)
#2 – drunkenness and other sins against one's body (9j) = 8 times
#3 – the divine nature and attributes of Christ (10) = 7 times
#4 – the nature of life after death and heaven (24) = 7 times
#5 – the need for personal witness and evangelism (30) = 7 times

Rest: #1 – magic, witchcraft, sorcery (9l) = 11 times
#2 – other pagan customs (9n) = 10 times
#3 – sins against God's name, cursing, etc. (9b) = 8 times
#4 – second coming of Christ, last days, judgment (23) = 8 times
#5 – the nature of hell and damnation (25) = 8 times

Some general trends and similarities in these topical preferences may be noted. First is the striking emphasis on practical, life related subjects and felt needs – the occult in particular. These evangelists have obviously learned to preach 'where it itches.' There is also an obvious concern for the last things (eschatology) – what is going to happen at the end of this life and the world age. Rather distinct is Wame's doctrinal emphasis on the person and work of Christ (eleven times when combined with those sermons focusing on his human nature [11])[25] as well as his encouragement toward a Christian's personal testimony of the gospel. Somewhat surprising, perhaps, is the attention devoted by the other preachers to the subject of God's name (cursing, etc.), but this also has a decided human interest in that 'cursing and swearing' in an African setting, whether any implicit or explicit reference to the deity is made or not, is invariably carried out in relation to one's fellow (wo)man (and is thereby closely related to the practice of sorcery).

Again, as was clearly shown by the Ross study, one observes "the massive importance of the Bible for mainstream Christianity in Africa."[26] In fact, in

---

[25] In future analyses, these two categories should probably be merged into one due to the difficulty of trying to distinguish between the various aspects of Christ's divinity and humanity as these are expounded and applied in a given sermon. No doubt, a less doctrinal, more moral grid needs to be developed in order to better reflect the current emphases that are being manifested by revival sermons of this nature. For Wame, as for Martin Luther, "the living breathing, loving, serving, and suffering Christ permeate[s] his preaching...the human Jesus of the Gospels" (Meusner, *Luther the Preacher*, p. 19).

[26] Ross, "Preaching in Mainstream Christian Churches in Malawi", p. 86. The great early Christian theologians, Ambrose, Jerome and Augustine, took this emphasis upon the Scriptures a step further in that the Bible served not only as the source of their sermon content, but also as the model for their preaching style. "The stylistic features Augustine found so appealing in the scriptures were clearness and simplicity, parallel and paratactic cola, antithesis, anastrophe [inverted word orders], interrogative cola,

most cases, a preacher will select several Scripture texts to serve as the basis for a sermon, and other related passages are also frequently quoted during the course of the presentation. Our corpus was further investigated with regard to this particular feature, and the results are listed below according to frequency in relation to each book of the Bible and the number of times that the references given were utilized either as an initial main text or as an internal minor citation:[27]

	Wame			The Rest		
	book	text	citation	book	text	citation
1.	Luke	10	4	Luke	5	12
2.	Matthew	5	4	Matthew	6	10
3.	John	3	5	John	4	12
4.	Psalms	3	1	Psalms	3	5
5a.	2 Corinthians	2	3	Ephesians	3	2
5b.	1 Corinthians	-	5	Isaiah	3	2

Again, it is rather surprising to observe the close correspondence here, namely, Wame's selection of main and minor Scripture texts in relation to that of his colleagues. The gospels (notably excluding Mark) clearly predominate, showing a general emphasis on the life and ministry of Christ. The Psalms, too, exhibits a comparatively significant number of occurrences, as does the book of Isaiah (three times in the Wame corpus). As for the other biblical books, the following are utilized either as a text or a citation once or more within the one hundred sermons studied:

---

rhyme, puns, and word play" (S.M. Oberhelman, *Rhetoric and Homiletics in Fourth-Century Christian Literature: Prose Rhythm, Oratorical Style, and Preaching in the Works of Ambrose, Jerome, and Augustine* (American Classical Studies 26), Atlanta: Scholars Press, 1991, p. 117). All of bthe verbal devices just mentioned are manifested to a greater or lesser extent in the sermons of Shadrack Wame (cf. ch 3).

[27] These results may be compared with those of Ross, who found the most commonly cited OT books to be Genesis (#1), Isaiah, and Exodus, while the most popular NT books to be cited in sermons were Matthew (#1), John, and Luke (Ross, "Preaching in Mainstream Christian Churches in Malawi", p. 87). "At the center of the slave preacher's oratory were stories from the Old Testament," especially those dealing with the Exodus (Jones, "The Sermon as 'Art' of Resistance", p. 14).

Wame	OT	Genesis, 2 Samuel, 1 Kings, 2 Kings, Job, Ecclesiastes, Isaiah, Daniel
	NT	Acts, Ephesians, Philippians, Hebrews, 1 Peter, 2 Peter, 1 John
Rest	OT	Genesis, Exodus, Leviticus, 1 Samuel, 2 Samuel, 1 Kings, 2 Kings, Nehemiah, Esther, Job, Proverbs, Ecclesiastes, Jeremiah, Ezekiel, Joel, Obadiah, Zephaniah
	NT	Acts, Romans, Ephesians, Philippians, 1 Thessalonians, 1 Timothy, Hebrews, James, 1 Peter, 2 Peter, Revelation

As these data indicate, there are several outstanding, and perhaps unexpected, omissions, that is, biblical books which were not referred to at all in the total corpus of sermons that were collected, namely Ruth, Jonah, Malachi (with its emphasis on offerings), Galatians (works of the flesh versus fruit of the Spirit) and Titus (instructions for church leaders). But my selection was restricted, and a wider collection would undoubtedly fill in most of the gaps.

In terms of the preceding evidence, I do not think that it is possible to conclude with reference to this study that "the figures represent a well balanced coverage of the Bible".[28] Neither can it be said that "a serious effort is being made to expound" the various texts that are used,[29] for an assessment of the *quality* as well as *quantity* of biblical exposition reveals some significant omissions or deficiencies in the area of exegesis. In other words, what we often find is that the Scripture passages quoted or referred to are not often explained in a systematic manner with regard to either the text itself or its original contextual (historical, geographical, ecological, political, sociocultural and/or religious) setting. Rather, the predominant tendency is to "amplify, illustrate and apply a given passage of scripture"[30] in terms of a contemporary situation. There are exceptions of course, but by and large, as far as these popular Chewa preachers are concerned, the Scriptures serve first and foremost to shed light on the present day and modern society.

---

[28] Ross, "Preaching in Mainstream Christian Churches in Malawi", p. 87.
[29] Ibid., p. 86.
[30] Ibid.

More will be said on this important issue after the Wame corpus has been examined in greater detail.

The preceding topical survey should be sufficient to set the stage for a brief discussion of popular Chewa sermonic discourse from the perspective of classical rhetoric, that is, with regard to compositional (stylistic) form and communicative (religious) function.[31] How do these popular preachers typically display their oratorical persuasiveness and power in the dynamic expression of conceptual content through the linguistic and literary resources available to them? By what means do they verbally enhance the meaning and organization of their sermons (in classical terms, the faculties of *inventio* and *dispositio*)[32] in order to augment the clarity, coherence, impact, appeal, appropriateness and relevance of their hortatory argument and main theological message? The following treatment is of a more general nature, and the details will be provided in chapter three with reference to the sermons of Shadrack Wame.

On the Power and Prominence of *Pathos* and *Pronunciatio*

The art and science of rhetoric as defined and demonstrated by its classical practitioners has generally taken as the focus of its concern the form and/or the function of communicatively effective oral discourse. This is "the knowledge of how to speak well" (Quintilian), i.e., eloquence, and/or "the available means of persuasion" (Aristotle).[33] As was pointed out above, the

---

[31] Generally speaking, most studies of rhetoric may be classified into two basic categories (allowing, of course, for various mixtures and overlappings): those which treat the subject as the art-technique of *composition* (a stylistic focus) and those that view it more as a more or less formal mode of *persuasion* (a functional focus; cf. P. Trible, *Rhetorical Criticism: Context, Method, and the Book of Jonah*, Minneapolis: Fortress Press, 1994, p. 32). Obviously, the investigation of *both* form (artistic devices) and function (pragmatic purposes) is important in any thorough rhetorical analysis of an oral discourse.

[32] For a brief but helpful summary of classical rhetorical distinctions, see Mack, *Rhetoric and the New Testament*, ch. 2.

[33] G.A. Kennedy, *New Testament Interpretation Through Rhetorical Criticism*, Chapel Hill: North Carolina Press, 1984, p. 31; Trible, *Rhetorical Criticism*, p. 25. A useful survey of the history of rhetoric in relation to Christian preaching is given by C.A. Loscalzo (W.H. Willimon and R. Lischer (eds.), *Concise Encyclopedia of Preaching*, Louisville, KY: Westminster John Knox Press, 1995, pp. 409-416). For a more general treatment of classical rhetoric from a cross-cultural perspective, see G.A. Kennedy, *Comparative Rhetoric: A Historical and Cross Cultural Introduction*, Oxford: Oxford University Press, 1998. The study of classical rhetoric "sharpens the preachers' [and their analysts'] sensitivity to different speech situations" by enabling one to pay more attention "to how a text makes a point and creates a reader experience" (O. Skjevesland, "Tracing the Dimensions of Homiletics", in A. Tangberg (ed.),

content, or subject matter, of a given composition is also considered, e.g., in the catalogue of traditional *topoi* or topical commonplaces,[34] but generally not with the same attention to detail, at least not in practice. These two basic distinctions of form and function must of course be combined in any credible rhetorical analysis. A presentation of the first without the second usually turns out to be a superficial display of stylistic sterility, while a focus on function, described without reference to the form, lies open to the charge of selective subjectivism.[35] It is hoped that the present study of Shadrack Wame's sermonody does not error too far in either direction.

Aristotle distinguished three primary ways of achieving the central aim of persuasion in formal discourse, namely, with an appeal to reason or the logic of the message (*logos*), to audience emotions and sentiments (*pathos*) and/or to the rhetor's own authority and credibility (*ethos*).[36] In other words, a speaker might focus upon three different, but interrelated, aspects of an oral communication event in order to best get his message (content

---

Text and Theology: Essays in Honor of Prof. Dr. Theol. Magne Saebo, Oslo: Verbum, 1994, pp. 283, 285).

[34] Kennedy, *New Testament Interpretation*, p. 20; Mack, *Rhetoric and the New Testament*, p. 32. According to Cicero, the content of an argument could be best arranged according to or in the form of the following sixteen "basic topics": definition, partition, etymology, conjugates, genus, species, analogy, difference, contraries, adjuncts, antecedents, consequents, contradictions, efficient cause, effects and comparison (R.A. Lanham, *A Handlist of Rhetorical Terms: A Guide for Students of English Literature*, Berkeley: University of California Press, 1969, p. 110).

[35] I was faced with a great problem in presenting my description and analysis of Chichewa rhetoric via the medium, or form, of a foreign language, English. The various features that I consider are often visible or apparent only in the original language; the latter, however, is probably not accessible to many readers outside of south-central Africa. Limitations of space also entered the picture, making it impossible to give the cited examples in both Chichewa and English. In the end, I made the subjective decision to include the Chewa text only in certain outstanding cases, including instances where my interpretation of the data is perhaps debatable.

[36] G.A. Kennedy (translator/ed.), *Aristotle On Rhetoric: A Theory of Civic Discourse*, Oxford: Oxford University Press, 1991, p. ix. In a generic sense, persuasion can be regarded as subsuming lesser rhetorical functions such as the three commonly cited: "to teach, to delight, to move" (A. Preminger and T.V.F. Brogan (eds.), *The New Princeton Encyclopedia of Poetry and Poetics*, Princeton, NJ: Princeton University Press, 1993, p. 1046). This is because an audience must somehow be persuaded in order to be effectively taught, delighted or moved to respond in word, feeling or action. Persuasion also incorporates the notion of conviction, which applies only to the conceptual level of one's psychology. Thus, in addition to a person's intellectual capacity, the operation of persuasion is also directed to one's volition and emotions. The purpose is not only to gain mental assent but also to motivate subsequent behaviour (speech, action; cf. L. Thuren, *Argument and Theology in 1 Peter: The Origins of Christian Paraenesis*, Sheffield: Sheffield Academic Press, 1995, pp. 51-54).

and intent) across in a given exigence or rhetorical situation:[37] the rationale or reasonableness of his argument, the feelings and attitudes of his receptors and/or his own ethical reliability, trustworthiness and personal character.[38] In the Western tradition of rhetoric, the *logos* component tends to be (over) emphasized – in presentation, analysis and evaluation – certainly as far as theological discourse is concerned, and this often includes the preparation and delivery of public sermons.[39] In other cultural contexts, however, this logical (particularly deductive), analytical approach is not nearly so privileged, especially in the originally intended oral-aural locus of rhetorical composition, utterance and assessment.[40]

In the particular Chewa sermonic setting investigated in my study, for example, the appeal to both *ethos* and *pathos* is decidedly pronounced,[41]

---

[37] I will use a masculine pronoun when referring to unspecified individuals for the sake of simplicity, due to the fact that most Chewa preachers are men, not simply because I happen to be male.

[38] A recent reformulation of the three classical categories is found in N.R. Leroux, "Perceiving Rhetorical Style: Toward a Framework for Criticism", *Rhetorical Society Quarterly* 22:4 (1992), pp. 29-41. Thus *logos* is specified more precisely by the "rhetorical functions" of "focus" and "presence." The former pertains to the various devices aimed at achieving topical/thematic foregrounding in a text, while the latter deals with the literary techniques that enlarge, enliven or create some special effect within it. The function of communion, on the other hand, combines the concerns of *ethos* and *pathos* with reference to the establishment and reinforcement of the bonds of interpersonal relationship between a speaker and his audience. Leroux applies these distinctions in a brief analysis of a sermon by Martin Luther.

[39] This relative imbalance with regard to both secular as well as religious discourse has given rise in recent years to a corrective movement, namely, the literary perspective and approach known as reader-response criticism or reception theory. As these terms would imply, there is little attention given here to the *ethos* of the message source (author) or even the *logos* itself in relation to its original setting. Such limitations severely reduce the value of this method for producing a credible literary-critical analysis.

[40] Kennedy briefly calls attention to this crucial cultural factor: "Rhetoric is a historical phenomenon and differs somewhat [I would omit this qualification] from culture to culture, more so in matters of arrangement and style than in basic devices of invention" (Kennedy, *New Testament Interpretation*, p. 8). This basic principle of communication may be restated, as follows, from a sociolinguistic point of view: "Language is the framework in which we live; it is the structure that gives meaning to our existence. People in different sociological environments operate with different linguistic forms. The interaction between their sociolinguistic perspective and the language of a text results in a unique understanding about the power and meaning of that text" (Blount, *Cultural Interpretation*, p. 4).

[41] Forslund concludes that "the ethos of the preachers is perhaps the most important of the internal proofs utilized in the sermons" (Forslund, *The Word of God in Ethiopian Tongues*, p. 230). This position is supported by Kennedy in his overview of "formal speech [secular and religious] in some non-literate cultures": "The primary means of persuasion is the authority or ethos of the speaker, deriving from such factors as age, experience, and skill at speaking" (Kennedy, *Comparative Rhetoric*, p. 79). I do not detect such a clear-cut emphasis upon the subjective, speaker-oriented element in my Chewa corpus, for an appeal to the feelings and attitudes of the listeners seems to be just as important in the preachers' rhetorical strategy.

and I will attempt to do justice to this prominence in my treatment, despite having to work through translation. Admittedly, it is not very easy to distinguish between a personally oriented argument or rhetorical device and an affective one due to the subjective nature of the qualities being investigated,[42] but where it is possible to see some clear demonstration of either type, this will be pointed out. In any case, it may be taken for granted that "effective preaching presupposes trust and credibility ... [and] aims at the free and grateful approval of the listeners".[43] The importance of the emotive element in preaching was recognized and stressed as far back (at least) as the great church father, Augustine.

> If...the hearers require to be aroused rather than instructed, in order that they may be diligent to do what they already know, and to bring their feelings into harmony with the truths they admit, greater vigour of speech is needed. Here entreaties and reproaches, exhortations and upbraidings, and all the other means of rousing the emotions are necessary.[44]

The primary appeals to *pathos*, *ethos* and *logos* in rhetorical argumentation are applied to varying degrees in the three basic species, or macro-genres, of formal oratorical speech that are posited in classical theory: judicial (forensic), deliberative (hortatory) and epideictic (demonstrative), with special attention being devoted to human reason, the will and personal emotions respectively.[45] The same is true of their usage in Chewa revivalistic

---

[42] The difficulty of this distinction is noted also in Preminger and Brogan: "This conceptually close relation between ethos and pathos is evident not only in Cl[assical] rhetorical treatises but also in the long trad. of writing 'characters'" (Preminger and Brogan, *Encyclopedia of Poetry and Poetics*, p. 389).

[43] Skjevesland, "Tracing the Dimensions of Homiletics", pp. 282, 284. Putting this in another way and adding an essential factor: "Upon the engagement of the physical matter of preacher, hearer, and text, the emotional field comes into existence. Once the emotional field exists, the Holy Spirit comes center stage to influence everything within the field" (F.A. Thomas, *They Like to Never Quit Praisin' God: The Role of Celebration in Preaching*, Cleveland: United Church Press, 1997, p. 42).

[44] Cited from Augustine's foremost work, *On Christian Doctrine* in Murphy, *Reasoning and Rhetoric in Religion*, p. 86. With regard to a contemporary of Augustine, John Chrysostom, it has been noted that "his clever but sanctified use of his rhetorical skills touched the intellect but at the same time stirred the deepest emotions among his listeners" (J. Pless, "Seven Pulpit Paradigms from the Prince of Preachers: John Chrysostom", *Wisconsin Lutheran Quarterly* 95/3 (1998), pp. 205f). Augustine's ideas on rhetoric in relation to homiletics have been influential right up to the present day. One typical expression of this is found in the words of Rev John Broadus, a well-known professor of homiletics of the last century: "The purpose of preaching...is to convince the judgment, to kindle the imagination, to move the feelings, and to give powerful impulse to the will in the direction of truth's requirement" (i.e., as stated in the Word of God; Murphy, *Reasoning and Rhetoric in Religion*, p. 87).

[45] Kennedy (translator/ed.), *Aristotle On Rhetoric*, pp. 47-50; cf. Trible, *Rhetorical Criticism*, p. 9;

sermons, which usually combine the three types to form a composite or mixed style that was apparently not so common in an ancient Greek oratorical setting.

Thus *judicial* discourse prevails when the subject pertains to moral right and wrong, or human sin, and divine judgment. The preacher attacks the guilty and defends the innocent as such human examples appear in history (normally the Scriptures) or, less often, the present day (including fictional examples). Furthermore, the congregation is vigorously called upon to evaluate their own lives in the light of God's law as revealed in the Scriptures and to repent of the (past) wrongdoing that they will invariably detect in their behaviour.[46] This commonly employed opening technique is often followed by a sustained *deliberative* exhortation to a more sanctified (future) manner of behaviour and lifestyle. This involves a sincere repentance of and departure from one's former (or present) way of living. Such change and commitment is a matter of the utmost expediency, not only for one's well being in this world, but above all, to avoid future punishment in gahena after death (the contrasting blessings of heaven are not as greatly emphasized). *Epideictic* speech appears regularly in conjunction with some familiar illustration or outstanding instance that is used to demonstrate or promote typically Christian ideals, qualities, attitudes and values and to discourage the opposite. This is seen, for example, in the praise accorded Christ and the blame that is verbally meted out to Satan, along with their respective well-known biblical representatives or agents (e.g., David/Saul, Peter/Judas, Paul/Elymas) as well as prominent contemporary religious heroes and villains.[47]

Skjevesland, "Tracing the Dimensions of Homiletics", p. 284.
[46] Forslund feels that the "judicial" species is relatively rare in sermons since the audience does not have "the authority to implement a judgement" (Forslund, *The Word of God in Ethiopian Tongues*, p. 108). In the strict sense, this may be true, but to then widen the scope of the "epideictic" category, as he does to cover all of these debatable cases (i.e., as "invective" discourse, *ibid.*), appears to greatly weaken the diagnostic power of this triad of rhetorical distinctions. Besides, the presence of an active, interacting audience in the Chewa sermonic setting does, in fact, allow for a considerable amount of impromptu personal and collective judging to take place as a particular sermon is being preached. There are, no doubt, many such cases of categorical overlapping, where strong censure (epideictic speech) may be used to provoke or evoke a negative, critical decision (judicial speech).
[47] According to Forslund, "Epideictic clearly predominates over the other two species employed in the material ... [since] the preachers emphasize the attitudes and values which a Christian ought to adhere to" (*ibid.*, p. 194). However, when he says that one of the principal aims of the Ethiopian sermon (in *Mekane Yesus* churches) is to urge "Christians to lead a good Christian life" (*ibid.*), it would seem that there is also a good deal of deliberative rhetoric that is also involved. In practice, at least with regard to

Three of the five major faculties, or stages, of a rhetorically conceived composition have already been referred to: *inventio, dispositio* and *elocutio*. *Inventio* deals with the initial selection of content categories (topics) and the preferred types of argument to be deployed in a persuasive composition. *Dispositio* is concerned with the larger organization and tectonic arrangement of the complete discourse, such as deductive reasoning (based on *enthymemes,* premise and conclusion) as opposed to an inductive (featuring familiar examples) method of structural development (see chapter 2).[48] Finally, *elocutio* involves the detailed stylistic features (schemes, figures, tropes) that are utilized to put the argument effectively into actual words, whether to teach (*docere*), to please (*delectare*) or to move (*movere*) the audience.[49] The first of the final two rhetorical canons is *memoria*, which applies to the process of committing a given speech to memory (e.g., by topical association and various other mnemonic devices) so that an effective, natural public delivery might be made. And lastly is *pronunciatio*, which focuses upon the actual oral presentation itself, that is, how one's voice, pauses, gestures, facial expressions and overall appearance may be utilized to give concrete audible and visual expression to the main semantic and functional elements of a particular speech. We do not read very much about these last two compositional dimensions in any discussion of classical rhetoric, especially in its modern applications. Instead, disclaimers such as the following are typical:

> Memory and delivery will not concern us here.[50]

> Discussion of memory and delivery is often omitted in the handbooks and will be omitted here, for they relate to oral presentation, about which we know little.[51]

---

the Chewa corpus, I found the three species of discourse usually very closely interconnected in one's presentation: the *judicial*, in relation to the repentance which must initiate the new life in Christ, and the *epideictic*, as setting forth the Christian ideal that serves as a model for the *deliberative* exhortation to specific acts pertaining to a renewed, Spirit-led lifestyle.

[48] As will be shown in chapter 3, the five deductively-based structural divisions of a classical oration do not apply at all to a typical Chewa sermonic discourse, i.e., *exordium* (introduction), *narratio* (presentation of the case/issue at hand), *confirmatio* (arguments for), *refutatio* (arguments against) and the *peroratio* (summary-conclusion) (cf. Forslund, *The Word of God in Ethiopian Tongues*, p.108; Mack, *Rhetoric and the New Testament*, p. 41).

[49] Quintilian, cited in Willimon and Lischer, *Concise Encyclopedia of Preaching*, p. 410; cf. also Kennedy, *New Testament Interpretation*, pp. 13-30; Forslund, *The Word of God in Ethiopian Tongues*, p. 109; Mack, *Rhetoric and the New Testament*, pp. 32-34; Murphy, *Reasoning and Rhetoric in Religion*, pp. 63-67.

[50] *Ibid.*, p. 63.

> Of the five parts of classical rhetoric, they [Perelman and Olbrechts-Tyteca] privileged *inventio* and *dispositio*, subordinated *elocutio* to its function within argumentation, and omitted *memoria* and *actio* [i.e., *pronunciatio*] as inapplicable to contemporary culture.[52]

This lack of attention given to memorizing a certain text can perhaps be understood since one rarely has access to the original speaker, even nowadays, to inquire about what strategy he employed to carry out this conceptual process. Moreover, it is almost certain that no Chewa popular preacher ever commits his sermon to memory before preaching it. In fact (although I do not have concrete proof), I think that it would be rare even to find one who works from a previously prepared, formal outline (other than a few handwritten notes perhaps).

The same applies to the matter of delivery where written compositions are concerned, which unfortunately form the great bulk of published scholarly studies. In such cases, the issue of manner or style of speaking simply does not apply. However, a neglect of the aspect of *pronunciatio* cannot really be excused when an audible presentation is the object of one's analysis, for "preaching is by its very nature an acoustical event".[53] Indeed, this is undoubtedly the most prominent feature of Chewa sermonic rhetoric in my corpus; it is the most important (powerful – or heart grabbing) rhetorical technique available for the evocation and manipulation of both *pathos* and *ethos* during these performance events involving public verbal religious communication.[54] Enunciation is thus the essential sensory tie that binds

---

[51] Kennedy, *New Testament Interpretation*, p. 14.
[52] Trible, *Rhetorical Criticism*, p. 56.
[53] Skjevesland, "Tracing the Dimensions of Homiletics", p. 284.
[54] This was and is true also of both traditional and modern Chewa oral narrative performances, including their adaptation to the radio (for a survey, see Wendland, "Stylistic Form and Communicative Function", ch. 5). In this connection, Okpewho writes, "This word-of-mouth medium of presentation implies that [African] oral literature makes its appeal first through the sound of the words that reach the ears of the audience and only secondarily through the meaning or logic contained in those words" (I. Okpewho, *African Oral Literature*, Bloomington, IN: Indiana UP, 1992, p. 70). The later Latin church fathers, Ambrose, Augustine and Jerome clearly composed their sermons for *oral* presentation and not according to the more formal canons of Classical rhetoric. On the basis of his careful analysis of the Latin original texts, Oberhelman concludes: "The vocabulary, phrasing, syntax, structure, imagery, all the 'tics' of the oral style, especially parataxis and parallelism, derive from the scriptures and popular literature" (Oberhelman, *Rhetoric and Homiletics*, p. 119). Evangelist Wame and his revivalist colleagues exhibit similar oral-oriented verbal features in their popular Chichewa preaching style – as dis-

rhetor and receptor(s) together with regard to their joint participation in a sermon's oral-aural realization.[55] This feature is a vital tactic in any effective preacher's delivery.

> Preachers who are raised in a cultural or subcultural region, when they are effective in their communicative endeavors, utilize the cultural linguistic keys of their community's speech in their sermons ... the preacher ... declares the gospel in the vernacular of the people.[56]

In the description and evaluation of chapters three and four, I will try, where possible, to indicate the nature and effects of especially noteworthy instances of such phonological rhetoric in the dynamic operation of this popular homiletical style in contemporary Chichewa.

There are many other aspects of classical rhetoric that are applicable in one respect or another to the analysis of sermons, in any language. Some of those that pertain to the micro-style of composition will be mentioned in chapter three, but the rest will be ignored so that our discussion does not become any more complicated than it already is. However, one final feature of potential significance needs to be mentioned and that is a listing of the "major moves of the rhetorical speech in terms of the major types of proof or argumentation" (an element of *inventio*[57]). For our purposes, it is not the sequential order or arrangement (the *dispositio*) of these elements that is important, for such standard, recommended outlines do not apply to Chewa sermonic discourse. Rather, it is the basic inventory of some of the more common of these techniques that is of interest; many of them are also utilized intuitively by the revivalistic preachers due to their fundamental oratorical competence, skill, and/or experience. The ancient Greek rhetorician, Hermogenes, provides us with a handy listing of eight such rhetorical

---

tinct from the more formal, 'churchly' type of composition and diction often found in the sermons preached during regular Sunday worship services. Wame's non-verbal style of presentation is also extremely effective in the pulpit. He is in almost continual motion, but not distractingly so – that is, in an over-dramatization of either his role as preacher or that of a character, biblical or otherwise, whom he happens to be describing. Rather, his facial expressions, gestures and body movements all serve to quietly enhance his varied vocal modulations and indeed the very words he is speaking.

[55] "*Actio* [was] claimed by Demosthenes as the *sine qua non* of persuasion" (Preminger and Brogan [eds.], *Encyclopedia of Poetry and Poetics*, p. 1050). Aristotle considered volume, pitch (accent) and rhythm to be the key features of a rhetorical "delivery" (*hypokrisis*) and claimed that even "written speeches [when orally recited] have greater effect through expression [*lexis*...including delivery] than through thought" (Kennedy [translator/ed.], *Aristotle On Rhetoric*, pp. 218f).

[56] Blount, *Cultural Interpretation*, p. 72.

[57] Mack, *Rhetoric and the New Testament*, p. 42.

strategies, which serve to promote the compositional characteristics of *pathos* and *ethos* as well as that of *logos*. Thus, they pertain, in an ever varying mixture and a cumulative progression as the sermonic text develops, to the fundamental cognitive, emotive and volitional components of the human psyche.

> The sermon is a series of ideas and images (moves) expressed in bundles of language that generate a certain nuance or shade of meaning that registers in the emotive. Each move builds upon the emotive effect of the previous move, heightening and enhancing what has already been created, until at the close of the sermon, one is left with a clear meaning or experience that registers in the intuitive.[58]

We will have an opportunity to experience, at least in part, something of this vital cognitive-emotive inductive development leading to one or more flashes of spiritual intuition when considering some actual samples of Shadrack Wame's sermonody in chapter 4.

In closing then, I will briefly define below the eight basic constituents that contribute to the rhetorical movement of a hortatory discourse in relation to how they might be realized in a typical sermon.[59]

a) *praise* – A word of praise (*encomium*) may be directed towards God (especially the Father-Creator or Christ the Son) or to one of his saints (biblical or church historical) as their actions or attributes relate to the main theme or thesis of the sermon. In the classical speech, such commendation usually initiated the discourse, but in sermons, it may occur anywhere, including the very end (i.e., a *doxology*).

b) *chreia* – This persuasive category refers to any memorable teaching or saying (proverbs, maxims, figures of speech, etc.) attributed to a well-known authority (biblical: God or a biblical writer/character; or traditional: common or conventional wisdom) that applies to the topic under consideration or to the recommended behaviour being enjoined.

c) *rationale* – Here we have the outstanding, widely recognized reason(s) given in support of the central theme or one of its main points, that is, why it is valid/true and/or relevant for the audience to carefully consider and/or

---

[58] Thomas, *They Like to Never Quit Praisin' God*, p. 11.
[59] Adapted from Mack, *Rhetoric and the New Testament*, pp. 44-47.

to act upon. An inductively based rationale will employ various kinds of life related illustration, whether factive or fictive, to make the case, rather than deductively logical proof statements.

d) *opposite* – The essence of a theological or ethical principle may be proved or confirmed if its inverse is also true. If it can be shown, for example, on the basis of Scripture or human experience (the latter being much less credible), that the righteous (faithful), either in general or with regard to a certain behaviour/attribute/attitude, are blessed both in this life as well as in the judgement to come while their opposite, the wicked, will be condemned, one position serves to reinforce the other and the argument as a whole.

e) *analogy* – An analogy is normally taken from the world of experience, the good as well as the bad, from the sphere of everyday life or natural phenomena. The basic similarity is typically of a general type that could be easily applied to many other, more specific instances – in particular, the one being propounded or illustrated in the case at hand. Christian sermons of course have a whole new field of data upon which to draw for their various moral and doctrinal analogies, namely, the Holy Scriptures.

f) *example* – As distinct from analogies, examples are to be historical in nature. They are presented either in the form of a straightforward narrative or, in the more dynamic speeches, as a dramatized or even dialogue embellished story. The Bible makes available to preachers a full case book of diverse examples of characters, both the righteous and the wicked. Such stories are the mainstay of the inductive method. They serve not only to focus upon a given (religious) principle but also to involve the audience in its personal evocation and experience.

g) *citation* – "The purpose of the citation was to show that other, recognized authorities had come to the same conclusion or rendered a similar judgment on the same issue".[60] In contrast to secular speeches, which depended on human words of wisdom (for conclusions, injunctions, admonitions, etc.), a Christian preacher will naturally turn to his source book *par excellence*, the Word of God, for the ultimate form of support, credibility or authority – especially as the climax to a particular argument, exposition or admonition.

---

[60] *Ibid.*, p. 46.

h) *exhortation* – This would be the main imperative conclusion that any and all of the preceding rhetorical devices lead up to, motivate, illustrate or reinforce, whether it actually comes last in the speech (as in strict induction) or earlier (an initial occurrence would be an instance of deduction). In a secular speech, such an exhortation would be expected to support the traditionally accepted beliefs, teachings, values, and customs of a specific culture and society, whereas in the case of a sermon, it would obviously promote biblical principles and practices and/or those of a particular church denomination.

As we will see in chapter 3, the sermons of Shadrack Wame provide many instances of these and similar devices in the development of his verbally dynamic and psychologically moving inductive style of oral discourse. It is to this major compositional method of *induction* that we now direct our attention for an introductory exposition that is clearly related to the eight rhetorical constituents just discussed.

2. The Inductive Art of Participatory Preaching

A Chewa Tale: *Konza kapansi kuti kam'mwamba katsike*

Once upon a time there was an entire village which moved to a new location. Among the villagers was a man who had two kittens. Now since the people happened to move their possessions at midday, this man left his kittens saying (to himself), "I will have a chance to come back and fetch these kittens this afternoon." Later when he came to collect them, he was able to catch one, but the other became frightened and ran away. The man returned for several days in succession, but he was unable to capture that kitten, for it would always climb high up into a tree.

One day a wise old man told him, "Give me the kitten which you have and I'll use it to go and catch the other one." The old man took some maize porridge and meat stew and went to the deserted village. When the kitten there saw him, it fled up into the tree again as usual. The man just sat down there along the path and started feeding and stroking the body of the kitten which he had come with. Upon seeing this, the kitten up in the tree became curious and was attracted not only by the food, but also by the kind behaviour of the man. The kitten began climbing down little by little in order to eat with its companion. The man kept calling to it enticingly. When it was finally down on the ground, the man gave the kitten some food and stroked it just like he had done with the other one. Then he gently picked it up, put it into a sack, and returned to the new village.

The owner of the kittens along with his friends were amazed that the wise man had succeeded so easily. The man explained, "I first took care of the one down below so that the one up in the tree would become tempted and come down. And that is just what happened – *konza kapansi kuti kam'mwamba katsike*, 'first prepare what's down below so that what is up above will descend'."[61]

Like the man who could not get his kitten to climb down to him out of a tree, so too most Christian churches working in central Africa have for many years been faced with a difficult problem of communication. What is the best method of getting people to respond to the message of the gospel? Indeed, great numbers have reacted eagerly, and the rapid growth of the

---

[61] I have translated this story from the original Chichewa text found in S.L. Kumakanga, *Nzeru za Kale* (Ancient Wisdom), Lusaka, Zambia: Longmans, 1949, pp. 36f.

church is a testimony to the mighty work of the Holy Spirit in this region. But others, like the kitten sitting up in the tree, are more resistant, and this includes not only those outsiders who have refused to respond when witnessed to, but also those nominal members who openly demonstrate that the gospel is having little or no effect upon their lives. What could be the reason for this? We know, of course, from Christ's parable of the Sower and the Seed that some hearers, due to their sinful nature, are more hardened to the Word than others. But is there something that the communicators are doing wrong perhaps or, to put it more positively, something right that Christ's messengers perhaps *ought* to be doing differently in order to more effectively carry out his great commission? In this chapter, I will present a general overview of one important aspect of this problem as it concerns the evangelistic and edificational ministry of the Christian church in Africa, that is, transmitting the essentials of the Word of God to people by means of preaching – the oral presentation of a prepared sermon, whether written out or prepared mentally in advance (i.e., in this discussion, not a completely impromptu or spontaneous address as may be the case in some of the recorded Chewa sermons).

When the first missionaries began their work in this part of the world, they quite naturally followed the basic church planting methods that they were used to in America (or Europe). This involved, among other things, the institution of regular worship services on Sundays (or Saturdays) – services which were rather closely based upon liturgies which they were familiar with from home. Apart from introducing preaching as a basic component of the order of service, these early missionaries also exemplified and taught a certain way of preparing and presenting the sermon. It was a very direct, logical (to them) and text based approach which they were accustomed to – one that was primarily *deductive* in nature. It begins with a biblical text, which is then analyzed, organized, explained, illustrated and applied to the congregation in a sequence of ordered steps or interrelated stages. It was sort of like the man in our preceding fable. He thought that he could simply return to his former village, walk right up to his two little pets, grab them and take them along back with him to their new home. But that is not how it turned out. One of the kittens did not appreciate this particular approach and ran up into a tree to escape what must have been an unfamiliar and therefore frightening situation.

Although a considerable amount of careful testing on this issue needs to be carried out yet, indications are that some, perhaps a great many, of those listening to the church's Western-oriented sermons over the years have reacted like that kitten. They have run away, so to speak, from what the preachers have been trying to tell them – if not physically, then mentally in terms of comprehension and interest. Hence, it may be that a somewhat different type of procedure is needed – a more indirect and, at the same time, a more dramatic and illustrative, method of getting the message across, such as was exhibited by the wise old man of our story. He paid a great deal of attention to "preparing the ground" first, before attempting to carry out the goal which he had set out to accomplish. But his patience and persistence, coupled with an overt loving and caring attitude, finally brought positive results.

It is this type of *inductive* approach to sermonizing which I wish to explore more fully in this study – a technique that we might also call *participatory* preaching.[62] Like a key aspect of Zambia's former political philosophy upon which this term is based (participatory democracy), the goal is to get people's thoughts, attitudes and emotions more fully involved with the sermon, the sermoniser and of course the Scriptures as it is being preached – to have listeners participate more actively in this presentation of the Word and especially its application. The assumption is that such an approach is already familiar to most audiences from the oral tradition of oral art (orature) which the majority of them have been exposed to in one form or another virtually all their lives. The aim then is to preach, beginning from the known (their experience) and moving to the potentially unknown (the message), not only with regard to the content of a particular sermon, but also with respect to its mode of composition (structure) and manner of expression (style).

The Indigenous Model of African Oral Tradition

In the search for more effective models, or proven examples, to follow in local sermon making, it is necessary to consider the cultural setting in

---

[62] I discuss certain aspects of the inductive method with respect to theological instruction in Africa in Ernst R. Wendland, "The Case for a 'Case-Study' Approach to Theological Education in Africa", *Africa Journal of Evangelical Theology*, 1998.

which we intend to communicate the biblical message. What are the specific means that were used to convey essential truths and traditional mores among African societies in the past? Are these methods still relevant to modern man? What can the ancient wisdom of Africa teach us about how to construct sermons for people living today? It would be unwise to simply import foreign models, conventions and strategies of discourse composition without first considering whether or not there is already a foundation that has been laid which will help us to proceed with the task of evangelistic and edificational preaching in a more appropriate and meaningful way.

Established custom and tradition carry a great deal of weight in the various social situations in which present day messengers of the gospel are working. Not only the ways, but also the words of elders should never be ignored in ignorance or summarily rejected without careful consideration. Those who think that they know better, whether foreigners or foreign trained nationals, must always remember that *mau a akuluakulu akoma akagonera* ('the words of elders become pleasant once they have spent the night'). That is to say, although one might at first be tempted to reject their advice as being old fashioned and out of date, the wisdom of what the elders had to say will sooner or later become apparent. The Tonga (Zambia) express the same idea in somewhat more graphic terms: *mupati usiigwa kuluno, kumaano tomusiyi* ('a big man (respected elder) may be outpaced in a race, but not in common sense').

The particular method of sermon making and delivery that we wish to consider in our discussion is based upon an ancient system of message transmission which is the norm in most oral-aural societies all over the world – communities which are also frequently characterized as being relatively homogeneous, small scale, face to face, pre-literate (functionally, that is) and non-urbanized. Here in Africa, despite the rapid and extensive technological development and modernization that is taking place all over the continent, this diverse communication complex, which we will refer to as *oral tradition*, still plays a prominent role in most social groups, urban as well as rural – the former due to its constant cultural interaction with the latter.

The term 'oral tradition' actually includes a wide variety of indigenous verbal genres, such as proverbs, riddles, dramatic narratives, dilemma tales, myths, legends, historical records, parables, praise epithets, prayers, divining incantations, curses, ceremonial initiation instructions and songs of all sorts (royal praise, pounding, hunting, field, dance, rain calling, spirit possession and so forth).[63] Although each of these forms of discourse is quite distinct, they all tend to have several important general features in common. One is that they are firmly grounded in the real life experiences and environmental setting of the audience, even the ancient myth of origin, which is clearly created in the image of man.[64] Secondly, they are strongly participatory in presentation. In other words, the audience frequently has an active part to play in the performance of such genres. And finally, these varied instances of oral literature are clearly functional in nature – that is, they are not engaged in just for the fun of it (though this, too, is a valid sociological purpose). Rather, each accomplishes one or more specific objectives in the particular social context in which it is used.

Take the dramatic narrative, or folktale (*nthano*, more precisely, 'fictitious-story-with-choral-song'), for example. In an initial study of this local genre as performed among the Chewa people of Zambia's Eastern Province, I had this to say about its purpose as a dynamic, functionally significant art form:

> Besides their obvious entertainment value, the individual narratives function as part of an elaborate and highly effective educational system, one that unites all the elements of oral tradition ... in serving to teach, explain, validate, sanction, and uphold the community's established ideals, institutions, and identity. Sometimes literally, but more

---

[63] For a detailed discussion and illustration of the various types of Malawian oral literature, see Steve Chimombo, *Malawian Oral Literature: The Aesthetics of Indigenous Arts*, Zomba: University of Malawi Centre for Social Research, 1988 (see Wendland, "Stylistic Form and Communicative Function", ch. 8 for some thoughts concerning *nthano*, traditional Chewa/Nyanja oral narrative; cf. also Okpewho, *African Oral Literature* for a recent Africa-wide survey of oral literature and H. Scheub, *The Xhosa Ntsomi*, Oxford: Clarendon Press, 1975 for an excellent in-depth study of Xhosa storytelling). Chimombo designates "the aesthetics of the Chewa people" by the coined term *Ulimbaso*, which he feels "underlies all artistic creation and perception" – and this would naturally include sermons preached in Chichewa according to an indigenous model. Chimombo describes this notion as follows: "-ul- refers to inspiration, -mb- to form and -so- to artistry. -ul- operates on the artist from the onset of inspiration to the production of the art object. -ul- is taken from **ula** or **laula**, oracle, and its divine connotations as the source of wisdom, creativity and human action. -mb- is at the centre of the verbal arts (**mwambi/mwambo**), (**nyimbo/chamba**) and the visual arts (**choumba/cholemba**). -so- deals with **luso**, artistic creation and **kaso**, the appreciation of the finished product" (Chimombo, *Malawian Oral Literature*, p. vii; boldface as in the original).

[64] For the text and a brief discussion of "the creation myth of Kaphiri-Ntiwa", see Schoffeleers, *Religion and the Dramatisation of Life*, pp. 9-11.

often metaphorically through reference to the world of nature, the magical, the absurd, and the supernatural, these tales all promote the well-ordered society, one in which every individual has his own distinct value and contribution to make, and one that is founded on the inherited wisdom which has accumulated over many generations ...

With a clear emphasis upon proper codes of behaviour at the key stages in a person's cycle of existence (birth – maturation – marriage – death), this artistic-didactic tradition affirms a harmonious model of interpersonal relationships where all types of antisocial action are dramatically by hyperbole and caricature discouraged. It provides each member of society with a set of norms whereby he may evaluate his own thinking and actions and then adjust these as needed in order to conform with accepted standards of behaviour in the community. Indeed, these precepts may be reaffirmed, re-examined, or, perhaps, even subtly rebelled against through a narration of the negative, the shocking opposite, which presents what is commonly regarded as improper action, a violation of the rules of normal conduct or social taboos; e.g. a man chops his brother-in-law down with an axe, two sons plot to kill their mothers, some hunters kill their companion for meat, a young woman refuses to get married, a mother tries to feed her child to a hyena. Tales of the latter type also provide opportunity for a psychological or vicarious escape from the strictures of social control and pressures toward conformity.

Finally, we note that these important topics and themes are regularly presented in a light-hearted vein, with an element of the humorous present in even the most solemn situations, e.g. a funeral or the installation of a new chief. This characteristic no doubt lightens the burden of didacticism which is a part of every story and greatly increases their overall entertainment value. Thus the subject matter, the style, and the aesthetic effect of each story can be fully perceived and appreciated only with a detailed knowledge of the socio-cultural experience and artistic tradition from which it springs. [65]

It is important to bear in mind the fact that these different functions of the folktale,[66] as is the case in any of the other oral genres, are carried out suc-

---

[65] Ernst R. Wendland, *Nthano za kwa Kwaza* (Tales from Kawaza-land), Lusaka: Zambia Language Group, 1976, pp. if.

[66] Okpewho examines four general and overlapping functions of oral literature in providing a measure of "social relevance" to the community concerned (Okpewho, *African Oral Literature*, ch. 5): (a) entertainment and relaxation ("offers delight and so relieves us of various pressures and tensions both physically and mentally," *ibid.*, p. 106); (b) asserting interests and outlooks ("making it possible for them to come to terms with the world in which they live ... [and] to establish securely an identity which they can

cessfully only with the full cooperation and personal involvement of the listeners to/for whom it is being told. This principle applies to a greater or lesser extent whether the art form concerned is relatively short (e.g., a riddle) or long (e.g., a narrative fable). In the tales, for example, we often find one or more series of songs which are sung at fixed places in the account. Such songs serve to structure the story into distinct episodes, to advance the plot forward to its climax and conclusion, and to build up suspense, or tension, in the story. But their most vital function is

> ... to provide an opportunity for the audience to actively participate in the "creation" of a tale, which is a very satisfying and enjoyable experience for every member of the group. Along with the other forms of audience participation, such as the stylized responses interjected at phrase or clause boundaries during the introduction and initial stages of a story's development (i.e., *tili-tonse* 'we're listening!' or *yeru* 'alright!'); spontaneous exclamations of dismay, joy, fear, anger, surprise, rebuke, etc. (including laughter, cries, whistles, ululations) in response to sudden changes and emphatic confrontations in the plot; rhetorical questions and repetitions that reflect upon what the narrator has just spoken; the clapping of hands; and verbal comments, promptings, and expressions of encouragement – or criticism! – songs allow the listener to play a significant role in the performance of a narrative, which is in effect a joint activity whose success or failure in many cases depends equally upon the ability and productive interaction of both artist and audience.[67]

Preachers today who are really concerned about getting their message across in a meaningful way cannot fail to take these traditional methods of artfully engaging instruction into consideration. This is what their listeners are used to – and this is what they most definitely respond to in thought, word and deed. To be sure, society is changing, especially in urban areas where the influence from cross cultural contact and consequent de-tribalization, the degree of literacy, further education, diverse employment opportunities and an exposure to new ideas and alternative ways of doing

---

cherish for as long as possible in the face of the vicissitudes of history," *ibid.*, p. 110); (c) teaching ideals and conduct ("presents constantly to members of contemporary society the standards of excellence that they should practice in their own interests and for the survival of the society," *ibid.*, p. 117); and (d) recording life ("the historical experiences of a people ... [and] the cycle of life which the average citizen is recognized by society to cover as he moves from birth to death," *ibid.*, pp. 118f). Cf. Chimombo, *Malawian Oral Literature*, chs. 5-6; Wendland, "Stylistic Form and Communicative Function", ch. 2.
[67] Wendland, *Nthano za kwa Kawaza*, p. v.

things is greatest. Nevertheless, people are still predominantly oral-aural, rather than print/script oriented, by nature. The emphasis upon sound as a vehicle of communication is thus greater than that on sight. These factors should certainly influence the particular communication policy and strategy that Christians adopt for transmitting "the whole will of God" (Acts 20:27), both to regular church members and in evangelistic outreach to others. Shadrack Wame is an outstanding example of a preacher who capitalizes on both his oral tradition and the phonic medium of speech to the maximum degree in order to convey his biblically based proclamation with the greatest possible impact and appeal.

This is a crucial area of endeavour where a much more thorough and widely practiced contextualization of Christianity perhaps remains to be effected, namely, as it concerns the contemporary ways and means of transmitting the ancient recorded message of the Scriptures via the various media currently available. The fundamental content itself (i.e., sense and significance) must remain essentially unchanged, but it is the specific language and culture based form or vehicle for conveying these truths that we are here concerned about. With regard to the practice of sermonizing in Africa then, to borrow a metaphor from the prophet Amos, what many mainline, Western trained (whether in actual location or in didactic technique) pastors need to do is to put the "roar" back into "prophesying" (that is, preaching) the "Word of the LORD!" (Amos 1:2, 3:8). In order to accomplish this essential objective, it is clear that they can, and must, learn a critical lesson from the fundamentally inductive method of their indigenous oral tradition.

Induction Versus Deduction – What's the Difference?

The following is a paragraph taken from a sermon on the need for Christian love:

> As Christians we surely ought to love all people. This includes our enemies. There are two reasons for this as expressed by our Scripture text for today. First of all, God is love. He showed his love in the beginning by creating mankind. He continues to show his love and mercy by providing for the needs and wants of all people, even those who do not acknowledge him or live according to his will. So if we wish to be like God, our heavenly Father, we will follow his perfect

example of showing love to everyone whom we know. That leads to our second point: love is characteristic also of the Christian life. Since we are the sons of God, we ought to demonstrate this by our actions. If we do not do so, people will not be able to tell any difference between us and the unbelievers around us. Thus we will fail to give a witness to the faith that lives within us. By our lack of love, we may even drive people away from the church. So love! That is what God is like, and that is how he expects his children to live.

The following is another treatment of the same topic that was presented above. Observe the difference in the two approaches.

You have heard that it was said, "Love your neighbour and hate your enemy." But I tell you: Love your enemies and pray for those who persecute you, that you may be sons of your Father in heaven. He causes his sun to rise on the evil and the good, and sends rain on the righteous and the unrighteous. If you love those who love you, what reward will you get? Are not even the tax collectors doing that? And if you greet only your brothers, what are you doing more than the others? Do not even pagans do that? Be perfect, therefore, as your heavenly Father is perfect.

The second quotation is, in fact, the biblical text upon which the first sermon portion was based (i.e., Mt 5:43-48, NIV). The two paragraphs reveal two different ways of presenting one's thoughts on the subject of love as it affects the Christian life. What is the difference between them? Which approach did you prefer and why? Is your preference related somehow to the different methods of presentation?

Notice first of all the neat, logically ordered progression that is found in the first approach. The central theme of the paragraph is stated right at the beginning. Christians should show love to all people. This exhortation is then explicitly supported by two reasons – or parts – which logically subdivide the theme in a positive-negative movement: (a) God our Father demonstrates love, and so as his children, we ought to manifest the same character; and (b) if we do not give evidence of love in our lives, then we are failing to give witness to the faith of our hearts and our standing as God's sons. Examples that illustrate these two parts are given in very general terms which are closely related to the subtopics themselves. One also observes that the second part is not really based on an explicit command of the text. It is rather implied (perhaps too weakly) by or inferred (perhaps wrongly) from a mention of the various categories of individual that is found in the second half of the passage, especially the negative types, e.g., unrighteous, tax collectors, pagans.

The arrangement and development of the second text, which is of course a portion of Christ's Sermon on the Mount, is quite different. The whole paragraph expounds only one theme: love *even* "those who are not your 'neighbour'." The point is thus taken to the extreme instance (enemies – plural!) and supported by a short series of specific illustrations and examples which runs throughout the passage. This sequence of cases is marked by two features that sharply distinguish this text from the previous one: contrast and confrontation. The paragraph leads off with a strong antithesis, namely, a well-known, but erroneous, popular belief as opposed to Christ's teaching on what was the true spirit of God's law. The contrasts and oppositions continue right through to the end where the practice of "pagans" is set next to the perfection of the "heavenly Father." Our Lord's instruction is also distinct in that it is given in very personal (and authoritative) terms, that is, directly to each and every listener. He uses "you," the second person plural pronoun (in Greek), instead of the more general, and perhaps pragmatically safer (since it includes the speaker), pronoun "we."

There are a number of other important stylistic qualities which are exhibited by the second passage. Christ begins where his hearers are, that is, with a familiar saying that all Pharisees (another extreme case) knew and put into practice in self-righteous justification of their separatistic attitude and behaviour towards religious rejects – racial outsiders (e.g., "pagans") as well as socially inferior insiders (e.g., "tax collectors"). But what most people did not know was that this popular tenet was completely wrong; the Old Testament said nothing at all about hating one's enemies. In fact, in texts such as Exodus 23:4-5, the LORD commands the exact opposite. Christ's examples are very specific, and they go so far as to push people to the very limits of putting love into practice: *pray* even for your *persecutors*! Common images from the world of nature are used to illustrate his point – the "sun" and the "rain." And there is no way of escaping the implicit rebuke which is conveyed by the series of audience involving rhetorical questions at the end. Surely his listeners had to admit that they loved only – or at best, mostly – those who were either seemingly worthy of it or in a position to love them beneficially in return. But such selective behaviour made them no better than the hated tax collectors (as the common stereotype went)! Mention of the latter group introduces a culturally specific reference to contemporary society and the bitter tensions which had split the community into a number of antagonistic groups – all virtual enemies of one another. Christ becomes even more pointed and provocative; in their restricted giving of the common greeting, many hearers were no better than the oppressive Roman colonialists (pagans)!

Through this carefully chosen sequence of instances, Christ brings his listeners at last to the theme of his discourse (and that of the sermon as a whole). Be *perfect* as children (implied) of your heavenly Father! This all embracing appeal, made manifest by love, comes as a climax at the very end of this section, and it hits his listeners especially hard because he has been building up to this impossible command all of the way. It is certainly *not* possible to fulfil if a person depends upon his/her own "righteousness," which even on its own terms should approximate that of the Pharisees (5:20). But an attributed perfection *is* possible if one comes to the merciful Father in repentance, and having received forgiveness (6:12-15), humbly asks for the strength to do God's will in the world (7:11-12, 21).

Lest anyone think that the Master Teacher – and Preacher – simply stitched together here a series of examples that happened to come to mind, like assorted beads on a string, observe the larger patterning of this text. It is truly an excellent specimen of the rhetorical power and the poetic appeal of the edifying words of Him who is the Word of God incarnate.

You have heard that it was said,
    "Love your neighbour and hate your enemy."
But I tell you:
    "Love your enemies and pray for those who persecute you,"

    That you may be sons of your father in heaven.
    He causes his sun to rise on the evil and the good,
        and sends rain on the righteous and the unrighteous.

    If you love those who love you,
        what reward will you get?
            Are not even the tax collectors doing that?
    And if you greet only your brothers,

> what are you doing more than others?
> Do not even pagans do that?
> Be perfect therefore as your heavenly Father is perfect.

To be sure, pastors may not be able to construct sermons as perfectly and powerfully as that, but they can certainly learn a general lesson from the Lord about sermonizing. It appears that his method of teaching his disciples was very close to the pattern that is commonly used in the traditional manner of instruction in central Africa. It would definitely be more familiar than the approach which was exemplified in the first, typical Western styled passage above. What we have illustrated here then is a basic contrast between the inductive and the deductive modes of presenting a certain subject. The truth that is taught may be virtually the same in both cases, but the particular way of expounding or manifesting it is not. Below is a comparative summary of seven of the main differences that serve to differentiate these two reasoning and compositional processes of induction and deduction (an *oral* presentation of the material is taken as the point of reference).[68]

	Induction	Deduction
1.	begins where the *listeners* are (their needs, wants, values, goals, fears, failures, knowledge, abilities) and works from that point of reference	begins where the *speaker* is (his knowledge, opinion, perception, attitudes, and conclusions about his audience) and works
2.	actively encourages audience *participation* and involvement, mental	assumes that the audience is mentally following along; they

---

[68] In his many important works investigating the relation between "orality and literacy" in human societies, Walter Ong stresses the vital importance of "the spoken word" in pre-literate, non-technological/industrialized, rural, traditionally-based communities. He offers the following "characteristics of orally based thought" (Walter J. Ong, *Orality and Literacy: The Technologizing of the Word*, London: Methuen, 1982, p. 37), which happen also to be features that often distinguish an inductively organized verbal text. Thus, "in a primary oral culture, thought and expression tend to be" additive rather than subordinate, aggregative (synthetic) rather than analytic, redundant or "copious," conservative or traditionalist, close to the human lifeworld, agonistically toned, empathetic and participatory rather than objectively distanced, homeostatic ("here-and-now" oriented) and situational rather than abstract (*ibid.*, pp. 37-57). Furthermore, these features "relate intimately to the unifying, centralizing, interiorizing economy of sound as perceived by human beings. A sound-dominated verbal economy is consonant with harmonizing tendencies, conservative holism, situational thinking, with human action at the center, [and] a certain humanization of knowledge around the actions of human beings and anthropomorphic beings" (*ibid.*, pp. 73f).

	and even vocal, depending on their situation and setting	are simply *receptors* to receive and process the information that is presented to them
3.	moves from *specific* facts to a *general* conclusion, with exhortations, admonitions, etc., usually following after, in this basic pattern of discourse development	moves from a *general* principle(s) to *specific* instances or applications, with various types of injunction and even conclusions being inserted at any time in the sequence
4.	works from the *known* and familiar to the *unknown* and unfamiliar, from a recognized 'problem' to an agreed 'solution' by the process of *analogy*	works from a *basic theoretical position* and established biblical/dogmatic principles, whether these happen to be known or unknown to receptors; starts with ready made solutions which are *assumed* to be true
5.	builds upon *common sense* and everyday experience; identification of the main point develops as a mutual search for the answer to a 'key question'; the discourse is *flexible* and practically rather than logically ordered	builds upon *formal logical progression* from the basic principles and facts which are taken for granted and from which all practical application must flow in a point-for-point fashion that can be diagrammed
6.	depends upon *concrete* images, figures, illustrations, facts, examples and natural evidence with an appeal to one's *senses*, imagination, and practical daily events or situation; the preferred mode of conceptual linkage in *analogical* (metaphoric) or *associative* (metonymic) in nature	concepts used to fill out the body of the text are more *abstract* with appeal to universal *reason* and basic human processes or assumed cognitive capacity; linkage of ideas is *logically* ordered, e.g., cause/effect, temporal sequence, spatial layout, major-minor, etc.
7.	*person* (receptor) oriented and effected, as revealed in interactive direct speech as well as by a more *informal*, even colloquial, style of discourse, i.e., that is characteristic of the audience itself	*subject* (topic/theme) oriented, which is often demonstrated by an impersonal 'objective', and passive manner of writing/speaking and a more *formal* literary and/or rhetorical style

It should be pointed out that in the context of informal argumentation these contrastive properties represent only broad, general tendencies rather than an explicit and rigid line of demarcation. Thus in actual practice, such as a sermon composition, there may not always be such an obvious boundary between these two types of reasoning, inductive and deductive.[69] Instead, induction and deduction are frequently combined, with a greater or lesser degree of emphasis and attention given to one or the other. The analyst normally finds a continuum of characteristics that extends from one pole to the other, and there will usually be a certain degree of overlapping with respect to one or another of the seven categories listed above. Nevertheless, the two methods are, considered as a whole or as complete discourse strategies, quite distinct though it is always possible to conjoin them in any given composition, either by accident (intuition) or by conscious design.

How do the differences noted above relate to the communicative activity of preaching? The following are four handy summaries of the chief distinctive features as they apply to sermons:[70]

> Deductive preaching starts with a declaration of intent and proceeds to prove the validity of what the preacher says is already determined to be true. Inductive preaching, on the other hand, lays out the evidence, the examples, the illustrations and postpones the declarations and assertions until the listeners have a chance to weigh the evidence, think through the implications and then come to the conclusion *with* the preacher at the end of the sermon.

---

[69] I am speaking here of informal usage. In the formal theory and practice of argumentation, however, there is indeed a precise difference, which may be stated as follows: "The difference depends on the relationship between the premises and conclusion of each type of argument. With a valid deductive argument, if the premises are true, then the conclusion *must* be true as well. This is not true for inductive arguments even when they place the conclusion beyond reasonable doubt ... [on the other hand] it is easier to establish the truth of the premise of the inductive argument than it is to establish the truth of the premises of the deductive argument" (R.J. Fogelin, *Understanding Arguments: An Introduction to Informal Logic* [Third Edition], New York: Harcourt, Brace, and Jovanovich, 1987, pp. 217, 219). This is because induction is normally based on concrete empirical evidence, whereas deduction depends on abstract conceptual reasoning. "In arguing deductively, we claim to establish the truth of one proposition by deriving it *necessarily* from other truths ... In arguing inductively, we put forward something as evidence *in support of* some further claim" (*ibid.*, pp. 219f, *italics* added).

[70] The following four quotations are taken (respectively) from: R.L. Lewis and G. Lewis, *Inductive Preaching: Helping People Listen*, Westchester, IL: Crossway Books, 1983, p. 43; Willimon and Lischer (eds.), *Concise Encyclopedia of Preaching*, p. 270 (C.L. Campbell); *ibid.*, p. 149 (T.G. Long); Thomas, *They Like to Never Quit Praisin' God*, pp. 5f.

Deductive preaching announces general, propositional conclusions and then breaks them down into various points and exhortations. As an alternative to this kind of deduction, the inductive method begins with the particulars of human experience and moves toward the often surprising conclusions of the gospel. In this process the preacher does not simply deposit conclusions in the hearers' minds but enables the congregation to participate actively in the movement and meaning of the sermon.

Instead of creating sermons with deductive movement (breaking a central idea down into smaller components and presenting these ideas systematically from the larger to the smaller – a logical pattern that does not reflect the way people really think, discover, and learn), preachers...should employ inductive forms that reverse the logical flow by moving from the smaller to the larger. Deductive sermons state a claim and then defend it; inductive sermons build, piece by piece, toward a claim.

Because the focus was primarily on words, the [deductive] method sought from the scriptural text a proposition or idea; a sermon was then written to elaborate deductively from this proposition, and persuade the listener. The sermon was rationalistic in approach and orientation, with little attention to emotional process. The goal of the sermon was to demonstrate truth, illustrate truth, logically deduce truth, and lead people to intellectually assent to truth. This by nature required an analytical, objective style that sought to impart information or give instruction. This style required people to be generally passive in the process, waiting for the minister to convince them of the truth of the [theological or moral] proposition. This analytical style was far removed from the experience and folk traditions of average everyday people, who intuitively understand (i.e., via inductive analogizing) the operation and the result of emotional process.

It may be noted that the cognitive logic of the deductive approach (which emphasizes rational coherence and intellectual development) is typical not only of Western formulated sermons, but also of other types of theological discourse, such as that found in a statement of belief (creed), a dogmatics textbook, catechism, instruction manual or even many a Bible study text. What may not be so evident, however, to pastors and theologians working in Africa and in many other parts of the predominantly non-literate world is that this method of composition, whether applied orally or in writing, is completely foreign to and more difficult to follow for the vast majority of the people whom they are trying to serve. The expression, instruction and promotion of African traditional religion, for example, is still, as it always has been, a process involving primarily inductive means and analogical association,[71] where the non-verbal (e.g., ritualized action) and verbal (e.g., prayers) elements complement each other to communicate a dynamic message, often communally, to some supernatural personage or power. Induction is also predominant in most other forms of popular communication in a traditional setting, e.g., judicial debates, initiation instruction or commemorative (royal) addresses, and even in such modern genres as political speeches. Here we have an emphasis upon emotive logic, which seeks to ensure that the cognitive truth of a given message "reaches the experience of people" so that they can more fully perceive, comprehend and act upon it.[72]

When it comes to sermonizing then, as a specific form of Christian instruction and edification, which approach should be followed? Do preachers really have a choice in the matter? The path of least resistance for many is merely to parrot or parade what they have been taught in seminary and Bible school. And this procedure, not surprisingly since it is the product of a Western oriented, culturally alien curriculum, strongly favours deduction, often to the virtual exclusion of any alternative. However, it is to the latter option – namely, induction – that we now direct our attention for the purposes of further description, evaluation and application.

Seven Prominent Inductive Devices

To begin with, we will examine some of the practical aspects of the inductive method more closely. To be specific, how does it operate to achieve greater listener participation and interpersonal cooperation in the process of communication? There are a number of important literary (i.e., text analyzable) means whereby such involvement may be stimulated, some of which we have already seen illustrated in the earlier example of Christ's teaching.

---

[71] With reference to African oral literature, Okpewho notes: "The mind of the oral artist works more conveniently in an associative way; in other words, the oral literary imagination is easily inclined – much more so than the mind of a writer [or, I might add, the Western mind] – to seek ways of linking or yoking ideas together [by analogy]" (Okpewho, *African Oral Literature*, p. 87).
[72] Cf. Thomas, *They Like to Never Quit Praisin' God*, p. 87.

Seven basic techniques are worthy of special mention.[73]

1. Examples

The use of varied, representative examples is perhaps the simplest and most straightforward type of induction. These should be familiar to the listeners and closely related to their lives, that is, to their own cultural setting and personal experience. They may be secular in origin or nature (e.g., taken from the realm of politics, kinship relations, traditional customs, popular farming techniques or the current economic situation). The daily newspapers and national radio broadcasts are often a good source of such material. Alternatively, the examples may be primarily religious in reference, like those found in the area of Christianity (including well-known biblical passages), indigenous beliefs, or those of mixed groups – the so called African Independent Churches.

When utilized as part of an inductive argument of some kind, such illustrations need to be carefully selected so that they will be seen as relating clearly and directly to the main theme or topic which the speaker (writer) wishes to convey to his audience. If a number of cases are cited, they should not be too long or detailed; otherwise, the audience may miss the unity of the forest on account of all the different trees. In more skilfully constructed sets or lists of examples, a certain pattern is developed, e.g., one instance builds upon another to form a conclusion at the end; there is a progression from less to more important evidence with a climax at the end; or the examples may be chosen so as to shed light on the diverse aspects of a subject, that is, to approach it from various angles in order to present a complete picture, as it were, of the topic under consideration.

---

[73] These are not the only verbal techniques to be found in good inductive discourse. Songs (hymns), for example, are sometimes incorporated into the text of a popular sermon. But the general types listed (which include more specific sub-types, e.g., riddles under the Puzzle category) are those that appear most commonly in my corpus of Chewa sermons. Such indigenous stylistic devices are discussed more generally (not with specific reference to the inductive method) in the recent major work by Healey and Sybertz (Healey and Sybertz, *Towards an African Narrative Theology*), which seeks to promote "an African narrative theology of inculturation" (the title of chapter 1). The authors adopt a topical approach in their promotion and illustration of a more effective, local value-and-image oriented mode of Christian communication in Africa, considering in turn the subject areas of God and Christology (2), the Church-family (3), hospitality (4), life and death (5), meal fellowship (6), sickness and healing (7) and mission work (8).

2. Narrative

A narrative is an event based and temporally arranged account, which may be told in order to illustrate or elaborate upon a certain point. In a sense, it is really just a longer type of example (cf. 1 above), but often it also has the distinct characteristic of incorporating a particular conflict or crisis involving the chief participants. Such a story sequence is built around a plot that builds up in tension or suspense to a climax and is finally resolved in the end. There are many different kinds of story, depending on the nature of the content that each presents: contemporary (current events) or historical, true or fictitious (imaginary), realistic or fantastic (supernatural), biblical or non-biblical, human or animal and so forth. African oral tradition provides a rich source of all types of narrative, usually plot based in nature, which are available for use as background material in the development of a certain argument or exposition (including, of course, a sermon).

If a biblical story is employed as an illustration in a sermon, it should be told in such a way that it does not detract from, overshadow or obscure the primary text of Scripture upon which the preacher is basing his instruction, exhortation, admonition, appeal, reproof, consolation or whatever. Furthermore, any narrative that is used, whether sacred or secular, must always serve to clarify, explain or focus upon the main theme and purpose of the sermon or text. In addition, it is also necessary to clearly relate an account which took place in the past, no matter how familiar it may be, to the present day life situation of the congregation. The other thing that one ought to keep in mind when considering the use of a narrative is that not everybody is a good storyteller, either orally or in writing – that is, able to relate the account with focus, proportion, balance, economy and drama. If a preacher, for example, does not possess this skill, which includes a certain degree of creative imagination and an interesting (if not dramatic) narrative style, he may be able to develop it through conscious mimicry and patient practice. Otherwise, it may be better for him to avoid using this particular method of induction too often, for a poorly told story can quickly turn an audience away from the speaker (i.e., detract from his *ethos*) and hence also his message.

3. Biography

A biography is a specific type of narrative, one which presents the account of a particular person's life from either a first person or third person perspective. It may or may not contain a prominent peak or climax as in a dramatic story plot. In the Chewa corpus, such a biography is usually that of the preacher him/herself.[74] Not everything that is known about a given situation or incident needs to be mentioned, of course, but only certain selected events which have a definite bearing upon a sermon's principal theme(s). I am treating this type of composition as a separate category, first of all, since it is so frequently found in the Scriptures (e.g., first person: Nehemiah, Daniel; third person: Moses, Christ), which is undoubtedly the most important source book for all the various case studies that might be profitably utilized in a sermon. And secondly, biography is an indispensable tool of the inductive method because it is so effective in stimulating a personal involvement of the speaker in relation to his audience.

A biography may be true or imaginary. While the former is generally more credible, even fictive accounts are believable when based upon the real life experiences of specific individuals. These involve familiar roles, played by personages who are confronted with situations, both good and bad, which are either the same or very similar to those of the listeners themselves. This enables people to more easily identify with the leading characters, that is, to mentally experience events or perceive things as he or she does when they occur in the narrative. Such identification allows the main point or application of the story, provided that this is clearly indicated, to make a greater impression on one's thoughts and emotions. Thus, it is usually not difficult for a well told biography to capture the interest and attention of an audience. And such a participatory attitude would lead each listener to say to him/herself, "Why, this could also happen to me!" Hopefully, then, s/he will be moved also to raise a question that is even more important. "What can I learn from that person's experience?"

---

[74] This form of "preaching from the 'I' position," that is, the personal experience and opinions of the preacher in response to the Word of God, is typical also of black American sermons (Thomas, *They Like to Never Quit Praisin' God*, p. 60). The intention is to reduce the "relational resistance" between himself and his audience (which is a factor of "distance, direction, and anxiety") so as to enhance his credibility (*ethos*) as a testifier to biblical truth and to encourage their "willingness to take responsibility for [their] own relationship with God" (*ibid.*, p. 57).

4. Analogy

An analogy is a concrete comparison which can range in length from a single word to an entire narrative. It may be either literal or figurative in nature, the latter involving some sort of pictorial representation of a given topic. Such imagery is generally quite specific, material that is selected from daily life and which makes a strong appeal to the senses (sight, sound, smell, taste, etc.). In its simplest literary form, this type of figure of speech is called a simile (marked comparison) or metaphor (unmarked; e.g., he is as strong as an *elephant*; women are *flowers* of the land). Such figurative language naturally needs to be taken from the hearers' own world of experience and cultural environment.[75]

An analogy in complete story form is known as a parable or allegory. In the case of the parable (e.g., The Weeds, Mt 13:24-30), there is usually only a single main point (or a closely related set of issues) which the story as a whole is intended to teach or illustrate by means of a more general comparison. An allegory (e.g., The Sower, Mt 13:3-23), on the other hand, tends to be more complex, with many of the specific persons, places and events of the account having a hidden, or deeper, sense or level of significance. The danger always exists, therefore, of pushing the various aspects of an allegory too far – of trying to get it to convey too much meaning so that it becomes artificial, or even so complicated that it is confusing. A proverb (e.g., Mt 6:24) is a conventional figurative comparison which normally does not extend beyond a single sentence. Its essential meaning, which incorporates some piece of traditional wisdom, is never stated directly, but is hidden by various layers of special linguistic form (e.g., brevity, ellipsis, allusion, word order) and culturally specific and/or sensitive content (e.g., sexual customs or religious practices). The analogy, in its various forms, is a common inductive device used in African oral tradition as well as the Bible. It is an especially prominent feature of the discourses of Christ, as any reading of the gospels readily attests to. Similarly, there is little doubt that this vital imaging device is an important element in the rhetorical repertory of effective preachers the world over.

---

[75] Cf. Ernst. R. Wendland, *The Cultural Factor in Bible Translation: A Study of Communicating the Word of God in a Central-African Cultural Context*, London & New York: United Bible Societies, 1987, pp. 110-124.

5. Contrast

A contrast is, in a sense, just a subtype type of analogy; indeed, it often forms the basis for a parable. However, instead of being based upon the relationship of similarity, the example, illustration, figure of speech or story that is cited involves some major form of difference, opposition or antithesis between the two items (persons, places, actions, situations, characteristics, etc.) which are being compared. As in the case of an analogy, this dissimilarity may concern a single key concept in the account, or it may be extended to cover several important aspects of the text's content. Similarities are often combined with differences to more fully convey the various aspects of a particular topic, issue, or appeal.

In Christ's parable of the two builders, for example, the first part of the discourse deals with the positive side of the matter, namely, the person who "builds" his thoughts and actions upon the Word of Christ. The second half then recounts the contradictory case (Mt 7:24-25), namely, that of an individual who constructs his life upon the sands of non-biblical principles of behaviour (7:26-27). Thus, a contrast is an effective means of highlighting the disparity or deviance between two states, characteristics or courses of action, and this makes it a useful resource in the preacher's repertory of inductive devices. A desirable attitude or attribute is often promoted with a greater measure of emphasis by dramatizing an opposing position, for prominent differences are usually more readily perceived by people than similarities, especially when they are receiving the message aurally as in a sermon. The use of contrast is particularly helpful when dealing with an established religious tradition (whether that of the Pharisees or a contemporary belief system) that needs to be radically revised with regard to many of its fundamental principles and presuppositions (e.g., Mt 5:27,31,33,38,43).

6. Puzzle

A puzzle involves some type of real or hypothetical problem that requires solving in order for understanding to occur or an action to take place. The speaker begins with a specific case, a situation which is familiar or at least known to the listeners, and then, during the course of a certain portion of the discourse, whether large or small, he proceeds to clarify, resolve, explain or interpret it together with them. Here, the matter of audience participation is especially crucial, for if they do not pay attention and thus get lost along the way, the whole point of the puzzle will of course fail to become apparent. On the other hand, a mystery of this nature tends to generate a great deal of interest, curiosity and even suspense, so people usually derive a certain measure of satisfaction in learning the truth or the solution that was at first hidden from them. This process of revelation, which may come all at once at the end (e.g., the parable of Nathan, the prophet) or may be progressively realized over the entire text (as we see in the books of Job and Ecclesiastes), helps in turn to reinforce the particular theological teaching or ethical admonition that is being set forth.

The same thing is true with the various other types of puzzle that can be used – a problem which needs to be solved, a question that lacks an answer, an error or mistake which has to be corrected, a difficult verdict that must be rendered, a controversial decision that must be evaluated, a discovery which is waiting to be made, an apparent paradox to be explained, a reversal or disappointment that needs to be overcome[76] or even a simple riddle that requires the right response. Sometimes a false or wrong solution, or solutions, may be presented first – and later rejected on the way to the right (or a more contextually appropriate) conclusion. Many of these instances deal with some type of cause-effect relation. One begins with true to life incident or situation which involves an effect and proceeds to answer the question, "Who or what caused it?" Alternatively, one can start out with a major cause and lead listeners along the path of discovering what will be its likely effect or outcome. These puzzles cannot be used too frequently or allowed to get too long and complicated, however, or they will not accomplish their purpose. Instead of enticing listeners to participate in the search for an answer, such a conundrum might only confuse them and drive them psychologically, perhaps even physically, away from the sermon.

7. Dialogue

Dialogue is the use of direct or reported speech involving two or more individuals. It is really a special literary technique rather than a separate text type; it may be introduced into any of the six categories previously dis-

---

[76] Thomas notes that such "reversals set the stage for fresh [spiritual] encounter," some new insight in relation to biblical truth and/or its moral imperative (Thomas, *They Like to Never Quit Praisin' God*, p. 15), or, we might add, some new direction or impulse in following the divine will (as illustrated, for example, in God's initial prevention from Paul going east [Acts 16:7], only to make possible his movement west into Europe [16:9]).

cussed. However, the importance of dialogue for achieving a genuinely inductive composition would justify our considering it as a distinct topic on its own. For one thing, since it is such a natural form of discourse, it strongly encourages the involvement of an audience. As they hear others talking in the text, they will be invited to join in the conversation mentally, at least, adding their own thoughts and opinions to the issues being discussed and hence learning through active participation in the sermon presentation. Dialogue also encourages personal, especially emotive, involvement by virtue of the fact that it normally deals with down to earth, life related topics. Such is the case, for example, in the dynamic folktale tradition of most African societies. It does not have to be this way of course; some very complex, philosophical subjects may also be effectively treated in this manner, as we see evidenced in the literary dialogues of Plato or Socrates.[77]

But for the most part, ordinary conversation is basically utilitarian in nature. In other words, it is used to carry out some of the most essential functions of human communication – not only to transmit or request information/knowledge, but also to convey one's emotions, to influence the thoughts, feelings, and actions of others and to institute and maintain harmonious interpersonal relations (e.g., discussions about health, wealth or the weather). Direct speech is also employed in literature, including virtually all of the books of the Bible, in order to foreground or give special emphasis to certain prominent ideas and attitudes. One frequently notices in the Scriptures, take Genesis and the Gospels for example, that the words of God and Christ are generally cast in the form of an actual quotation rather than as indirect speech. Such a feature automatically attests to the importance of what the Lord had to say, and this discourse characteristic holds true for people in most oral-aural societies as well.

The same thing applies if we consider the possibility of dialogue between a public speaker and his audience.[78] During a traditional oral narrative per-

---

[77] Complex, philosophical subjects are also reflected or commented upon in African oral narratives, but this is normally done below the obvious surface of a text – that is, on a much deeper, metaphorical or often symbolical level that is not immediately apparent to the uninitiated among the audience.
[78] "The preacher who is concerned about emotional process must use language that fosters dialogue between the preacher and the people ... [for this] involves the listeners as partners in the preaching process ... When people become a part of and invest in the sermon, they move more easily at the level of emotional process and experience the Gospel more deeply and profoundly" (*ibid.*, pp. 7f).

formance in many parts of Africa, for example, the audience participates not only with their minds, but periodically also with their words as well. As was noted earlier, this takes place in a more formal way during the song-choruses and stylized responses that are inserted into the story. Informally then, listeners may also be moved to spontaneously interject their own comments (exclamations, encouragement, acclaim, criticism, etc.) into the account, especially when the conversation of the characters reaches a climax or very critical stage. Certainly, such an overt form of involvement, if uncontrolled, would no doubt be very distracting to a preacher and disruptive of his sermon. But there may be ways of organizing or guiding the situation so that it serves a productive purpose – not only to help keep listeners mentally alert, but more important, to give them the opportunity of contributing their spontaneous ideas and reactions to the development of a particular theme and to stimulate them to make some of the important personal applications for themselves.

Probably the most obvious way of doing this (a method which I have tried out with some success myself) is to inject a number of key *questions* into a sermon presentation, both real (those which demand an answer of specific information) and rhetorical (those which demand some other form of response, such as assent, refusal or disagreement). This technique of course depends on the specific liturgical situation and nature of the congregation being addressed. It may not be appropriate or effective on more formal occasions (e.g., a Christmas sermon or at a funeral) or when the group concerned is relatively large (e.g., over one hundred) or older in age (i.e., this technique works especially well with the youth). Furthermore, it ought not be overdone or it soon loses its effectiveness. The best way might be to use this dialogue-provoking, question and answer technique as a means of introducing, concluding and/or summarizing the main point(s) of a particular portion of the text, or indeed, the sermon as a whole. We might just note in this connection that Christ asks nineteen key questions in his Sermon on the Mount to accomplish several important audience involving objectives (e.g., to generate thematic emphasis, as in Mt 5:46-47).

These seven crucial tools of the inductive technique are not often used in isolation. Rather, they perform best when employed in conjunction with one another within any composition that features the inductive method. Their basic interrelationships may be shown in a general sort of way by means of the following diagram:

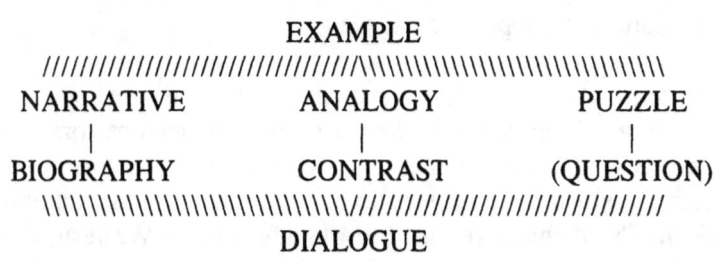

To explain, the example may be viewed as being the broadest category of the set as a whole. But 'example' may also exist as a class of its own, especially when multiplied to form a related series which together illustrate and illuminate a particular topic or issue. As a generic term then, the example may include at least three distinct subtypes: a narrative (story), analogy (comparison) or puzzle (problem to be solved). Each of the latter three may in turn be represented by an especially prominent instance, respectively: the biography (a personal life story), contrast (a comparison based on difference[s]) and question (motivating the search for an answer to the puzzle). And finally, all of these individual literary types may incorporate the device of dialogue, or direct speech, in order to increase the overall appropriateness, relevance, impact and appeal of the discourse.[79]

The inductive method, as we have seen, is an outstanding feature of traditional oral literature in central Africa. Due to the familiarity of this approach, therefore, as well as its undisputed effectiveness in an oral-aural

---

[79] Within these seven larger compositional forms, various other types of inductive or deductive development may be included on the paragraph level, such as the following sequences: "What is it – what is it worth – how does one get it?; explore-explain-apply; problem-solution; what it is not-what it is; either-or, both-and, promise-fulfillment, ambiguity-clarity, major premise-minor premise-conclusion, not this-nor this-nor this-nor this-but this; flashback (present-past-present); flash forward (present-future-present); lesser-greater" (F. Craddock, *Preaching*, Nashville: Abingdon, 1985, p. 177).

situational context, one might well assume that it would have considerable relevance to communication in general and the field of homiletics in particular. How might this technique be used to enhance the effectiveness of Christian sermon composition and delivery? In what way(s) can it be utilized to encourage a greater level of participation on the part of a listening audience (congregation) – an involvement which might not only increase the degree of message comprehension but also the amount of individual or joint appropriation and application as well?

What has been described here, namely, the inductive compositional approach, is surely quite familiar already to most African pastors and evangelists since they have without a doubt participated in one form or another of this method, which is characteristic of their ancient oral tradition, from childhood on. But many have also been taught a more Western, deductive procedure for sermon composition and delivery in their seminary or Bible school training program. This latter format may even have been impressed upon their thinking as the only correct way of Christian preaching. Thus, a certain tension or conflict may have been created in their minds. Is one method better than the other (the traditional versus the modern), or are they both equally suitable for use in Africa? Does each system have certain strengths which should be promoted, coupled with some critical weaknesses that need to be discouraged in their sermonizing? Could a combined methodology possibly be the answer – that is, a more flexible approach which at least leads one off in the right direction and which may be modified as called for by the situation or occasion at hand? In the final section of this chapter, I will offer a few suggestions that will hopefully lay the foundation for a constructive debate on this issue (to be followed up in chapter 5). The principal goal, it would seem, is to set our course towards developing a more indigenous, hence more practical, productive, teachable and contextualizable model to follow in this vital aspect of the pastor's ministry.

Application of the Inductive Method:

A.   Teaching through Participation
B.   Learning through Practice

I will comment first on the word *teach* in the heading above. Preaching (or public oral proclamation) is a means for *transmitting* a biblical message The essential goal is *teaching*, which consists of two distinct but closely interrelated activities: instruction, that is, imparting a certain amount of relevant information to people which they can understand; and *persuasion*, that is convincing them of the value of the material and motivating them to apply it in their hearts and/or lives. There are also other ways, besides or in addition to vocal preaching, that one can use to teach. Accordingly, one might employ large pictures or diagrams, slides or video film projected on a screen, a dramatic presentation, a selection of songs or the medium of the printed word. The content and objective might well be the same; only the form of the message and the method of conveying it is variable. In the present section, we want to consider this communication means and manner in somewhat more detail, based upon what has already been presented and from a didactic perspective. Is there an explicit set of procedures that may be taught in a group, or class situation, which may be used in order to improve sermon skills so that preachers might better accomplish the purpose(s) for which preaching is included as part of the regular worship service?[80]

To begin with, it is important to reaffirm the position of the Holy Spirit in this whole process. We are dealing with different ways of conveying the same basic Word of God. It is the Scriptures that are divinely inspired, not our various human modes of presenting them. And secondly, we must never forget that it is not our powerful preaching or our excellently conceived and fashioned sermons which convert people. This essential task is performed solely and alone through the distinct and diverse operation of the Holy Spirit. The best prepared, most beautifully presented sermon in the world will neither convict nor convince a single soul, let alone transform his sin-sick heart, if the Spirit is not working behind it. This essential homiletical principle has been well stated by Frank Thomas.

> The Holy Spirit causes and allows [spiritual] transformation to occur through [sermonic] celebration, and we preachers are junior partners and facilitators in [the] celebrative emotional process. We assist the

---

[80] Many able and experienced preachers, like a majority of the popular Chewa evangelists, carry out their communicative craft intuitively, using their God-given gift to convey the gospel in an effective manner (1Cor 12:4-11). I am not necessarily proposing a change in their accustomed way of doing things. What I am discussing in this section is merely a very tentative and provisional plan for introducing a more inductively based component into the homiletics classes of theological schools and seminaries. Of course, these preliminary ideas will need to be changed, supplemented and/or adapted as necessary to fit a particular curriculum or didactic setting.

Spirit, but the work is that of the Holy Spirit. ... The Holy Spirit goes along beside us in the journey from preparation to actual delivery of the sermon. ... If the Holy Spirit is going to do transformative work in the lives of people, the Spirit must be involved at the point where we commence sermon preparation. Involving the Spirit from the very beginning through prayer allows us to get in contact with God's intention for the sermon.[81]

In the present discussion we are simply considering different methods of proclaiming the gospel – human means which a sovereign, but gracious, God may use to accomplish his saving purpose in the world – to sanctify his name, to let his will be done, to make it possible for his kingdom to come. Preachers are but frail and fallible instruments in his almighty hands. They invariably require his wisdom to guide them in this task (and to begin with, a sure conviction of his calling). He is the power, and to him belongs all the glory. That is the fundamental presupposition upon which all biblically based sermonizing rests.

Our next major decision is to agree that we cannot do away with the sermon altogether, as some radical revisionists have proposed. That would not really accomplish very much because we would just have to replace it with some other mode of communication in the regular service of worship (which is itself a divine injunction – Heb 10:25) so that we might be faithful in carrying out our Lord's command to "make disciples of all nations" by publicly proclaiming his Word (Mt 28:19; cf. Rom 10:13-17). We remain, therefore, with the sermon as an essential form of message transmission, but what sort of organization should it manifest? A manner of arrangement that differs significantly from that of a standard Western deductive format is the focus of consideration in the present study.

The second thing that we do not wish to abolish are some of the fundamental principles of homiletics, especially those that are important and have proved their worth, at least from a Protestant evangelical perspective. It would seem that the following seven summary guidelines are more or less valid universally, that is, in Africa as well as America (or elsewhere):[82]

---

[81] Thomas, *They Like to Never Quit Praisin' God*, pp. 35, 64f.

[82] A more complete discussion and exemplification of these points in relation to a sermon teaching situation may be found in E.H. Wendland, *Preach the Word: A Study in Homiletcs*, Lusaka: The Lutheran Press, 1988. These principles arise out of a specifically Lutheran theological framework and

1. The *Word of God* must be the basis and primary focus of all preaching. It alone gives divine authority to the preacher's message. The text is a selected portion of the Scripture which serves as the foundation for a particular sermon and all that it contains: background, exposition, application, motivation and, to a considerable extent, also illustration.

2. The central purpose of preaching – in addition to giving glory to God – is fourfold: to instruct hearers concerning the truths of Scripture (*education*), to lead sinners (through the effective operation of the Holy Spirit) to faith in Christ (*evangelization*), to strengthen the faith of believers so that they might demonstrate it more deliberately and openly in their lives (*edification*) and to inspire people emotively to make God's Word a more active part of their consciousness and everyday experience (*evocation*).

3. A pastor needs to include both *law* (regarding human sin) and *gospel* (regarding divine grace) when preaching his sermons and to do so in a way which carefully preserves the distinct nature and function of each of these two basic biblical principles.[83] A similar distinction, but also manifesting a close theological interrelation, should be maintained with respect to the two chief doctrines that concern regenerated (born again) Christians: *justification* (new life) and *sanctification* (life renewal).

4. A pastor should choose his sermon texts so that he proclaims the whole counsel of God and thereby allows his people to grow in their knowledge of *the complete Word*, from Genesis to Revelation. It must be recognized, of course, that certain Scripture texts are more difficult to understand than others, and that some passages may be less contextually suitable for, or

---

praxis, but they would probably be acceptable, if not affirmed, by all evangelical churches that have their roots in the period of the great Reformation. The issue of developing a more natural, user-friendly and contextualized curriculum and method of theological education in Africa is one that needs considerable attention. Certainly the inductive approach would play a major role in such a plan, including such correlates as the case-study technique, dialogic (preferably vernacular) instruction, more group learning assignments and communal project work and holistic courses (i.e., ones that incorporate as many traditionally separate theological disciplines as possible: exegesis, isagogics, dogmatics, catechetics, church history, comparative religion, homiletics and so forth; cf. Wendland, "The Case for a 'Case-Study'").

[83] These fundamental principles may of course be expressed in different theological terms so long as no confusion results, such as we find for example in the following statement: "The Gospel [i.e., Law!] faces people in their sin and invites them to leave it for the life of freedom in Christ [i.e., Gospel]" (Thomas, *They Like to Never Quit Praisin' God*, p. 95). "Helpful criticism [and/or *reproof* and *condemnation* as necessary, i.e., Law] belongs early in the sermon, but further along we are, the more we present biblical affirmation [i.e., Gospel]" (*ibid.*, p. 95). There is thus a basic *law* => *gospel* movement in most evangelical sermons, which may be effectively climaxed, especially in an African setting, by an enthusiastic-emotive response to God's good news, termed "celebration" by Thomas (*ibid.*, ch. 5).

relevant to, a particular cultural group, specific social occasion or time of the year. In addition to the whole Bible, homiletical pericopes need to be selected so as to apply to the *whole life* of the audience, including both their perceived felt needs (or concerns) as well as their possibly unrecognized actual needs (or spiritual problems) as revealed by a thorough study of the Word.

5. A careful *preliminary study* is the first step in biblically based sermon preparation. This involves attentively reading and prayerfully meditating upon the chosen text itself, examining its total context (both textual and situational, biblical and contemporary), considering any parallel and other related passages (to allow Scripture to interpret itself), utilizing the insights of reliable commentaries, textual notes, cross references, study guides, doctrinal works, etc., and noting (by the methods of free association as well as deliberate investigation) all important theological truths and ethical applications that come to mind during such initial investigation of the pericope at hand.

6. Next, a *thorough analysis* of the biblical pericope must be carried out, preferably in the original languages of Scripture. This involves determining the chief, author intended, text specified communicative function(s) of a passage in its given textual context and situational (historical and ecological and socio-cultural) setting; observing the larger discourse structure of the text as the biblical writer arranged it; doing a complete exegesis of the individual verses (a lexical, grammatical, literary and rhetorical study with interpretation); summarizing the main thoughts of the passage under consideration; selecting several ideas which appear to be of greatest importance in the original setting; noting how these key ideas are related to one another within the text; and finding the central thought, or theme, of the pericope based on its overall structure, content and purpose.

7. Finally, a *basic outline* for the sermon is prepared by relating the preceding analysis of the biblical text to the particular social occasion and/or liturgical setting for which it will be preached. Such a sermon format will naturally focus upon the main thought of the passage and develop its own structure from there, generally following the organization and emphases of the original as much as possible. This thematic and topical framework may be composed in whatever degree of detail is desired, or as time allows, but it should be done using a receptor oriented level of language so that these basic thoughts may be readily transformed from the outline into actual

speech (e.g., without complex theological terms or concepts and churchly jargon).[84]

At this point in one's preparation – namely, the formulation of an outline – an important decision will generally have to be made. According to which method is this sermon going to be conceptualized, organized and developed – inductive or deductive? In more practical terms, the choice then actually boils down to this: will it be essentially a theme-and-parts or an examples-with-conclusion sermon (taking 'example' in the wider sense as noted earlier). But does such an either-or decision really have to be made? Is it desirable and/or necessary, in fact, to choose one method in preference to, or in virtual exclusion of, the other? Is there no way of combining the two approaches in such a manner that the strengths of each are retained while their major weaknesses are overcome?

A careful consideration of these two ways of compositional organization reveals an interesting relationship between them. Each method tends to have a principal deficiency, one which turns out to be the strong point of the other procedure. The following diagram summarizes these contrasting features:

Method	*Strength*	*Weakness*
Inductive	Illustration	Exposition
Deductive	Exposition	Illustration

Thus, an inductive procedure usually has plenty of illustratory material (stories, analogies, contrasts, puzzles, etc.), but there is always the danger that this may have the cumulative effect of diverting one's interest and attention away from the Scripture passage upon which the sermon should be based.

---

[84] To this point, the preceding guidelines are quite similar to those advocated by Thomas in his helpful notes on "sermon preparation" (*ibid.*, pp. 63-74). However, in his written sermon plan, or "preaching worksheet", Thomas goes further to present ideas that encourage a greater "experiential orientation" within the sermon, with special reference to a "behavioral purpose statement ... [which] state[s] specifically the way in which the sermon is to influence the behavior of the listener" and also a "strategy for celebration," which as "the final stage of the sermon functions as *the joyful and ecstatic reinforcement of the truth already taught and delivered in the main body of the sermon*" (*ibid.*, pp. 74, 85; original italics). These additions that pertain to both the emotive **experience and volitional** response of the audience would also be important factors to consider in the composition, presentation, teaching and evaluation of a more inductively developed sermon model for central Africa.

Furthermore, this method does not really encourage a thorough exegetical study of the original text. Frequently, then, either the message of such a sermon will be defuse and unfocused – that is, without a central, biblically based theme for the congregation to hold on to and remember. Alternatively, the exposition of the Scripture portion will be deficient and perhaps even deviant in spots where not enough concrete (or correct!) explanation has been supplied. As a result, the application of a poorly prepared inductive sermon may well turn out to be inappropriate, inaccurate, mixed up or misleading – that is, with respect to the biblical text(s) upon which it is supposedly based.

A deductively organized sermon, on the other hand, prepared by a skilled exegete, may be expected to offer a thorough exposition of the text (in its original context). But often this type of presentation is too detailed and finely argued, especially in a Western, more abstract, deductively analytical sort of way. In addition, it is often weak in the area of illustration and experiential application, and this will make it harder for listeners to understand and relate the logically ordered points as they are unfolded. This is a danger particularly in places like central Africa, where people are not used to this style of composition in the first place. The practical application of this type of sermon, one which concentrates too heavily upon a rational and elaborate explanation of a passage from Scripture, will probably end up sounding rather too deep, difficult or distant. Deemed irrelevant to everyday life, it will consequently fail to adequately meet the needs of the congregation and to come to grips with the real spiritual problems the members are facing.

The inductive method encourages active emotive participation; the various examples, illustrations and so forth which are introduced serve to get the audience personally and psychologically involved with the message. People learn by doing. That is to say, by imagining and putting themselves empathetically into the specific, everyday situations which are called to mind by the preacher-teacher, they gradually arrive at the conclusion, thematic point or exhortation that he is leading them to. They progressively grasp the lessons and principles that he is teaching since he has started out from where they are located conceptually – their beliefs, needs, values, goals, opinions and so forth. In short, he has taken their culture seriously, that is, their own worldview and way of life, and has employed it as a conceptual bridge to cross over into the Word of God and a consequent Christian perspective.

This method of moving – in a spiral (funnel or whirlpool) shaped manner, as it were – from the known to the unknown, the specific to the general, from concrete to abstract, question(s) to answer, from problem to solution, is quite familiar to the people of central Africa from past experience. Thus, their extensive oral tradition and corpus of customary lore can easily supply much of the background material which the preacher may wish to use in writing a sermon along these lines: the real life personal accounts, tribal histories, local descriptions (of familiar objects and events) or comparisons, initiatory instruction (if not contrary to the Scriptures), familiar folktales, proverbs, riddles, figures of speech and even popular songs (religious or secular). There should be little difficulty in capturing the immediate interest and sustained attention of his congregation while performing such a sermon as he employs some of the conventional illustrative and supporting techniques of the local storyteller – the lively enunciation, facial expressions, dramatic gestures, mimetic movements, vocal impersonations and so forth.

Of course, one should not overdo it. The preacher must never, albeit unwittingly, de-sacralize or trivialize either the Scriptures or his sermon through the chosen mode of presentation. Neither should he allow the attention of his captivated congregation to focus upon himself and his preaching technique, instead of the divine Word that he is proclaiming. There is an obvious danger here and a fine line to follow. Surely the speaker, who is in control of the message transmission event, must always be on guard against any such self-magnifying distortion. But neither should he bind himself to a manner of presenting a sermon – some textbook model perhaps – that is both unnatural to him and foreign to the people to (or better, *with*) whom he happens to be communicating good news of God.

There is another danger that needs to be mentioned here. One cannot simply string together a collection of stories, proverbs, comparisons or contrasts, mix in a little dialogue and assume that one has adequately prepared a sermon according to the inductive method. Not just any illustration will do, nor will a mere multitude of examples be effective in and of themselves. Each and every instance should be carefully chosen to fit into the larger pattern of thought and organization of the sermon as a whole. First of all, it must be related in some definite way – immediately perceptible by the listeners – to the textual base of the sermon. Secondly, the exemplifying material needs to be connected in a recognizable manner to the particular point (whether the central theme or a subpart) which the preacher happens to be developing at a given place in his presentation.[85] And finally, it is often considered to be the mark of a good style (at least in a Western sense) to have the various illustrations relate to one another so that each moves smoothly into the other, that is, with clear transitions, so that the sermon does not bump along, jumping from one example to the next with no apparent direction or goal in mind. However, this criterion may prove to be not as important in an African setting, that is, as long as the inductive devices all link up somehow with the main theme and purpose of the sermon as a whole.

So the inductive approach, if correctly carried out, can be utilized to build up a perceptible rapport between the preacher and his congregation (i.e., *ethos*) as well as to encourage their active participation in the sermon which he is delivering to them (i.e., *pathos*) – to get their thoughts and emotions flowing with him, so to speak, along the course prepared by the obvious current of his text (i.e., *logos*). There remains the appreciable difficulty of maintaining an appropriate or sufficient focus and emphasis upon the biblical passage which he has chosen to base his message upon to balance up with the important life related, experiential, emotive encounter that is fostered by the inductive method. Here is where the deductive mode of organization can help. In other words, once the preacher has achieved the goal of getting his listeners mentally involved in his communication through the use of inductive examples, stories, comparisons, etc. and has thus guided them to his main theological truth, conclusion, theme or exhortation, he is ready to expound and apply the particular portion of Scripture upon which everything should be firmly grounded.

This part of the presentation will manifest the typically deductive processes of text organization, interpretation, explanation and argumentation, along with the life related practical appeals of exhortation, admonition, recommendation or whatever is contextually needed or relevant. At this point, one of the three principal ways of unfolding a sermon deductively might be

---

[85] Thomas emphasizes this same point in his guidelines for a well-formed sermon of "celebration" (in an Afro-American setting): "I have seen preachers ride roughshod over the main body of the sermon, totally ignoring the situation, complication, and gospel assurance to spend most of the sermonic discourse moving to a crescendo unrelated to the biblical truth of the sermon" (*ibid.*, p. 96).

used, namely, the analytic, synthetic or diachronic (homily) outline,[86] depending upon the text which has been selected and the interpretive (biblical) competence or intellectual capacity of his congregation. Although there are three main homiletical possibilities to choose from here, it would seem that, within the larger framework of a primarily inductive approach, an elementary analytical or a diachronic, sequential and explanatory format would be preferable. This is because a closely text based expository procedure is better suited to expound the pericope as a *whole* from a *unified* perspective, with the principal stress upon *one* main idea, which leads in turn to a single major application. Accordingly, the simplest possible format of such a mixed, or combined inductive-deductive homiletical technique may be illustrated by the figure below:

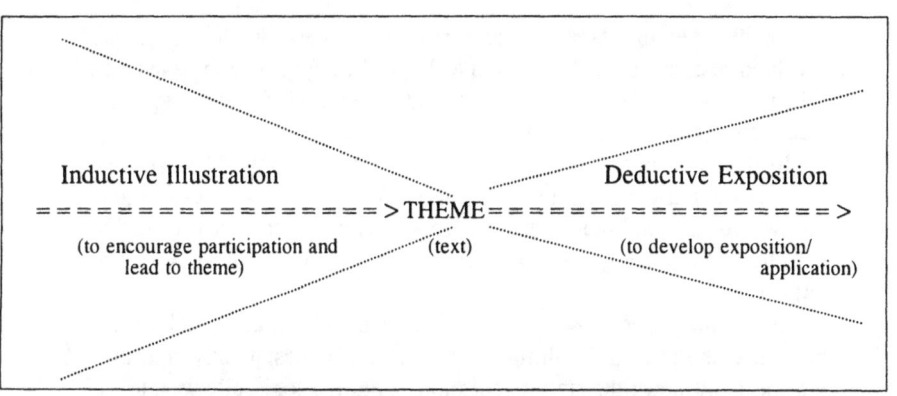

This overall process of progressively narrowing down inductively (major portion) to the central sermon theme (teaching or exhortation) and expanding out from that again deductively (minor portion) may be repeated, or recycled, several times; for example, *Induction* $> > > -- <$ *Deduction* / *I* $> > -- < D / I > > > > > -- < < D$, (where [--] signifies an exclusive focus on the biblical text; [/] indicates a new compositional "move" or section; and [>] or [<] refers to the relative amount of space/time devoted to induction or deduction respectively). This might be done in order to demonstrate a principal truth, first of all, and then – depending on the Scripture passage being studied – each of its major parts, or subtopics (generally, no more than two – to allow for comparison and contrast). Any number of variations are possible, which would change according to differences in

---

[86] Cf. Wendland, *Preach the Word*, pp. 40f.

factors such as the text, the occasion for the sermon, the type of congregation or group that it is being preached to, the formality of the setting and so on; e.g., for a children's sermon: [$I >>>>>-<D-$].

It is interesting to compare the basic model proposed above with that outlined by Thomas for his plot related (i.e., situation => complication/problem => resolution) type of celebratory sermon that seems to be especially effective in black American preaching.[87] Here, too, we have an essential three stage process of induction (complication), followed by deduction (gospel assurance) and climaxed by an even greater measure of induction (celebration). The homiletic intent of each of these segments may be described as follows:

> In the opening stage of the sermon, the need is to get people involved and 'on board' so emotive logic through sense appeal takes priority over cognitive logic. The situation and complication are localized in the experience (senses) of the listener.
> In the main body of the sermon, the gospel is applied to resolve the experiential complication. Cognitive logic through exegesis, interpretive insight, and theological reflection come centre stage to establish the truth of the gospel. The truth of the gospel resolves the complication.
> Once the gospel resolves the complication, emotive logic mandates that the preacher culminate the sermon by ecstatically reinforcing the good news through celebration. Emotive logic allows intensification of the good news at the core of people to effect a shift and transformation of perspective, attitude, and feeling [through the overseeing operation of the Holy Spirit].[88]

---

[87] The similarity here is especially noteworthy since Thomas' significant work has only just recently been published (Thomas, *They Like to Never Quit Praisin' God*), long after the ideas of this chapter were developed and composed in their present form. Blount too proposes a basic tripartite design for "the black [American] sermon": "In the first phase ... the preacher establishes the biblical theme for the sermon by using textual and ideational controls. Phase two begins the interpersonal phase of the sermonic presentation: the preacher interprets the biblical theme in a manner appropriate to his or her personality [*auto-application*]. ... In phase three ... the preacher interprets the text by means of secular examples that make modern illustrative contact with the biblical materials [*audience-application*]" (Blount, *Cultural Interpretation*, p. 75). However, it appears that according to this model, the preacher would begin more or less deductively and then move on to develop the biblical text by various types of induction.
[88] Thomas, *They Like to Never Quit Praisin' God*, p. 88.

It is during the crucial climactic stage of celebration that an activation of the *intuition* of individual Scripturally (spiritually) engaged listeners normally occurs. Such an intuitive "capacity for direct knowing or learning beyond the conscious use of reasoning",[89] whether deductive or inductive, makes possible or facilitates (there may be some debate here) a person's implicit interaction with his or her core beliefs and essential values in terms of their elimination, reinforcement, addition or some other significant conceptual or behavioural modification. It is not possible to expand upon these rather complex, psychological compositional notions here, except to stress their potential relevance to the development of a more natural, African oriented homiletical model, one that will have to be proposed, constructed, adapted and perfected by mother tongue speakers/thinkers for the ultimate spiritual benefit of their own people.

The totally inductive style of preaching that characterizes the Chewa revivalists differs considerably from all of the models previously discussed. It will be considered and evaluated in relation to the Wame corpus in the next two chapters. But before we reach that alternative, it may be useful to point out several other options that issue from the inductive-deductive compositional approach that was presented above. One important modification may be necessary for those congregations which are accustomed to, and actually prefer, a sermon which begins with a reading of the Bible text. In this case, the preacher would read this passage (with or without a brief introduction) and then proceed to develop his sermon along the lines suggested above. The difference here is that his first major point of transition (that is, the break between induction and deduction) occurs at his central theme, at which stage the text (or some relevant portion of it) is reintroduced and explained or expounded in considerably more detail. The procedure could be repeated subsequently for each of the parts according to how the theme has been divided in the sermon outline. The organization of the message would thus alternate between an inductive, a deductive and a mixed mode of arrangement throughout.

The important principle to keep in mind when applying this combined method in an African setting is that the process ideally *begins and ends with induction* (with or without an explicit citing of or reference to the biblical

---

[89] *Ibid.*, p. 9.

text). This would constitute the sermon's major development style, first of all, to effect entry into the discourse in order to initiate the essential stage of conceptual engagement and emotive interaction. Then, once a main point, conclusion or appeal has been reached through such familiar, participatory exemplification, the preacher would carry on with a minor (in terms of quantity), deductive exposition of the biblical text. This alternation between induction and deduction could be repeated for every aspect of the main theme and/or exhortation that is being proclaimed, along with appropriate life related applications according to the Word of God that is serving as the foundation for the message. But the close of any experientially engaging sermon will normally be characterized by an emotionally heightened type of induction, or celebration, which serves to reinforce, through thanksgiving, praise and worship, the gospel centred resolution (whether a proposition or an imperative) of the main problem (complication) of the message. As Thomas describes it,

> Any material based on sense appeal that puts us in touch with festive and positive emotions is suitable for use in celebration. Any material that triggers the imaginative capacity by releasing affirmation, hope, peace, joy, and love in core belief is potential material for celebration ... [such as] poetry, music, images, metaphors, stories, personal testimony, anecdotes, [references to] plays, novels, etc. And then there is the preacher's own spirit, gestures, facial expressions, and personhood that can generate a contagion of celebration.[90]

The question of whether such an outburst of celebration should occur only once in a sermon – namely, as its concluding segment[91] – or whether several minor, mutually reinforcing instances might have a similar impact and effect is debatable. This issue might be better considered and assessed after presenting the Wame relational-inductive model, which seems to more closely exemplify the second alternative.

As far as the actual composition of an inductive, or an inductive-deductive, sermon goes (if we consider a classroom situation), the preacher ought to

---

[90] Thomas here (*ibid.*, p. 99) mentions only the "positive" aspects and emotions that might pertain to what he terms the final "celebration" of a sermon. However, I think that in certain instances some negative counterparts could also serve as an effective concluding force of motivation, e.g., sorrow and penitence in conjunction with a Good Friday sermon, one preached at a sad-case funeral or where the entire congregation is in need of rebuke (as Paul does in First Corinthians).

[91] Thomas, *They Like to Never Quit Praisin' God*, p. 96.

follow the basic advice of the method itself; learn to carry out and perfect it on the basis of actual experience, that is, through extensive personal (communal) participation and practice. To begin with, the minister (in the full sense of this term) has to involve himself fully in the life of the parishioners whom he has been called to serve. He must first know their various weaknesses, needs, fears, values, desires, goals, etc. before he can begin to communicate with them effectively.

Where will he find all of the examples, stories, analogies, and case studies which will constitute the backbone of the inductive part of his sermon? From the culture of his people, of course – from their everyday experience, life style, oral art forms, conversations, surrounding environment and the like. To be a good teacher, he must first be a good learner. It has been said that "a pastor finds the themes of his sermons among his people"[92] This applies not only to the Scriptures, which are to be his life long subject, but it also involves all those individuals who comprise the object of his ministry – young and old, male and female, educated and non-literate, wealthy and poverty stricken. He must be able to relate in some way to them all and apply the Word to the hearts and lives of each and every one – beginning with his own inner self (i.e., his personal core beliefs and central values[93]). The preacher who does not know himself or his people, and know them well, will never be able to compose a successful inductive, person to person and experience oriented, sermon. It is as simple – and as difficult – as that!

The same thing could be said, of course, for the deductive sermon. But here, all too often, for one reason or another, the experience driven, people-oriented aspects of one's preparation are left to suffer, while the greater portion of one's time and effort is devoted to text study, developing a logical outline (whether basic or expanded), writing out and learning the sermon. To be sure, these also are important elements in a discourse that is primarily inductive in nature. The biblical text, as has been stressed repeatedly, is the heart and life of the sermon, and one simply cannot do without an adequate background study and analysis of this selected and highlighted portion of Scripture. But the preacher, who wishes also to be a genuine teacher, an effective communicator and a successful motivator cannot stop there. He must not assume that, because his exegesis is correct and he has

---

[92] Cited in Pless, "Seven Pulpit Paradigms", p. 201.
[93] Cf. Thomas, *They Like to Never Quit Praisin' God*, p. 71.

formulated an exemplary, well-constructed theme-and-parts, he will automatically convey the central teaching of his text in a way that is really meaningful to his listeners. He needs to explicitly, empathetically and energetically relate to their way of thinking and feeling. He must constantly refer to real life experiences, the sad as well as the glad, both for the illustrations which will involve his audience in the message and in order to follow up on the exposition of his text by means of a contextually appropriate, emotively captivating and behaviourally challenging application.

Summary: Five Basic Homiletical Steps

The compositional outline or framework of a combined inductive-deductive sermon as proposed above will naturally differ in certain key respects from that formulated for an analytic, synthetic, or expository sermon. I will conclude with a summary of some of the suggestions that were given above concerning how one might go about organizing more precisely or deliberately such an outline which incorporates elements of both induction and deduction into its homiletical development.[94] There are five basic steps in this procedure.

1. Determine the Textual Focus and Flow

One must first decide upon the main principle or teaching of the passage of Scripture that one is basing one's sermon on. What is the central idea which all of the other thoughts relate to; what is the key question that the rest of the material serves to answer? How do these thoughts flow together to comprise the portion or text as a whole? What is the main problem of physical or spiritual need that is being addressed? What is the primary exhortation (proscription or prescription) that is set forth in the text at

---

[94] These procedures, which more or less summarize those that were presented earlier, presuppose a literary composition. However, the method under consideration may also be applied to a sermon which is prepared completely within a vocal-audio framework, that is, without writing anything down on paper. It is likely that the use of a cassette tape recorder could be effectively adapted for this purpose. Such a totally oral-aural approach would naturally be more difficult, though not impossible, to teach – or perhaps model would be the better term to refer to this practice. As was mentioned earlier, most popular Chewa preachers who utilize the inductive method probably do not write much, if anything, down as part of their preparation (Shadrack Wame usually does compose notes). Nevertheless, it might be good for them too to keep some of the positive features of deduction (biblical principle = > practical application) in mind as they either conceptually work through their sermon in advance or as they intuitively preach a given text of Scripture.

hand? As was noted above, such focused conceptualization is one of the most important aspects of the analysis process that needs to be carried out as part of one's preparation for composing any kind of sermon, whether inductive or deductive in nature.

2. Consider the Contextual Occasion

A given idea or injunction may be expressed in different ways. The underlying content might remain essentially the same, but the manner in which this is stated can be modified in order to fit different situations. A preacher must carefully consider the particular setting in which his sermon is to be preached – the time of the church year (e.g., Christmas), any special problems that his members may be facing (e.g., a recent funeral in the congregation), the secular context (e.g., news of local or national importance) and the environmental setting (e.g., a widespread drought). Such circumstantial factors will determine the specific form in which he words the central theme that he intends to use as the basis for his sermon. They will also influence to a great extent the direction that he will take in developing this theme. In fact, the occasion concerned may determine the biblical text that is chosen, in which case steps 1 and 2 would have to be reversed.

3. Collect the Relevant Illustrations

The preacher now starts to gather the various life related examples, narratives, proverbs, analogies, Scriptural parallels, and so forth which will serve as the foundation for the inductive approach. One way to organize this process (at least for beginners) is to take a piece of paper and write the central theme of the text at the top and underline it. Then make two columns underneath, the one on the left for any implied thoughts or theological insights which may be related to the main idea; the right column for listing all types of practical examples which may be used to illustrate either the main topic (imperative) or any of the chief subpoints that are potentially associated with it.

Begin with the rich resource of the Bible itself[95] and only after that motherlode has been fully mined, turn to other religious and secular sources. Particular attention should be given to what may be termed the 'emotive-volitional value' of the illustratory elements that are selected. How closely are

---

[95] Cf. Thomas, *They Like to Never Quit Praisin' God*, p. 99.

they related to one another and to the sermon's major message? How well do they actually develop, enhance or unify that message (without detracting or distracting from it)? A preacher should not attempt to carry out this brainstorming procedure all at once, at a single sitting. Rather, he ought to meditate on his text for several days (if possible), first to review his previous study and then to note down any more relevant ideas, illustrations, applications and implications as they come to him.

4. Sort Out the Data

At some point, one must stop the additive process of gathering and begin to meaningfully organize what has been collected. This is largely a matter of subtracting extraneous material and connecting the more closely related items among what is left. It will become obvious that some thoughts simply do not belong – at least they do not seem to fit within the general framework of thought that is emerging for this particular sermon (text, occasion and purpose). These may be crossed out. The remaining ideas, illustrations and applications need to be linked up with each other. This may be done by drawing lines to the various concepts or exhortations which appear to fit most closely together.

The author also has to think about a particular order in which he wants to arrange his material – an order of importance as well as one of natural succession. The major ideas as they relate to the central theme can be indicated with capital letters (so as not to be confused with Bible verse numbers), the minor ones by small letters. In the case of the various emotive or provocative elements, it may be helpful to organize these as well so that a progressive build up and a final climax, or end stress, is created (with or without one or two minor peak points within the body of the sermon). Alphabetical order will suggest the sequence in which the preacher will present the selected topics of his sermon. It is a good idea to do this sorting out process in pencil because one normally finds that it is necessary to keep revising things as one goes along.

5. Construct an Outlined Plan of Development

After he has organized his data roughly on a page of paper, the preacher will find it helpful to tie his ideas together more tightly in the form of an planned outline. This is best done on a separate sheet from the data page of step 4 to avoid complication or confusion. If a spiral notebook with facing pages is available, one side may be used to record all of the preliminary work (steps 1-4), and, next to this, one can write down the final outline, which will, we assume, include both inductive and deductive arrangements consisting of various cognitive, emotive and volitional elements in an appropriate proportion and balance for the particular sermon occasion. This will contain all of the main points, including the theme and its parts (if any), along with the various examples which are cited to illustrate them as well as the specific real life situation(s) to which they will be applied. A good rhetorical outline is like a road map; it shows the preacher the direction in which he will travel in the sermon and why. It can also help to prevent him from getting lost – that is, from leaving out, adding to or mixing up his basic material (yet allowing for the freedom to modify extemporaneously as needed – or inspired – during the actual delivery).

Once such an compositional guide has been prepared, and perhaps revised as the author rethinks this and continues to meditate on his text and context during the week, it is not difficult to go ahead and write the sermon out completely in readiness for thorough learning and a smooth delivery. More experienced orators may not feel the need to write everything, or even anything, down.[96] But the basic conceptual affective plan, one which is essentially tied to the text of Scripture that the pastor intends to preach about, is a helpful (some would say, crucial) aspect of adequate sermon preparation, no matter what method one is following.[97]

We turn now for some specifics to an expert in the art technique of more purely inductive, participatory proclamation, Mr Shadrack Wame. In the next chapter, I present a detailed description and exemplification of the main distinguishing features of his compositional rhetoric and style of

---

[96] Thomas emphasizes the importance of writing out one's sermon, several times in fact. "Experience teaches that writing sharpens sermonic focus, and allows careful attention to the movement and unity that are critical to any quality sermon ... *clear and precise writing that develops clarity of thought is indispensable to clear and precise preaching*" (Thomas, *They Like to Never Quit Praisin' God*, p. 80; original italics). Perhaps the oral-aural equivalent for a sermon that is being composed with a minimum of writing or none at all would be several *vocal* preach throughs (ideally *recorded* for subsequent evaluation) once the initial conceptual preparation (text study, illustration gathering, etc.) has been completed.
[97] As was noted earlier, on his "preaching worksheet", Thomas gives some good suggestions for other items to be considered that will contribute to the formulation of a well-constructed, rhetorically effective sermon outline, with special reference to the text-culminating activity of "celebrating" its central gospel message (*ibid.*, pp. 74-80).

sermonizing. This is based on a prior analysis of a relatively large corpus of texts (about forty) that he has already preached over a number of years in both Malawi and Zambia. These features do reflect, to a greater or lesser degree, also the essential pattern or plan of the basic Chewa iterative relational-inductive type of sermon that characterizes most of those that are included in my wider collection (over one hundred sermons).

3. Ten Verbal Power Tactics for Rhetorical Proclamation in Chichewa Preaching

Introduction: The Word at Work

There are ten interrelated and partially overlapping tactics from the point of view of rhetorical strategy and stylistic technique which the popular Chewa preachers all seem more or less to rely upon in the compositional development of their revivalistic sermons – that is, to enhance the appeal of their discourse to *pathos, ethos,* and *logos* (in that order of relative importance).[98] They thereby seek to foreground or to magnify (in a supplementary, supportive sort of way) the divine power of the originally inspired Word by means of the human power of the contemporary spoken word.[99] These devices, all of which serve in tandem to mentally and emotionally engage the congregation during this *participatory* manner of preaching, are as follows: narrative preference, personal exemplification, traditional allusion, dramatic delivery, affective appeal, evocative description, strategic reiteration, verbal intensification, idiomatic figuration, and audience involvement.[100] The first three are particularly applicable to

---

[98] By terming these sermons *revivalistic* (or *hortatory*), I am simply attempting to classify them rather broadly as religious proclamations that are designed primarily to inspire, excite, admonish, warn, and/or encourage believers in their Christian life. Thus, the *principal* aim is not evangelistic (to win the lost/new converts), edificational (to build believers up in their knowledge of the faith), or expositional (to systematically interpret a particular biblical pericope).

[99] I am assuming the best motives and consequent performance on the part of this group as a whole. Although it does seem at times that one preacher or another will get carried away by his rhetoric, I believe that a final evaluation in this regard awaits the detailed study of competent Malawian scholars based on their own research. In any case, the position of Augustine on the matter is worth noting: "...eloquence cannot be separated from Christian truth ... eloquence without [biblical] truth is empty, false rhetoric ... eloquence must show truth, make truth pleasing, and make truth move the audience" (Oberhelman, *Rhetoric and Homiletics*, pp. 116f). Conversely, in the words of John Chrysostom, "the [preacher] who is carried away with the desire for eulogies may have the ability to improve the people, but chooses instead to provide nothing but entertainment. That is the price he pays for rounds of applause" (cited in Pless, "Seven Pulpit Paradigms", pp. 197f).

[100] It is interesting to compare this list with the inventory of usages that Mitchell regards as being characteristic of traditional "Black preaching" in America: personal mannerisms, tone, rhythm, call and response, repetition, role playing (story telling), subjectivity, rhetorical flair, slow delivery, aphorisms, and hesitation (H. H. Mitchell, *Black Preaching: The Recovery of a Powerful Art*, Nashville: Abingdon Press, 1990, ch. 6). I will be referring to these in more detail for comparative purposes in the following discussion (cf. H. H. Mitchell, "African-American Preaching", in Willimon and Lischer (eds.), *Concise*

the larger *structural* development, or constitution, of a homiletical-hortatory discourse; the second three pertain especially to an *emotional* stimulation of the audience; the third triad features the *stylistic* microstructure of composition and its diction. The last tactic relates to the primary purpose of an inductively fashioned text as a whole, namely, a *communal* engagement of the thoughts, feelings, values, and volition of the intended receptors, together with the speaker-source himself, with regard to some message of deep religious and ethical concern.[101]

One preacher will usually differ from another in his/her chosen or preferred combination and ordering of these devices as well as in the proportion or degree to which s/he utilizes them within a particular sermon.[102] However, the most effective orators utilize an effective balance of such tactics – not as an end in themselves or purely to draw attention to their own verbal skills[103] – but to highlight and to impress upon one's memory the main theme of their message along with any related subpoints through the use of this culturally conditioned "mother tongue of the spirit"[104]. I will exemplify these techniques by means of a *paradigmatic* selection from the outstanding cor-

---

Encyclopedia of Preaching, pp. 2-9; J. M. Spencer, "Folk Preaching (African-American)", in Willimon and Lischer (eds.), *Concise Encyclopedia of Preaching*, pp. 142f). My ten features also include or overlap with the main "stylistic qualities" that have been identified by Okpewho for "African oral literature," namely, repetition, parallelism, piling and association, tonality, ideophones, digression, imagery, allusion, and symbolism (Okpewho, *African Oral Literature*, ch. 4).

[101] The typical Chewa sermon audience tends to interact quite closely with a preacher through a variety of verbal and non-verbal means throughout a given presentation. Such an active group of receptors differs quite markedly from the passive Ethiopian congregation noted by Forslund: "... no immediate feedback from the audience is usually possible. Communication between the preacher and his audience takes place mainly outside the formal setting of the sermon" (Forslund, *The Word of God in Ethiopian Tongues*, p. 111). Indeed, such quiescence would appear to be atypical in relation to most sermon settings in Africa.

[102] I will use the masculine pronoun when referring to a certain preacher in the abstract simply for convenience and because most of the group that I have collected are men. Mitchell refers to this personalized attribute as a preacher's use of "mannerisms," or individual peculiarities of oratorical style that distinguish him to a greater or lesser extent from his colleagues. This would include any distinctive stylistic features that are not described below. He notes that such "mannerisms add interest and signal a freedom and authentic personhood in which the congregation participates vicariously, by identification" (Mitchell, *Black Preaching*, p. 89). I would suppose that this observation is largely true also as far as the Malawian preachers are concerned. A more content oriented overview of "the sermon in the Black [American] church" is found in ch. 5 of Blount (Blount, *Cultural Interpretation*, ch. 5).

[103] Martin Luther warns against such a temptation: "The preacher must avoid laying emphasis on his own words in order to show off (*glaenzen*)....That is pure noise, serving one's own vanity....To say much in a few words, that is [the art of preaching]" (cited in Meusner, *Luther the Preacher*, p. 54).

[104] Mitchell, *Black Preaching*, p. 76.

pus of Shadrack Wame's sermons (about forty in total).[105] In order to illustrate the unified, stylistically and thematically integrated, quality of these inductively organized homiletical compositions,[106] I will present in the next chapter a partial analysis through annotation of the *diachronic* rhetorical development of three complete examples, the first and most extensively examined being Mr Wame's sermon proclaiming Christ as the "rock" solid "foundation" who enables his people on the one hand to stand firmly against the formidable powers of evil that trouble them in this present world, and on the other hand to enter upon a life of genuine discipleship (Mt 7:21-24; 1Cor 3:11, 10:4; Lk 9:23 – note this typical juxtaposition of topically related texts).

Narrative Preference

"There is much storytelling at work in the Black approach to the Bible," observes one recognized expert with reference to the typical African-American sermon.[107] The same homiletical preference holds true with respect to the vast majority of Chewa sermons that I have experienced, including the many that I have only heard over the years but not collected. Most preachers prefer biblical narrative texts, whether found in the Old or the New Testament, and even when starting out with a pericope or passage of another literary type, e.g., from the psalms, prophets, or epistles, they will usually find a way of linking this to some familiar historical account.[108] One common mode of sermon development is for the preacher to dramati-

---

[105] Many noteworthy examples occur also in the sermons of the other preachers, but in order to limit the scope of my study somewhat I decided to restrict my consideration to the Wame collection. This further enabled me to get a better picture of the interactive nature of these stylistic-rhetorical devices as they are manifested both paradigmatically and syntagmatically within the corpus of a single, preeminent practitioner. My original analysis was based upon the corpus of forty Wame sermons; I subsequently obtained recordings of another fifteen but did not have the opportunity of analyzing these as thoroughly.

[106] From an analytical, Western perspective, these inductively fashioned sermons at first appear to be rather loosely organized, which results in typically negative evaluative characterizations such as circular, repetitious, rambling, or disjointed. As we shall see below, the inductive arrangement is decidedly more paradigmatic (topically related) in nature and hence not so apparent perhaps as the syntagmatic (temporally ordered, logically linked) development that marks a deductive composition.

[107] Mitchell, *Black Preaching*, p. 69.

[108] This same narrative emphasis is found in the collection of sermons analyzed by Ross (Ross, "Preaching in Mainstream Christian Churches in Malawi", p. 87). Texts from other types (genres) of books tend to be rather short and appear to be chosen primarily for their topical relationship to the preacher's main theme or pericope, often by means of some prominent hook word or key concept.

cally *retell* the story that he has just read from the Scriptures.[109] This will be done after the manner of a teller of traditional tales (*nthano*) where the speaker performs or impersonates the key narrative roles, including the antagonistic parts of God and/or Satan, e.g., through vocal mimicry and selective sound effects.[110] In such cases, the application of *pronunciatio* would involve the appropriate vocal representation of the particular character, interpersonal situation, and social setting concerned (cf.ch.1). The narrator would also incorporate various comments or asides as needed, for example, to provide further explanation or illustration of some aspect of the account, or to make an appropriate religious application.

To be sure, there may be a considerable amount of imaginative *elaboration* involved in this rhetorical technique, for example, when Shadrack Wame speculates about why God brought the family of Jacob/Israel *en masse* to Egypt (his answer: so that the clan leaders might learn how to write from the Egyptians and thus be able to keep better records of God's saving activity on their behalf; SW14).[111] On other occasions, a narrator will not only elaborate upon a particular narrative detail, he will proceed to expand this into a powerful *exhortation*. When reflecting, for example, on why Jesus stumbled when carrying his cross (a possible implication from reading Mt 27:32), Wame suggests that it was not the physical weight of the wood that caused this, but rather the overwhelming spiritual burden of the sins of the whole world – including in particular those of the listening audience. The only proper response to such a great manifestation of personal vicarious self-sacrifice would be a sufficiently sorrowful repentance (SW42).

In many instances such narrative augmentation serves the essential function of enabling the audience to mentally visualize the events that are being recounted and to empathetically identify with (or feel revulsion for) certain personages as if they were actually present there as observers on the scene.[112] The more accomplished practitioners always carefully structure

---

[109] Forslund noted a strong preference for narrative retelling in his Ethiopian collection, especially among "preachers with only informal theological training or none at all" (Forslund, *The Word of God in Ethiopian Tongues*, p. 242).
[110] Cf. Willimon and Lischer (eds.), *Concise Encyclopedia of Preaching*, p. 4; Wendland, "Stylistic Form and Communicative Function", ch. 8.
[111] The special references, e.g., SW14, denote individual sermon texts in my collection, i.e., SW = Shadrack Wame; 14 = number 14 in Mr Wame's personal corpus.
[112] The same is true of the Black American use of stories in sermons: "At all times while the story is

and shape the original account to highlight the main theological topic and/or religious purpose of their sermon so that the retelling does not become a mere entertaining end in itself. The story rather lays the foundation both for thematically unifying the discourse as a whole and for motivating the principal effect (impact and appeal) that the preacher aims to achieve. Through this means, the central, everyday conflict of the Christian with the various internal and external forces of evil is made immediately personal and vividly real so that listeners are strongly encouraged to commit themselves to the power of Christ for both temporal and ultimate (eternal) victory. In this way, then, these dramatic narrative pieces powerfully "engage the vital emotions of an audience [i.e., *pathos*!], making possible new understanding and a fresh orientation".[113] That is to say, the grievous, demoralizing problems caused by sin in one's life are confronted with a renewed resolve, through divine enablement (which is rarely lost sight of), to overcome such adversaries and adversities.

An outstanding example of Evangelist Wame's evocative narrative skills is found in his sermon based on the story of the raising the Nainite widow's son (Lk 7:11-17; text SW8). Wame first sharpens our perspective on the scene by focusing upon two large companies of people and their opposing movements. One is composed of the itinerant Rabbi (Jesus) and his disciples happily moving into the town (*mudzi*) to begin a new 'crusade'; the other is made up of a sad company of mourners accompanying the bier of the only son of a widow and heading for the graveyard (*manda*) outside of town. The two groups eventually meet near the main gate (where there would most likely be another crowd present conducting civic and personal business) to witness a dramatic resurrection event performed by the Lord.

Wame heightens this unusual encounter by briefly contextualizing the events. In a Chewa cultural setting, the only person who is believed to have the mystical power to halt a funeral procession or handle the coffin of a dead body and cause it to rise up (v.14) is the infamous, nocturnal, necrofagous witch (*mfiti*) of traditional belief! Jesus, however, operates in broad daylight and touches the young man's corpse to give life, even as he

---

being told, the teller is caught up in it as if it had been witnessed personally. ... Members of the audience then feel as if they too have seen the action; they participate vicariously" (Mitchell, *Black Preaching*, pp. 69f).

[113] *Ibid.*, p. 70.

encourages the surrounding survivors with the words, "Don't weep!"(v.13). The notion of weeping is rhetorically developed in the form of a paradox which emphasizes the sermon's main point: We should not mourn over the *death* of a person who was spiritually alive on earth (having been raised up by faith in Christ); rather, we ought to weep for the *life* of someone who is spiritually dead. The latter is the real "corpse" (*mtembo* – a key thematic hook word), which may be characterized by the nature of the mortal sin of the individual who inhabits it, e.g., sexual immorality, stealing, slander, or avarice. Wame goes on to illustrate the notion of a living corpse by telling the account of his son whom he found sleepwalking one night but who could not remember the event at all the next morning. In this way, Wame narratively captures the imagination of his listeners and thereby encourages them to emotively experience the nature and the effects of life and death in a spiritual sense and from the viewpoint and judgement of God.

Most narrative retellings or paraphrases are based more or less on some Scripture passage, but the Chewa sermon inventory includes several other important story types, which may be classified as being either true or fictitious in quality and traditional or modern in setting. Many true, non-biblical narratives are personal in nature, but there are others that recount a series of historical, usually relatively familiar, events that occurred either in some distant age (e.g., of colonialism) or in the more recent past. The fictional category includes stories of a customary oral variety, i.e., folktales (*nthano*), either retold or newly composed, and those that are set in a more contemporary sociocultural context.

The rhetorical objective of any of these narratives, as in the case of Christ's parables,[114] is to draw the audience psychologically into the account – and thereby also into the topical framework of the sermon itself. Here, especially through empathy with one or more of the key characters, listeners experience its actions, attitudes, feelings, and motivations more immediately and hence memorably. The central thematic (theological and/or ethical) point being implicitly conveyed (but later explicitly revealed and expounded by the preacher) thus makes a greater impression on listeners'

---

[114] Ernst R. Wendland, "Finding Some Lost Aspects of Meaning in Christ's Parables of the Lost – and Found (Luke 15)", *Trinity Journal* 17NS, 1996, pp. 54-59.

minds and hearts, which is the primary purpose of rhetorical *pathos*.[115] Consequently, it is more readily acted upon (or rejected) as a deliberate act of the Spirit led (or unregenerate) will.

I cannot illustrate all of the different, non-biblical narrative type distinctions mentioned above, but it may be helpful to consider just one example in order to observe in summary fashion how Evangelist Wame tends to utilize this prominent device (in terms of form, content, and function) in his discourse. In a sermon based on John 10:9-10 that promotes the full life (*moyo wochuluka*) that believers have in Christ (SW12), Wame dramatizes the on going conflict that exists between them and the personal spiritual power who wishes to destroy them, namely, Satan – the thief. He utilizes a little animal tale composed in the traditional mode to highlight the precariousness of man's position and the need for constant vigilance against a life threatening foe. One day a mother hen (*nkhuku*) hatched out a new set of chicks (*anapiye*), but an immediate problem arises. How would she protect them from a house-cat (*mphaka*) that lived on the domestic premises? Would the cat wait until these chicks matured so that it could make a fuller meal of them? No indeed, moved by instinct and greed, it would strike and devour at the first opportunity, no matter how small a morsel. Similarly, there is no time when a Christian can consider him/herself immune from Satan's deadly strike.

Now it so happened that the owner (*ambuye*) of the farm kept careful watch on his flock and did not allow the chicks to fall prey to the cat, which had to satisfy itself in the meantime with lizards and mice (non-believers and hypocrites). Thus the chicks all matured and started making optimistic plans for their future (e.g., one decided to build a house the following year!). Then one day, a guest arrived at the farm, and the master himself entered the hen house to grab several handy victims for a special meal. It was all so sudden and unexpected. Which of the chicks would have guessed that its former defender would eventually turn out to be its devourer? So, too, Satan's attack will come in different forms; one must simply be ready for

---

[115] Thomas suggests a basic narrative format for the whole of an ideal Black American sermon: "The sermon is structured in the intuitive form of situation-complication-resolution-celebration ... The preacher manages the emotional process of the sermon by clearly and experientially setting forth the situation and complication, then the good news is supplied to resolve the complication, and the sermon moves up to celebration" (Thomas, *They Like to Never Quit Praisin' God*, p. 79).

this danger all the time – that is, by remaining within the corral (*khola*) of Christ (*Kristu*), who provides the only safe gate (*chipata*) to the future and life secure.

By thus linking his sermon style to that of the didactic oral narrative tradition, today's Chewa preacher forges an immediate bond (*ethos*) of personal familiarity, authority, credibility, and interest that renders any audience more mentally receptive to the new or renewed lessons on religion, life, and morality that come from the Word of God. Narrative is a dynamic, dialogue driven means of communication, including also ethical instruction (*logos*), that people have been accustomed to (or acculturated into) from earliest childhood. Hence it is the 'default mode' of universal message transmission that operates most efficiently in any sociological setting or rhetorical exigence.[116]

Personal Exemplification

Like a traditional Chewa oral storyteller, the inductive preacher of today does not hesitate to introduce himself and his own life history within a sermon. As an integral component of his strongly inductive-relational approach, he feels free to preach directly to and about himself so that he becomes as much a part of the discourse as he expects his hearers to be through their psychological participation in the various scenes, images, case studies, examples, and illustrations that he depicts for them. These, along with the periodic explanatory or elaborative comments and asides that he inserts into the text, perform the essential rhetorical function of creating for him a positive, personally familiar *ethos* in relation to his audience. They should listen to, trust, and heed him because he is actually one of them – someone who has had similar experiences and has encountered corresponding trials, temptations, and troubles in living the Christian life while confronting Satan and the demonic "powers" of this world (Eph 6:12).

The establishment of such personal affinity and credibility is especially important when the preacher is presenting his message to a new receptor group, to those who do not know him personally and may have never heard him (or even *of* him) before.[117] This is frequently the case as far as the ser-

---

[116] Cf. Kennedy, *New Testament Interpretation*, pp. 34f.
[117] Forslund's observation is pertinent here: "... the older preachers have a stronger ethos than the younger ones thanks to their long experience in the work of the Church. Through their experience they

mons of the Chewa revivalists are concerned. Why should people take the advice of a stranger or outsider (if he happens to be preaching to a group of mixed denomination)? A basic rhetorical progression thus seems to be operative here; a satisfactory level of *ethos* needs to be first stimulated with respect to the preacher so that the necessary audience *pathos* can be generated in order to reinforce the essential *logos* of his religious message to them. The *ethos* and *pathos* of interpersonal participation must be sufficiently grounded and then upgraded before serious consideration will be given to what a speaker has to say, particularly regarding the deep things of life and death, of this world and the hereafter – where such a critical conceptual gap exists between the biblical faith and that of African traditional religion.[118]

During the course of a given sermon, most Chewa preachers will recount some personal experience or another, either from their biography and the surrounding world in general or more specifically from their Christian ministry. Evangelist Wame, for instance, makes a number of keen references to life as he lived it along the shores of Lake Malawi at Salima, e.g., to the stealthy, subversive behaviour of the lethal crocodile (a more relevant figurative type of Satan than the lion, SW10); to the elusive "rock rabbit" (or 'coney', *mbira*) that prefers to hide among the rocky ledges along the lakeshore (like many Christians do with their faith, SW43); or to a tiny species of fish that builds elaborate trenches in the sandy lake bottom as a refuge for the time of a storm (what Christians ought to do in relation to the Word prior to trials and testing, SW6).

Many such anecdotes have to do with some memorable situation of religious conflict involving those whom the preachers were trying to teach or reach with the gospel. For example (during sermon SW12), Evangelist Wame tells of one occasion when he was facing a rather hostile audience at the University of Malawi. "What can we learn about this 'life' from Christianity?" he was asked by one particularly disruptive student (i.e., in relation to the text of John 10:10). Wame replies with a sequence of incisive,

---

have a background to refer to in their sermons, including a wealth of events and memories from which illustrations for the sermons may be drawn" (Forslund, *The Word of God in Ethiopian Tongues*, pp. 230f).

[118] Cf. Ernst R. Wendland, "Traditional Central African Religion", in P. C. Stine and E. R. Wendland (eds.), *Bridging the Gap: African Traditional Religion and Bible Translation*, New York: United Bible Societies, 1990, ch. 3.

unanswerable rhetorical questions, queries that (in the Chewa context) expose the skeptic's ignorance about religious matters in general and his supreme spiritual enemy in particular (a technique similar to that of Yahweh in Job 38-41). He first calls attention to the fact that these university students have been blessed with a privilege that the vast majority of their agemates in the country do not have access to, namely, a college education with all that this implies for future job opportunities and leadership potential. Then he asks,

> Have you ever questioned Satan, "Say you [familiar, minus-respect vocative pronoun], Satan, do you have a degree?" There is no reply [*zii!* 'complete silence' – an ideophone] from the audience. "OK, Satan, do you have a diploma then?" Quiet. "Say what [secondary school] form did you complete – form II, form IV?" Silence. "Say Satan, did you ever attend primary school?" No reply. "Hey Satan, have you ever been educated at all?" All quiet. (Wame goes on to conclude as well as to chide.) Since no one has been able to answer any of these questions, we would have to say that Satan is completely illiterate. How sorry I feel to see such learned people like you, following the advice of a 'wretched person' [*chimunthu*] who is totally uneducated! What has allowed him to make such fools of you – to get you to listen to someone who has no degree, no 'science,' nothing! I just cannot understand it at all! ... He has nothing to attract you with, only a [wicked] life-style. Why have you fallen for that?!

Thus like his African-American counterpart, Evangelist Wame "effectively combines imagination with role playing and spontaneous dramatization [which] can hardly fail to reach, hold, and lift the Black audience".[119] At times the very setting for the sermon itself is concerned, as happened during one Good Friday service when Wame felt compelled to introduce his sermon for the event by recounting the sad circumstances surrounding a funeral that he had officiated at just the day before (Kamwala Reformed Church in Zambia, Lusaka, Zambia, 10 April 1998). Similarly, there are instances when he mentions at the very beginning that he has had to either determine or modify his selection of sermon texts in response to something which he has seen or heard in the immediate congregational setting so that he can focus his message to better meet a particular need or problem, e.g., a preponderance of women over men in the audience. There are even

---

[119] Mitchell, *Black Preaching*, p. 93.

instances when, as an attention grabbing rhetorical device, he must make a confession similar to this one by John Chrysostom, "I have no idea what I shall say to you today" (but of course he knows perfectly well what his message is going to be about).[120]

In addition to personal anecdotes from his own life, the Chewa preacher often extends this technique and its impact by means of personalized examples and true to life citations from, or references to, his common sociocultural life setting, including the latest local or national news and current events. This is all part of their shared everyday experience, which includes a host of events or situations, both good and bad,[121] that they may have heard about, witnessed, or personally gone through. The preacher thus induces his audience to trust him also with respect to the spiritual application that he wishes to make on the basis of the realistic incidents that they have participated in together or the exemplifying events that he has persuaded them to identify with in his sermon.

How many of us have not experienced, for example, being confined in some vehicle (auto, lorry, bus) whose engine is either dangerously overheating or which has already boiled over on account of the strain of its journey – climbing up a hill, plowing through sand, or spinning in the mud? Wame transforms this familiar predicament from everyday life into a metaphor that applies to an experience that many Christians have also in their daily walk of faith (SW6). The engine (*injini*) of their body – that is, their heart (*mtima*) – may suddenly begin to heat up (*kutentha*) because of

---

[120] The preceding quote is from Pless, "Seven Pulpit Paradigms", p. 203. Chrysostom goes on to specify his problem: "I see that since the Feast of Pentecost the attendance at divine service has fallen off, the Prophets neglected, the Apostles are little valued, the Fathers are set aside ... As a matter of fact the whole city is at the circus [i.e., equivalent to the local sporting arena or football stadium]" (ibid.). Wame, like John Chrysostom, has "the ability to turn a phrase instantly, to respond immediately and extemporaneously to an event [that is taking place] at the moment" (Ibid., p. 207). For example, during one evening sermon, Chrysostom suddenly interjected, "Please listen to me; you are not paying attention. I am talking about the Holy Scriptures and you are looking at the lamps and the people who are lighting them. ... After all I, too, am lighting a lamp, the lamp of God's Word" (H. T. Kerr, *Preaching in the Early Church*, New York: Fleming H. Revell, 1942, p. 180).

[121] Often the good and the bad, the positive and the negative, the helpful and the dangerous, etc. are juxtaposed in antithetical fashion to respectively highlight one another. This is particularly true where spiritual behaviors, attitudes, and values are concerned—the divine versus the satanic, with man floating somewhere in the middle. Thus for Wame, as for Luther, "the sermon of part of the battle still going on between God and evil for the universe. And a battle has two sides. The sermon is not just instruction, but conflict—of truth with error, God with Satan" (Meusner, *Luther the Preacher*, p. 50).

the powerful heat (or fire – *moto*) of certain sinful lusts in their lives. If this dangerous process is not checked, e.g., by putting an end to the stressful trip (i.e., by getting away from the place or source of temptation) or by adding the cooling and cleansing water (*madzi*) of God's Word, the heart engine will eventually boil over into some overt wicked behaviour that can completely destroy it as well as the larger vehicle body (*thupi*), either physically and/or spiritually.

Such simple, but insightful, illustrations and confirming instances from the familiar surroundings of one's world of reality serve to personalize a sermon in the sense that they engage hearers both mentally and emotively in the realm of the known. This captivation then becomes the vehicle for taking them further into what may be a relatively unfamiliar mode of applied Christian reflection, discourse, and action, especially with regard to traditional religious beliefs and practices concerning spiritual and mystical powers, now subsumed under the authority of Satan and lesser demonic beings. Virtually all of the Chewa revival preachers are very skilled in the selection, composition, and incorporation of these concrete, down to earth examples both to vivify and to amplify their sermon texts.

A final, rather controversial type of personalization of the Chewa revival sermon takes the form of some manner of appeal or reference to a *vision* or *dream*, usually divine in origin, that the preacher has experienced. This does not occur very often because these preachers generally as a group have too high a respect for the authority of the recorded word of Scripture to allow such additional revelations lightly (despite their obvious enhancement of one's *ethos*). Evangelist Wame, for example, does recount several occasions when he received a dream (*maloto*) or vision (*masomphenya*) from the Lord (cf. the Appendix). Once was in 1972 when his eldest son lay on a sickbed near death. At that time, an angel first announced that the child would indeed die, but s/he later returned in another dream to reveal that his son would eventually recover as a result of God's great mercy towards his friend, Wame (cf. Gen. 18, SW23).

Then, in a somewhat more debatable case, Wame appeals to a vision that he received to support his preferred interpretation of the sacred 'books' of heaven mentioned (appropriately enough) in Revelation 20:12. He takes these to refer to three distinct inventories: one in which every person's deeds are recorded, a second which lists the names of the condemned, and a third – the book of life – where the names of all the saved are found (SW29). In his actual sermons (as distinct from personal conversations or interviews), Wame does not make a big issue of his reception of dreams and visions in which he feels that God speaks to him, giving guidance, spiritual insight, encouragement, and on occasion, also some correction. On the rare instance that he mentions such an experience when preaching, he does so either to reinforce a concrete theological or moral point already revealed in the written Word, or to derive some new implication from a particular passage of Scripture.

A final aspect of the homiletical quality of personal exemplification might be better termed self appropriation since it refers to the preacher's being enthusiastically caught up, so to speak, in the spiritual message that he is proclaiming. Thomas describes such personal captivation in the following terms:

> By the time the emotional process of the sermon reaches its final stage of celebration, the truth of the sermon should have become conviction for the preacher, and therefore available to be spread contagiously until many are affected. ... The preacher's [own] conviction of the assurance of grace results in joyous celebration (praise and thanksgiving) that spreads from person to person [throughout the congregation].[122]

The contagious effect of the Chewa revivalist's own emotional involvement in his pastoral message is reflected in various types of audience response (exclamations ["amen!" – "hallelujah!"], cheers and shouts, clapping, choruses, and so on). However, in keeping with the basic iterative-inductive mode of compositional development, such especially overt outbreaks may occur on a number of occasions during the sermon – that is, *within* the discourse – not necessarily at its close, which may in fact be relatively undistinguished in terms of overall affective intensity.

Traditional Allusion

This category is similar to the preceding, but the focus is slightly changed

---

[122] Thomas, *They Like to Never Quit Praisin' God*, pp. 91f.

to better illustrate the diversity of everyday instances, well-known cases, practical proofs, etc. that the more skilled preachers make use of in the inductive development of their sermon theme and its rhetorical purpose. Here we are not dealing with narrative accounts or personalized examples of the here and now (as discussed above), but the reference is more to that ancient treasure store of wisdom which is embodied in a people's oral traditions and related tribal customs.[123] Of course there is overlapping, but we focus now more on the *past* and the concrete corpus of beliefs, sayings, or practices that have been handed down from the ancestors to the present day, where they continue to exert a great deal of influence on all aspects of life, including religion and public morality. Some of the popular preachers are more open about, or seemingly cognizant of, this vital indigenous heritage than others. But all, to a greater or lesser degree, see the need for evaluating these elements in the Chewa tradition, in particular those features that bring people into conflict with certain aspects of the Word of God. Such ethnically specific allusions may be verbal or non-verbal in nature, and either brief or extended in their textual development within a given sermon.

It is going to take considerably more research efforts before I have gained an adequate grasp of the extent to which the root of traditional African oral literature is tapped in the sermon construction of Chewa revival preachers. Preliminary indications (i.e., the Shadrack Wame corpus) are, however, that such local intertextuality is not as great as might be expected in the overall repertory of this contemporary group of verbal artists. Well-known folktales (*nthano*), for example, do not appear to be retold or alluded to very often in order to illustrate some moral point. Rather, as was noted earlier, the preachers seem to prefer to compose their own traditional-*like* stories for this purpose, or better yet, they will utilize some appropriate biblical narrative, usually adapted to fit the situation.[124] The inventory of Chewa mythic or legendary accounts (*mbiri*) is not large to begin with, so it

---

[123] "This technique shows how a people's language grows by borrowing images and ideas from real experience or from imaginative literature such as folktales. ... Allusion is a device whereby such an idea or image is used in a highly compressed form ... the user has assumed that the speakers of the language already know that source" (Okpewho, *African Oral Literature*, p. 100; cf. Wendland, "Stylistic Form and Communicative Function", pp. 553-572).

[124] As Mitchell observes from the perspective of an early American setting, "In the evolution into Christianity, the [African] slaves simply substituted the Bible's story collection for their original repertoire of tales" (Mitchell, *Black Preaching*, p. 31).

is not a notable source of allusion either – nor are traditional songs (*nyimbo*), which are replaced with hymns (i.e., Christian songs) or riddles (*zirapi*), which may be too closely associated with the verbal play of smaller children.

By far the largest body of indigenous oral art that is either quoted or, more boften, simply alluded to is the great treasury of 'wisdom literature' – aphorisms, maxims, proverbs (*miyambi*) – which inevitably colours the language of gifted Chewa orators and speakers. But here again, more study is needed because of the reduced, adapted, or paraphrased form in which such material frequently appears, no doubt, because everyone is expected to know it, including the preferred settings of use and application. These sayings are always used with some spiritual implication – that is, over and above their social-secular sense: e.g., *m'lereni, aiwale kwao* ('nourish him [a guest or visitor] so he forgets about home') (SW6, applied with reference to Satan's attempts to get Christians to get "fat" on the riches and pleasures of this world so they "forget" about heaven); or *mkango ukasauka, ukudya udzu* ('when the lion is suffering [with hunger], he'll even eat grass') (SW1, now speaking of Satan who does not hesitate to make a "meal" of even the most emaciated believer). The following then is Wame's interesting play on the proverb *nkhwangwa ikoma pokwera* ('an axe seems good when climbing [a tree]'); in other words, once you have cut down a desired branch, the axe is no longer needed [and may be dropped]. Wame's version goes *chikristu chikoma pomwalira* ('Christianity seems good when you are dying') (SW18, i.e., the faith has served its purpose now that you are about to enter heaven!). The use of traditional aphoristic allusions not only serves the purpose of concise and concentrated illustration, but it also helps to establish and/or solidify the essential rapport (*ethos*) of a common ethnicity between preacher and audience that facilitates the interactive communication process.[125]

Much more important in the preachers' repertory than such folkloristic allusion, however, is reference to the wise words and well-known examples of the more recently developed biblical tradition.[126] For most established

---

[125] "... it would appear that the use of aphorisms is more frequent among the great Black preachers of America" (*ibid.*, p. 97).

[126] Forslund notes in his Ethiopian sermon corpus a similar emphasis on biblical and related material in forming the bulk of "external proofs" (i.e., not speaker-generated) pertaining to the *logos* aspect of mes-

Christians, this embraces quite a corpus, found especially in the dramatic sayings of Jesus or in various graphic images employed by the biblical writers and characters, which frequently serve as the major theme or key motif of an entire sermon, e.g., the full life (*moyo wochuluka*) that Jesus promises to all his followers (SW10, cf. John 10:10) in contrast to the full wealth (*chuma chochuluka*) of the rich fool (SW22, cf. Lk 12:16-21) or believers being chosen vessels (*zotengera*) of the Lord, like Paul (SW2, cf. Acts 9:15), despite the fact that they must live in corporeal temporary stick-and-grass shelters (*misasa*) during this life (SW6, cf. 2Cor 5:1-5). This extensive Christian *verbal* tradition, many examples of which appear in the various Wame citations below, is also appealed to in the well-known hymn tunes and choruses that may be either mentioned in passing or actually sung during a sermon.

The *non-verbal* tradition that is relied upon as a basis for allusion in the revivalistic sermons consists of ancient customs, social institutions, celebrations, and other cultural practices – some explicitly religious, others just implicitly so, still others having only secular significance – that played a great part in the Chewa way of life and often still do. For example, Evangelist Wame employs the well-known former practice of travelling by foot from Malawi to South Africa to seek employment in the mines (*wenela*) as an illustration of the arduous Christian life (SW6). Both experiences were/are very goal centred and demanding, physically as well as mentally, but they are also prone to a diversity of dangers all along the way. Neither trip could tolerate any sort of reverse (*liveesi*, an English loanword) from the intended direction and desired goal!

A more traditional example plays a key illustrative role in a sermon on the wisdom (*nzeru*) of God in contrast (or opposition to) that of sinful humans (1Cor 1:17-25, SW15). Wame first points out how different the divine perception and plan is from ours. God begins on the inside and works outwards, whereas man typically gets captivated and impressed by mere externals (e.g., 1Sam 16:7, which is cited). How then can a surface bound

---

sage composition (Forslund, *The Word of God in Ethiopian Tongues*, pp. 232-235). This is a practice well-rooted in church history. For instance, Pless comments as follows concerning John Chrysostom's reliance upon the Scriptures for his examples and allusions: "[He] wanted his hearers to grasp spiritual truth and to come to know the personages of the Bible as if they had actually met them. Most of John's illustrations were either examples from everyday life or they were biblical allusions" (Pless, "Seven Pulpit Paradigms", p. 206).

human being learn about true inner wisdom? To illustrate his emphasis upon the importance of a thorough instruction in the Word of God, Wame takes listeners back to an old tribal custom, now gradually dying out or being modified to fit into the modern world. Just as newly matured maidens were initiated by elderly women into the Chewa life and lore by being isolated at a special camp (*tsimba*) out in the bush, so Christians must make the effort to separate (sanctify) themselves from the world around them in order to be initiated, so to speak, into the wisdom of God and the secrets of true discipleship. Then, just as these young ladies were ritually reborn and became new persons in the eyes of the community as a result of their formal, customary initiation, so also believers become transformed, spiritually and morally, by means of the renewing experience that takes place through their conceptual, emotional, and volitional immersion within the Scriptures.

To be sure, such allusions may not be so familiar to many of the younger generation, especially to those who have grown up in towns. But it will not be many listeners who pass up the opportunity of finding out more about these fading ancestral traditions from those who still remember them. In the process, the Christianized, didactic point (*logos*) being conveyed by the preacher is correspondingly elucidated, strengthened, and made relevant to one's current thinking and behaviour. The past is thus resurrected metaphorically and transformed to function on a higher, a spiritual plane by such a well placed reference and application.

The Chewa revivalists do not ignore or detour around current controversial issues in the ongoing debate with religious syncretism or spiritual dualism (African traditional religion versus [theologically conservative] biblical Christianity). Wame, for example, alludes to the infamous *nyau* traditional male cult[127] in the conclusion of one sermon dealing with the "jaws of death" (Job 41:14, SW10). Like a fierce crocodile (*ching'ona*, cf. Leviathan, Job 41:1), Satan will not release his deadly grip from those who are adhering to such pagan practices at the time of their death. Accordingly, their alternative, earthly indigenous church (*chalichi*) and its sacred beliefs will not be able to deliver them when final judgement calls.

---

[127] For a good summary-description of the basic character and significance of the traditional *nyau* secret brotherhood (which reverences ancient religious cosmology and nature spirits), see Schoffeleers, *Religion and the Dramatisation of Life*, pp. 11-13.

Evangelist Wame does not usually delve too deeply into the customary lore of witchcraft, sorcery, and spiritism, but he does make frequent reference to this corpus of the occult and occasionally alludes more concretely to such strongly believed and persistently practiced activities. When encouraging believers, for example, to be prepared for the second coming of Christ (SW28), he refers to all those who are captivated by the works of this world, sinful and otherwise (cf. Mt 24:38), as engaging in games (*masewero*). To give oneself over to such behaviour would be as foolish and wicked, Wame goes on to say, as for one to take part in the mysterious football 'games' that witches play at night in their graveyard 'stadiums' and the supernatural trips that they make with the help of their magical airplanes, buses, and automobiles (i.e., inanimate: old, worn out mats or winnowing baskets; animate: an owl or hyena). These mystical phenomena are not denied, but they are all denounced and attributed to the power of the Prince of this world, *Satani* (John 14:30). The sad fact is, warns Wame, that people who participate in such traditional heathen beliefs and practices will one day end up being shocked and dismayed in the other world that they were really living in all along, namely, in the diabolical realm of fiery Gahena.

Thus far we have been dealing with the three major *structure-topical* preferences that are involved in inductive composition with reference to Chewa revivalistic preaching, i.e., narration, exemplification, and allusion. We turn our consideration now to three prominent techniques for achieving a more complete *emotive* (em-*pathetic*) engagement of the audience in the actual oral presentation of a sermon, namely: the use of a dramatic delivery, a strongly affective appeal, and evocative description. As in the preceding discussion, these features will be described and exemplified individually, though they are obviously related and often combined in actual usage.

Dramatic Delivery

One cannot fail to be impressed by the vocal energy and enthusiasm that the popular preachers put into their preferred manner of sermon proclamation. This turns out to be as dynamic as the religious subject matter that is being thereby conveyed. Unfortunately, this vital feature of Chewa sermonody cannot be illustrated via the printed word; it can only be very imperfectly described. An exceptional preacher like Shadrack Wame, for instance, displays a highly effective, rhetorically controlled use of such paralinguistic qualities as volume, stress, pitch, tempo, pause, vowel elongation, vocal mimicry, and intonational variation in order to convey connotative implications like urgency, importance, excitement, anticipation, disappointment, doubt, and frustration.[128] These are often accompanied by emotional overtones that are appropriate for the setting, occasion, mood, situation, character, or compositional section concerned, e.g., anger, sorrow, joy, despair, anxiety, fear, courage, pronounced pessimism and unbounded optimism. Such phonologically conveyed feelings and attitudes may be set in contrast or attributed to some real or fictitious personage within the sermon, e.g., Christ's controlled, objective intonation vs. Peter's passionate, subjective speech style in John 6:61-69 (SW26).[129] Sound shaping and shading of this nature thus serves to foreground and/or reinforce key pragmatic (illocutionary) notions like warning, rebuke, encouragement, conviction (indictment) and blessing, which are related to the central theological message and primary rhetorical purpose of a given sermon (or portion thereof).[130]

Overall, there tends to be a perceptible modulation in the ongoing flow of utterance; that is, most preachers do not sustain a fever-pitch level of articulation throughout a sermon.[131] Rather, periodic areas of dramatic

---

[128] For a detailed description of the use of such dynamic phonological features in Nyanja (Chewa) radio narrative performances, see Wendland, "Stylistic Form and Communicative Function", pp. 611-669. Oberhelman notes the relative absence of "prose" rhythms in the Latin sermons of Ambrose, Augustine, and Jerome. In short, "...the greater the frequency of rhythm, the greater the amount of [literary] revision" (Oberhelman, *Rhetoric and Homiletics*, p. 109). A different sort of rhythm perhaps - balanced syntactic parallelisms - is typical of the Chewa revivalist sermons, especially those of Evangelist Wame.
[129] In his dramatic re-interpretation of Peter's reply to Christ's question of faith, Wame focused on the emotive implications of the rhetorical question of v. 68a: "Lord, to whom shall we go?" This was done in order to set listeners up for Peter's subsequent confession of trust in his Lord's divine nature and mission.
[130] Thomas adds a relevant caution with regard to the use of the device of phonological manipulation: "Intonation can be an appropriate and powerful vehicle for celebration when it is natural and authentic to the preacher and congregation, and when it reinforces the truth already taught. But divorced from biblical substance (cognitive logic), it is emotionalism, a cheap replica of celebration" (Thomas, *They Like to Never Quit Praisin' God*, p. 105).
[131] This is in contrast to what appears to be an increasingly popular manner of preaching in local central African congregations (English and vernacular), where the pastor virtually shouts his way through the entire sermon, often attempting to duplicate the rhythmic cadences of well-known television evangelists (from America). Wame's vocal style tends to be much more nuanced and subtle than this melodramatic sort of speech mode.

release and a reduction in emotive tension are introduced, not only for the sake of artistic variety, but also to allow the audience a chance to make a psychological pause in their compositional involvement. Otherwise, they might easily burn out in terms of their attention span or, on the contrary, become so psyched up that they lose or miss the specific point(s) of the theological thought, ethical argument, or concrete exhortation being communicated. Evangelist Wame, for example, prefers to begin and end his sermons on a relatively quiet note. Similarly, those portions that deal more with *logos*-like instruction or even exhortation will generally be less forcefully or passionately presented. The drama increases noticeably, however, as a particular story or example is being told or as his chosen application is being made to the lives of his listeners. This is accompanied by a corresponding rise in the level of verbal (as well as gestural) dynamics, that is, in the number and intensity of the vocal modifications which are used both in the evocation of *pathos* and to audibly structure, shape, and selectively stress the various components his message.

In keeping with a dramatic, oral mode of presentation, these Chewa sermons are characterized by a relatively simple sentence structure, that is, short and to the point, with not a great deal of complex or embedded modification.[132] There is considerable variety in syntactic construction so that any possible monotony or predictability is avoided. A notable exception occurs, however, in the rhythmic, reiterative sequences which are frequently introduced, either to emphasize a given point or to build up to some type of thematic peak or pragmatic climax. For the African, as well as his Afro-American counterpart, "rhythm...is the single ingredient that gives the melodiousness of black preaching its momentum."[133]

These phonologically foregrounded portions, which are especially prominent in Wame's style, at times approach the quality of a tonal chant, except

---

[132] "To this day, this great inner simplicity [of basic form and content] has remained a mark by which to distinguish truly evangelical preaching" (Hirsch, cited in Meusner, *Luther the Preacher*, p. 55).

[133] Willimon and Lischer (eds.), *Concise Encyclopedia of Preaching*, pp. 142f. J.M. Spencer goes on to point out that an important aspect of such "rhythmic usage" is the "fitting [of] their sermonic phrases and sentences into quasi-metrical units" (Spencer, "Folk Preaching (African-American)", p. 143). Wame's style approaches this when he goes into one of his periodic "rhythmic-reiterative sequences" of religiously challenging utterances (see examples below). For a brief consideration of prose rhythm in the Classical Greco-Roman tradition, see F. Siegert, "Mass Communication and Prose Rhythm in Luke-Acts", in S. E. Porter and T. H. Olbricht (eds.), *Rhetoric and the New Testament: Essays from the 1992 Heidelberg Conference*, Sheffield: Sheffield Academic Press, 1993, pp. 42-58.

that they are more forcefully rendered by means of several kinds of verbal intensification, including the vocal ascent to a dramatic call utterance or a series of them, e.g., "Adam, where are you?" (to highlight man's loss of the divine image, SW9; cf. Gen 3:9).[134] An audibly pronounced text portion of this nature may then be followed by a deliberate dramatic downshift, e.g., through a lessening in the volume and rate of speech or by the insertion of an extended pause, hesitation, or stretch of elongated enunciation.[135] I have not yet detected, at least not in the Wame corpus, any unusual amount of rhetorically motivated phonological manipulation other than that already effected by rhythmic patterning and contrastive intonation.[136] This is

---

[134] In Chichewa: *"Adamuuu, uli kuuuti?"* – notice the emphatic, moan-like /u/ assonance. Mitchell observes that a common stylistic feature of African-American sermons is "the use of a musical tone or chant in preaching. ... (Such) intonation has general significance as an identity signal [NB – also in the Chewa corpus], (and) it has come to be used widely by Black preachers to indicate celebration" (Mitchell, *Black Preaching*, pp. 89f). "[This] use of musical tone or chant...add[s] another dimension or 'wave length' of celebrative meaning in the final stage of the sermon" (Thomas, *They Like to Never Quit Praisin' God*, p. 104). While the Chewa examples might not reach the vocal prominence of the celebrated 'moaning,' 'whooping,' 'tuning,' or 'zooning' portions of Black American sermons (*ibid.*), they are very distinctive in their own right and effective as stimulators of both *ethos* and *pathos* in the rhetorical strategy of their speakers, namely, to lead listeners along to a hortatory climax of some type – not necessarily at the end of the sermon, but at any appropriate point during the development of its central message. Thus the selective, carefully positioned use of rhythmic sequences of partially repeated utterances (paradigmatic "frames") is possibly more crucial to the effective execution of a Chewa revivalist sermon than it is in a typical Black American one (cf. Mitchell, *Black Preaching*, pp. 91f). Okpewho has observed that "diverse uses of tonal changes in song and chant ... [serve] to enhance meaning and to indicate extent or variety" (Okpewho, *African Oral Literature*, p. 92). My data leads me to conclude that such "tonality" (as Okpewho terms it) – and indeed intonation in general – plays a vital role in Chewa oral *prose* literature as well, these revivalistic sermons in particular.

[135] It would appear, at least from Mitchell's description, that most Chewa preachers (there are exceptions of course) manifest a *rate of speaking* that is considerably higher than of their average American counterparts, who tend to employ "a significantly lower-than-average number of words per minute" (Mitchell, *Black Preaching*, p. 96; cf. Blount, *Cultural Interpretation*, p. 73). The rhetorical intent of the latter is to "increase comprehension and influence as much as possible," namely, to create an "impact on the whole person: on cognitive, intuitive, and emotive consciousness" (Mitchell, *Black Preaching*, p. 97). The Chewa orators achieve the same effect by other means, especially through reiteration and the diversified vocal modifications being described in this section.

[136] In other words, Evangelist Wame – like most of his Chewa colleagues – appears to deliberately avoid an insincere, artificially contrived oral-oratorical style, one designed to attract listeners only on a superficial level and for a self-serving purpose. Mitchell has some good words of warning on this point (*ibid.*, p. 91). Already in the early Christian era, John Chrysostom warned, "[If a preacher] is a slave to the sound of applause, again an equal damage [i.e., to that of lackluster preaching] threatens both him and the people, because through his passion for praise he aims to speak more for the pleasure than the [spiritual] profit of his hearers" (cited in Pless, "Seven Pulpit Paradigms", p. 197). Luther adds: "Because they praise him, he must, in turn, praise them. So they praise one another until one goes to the devil with the other" (cited in Meusner, *Luther the Preacher*, p. 49).

because the concordial prefix arrangement and five vowel inventory of a typical south central Bantu language brings to any text its own characteristic euphony of alliteration, assonance, semi-rhymes, and partial puns.

The effective sound shaping of any skilfully constructed Chewa sermon is invariably accompanied by another important and closely related dramatic device that is utilized to heighten certain chosen segments of the composition. This is *direct discourse*, that is, actual quoted speech as distinct from the personal address which is natural in any speaker-hearer form of communication. Such cited speech is a dominant feature of Chewa oral narrative tales (*nthano*) as discussed above.[137] There is thus a natural carry over of the device into sermonic discourse, which despite its differing structure and function, maintains a close continuity with the style of traditional verbal art forms due to its similar oral, performer-audience setting and its frequent inclusion of speech oriented stories and examples. One might say that there is a decided predilection for direct discourse in the presentation of popular Chewa sermons, a strong preference that may be summarized in the principle: If it is possible to say something directly (as opposed to an indirect style or a pure reportative mode), then do it! This means of course that there will often be a certain amount of imaginative *elaboration* necessary, that is, to fill out a given biblical dialogue or monologue and make it sound more natural in personal terms (i.e., *ethos* and *pathos*). This serves in turn to augment the human credibility, on the one hand, as well as the theological relevance of the *logos* message that is being implicitly conveyed.[138]

The pre-eminence of dialogue in the Wame corpus is brought out very nicely in his "Potsherd" (*"Phale"*) sermon (SW6). The topical foundation is laid by an interesting and quite typical instance of the inductive-relational, text reflection technique. Wame begins with a dramatized re-telling of the dialogue recorded between God and Ananias (Acts 9:10-16), one which focuses upon the Lord's choice of Saul the persecutor to be his "chosen vessel to proclaim his name (message) to the Gentiles" (v. 15). This divine commission of gospel proclamation is then applied to every chosen disciple, including its frequent association with personal suffering for the sake of the good news (v. 17). Like

---

[137] Cf. Wendland, "Stylistic Form and Communicative Function", ch. 6.
[138] Martin Luther too utilized the device of dramatic dialogue to the full: "Usually he spoke in the first person for both parties. There is a conversation between Luther and his hearers, between God and humanity, God and Adam, Jesus and the disciples...[etc.]" (Meusner, *Luther the Preacher*, p. 50).

the mission minded apostle, Christians can and should serve as the Lord's mouthpiece to bring a specific word of warning, rebuke, comfort or encouragement to their fellow believers whenever the need arises.

The key thematic image (see below) of a vessel (Greek *skeuos*) is next transported back into the Old Testament to introduce the admonition that Christ's followers nowadays are all too often broken and useless vessels because they fail to perform their God given function. Consequently, they become mere 'potsherds,' fit only to serve as temporary carriers for removing chicken dung, garbage, and other types of rubbish from the front yard of their houses – Isa 45:9a, here vividly contextualized! Wame imaginatively and ironically develops and expands upon the silly debate between the clay and its potter, then the human being and his creator, as the former complains about what, how, and why the latter made it to be (v. 9b-c). Finally God exclaims, "I have been *augured*[139], I have! Never did I see (experience) such a thing before!"

Finally, the punitive implication of this sort of rebellious behaviour is dramatized in a brief fictitious divine monologue that is rhetorically negativized, that is, it could never take place. God would not find occasion to call out to one of his angels, saying, "Hey, come give me a hand with this hardened, dagga-smoking fellow here. Hold him down, and I'll put an end to him!" Just as a potter has no difficulty in destroying a misshapen pot and replacing it with another, so the Lord will not fail to discipline any deformed and defiant disciple. In a further development (i.e., of Isa 45:10), Wame goes on to present a snatch of conversation which illustrates the shameful lack of respect that children often show towards their parents (and God, cf. Exo 20:12) nowadays: "Why did you make me like this?"

These little dialogic vignettes, whether based upon a particular passage of Scripture or specially created to amplify one, are always idiomatically phrased and naturally expressed, thus lending a touch of everyday realism, verbal naturalness, and *humour* to the sermon. However, such humourous elements are often coupled with the incisive device of *irony* and suddenly turned

---

[139] The abnormal verb *augur* is an attempt in English to concisely render the unfamiliar Chewa notion of *-laula*, that is, to meet with a bad omen, whether in the words or actions of someone or in the world of nature, e.g., to have a puff adder quickly (contrary to its normal movement) slither across the path in front of you. In this section, Wame also uses a culturally and connotatively more powerful term, *malodza* "a sign/omen of witchcraft or bewitchment" – but in a transferred, non-religious, humorous sense to denote God's utter shock and amazement at the impudence of his ungrateful human creation.

around like a hook and set directly into the ears and hearts of the listening congregation (see Audience Involvement below). In any case, the overall evocative effect stimulated by the use of these dramatic devices contributes both to the *ethos* of the preacher and to the forcefulness of the homiletical point that he is attempting to make.

Affective Appeal

Whenever a Chewa (or any) preacher exhibits a dramatic delivery – a speech style that displays a malleable intonational overlay and a great deal of natural dialogue – there will automatically be some measure of an accompanying appeal to the *affections* of his audience. In other words, he will make a deliberate play upon their feelings (lesser), e.g., hope, happiness, sadness, frustration, disappointment, fear, and emotions (stronger), e.g., love, hate, grief, joy, despair, dread – plus the many variations of these. However, such emotive engagement (*pathos*) is not an artificial rhetorical device, i.e., emotional*ism*, which is unrelated to the principal biblical truth of a sermon.[140] Rather it is simply an expression of the preacher's own deep participation of the Word that he is proclaiming (*ethos*). Furthermore, it is an indication of the spontaneity of the Bantu rhetor and his ability "to express deep feeling without shame."[141] For example, how could any person (in this case, Wame) *not* get emotionally involved as he recalls his fervent prayers to the Lord at the deathbed of his son (in a sermon about prayer with reference to Abraham's example of Gen 18, SW23)? Such an open baring of the soul, as long as it is not prolonged or overdone, is generally reacted to in a positive way by the congregation.[142] It helps to

---

[140] Thomas suggests that any affective appeal "must be based in the great affirmative themes of the Bible: mercy, compassion, hope, healing, justice, forgiveness, peace, salvation, and most of all love" (Thomas, *They Like to Never Quit Praisin' God*, 93).

[141] Willimon and Lischer, *Concise Encyclopedia of Preaching*, pp. 3f. Mitchell adds: Black preachers are "expected to be caught up in sharing the Word. [They] have to let go. They feel what they are preaching about. ... They must make no pretense of so-called objectivity" (Mitchell, *Black Preaching*, p. 95). This does not mean that there is no objectivity in their sermons (the Chewa corpus included); they simply do not make a show of scholarly (or any other) erudition.

[142] The audience reactions referred to, both verbal and non-verbal, are those heard in the background of my sermon recordings, as well as those observed when I played tapes of these sermons for the evaluation of my seminary classes. I further witnessed this in the several Wame sermons that I was present for. In addition to actual verbal responses, many instances of laughter, clapping, and ululation were noted. Again, such overt emotional reaction has precedent in early Christian church tradition; for example, "...following the custom of the day...at the end of [John Chrysostom's] sermons, the audience often

reassure them that the preacher has human feelings and reactions too; he is (just like) one of us!

An important general emotive affection that is frequently introduced and developed in a Wame sermon, particularly in the narrative portions, is *suspense*. This too is a vital element in many Black American sermons, as described by Thomas:

> Suspense spurs the listener, through growing excitement and interest, to seek equilibrium when confronted with the [thematic] complication. The complication is the presentation of situations, circumstances, or facts that throw the listener off balance and cause a feeling of anxiety/uneasiness. The human personality naturally seeks balance, stability, and equilibrium, and it is the management of this anxiety that keeps the listener engaged. ... It is the suspense, and the preacher's experiential presentation of the suspense, that helps people to listen. Effective timing is to maintain suspense as long as possible before resolution with the gospel, and the [emotional] celebration of that resolution.[143]

It is more typical of the inductive revivalist sermon to incorporate several dramatic sequences of [*complication* => *suspense* => *resolution*] within a given sermon, rather than a longer, more sustained development as recommended above. Perhaps the latter alternative would be a viable model for the Chewa preachers to consider. But as noted, any critical evaluation of this affective device also needs to take into consideration the need for definite suspense *resolution* within the sermon and to ensure that any such suspense generation is perceptibly *related* to its central, biblically based theme and purpose. Artificial suspense evocation is, like emotionalism, a negative force that only confuses or deflects a sermon's main rhetorical progression and conclusion.

Certainly not all of the emotions mentioned above are manifested – or evoked – in any given sample of the corpus of sermons under examination. But I have no doubt that individual instances of affection covering the whole range of the primary ones, at least, are found in the Wame sermonic set as a whole. There are several strong sentiments and emotions, plus their variants, in particular that he seems to excite with great regularity in his

---

would break out in wild applause and stamp their feet" (Pless, "Seven Pulpit Paradigms", p. 205).
[143] Thomas, *They Like to Never Quit Praisin' God*, pp. 53, 97.

hortative presentations, namely: (a) total *revulsion* with regard to sin(fulness) as well as spiritual apathy in the Christian's life; (b) a healthy *fear* of Satan, his varied demonic manifestations in the world and gahena, the destiny of the damned; (c) an affectionate *attraction* to Jesus, the truest friend one can have both now and in eternity; and (d) a longing *anticipation* of the peace and joy that will be ours in heaven. All of these are represented in the first sample sermon reproduced in the following chapter (SW5).

At times Wame becomes almost vehement in his verbal appeal for listeners to resist the power of Satan, to forsake their wicked behaviour, whether internal or external, and to follow the will of God in their lives. Reiterated sequences of pointed commands or barbed rhetorical questions, all vocally coloured with heartfelt intensity and emotion, frequently rise to a climax when the preacher nearly breaks down in tears as it were (particularly when speaking of Christ's redemptive suffering on our behalf).[144] At other times, Wame utilizes sharp irony and sarcasm to dramatize the danger of any hypocrisy, obstinacy, or outright rebellion against the Lord. On such occasions, he often rises to a fit of subdued (mock, or is it real?) laughter as he highlights the blind folly of the wicked. Feigned weeping as well as laughing (the latter being somewhat more common in his sermons than the former) are alternatively combined, for example, in his powerfully emotive plea (SW5, see ch 4) to build genuine discipleship upon the sure "Rock" of your salvation (cf. Mt 7:24-25; 1Cor 10:4): deny yourself, take up your cross, and follow Christ (Mt 16:24). No listener could conclude that the believer's walk is smooth and straightforward after such a homiletical performance. The problem is of course that one must actually *hear* such a hortatory segment to believe or appreciate it – in contrast to reading a flat, silent, written description that is.

Now the term 'performance' might well be interpreted negatively in the sense that a preacher like Wame is simply playing for and upon the emotions of his audience, rather than basing his appeal on the textual foundation of the Scriptures. Admittedly, the border between effective as opposed to manipulative, melodramatic communication is rather hard to define at times. Being a subjective and personal evaluation, this can never

---

[144] Cf. Martin Luther: "...preaching Christ meant, above all, preaching his passion and resurrection" (Meusner, *Luther the Preacher*, p. 19).

be determined with certainty, particularly when one is not physically and psychologically present right there on the scene of the sermon event. But my personal, and partially alien, impression is that Evangelist Wame handles the emotional dimension of his discourse with tact. That is to say, for the most part (any preacher may experience occasional lapses in this respect) he remains in overall control of the connotative techniques that he employs and does not allow such dynamic rhetorical forces to get distractingly out of hand, to the ultimate depreciation of the Word that he is preaching. To put it another way, Wame does not permit his chosen oratorical means, or medium, to become the message, thus lifting listeners up to a mere emotional high (without solid Scriptural substance) that cannot be sustained for very long after the moving but transient sermon experience has passed. That sort of counterfeit preaching would be tantamount to building one's homiletical house upon the unstable sand of subjectivism and self-serving personal aggrandizement (cf. Mt 7:26-27).

The segments of affective augmentation or emotional climax that Wame (and several other Chewa preachers) displays in his sermons are intended to produce a *pathos* inducing appeal for the purpose of emphasizing some point of instruction, exhortation or admonition. They are comparable to what one authority has described as "the one aspect of the [African-American] sermon that most nearly deserves to be called typically black," namely, "celebration".[145] The latter may be more fully defined as follows:

> Celebration dramatizes the main idea of the sermon and supports the behavioral purpose or motivational goal. The function could be called "ecstatic reinforcement." People relate to and remember what they celebrate, and it influences their behavior. ... There simply must be a biblical lesson and behavioral objective that justifies stirring people's feelings. The emotional is most essential; it may not be omitted.[146]

The final remarks are a warning against "irrelevant celebration," gratuitous emotional evocation for its own sake – or worse yet, celebration of the preacher himself. Some (printed only!) examples of a Chewa celebratory style will be given in connection with our consideration of strategic reiteration below.

---

[145] Mitchell, *Black Preaching*, p. 119.
[146] *Ibid.*, p. 121.

One other important affective resource in a Chewa preacher's inventory of rhetorical devices is a limited amount of strategically placed, carefully managed *humour*. Mitchell's observation is directly on target in this regard.

> The positive side is that humor can do much to help both speaker and audience to relax and open up to each other. But humor must be in the best of taste and held to a minimum.[147]

Evangelist Wame is a past master in the use of the humorous (including the incongruous and incomprehensible) in life to influence his listeners to look at a particular issue, often the foolishness of some sinful behaviour, in a new, more critical and biblical light. This snatch of the funny side of human nature may occur at any place in one of his sermons, where it may serve different purposes, e.g., at the beginning to loosen up his audience and to generate some positive *ethos*; in the middle somewhere to diffuse an emotive build up (too much *pathos*) that is threatening to overshadow a major theological thought or some pragmatic implication; towards the end either as part of his ascent towards a hortatory climax or on the downside of its denouement to act as a foil for his main theme (*logos*). Humour, often coupled with *hyperbole*, may thus be utilized to 'prime the pumps' of people's emotions either for a bit of lively encouragement or, more frequently, to soften the blow of a vigorous warning to desist from some evil, worldly activity.[148] The following are two examples of the second function (both from SW6). The first is related homiletically to the apostle's image of a "temporary [grass] shelter" that we are living in here on earth (2Cor 5:1); the second plays off of the psalmist's warning to "kiss the Son" in reverent submission to his royal rule over your life (Ps 2:12).

> Now when constructing this type of overnight shelter (i.e., while on the old journey by foot down to South Africa), they did not put a lot of effort into it. They just built it anyhow because it was merely a dwelling to sleep in while on this trip. And after they rested, they proceeded with their journey without looking back. Say, did you ever see (hear of) a person who bought a big sofa to fill up the inside of such a shelter? Did they ever buy a big iron door for the entrance or put windows in the openings? Did they ever start a farm nearby a trip

---

[147] *Ibid.*, p. 116.
[148] This is a personal assessment, but I believe that the following characterization of the light-hearted vein sometimes found in the sermons of Martin Luther applies in large measure also to those of Evangelist Wame: "Although there was humor, there was never levity, or anything calculated to produce laughter. Yet the congregation frequently must have chuckled" (Meusner, *Luther the Preacher*, p. 52).

shelter, or a grocery right beside it, or a store on the other side? Did they set up a maize mill at a shelter like that? ... Is it wrong to set up a maize mill there? Is it wrong to buy a sofa [and put it inside]? Is it wrong to put your car inside? Is it wrong to use it for a cattle pen? Is it wrong to start a farm right there? Is it wrong, is it wrong? So why then do you say, "That's insane!"? Why is that, why is that? Let me tell you why: At a shelter one doesn't herd cattle – they'll all be left behind [i.e., when you continue your journey]! Alleluiaah! (Amen!)

Kiiiiss the Son lest He become angry at you while [you are] on the journey! You are on a dangerous trip – no reverse! Blessed is the person who travels along with Jesus on this journey, in this wicked world! Some people, instead of kissing the Son, they kiss a bottle of beer! Ah! (laughter) Now if he gets angry at you and that bottle of beer, you're finished! Some of you are kissing a bar girl. Ah! If he gets angry at you and that bar girl, you're finished! Some of you are kissing a big [good luck] charm. If he gets angry at you and that big charm, you're finished! Some of you are kissing a lie. If he gets angry at you and that lie, you're finished! Kiiiiiss the Son, lest he become angry at you! You are on a daaaangerous trip – no reverse! No reverse! Blessed is the person who travels along with Jesus...

The preacher's humour here serves to lighten the load of his rather heavy hortatory appeal for the audience to take their Christianity seriously. He thereby 'tickles' their emotions while simultaneously 'pinching' their conscience and heart felt affections. The abundant imagery that is evident in the preceding selections leads then to the next prominent rhetorical technique.

Evocative Description

With this category we encounter another little problem of definition, that is, how to distinguish its manifestation from that of the preceding, affective appeal. Obviously, they are very closely connected, but in the case of the present technique, I would like to focus on the instances of vivid description whereby the speaker evokes feelings that pertain to the five main external *senses* (sight, sound, taste, smell, and touch), as well as to those that affect one's bodily *sensation* (e.g., heat, cold, pain, itching, and so forth). Jay Adams explains the relationship as follows:

> When a preacher says what he relates in such a way that he stimulates one or more of the five senses, thus triggering emotion, then the listener may be said to "experience" the event. In that way, the event will become "real" to him, which means that it has become concretized (or personalized), memorable, and in the fullest sense of the word, understandable.[149]

Evangelist Wame's sermons in particular feature certain graphic descriptive passages which readily stimulate a strong, familiar sensory impression in the imagination of his audience. Some of these images are positive (attractive), while other illustrations and analogies are definitely negative (repulsive) in nature. But all of them are designed to depict in a memorable way a specific thematic point that he is trying to make in relation either to biblical theology, or more often, to morality, that is, a sanctified Christian lifestyle. The purpose of such sense provoking imagery is to promote a greater measure of personal engagement, identification, or application among members of the audience.

> Once identification occurs, emotion is stirred and the listener becomes interested. When the preacher cultivates this interest, the listener is open in a fresh way to the preacher's message, open for reversal in the emotional field, and open to the gospel call for change. *The ability of the preacher to stir identification, emotion, and interest through sense appeal is what is meant by the term experiential preaching.*[150]

Mitchell refers to this faculty as the "picture painting art" of the black preacher[151] which is fashioned largely by the addition of elaborative detail to either some portion of the text of Scripture during its dramatized retelling or to some illustrative story, example, allusion or other real life reference (as discussed above).

> Black preachers often use the best of biblical scholarship to add living details that would not otherwise be evident to the laity. These fresh insights are used to enhance the gripping realism of a message. ... In addition to the scholar's details, there is a great need for more vivid

---

[149] Jay E. Adams, *Preaching with Purpose*, Grand Rapids: Zondervan, 1982, p. 86.
[150] Thomas, *They Like to Never Quit Praisin' God*, p. 37; original italics.
[151] Mitchell, *Black Preaching*, p. 34.

> but not less valid details, often not given in the Bible or anywhere else. These details help the hearer to be caught up in the experience being narrated and, as a result, to understand better and to be moved to change. Black preaching, at its best, is rich in the imaginative supply of these details and in their dramatic use in telling the Gospel stories.[152]

As already noted, Chewa preachers like Shadrack Wame do not limit their usage of evocative description to biblical narrative or to some other Scripture text type. Instead, they may attach it to any portion of the sermon – an exhortation for instance – which they feel needs a bit of creative embellishment in order to help listeners focus upon a given point and to stimulate them imaginatively to identify more deeply with the religious issue at hand or the rhetorical means that are being used to coax it home to the heart. These descriptive passages normally feature figures of speech like metaphor or simile, a special concentration of adjectives and other modifiers, or above all, the oral descriptive action predicate par excellence – the dramatizing *ideophone*. Ideophones are worthy of special mention because, as emphatically vivid, phonologically distinct and attractive expressions that evoke immediate sensations and images, they are so characteristic of good African traditional narrative:[153]

> The language of (Chichewa) storytelling is rich in ideophones. The storyteller exploits this advantage and employs ideophones which vivify his speech, lend him eloquence, complete his thought and help him to create a fresh picture of an event, and to convey contrasting images. ... The images created by using ideophones help the audience to see, hear, feel, smell, touch and enjoy the narrative.[154]

A number of the prominent pictorial devices just mentioned are demonstrated in the several segments of evocative, *pathos* arousing description that are cited below.[155] In the initial passage (from SW10), Wame first

---

[152] *Ibid.*, pp. 61, 63. Albrecht calls attention to this function of figurative language in his Tanzanian corpus: "African preachers employ metaphors as analogy and identification to draw biblical events of the past into the present-day existence of African Christians. The use of metaphors has the effect that African sermons transform remote happenings recorded in the Bible into an existential *hic et nunc*" (summarised in the review by F. A. Dierks, Review of Rainer Albrecht, 1996 (q.v.), Missionalia 27:1 (1999), p. 140).
[153] Cf. Okpewho, *African Oral Literature*, pp. 92-96.
[154] E.S.T. Mvula, "Four Songs from Malawi", *Kalulu* 3 (1982), p. 62.
[155] The combined use of these descriptive devices in a given passage illustrates what Okpewho calls "piling". "In African oral literature, it is perhaps true to say that fullness, not economy, of expression is

describes the fierceness of a crocodile (cf. Job 41), which is like Satan in the terror and tenacity of its attack. Later, at the end of his sermon he recounts the horrible death (by murder) of a person who during his life "worshipped" at the riotous rites of the "church of Satan," i.e., the pagan *nyau* traditional male socio-religious cult.

> Who can open the door to the mouth of a crooocodile? If a person strikes it with a sword, it simply bounces off – even a spear, no way! Or an arrow, no! Or a lance, no! An iron bar it treats like a reed, and a brass one like green twig. You can't chase it away with an arrow. As for stones from a sling, or legging, it laughs, "Haaa!" and treats it like a clump of dry grass. War clubs too are regarded as grass. Yes, it just mocks at the stabbing of a spear. If you raise a spear at it (*chii!*), it says, "Let them come (*thii!*)," and laughs (*khakhakha!*), and slips away, out of sight (*zii!*). Who can open the doors of the mouth of a crocodile. In this world there's nothing like it, a beast without fear. It looks upon everything with boastful pride, the king of braggarts. Its heart is as hard as a rock!
> So her husband went off to that "church" of his, to the beer-drink. And there really was a lot of beer there, but it was also a celebration of the *nyau* cult (*gule wamkulu*, "the big dance"). And what happened there was that his fellow cult members, his fellow "Christians," they poured 'medicine' (*mankhwala*) into his beer mug, lethal poison! They poured it right inside (*phwi!*). He merely said, "My beer tastes mighty good!" – not realizing that his mates had put "medicine" into it. After he had drunk that beer, right away he began to "see" a lot of sweat (*chithukuta*). Right away he exclaimed, "I'm feeling very hot!" Right away he said, "My heart is racing!" Right away – down he fell to the ground (*thii!*). The fellow members of his "church" came to grab him, some to remove his clothes. "What's wrong? what's wrong!" [they cried]. Right away a lot of foam began to emerge from his mouth. Right away his tongue began to hang out of his mouth. They said, "Well, there's nothing that we can do for him here, let's just get him home." ... She (his wife) came back to find a group of people there; they had laid the body out at her house. She saw her husband – speechless, frothing with foam at the mouth, his tongue all hanging out – but he was not yet dead, he was still alive.

---

a fundamental virtue. .... One way in which this fullness can be achieved is by piling or coupling one detail or idea to another so that the performance build up to a climax" (Okpewho, *African Oral Literature*, p. 83; cf. Wendland, "Stylistic Form and Communicative Function", ch. 4).

In one of his most powerfully expressed sense related sermons (based on 2Cor 2:14-17), Evangelist Wame uses a diverse assortment of descriptive images of scent and smell to highlight the contrasting lives of genuine Christians and good hypocrites. In building up to his punch line of application to the spiritual dimension (i.e., fight fiercely against the forces of sin to retain your victory in Christ, 2Cor 2:14), Wame captivates his audience with the following vivid piece of abundant antithetical sensory evocation (only part of which is cited here).

> When a person roasts a chicken and its aroma reaches us, we ask, "Say friends, how do you feel in your noses now?" "Iiiih!" they reply, "Somebody has cooked a big chicken – my, it must be a big fat one!" As you are talking there, you see someone else arriving to ask, "How do you feel in your noses now?" You see, a good smell attracts [people]. After discussing the matter at that place, you begin to get closer, asking one another, "Say, do you think it's coming from here?" One says, "It seems like it's from over here." Another says, "No, it's coming from over there." You cannot forget a good smell – it's attracts [you]! Ah, but a big chicken like that, you simply have to snuff its aroma out by cooking some maize meal mush (*nsima*, i.e., to eat along with it). A good smeeell! It attraaacts! Some can't get it out of their minds, saying [to themselves], "If you could only find that [roast] chicken, ah indeed, that would be wonderful!" A good smeeell – it attraaacts! That is its goodness!
>
> But a bad odour, e-e-eeh! There were some men who were on a journey [on foot], and they had taken along some lunch. After travelling for some time, they reached a shady place, nice and cool. "Let's rest here," they said. So they unpacked their lunch and began to eat. Now while they were eating there, they said, "M-m-mm! How does it feel in your nose right now?" At that point one fellow grumbled saying, "A-a-aah! A terrible stench is coming out here! Hey you, this stench, what could it be?" Another said, "M-mm, it's hyena [meat], and it has gone bad! It's rotten! (i.e., a bad smell coupled with meat that is taboo). I too wanted to ask [about this]. M-m-mm!" Immediately they wrapped up their lunch [and left it there]. They didn't finish it – due to that heavy stench everywhere (*phaa!*). They took ooooff [far away]! A bad smell – it repeeels. They left, yes, they left. A bad smell really repels!

It is sensory attuned, culturally significant, spiritually relevant descriptive sequences such as these that captivate listeners, bringing them mentally into a sermon along with all their faculties – not only the cognitive, but also the emotive, the sensuous and ultimately also the intuitive, whereby a fresh encounter with the Word may be experienced.[156] This renders them more receptive to intellectual and volitional stimulation as well, that is, to some biblical teaching coupled with an exhortational appeal to their values, will and an associated way of life.

Finally, in connection with the technique of rhetorically motivated description, it is important to note the degree of *contextualization* that a preacher applies in order to bring the biblical message vividly home to his listeners, to plant it solidly in local soil by means of some familiar, evocative reference(s) to the indigenous environment and the local way of life.[157] Such application involves not only the *manner* of discourse as we have been considering – the genre, style and mode of text organization – but it also includes the *matter*, that is, the content of what is being preached. In order to assist the audience in applying its primary admonition or exhortation, the message must be stated in terms that are appropriate and relevant to their needs, interests, concerns, values and goals. As Mitchell observes in an American setting, "Black preaching at its best has remained focused on problems that people confront daily and feel real needs in meeting. ... The dialogue [i.e., between preacher and congregation] is lively when needs are met and the concepts uses are within reach of the hearers".[158]

For example, during a certain biblical text retelling, Evangelist Wame will often transpose certain incidental details found in a given narrative, exposition or description of Scripture to fit a typical Malawian setting. Accord-

---

[156] Thomas points out that evocative description is effected not only verbally, through figurative language and sensual imagery, but also non-verbally as well, that is, by a preacher's entire body: "... our gestures, our facial expression, our tones/sounds, our bodily movement, and our posture stimulate or limit the operation of sense appeal in the emotional field" (Thomas, *They Like to Never Quit Praisin' God*; original italics). Okpewho notes that when uttering ideophones during an oral narrative, "the artist may accompany the words with certain dramatic movements" (Okpewho, *African Oral Literature*, p. 95).
[157] For Wame, like Luther, most "words and illustrations [are] those of the common people .... [for example] Just going to church and hearing the word of God will not make one a Christian: 'Dogs also occasionally stray into church and remain dogs as before'" (Meusner, *Luther the Preacher*, p. 54).
[158] Mitchell, *Black Preaching*, pp. 105f. In the corpus of the Chewa revivalist preachers, 'felt need' and 'daily problems' in a physical or social sense cannot be easily separated from those that are religious and spiritual in nature (cf. section 5). The former, worldly variety of trial or difficulty is often viewed as being a manifestation of the latter, in particular, the result of believers being assailed by the demonic powers of darkness led by their chief (*mfumu*), Satan himself.

ingly, the various kinds of crops that the selfish rich man of Christ's parable (Lk 12:16-19) had packed into his granaries turn out to be maize, millet, cassava, groundnuts and sweet potatoes (SW22), while the drinks that were flowing freely into the sacred cups at the great feast of Belshazzar (Dan 5:2-4, 23) are reported (SW24) to be local whiskey (*kachasu*) and beer (*chibuku*), as well as imported gin (*jini*) and brandy (*bulande*).

More important perhaps is the special attention that is directed towards particular sins and evils which are problematic in an African/Chewa cultural context. Thus in addition to the iniquities that are more or less common to a fallen humanity, including so called Christians, e.g., lying, hatred, jealousy, sexual immorality, disrespect for the Lord's Day and Church elders, the popular revivalists do not hesitate to zero in on those traditional sins that are prevalent in society. So it is not surprising that at Belshazzar's ball, in addition to drunkenness, the degenerate guests were also participating in wicked practices such as witchcraft, smoking dagga (Indian hemp), divination and praising the ancestral spirits (*mizimu*, cf. Dan 5:4). As an especially graphic instance of how the infidels of this world take pleasure in tormenting the weak and those whom they consider to be inferior, including believers (SW28, cf. Ps 137:3), Wame tells the shocking story of an old man, a practising night-witch (*mfiti*), who delighted in scaring his little grandson to death with his demonic nocturnal activities. Description then is most evocative and rhetorically effective if it is based upon images that the audience can easily conjure up for themselves in their own minds, based on their own personal experiences, worldview (*Weltanschauung*) and life setting (*Sitz-im-Leben*).

We direct our attention now away from the broader or more comprehensive features of Chewa sermonic rhetorical technique to a trio of compound strategies on the *microlevel* of discourse organization: reiteration, intensification and figuration. As their general titles would suggest, each of these categories includes a number of different devices that contribute, often in close combination, to the overall cognitive impact and/or emotive effect that is being generated, namely, by sharpening or focusing upon crucial aspects of the primary message.

Strategic Reiteration

Linguistic reiteration in some form or another is the mainstay of any comprehensive and convincing rhetorical strategy, particularly in oral discourse where it tends to be more noticeable in terms of both quantity and quality (i.e., diversity). Again, this stylistic feature was/is also important in secular African verbal art forms:

> Repetition is no doubt one of the most fundamental characteristic features of oral literature. It has both an aesthetic and a utilitarian value: in other words, it is a device that not only gives a touch of beauty or attractiveness to a piece of oral expression (whether song or narrative or other kind of statement) but also serves certain practical purposes in the overall organization of the oral performance.[159]

This principle of recursion is certainly operative within the complete Chewa sermon corpus, but it is especially evident in the preaching of Evangelist Wame.[160] This is not *mere* repetition, the aimless reproduction of words uttered to avoid silence and to fill out the space of a discourse or to give the speaker an opportunity to think of what to say next.[161] Rather, such repetition is always *meaningful* in the sense that it is motivated according to some specific rhetorical purpose, beginning with the subject at hand.[162] This fact is evident in the great variety of types that are manifested within the collection, namely: phonological, morphological, syntactic, lexical, literary (i.e., duplicated stylistic devices or major themes), structural (e.g., parallel discourse portions in the larger argument of the message) and practical (e.g., involving a return to the topic line after a digression.[163] Each distinct form of recursion is intuitively selected to perform a particular communicative

---

[159] Okpewho, *African Oral Literature*, p. 71.

[160] Repetition is also a prominent feature of Ethiopian sermons, especially in the compositions of "preachers with only informal theological training," where it serves to give special emphasis to the biblical text in a way other than by means of a thorough exegesis of the original (Forslund, *The Word of God in Ethiopian Tongues*, pp. 241-243).

[161] Such a "spouting of words," Luther once remarked, sounds "as if you knocked the bung out of a full barrel. There it spouts because it is full inside. But this verbosity does not impress or edify, though it may please some" (cited in Meusner, *Luther the Preacher*, p. 93).

[162] Leroux notes that "Repetition [is] perhaps the most common rhetorical device for creating presence [i.e., of topic or theme, foregrounding] – the deliberate portrayal of events, characters, and ideas in such a way as to make them visible, dominant, and true before their hearers" (Leroux, "Perceiving Rhetorical Style", p. 29).

[163] Cf. Luther: "In many sermons he chased some rabbit or other across the landscape, and then had to come back to what he was talking about" (Meusner, *Luther the Preacher*, p. 57).

purpose within its immediate context and often within the framework of a certain text as a whole. In short, we may have a significant restatement for the sake of semantic and/or aesthetic "emphasis, memory, impact, and effect,"[164] and the scope or range of any such function may be either *local* or *global* in its textual extent and compositional significance.

Some of the principal kinds of reiteration to be found in a Chewa sermon can be roughly classified as follows:[165] the recursion may be either *exact*, which is of course the easiest to detect, *synonymous* to a greater or lesser extent,[166] or it may take the form of a flexible *filler-frame*, which is Wame's specialty. In this last type, we typically have a sequence of relatively short, parallel utterances that are virtually the same, except for a single word or phrase which occurs in the same syntactic position each time. This "blank" is then "filled in" with a different expression which is related paradigmatically to the others, that is, by "association".[167] In other words, it belongs to the same basic semantic field, e.g., grace, love, mercy, kindness, pity, etc., within a specific textual context.

The reiterated term or lexical set may be *contiguous* (found right after or in the immediate vicinity of its base) or it may be *removed*, that is, located at some distance from the expression that it is repeating. The reiterated items may be *thematic* in the sense that they are related semantically to the main instruction, implication, or injunction of the sermon, or they may be *topical*, that is, pertaining only to the particular subject or issue at hand, whether this be part of a story, example, illustration, explanation, or description of some kind. The set or sequence of repeated items may be arranged in *parallel* (corresponding) or *chiastic* (transposed) fashion, that is

---

[164] Mitchell, *Black Preaching*, p. 93.
[165] At some point in a more complete analysis, it might be helpful to determine which recognized 'classical' forms of repetition are found to a significant degree in Chewa oral rhetoric, in comparison, for example, with a listing such as that found under "figures involving addition" in E. W. Bullinger, *Figures of Speech Used in the Bible, Explained and Illustrated*, Grand Rapids: Baker Book House, 1898 (reprinted 1968), pp. xxii-xxx. For the various types of reiteration found in the repertory of a Nyanja radio narrator, see Wendland, "Stylistic Form and Communicative Function", pp. 749-771.
[166] A lesser degree of synonymy would include that of the generic-specific variety, e.g., "It was a huge snake - a big mamba, a cobra..." (SW25). Synonymous reiteration is termed "parallelism" by Okpewho, who describes it as follows: "Essentially, the device is a form of repetition in which a single idea is restated in a variety of ways. It is, in other words, a repetitive device that puts more emphasis on diversity and contrast than on similarity between details" (Okpewho, *African Oral Literature*, p. 82).
[167] Ibid., p. 86.

to say, A - B, A' - B' or A - B, B' - A'. Furthermore, the set may be constructed in the form of a *climax*, where the most graphic, shocking, revealing, or important items occur at or near the end, or it may merely constitute an illustrative *listing* that is intended to highlight in its entirety, as a whole, some point that the preacher has already made or wants to introduce.

In addition to the preceding types of *intratextual* recursion, instances of *intertextual* iteration also appear in the form of a given preacher's verbal trademarks. At the beginning of a Wame sermon, for example, we often find these words, "Today we have a warning (*chenjezo*)"; somewhere in the middle, "These are painful words (*mau osautsa*)"; and toward the ending, "Blessed (*odala*) are those who..." Such intertextual repetition would of course include those favourite passages that a certain preacher likes to cite again and again. One of Evangelist Wame's preferred texts, one that he uses especially at the close of a sermon prayer, is Zechariah 4:6: "Not by might, nor by power, but by my Spirit, says the LORD of Hosts!"[168]

The basic types of verbal recursion listed above are all exemplified in Wame's homiletical admonition based on Psalm 57:1 (the *primary* text) and Matthew 11:28 (a *secondary* text).[169] Space allows us to consider only several outstanding and easily recognizable instances of reiteration in this sermon, which somewhat resembles Ecclesiastes in style (SW25):

> But the thing that troubles me [is] the bane of a shady spot that shifts all about (*chosunthasuntha*, morphemic repetition).[170] "Drag that mat over here, the sun is now breaking through [the shade]." "Drag that chair over here; let's sit right here, the sun is now breaking through." "Go get that rug; let's move over here, the sun is now breaking

---

[168] Wame re-expresses the literal Nyanja Bible translation (*Buku Lopatulika*) more naturally as follows: "*Si mphamvu, si nkhondo, koma ndi Mzimu wanga, akutero Yehova Mulungu.*"

[169] Wame often begins a sermon with the advice that it is intended to be a *chenjezo*, that is, a warning or admonition to the audience, one that encompasses believers, those who are undecided, as well as the manifestly unfaithful. A *primary* Scripture text is the passage that the preacher begins with, derives his main theme from, and/or bases most of his message upon. There is normally only a single primary pericope, consisting of one or more verses. A *secondary* text is some passage that is clearly related to the primary passage, which the preacher uses to support, develop, or elaborate upon the latter in a significant way (i.e., more than just a passing reference or citation).

[170] The reiterated notion of "shifting shade" is also thematic for the greater (admonitory) part of this sermon, that is, as a metaphor for the various earthly entities that worldly people attempt to "shade" themselves "under" (e.g., money, wealth, fame, family) - away from the scorching "sun" of the different problems and pains of life.

through." "Ah, let's get away from here; we can sit behind the house, the sun is now breaking through."[171]

This earthly life is tiresome (*wotopetsa*, another key intertextual term of Wame's). When troubles come, they don't first look to see whether this person was troubled yesterday as well. Before these are finished, others are on the way; before these are finished, others are on the way. Tired of sickness, tired of being cursed, tired of debts, tired of hunger, tired of poverty, tired of court cases, tired of being a "survivor" (*umasiye*). (But) when we look at one another, we say, "My friend is pretty well off." So sorry – the life of this world, we travel it huffing and puffing (*wefu-wefu*) along. It's a tiresome life. If you are lying down here, don't get up – it's too tiresome! If you are standing upright, don't lie down – it's too tiresome! If you are running along, don't stop – it's too tiresome! If you are quiet, don't say anything – it's too tiresome! If you are speaking, don't get angry – it's too tiresome! You folks, even eating [can be] tiresome, even bathing [can be] tiresome! You folks, your car may look like it's in good condition, later it lets you down, saying, 'I'm tired, send somebody else [to ride in me], I'm tired!' Every single thing is tiiiiiiresome (*chotopetsaaaaa*, emphatic final vowel extension)! It's a painful life, a painful life – every single thing is tiresome!

As I am speaking here some "big people" are beginning a business saying, "Perhaps I'll find a shady spot here." Children as well as old folks are busily occupied in the search for shade – a tiresome life! Some [women] knit little dolls saying, "Perhaps I'll find a shady spot here" – a tiresome life! Some sell groundnuts perhaps, saying, "I'll find a shady spot here." Some sort through little fish [to sell] saying, "Perhaps I'll find a shady spot here." Eeeeeveryone, young and old – buuuusy! (*biizi*) seeking shady spots. My friend, it's not wrong to buy a minibus. It's not wrong to sell tomatoes. It's not wrong to sell charcoal. It's not wrong to buy a maize mill – cattle – stores. It's not wrong to open up a business or a farm. But the thing that pains me at heart [is] fickleness (*chosinthasintha*)!

And when we find those small shady spots, [what happens is that we] forget the things of God! Our backs are covered up (*fundu!*) [so we think]. He thinks he's found a little shade as he sells charcoal – [but] he stopped going to church long ago. He thinks, the little shade of a minibus – he stopped going to church long ago. He thinks, the

---

[171] There is a sequence of quotations in this section – different speakers who are distinguished despite the absence of speech margins (e.g., "he said") by means of the preacher's effective use of intonational patterns and pauses.

little shade of a maize mill – he stopped going to church long ago. He thinks he's in a little shade, he has his business – he stopped going to church long ago. But bewaaare! Let's not play with the world! After [only] two days or three, the sun strikes (*phaa!*). It beats down [again]!

Let us not play with the world – this changeable thing! Is this real shade? For this reason Jesus tells us in Matthew 11:28, "Come here all you who are tired and troubled, and you will find rest for your lives." There in heaven – if you draw near, there's no hunger. If you draw near, there are no sicknesses. If you draw near, there are no curses. If you draw near, there are no sins. Life unbounded! Our hope is Jesus, our rest is Jesus!

Please call upon Jesus, he is the shade! Call on Jesus, he's your hope! Do not quarrel and fight! ... Remain in Jesus where there is rest. Don't kill one another, pleeease! Don't kill one another [because of] little shady spots! Don't attack one another [because of] little shady spots that shift! Do not oppose the government; it too is moving along in a discouraged manner (*khumakhuma*). [Yes,] there is democracy, [but] we received it at a bad time (an ironic reference to local political developments)!

By means of such skilful reiteration – a basic *theme* complemented by many *variations* – the point of the Scripture (*logos*) and the motivational purpose of the sermon is made crystal clear and is strongly impressed upon the memory. Indeed, it often reaches the point where certain graphic segments could surely be reproduced almost verbatim by the audience.[172] Thus the impelling message retains its verbal life, meaning, impact, and significance far beyond the scope of its initial setting of proclamation. That is to say, the message enters what we might call "Chichewa religious oral tradition" via the impressed original listeners, many of whom become selective text transmitters in their own right as they retell such a memorable sermon (or selected portions of it) to their family and friends – or repreach it to another congregation.

---

[172] While such a capacity for memory retention and message reproduction may seem a bit far-fetched to Westerners, it is a present reality among those who are living wholly or partially within a world that is still keenly sensitive to the dynamism of the purely spoken word and who are correspondingly much more oral-aurally proficient and hence also active in their practice of this talent. Certain key Christian phrases and vivid images are particularly prone to informal re-transmission – a popular, vernacular process that may be stimulated in the case of the broadcast sermons by the radio medium itself (cf. D. Spitulnik, "The Social Circulation of Media Discourse and the Mediation of Communities", *Journal of Linguistic Anthropology* 6(2), 1997, p. 162).

Verbal Intensification

It is not surprising in orations as dramatic (expressive, affective, and evocative) as those of the Chewa sermon corpus to find (hear) a variety of devices that are employed either individually or (more often) in conjunction to intensify some verbal, nominal or adjectival concept to a greater degree. This augmentation or heightening may be effected *phonologically* (e.g., by volume, pitch or tempo, considered earlier); *syntactically* through repetition, or via some deliberate modification in the normal order of words; *textually* through the juxtaposition of segments (pertaining to character, quality or activity) that are in obvious contrast or conflict;[173] and *lexically* in use of intensifiers such as vocatives, imperatives and hortatives (usually directed at the audience), exclamations (to express strong emotions and attitudes), ideophones, nominal prefixes (e.g., the augmentative *chi-*), emphatic pronouns (i.e., independent or separable forms), verbal suffixes (e.g., the causative *-tsa* and emphatic enclitics such as *-di/-tu* greatly), plus an assortment of assertive adverbs (e.g., *kwambiri* 'very much,' *ndithu* 'indeed,' *zoona* 'truly' and *zedi* 'surely').[174]

Through these diverse means – their varied combination as well as their nuanced modulation – the power or forcefulness of the discourse is stepped up to a higher level. It thus rises to a more intense emotive pitch in order to foreground certain aspects of the preacher's exhortation to the faithful to be active in their fight against the evils and religious enemies of this world – the seen as well as unseen, external and also internal, human or non-human powers. In other words, such intensifiers serve to mark various *peaks* (in narrative) or *climaxes* (in non-narrative discourse) during the progressive development of the text. The rhetorical skill and homiletical competence of a preacher is demonstrated then in the variety of intensifying devices that he utilizes, in their harmonious deployment or incorporation within the composition and also in the control that he exercises over them. That is to say, a certain amount of balance and restraint is required so that these techniques

---

[173] A recent innovative development in Chewa popular sermonody is the extratextual use of backgrounded traditional drums or even an electric guitar to highlight or punctuate selected, verbally intensified portions of the discourse. The drummers or strummers of course have to be attuned to the preacher's particular compositional and rhetorical style for this device to be effective.

[174] The English glosses supplied here are only general approximations of the semantic force of a particular word or affix, which can be specified more precisely only within a given cotext of discourse and with reference to a complete Chichewa lexicographical framework.

do not turn out to sound rhetorically overdone or appear to be merely a gratuitous attempt to enlarge his own *ethos*, or that they generate so much *pathos* within the audience that it detracts from the *logos* of the intended spiritual message.

Again, perhaps the best way to illustrate the quality of such intensification within a Chewa sermon is to present a few representative selections from the Wame corpus. In the extended example below (from SW32), as is typically the case, they are found concentrated at a point of high emotive tension in the discourse, namely, as the preacher dramatizes the nature and significance of Christ's vicarious sacrifice on behalf of all people. A number (only a fraction) of the intensifiers manifested in this text are identified in parentheses simply to indicate something of the diversity and density that is present:

> That's right (*eeeh!*, exclamation), you cannot gain heaven at all (*-di*, intensifying suffix), but gahena (vocal stress and volume) you will gain (chiastic syntax), indeeeed (*ndiiithu*, assertive adverb and vowel elongation) – you will indeed gain [it] (repetition)! Take care (audience imperative), my brother (vocative and utterance brevity)! We became guilty of a teeeerrible (vowel elongation) crime! It was necessary for someone else to enter into our place, someone who was not affected by our sin and its reward (contrastive apposition). God commanded that all people on the whole earth (augmentative attribution) – gahena (anacoluthon and stress)! The someone who entered our place (syntactic front-shift), he is our Lord Jesus. Up there in heeeaven, seeing (emphatic infinitive) the souls of boys, the souls of girls, the souls of fathers, the souls of chiefs, the souls of children (frame reiteration) – he saw them, the Lord Jesus did (syntactic reversal), going to gahena! The case has gone badly (exclamation)! There's no one who could have paid for it! (condensation) Mercy grabbed the Lord Jeeeesus (idiom). "Father, can't you allow me to go, yes meee (*iiine*, intensive pronoun)? I'll go and pay for this very crime (*umenewu*, demonstrative elaboration) instead, in their place (pleonasm). Let me (*ineeyo*, intensive pronoun) just go and die, let me just go and die!"
>
> ... I (the preacher) am sorry (personal interjection) – the separation from God who hates sin (anacoluthon) – when the Lord Jesus carried my adulteries, my lies, drunkenness, witchcraft, all [my] evils (emphatic enumeration and syntactic front-shift) he bore the Lord Jesus [did]. When we have a look at that head [of his] – he wore a cap of thorns (imagery) – today I reveal to you [that] it wasn't those

very thorns (demonstrative elaboration and condensation), but it was sins that caused him to suffer, and they entered into his whole head, all bloody (*magazi okhaokha*, vivid metaphor and augmentation). My sins he bore and my sins caused him to suffer. And they condemned him [to] an awful death on the cross – my sins (syntactic back-shift)! Because God hates a sinful person, his very own only begotten one (attributive concentration and front-shift) he cast him outside, he cast him outside. And it reached the point where the Lord Jesus knew this, saying [to himself], "That's it (*basi!*, exclamation), me and my Father – we will not see one another again (*pathos*)!" He knew that, "Me and my Father (front-shift), there is enmity [between us]. Me and my Father, I have no more rights with him (*ndilibenso gawo*, idiom)!" It reached the point of weeping – he wept saying these words (Wame himself is weeping!), "My God, my God, why have you abandoned me? ..."

"... Why have you abandoned me, Dad (*Baba*, familiar vocative)?" [The Father replies], "You are carrying the sins of the whole wide world; [that is why] I have indeed abandoned you!" (condensation) So now if you (the listener) say (object) saying, "God is merciful." (Wame replies:) It failed with his son (i.e., to show mercy), so you, who are you if he should assess you, yes you (i.e., what would happen)? (condensation and rhetorical question and emphatic pronouns) Watch out (*basopo!*, exclamation), take care! How would he assess you – you? Aah! (interjection) It failed with his very own son (repetition)! God is righteous, and he could not possibly receive any sinner at all (*m'pang'onopang'ono pomwe*, emphatic adverbial)! And (polysyndeton) God wants a person to be one hundred percent (*handredi pasenti*, emphatic loanword) [in] holiness before him – ninety nine percent no! (negative intensive) no entering heaven! One hundred percent [means] entering heaven, but one hundred percent you cannot achieve. It is found [only] in Jesus. When you receive Jesus, you – that is, your righteousness – [is] a full one hundred percent! That it could come from you (prolepsis), this is impossible, this is impossible, this is impossible, no way at all (comprehensive negative repetition)!

The oral-audio version of this text is an intense, tremendously moving piece of *pathos* inspiring preaching, obviously involving several other rhetorical techniques as well, such as dramatic delivery and affective appeal. Even a vocally reduced (and sometimes unclear) cassette recording of this portion never fails to have a pronounced effect upon all who listen. Some hearers are even moved to tears themselves as they are progressively attracted to the emotional state and clear conviction of the preacher with regard to his message concerning this central theological truth of the Scriptures. Clearly, this is rhetoric in service of the gospel!

Idiomatic Figuration

This category encompasses all the different figures of speech (from word to sentence level) and other types of idiomatic diction, including selective intensification (as just surveyed), that are utilized to enliven a sermon and to render its central message (truth and application) in a style that sounds more natural and down to earth to its listeners.[175] Through this means the *ethos* of the preacher is enhanced in that his audience is led to conclude that, "He speaks like one of us!"[176] (even more, he is *walilime laluntha* 'one having a clever tongue') and does not talk *mwachibusa* ('in the [artificial]

---

[175] This sort of idiomacity of speaking style seems to be missing in the average sermon preached in the Ethiopian Mekane Yesus churches (in the Amharic and Oromo languages). According to Forslund: "The language of the sermons is frequently close to biblical language. This means that the style of biblical texts influence [sic] the style of the sermons. The sermon language is frequently on a formal level of style" (Forslund, *The Word of God in Ethiopian Tongues*, p. 238). Thus it is not surprising to find that "the majority of the figures of speech used in the sermons are [sic] closely related to biblical language. ... [and that] relatively few figures of speech originate from the Ethiopian background" (*ibid.*, p. 224). The Chewa corpus and that of Wame in particular give evidence of a much larger percentage of indigenous figures and locally-colored imagery. We note once more the corresponding goal and method of Ambrose, Augustine, and Jerome in this whole matter: "The[ir] sermon[s] explained in simple yet colorful language the mysteries of the scriptures; the style was constructed to guide the audience to an understanding of, and belief in, the truths of Christianity. The formal characteristics of [formal, literary] rhetoric were minimized; instead, vivid imagination, sound play, parenthesis and antithesis, vignettes, rhyme, paratactic cola, and all the other elements typical of colloquial speech and popular novel were used to make that truth accessible to all" (Oberhelman, *Rhetoric and Homiletics*, p. 125). Indeed it would appear from this list that if these renowned church fathers were alive today and preaching in Chichewa, they too would be included in the ranks of the popular evangelists along with Wame and his colleagues!

[176] Blount notes the importance of this characteristic of the American Black sermon: "The preacher must not only, in a broad sense, speak the language of the listeners, but must also, in a more specific sense, use that language according to the particular linguistic prescriptions, verbal and nonverbal, of the cultural or subcultural group with whom he or she is conversing" (Blount, *Cultural Interpretation*, p. 71). This quality of basic communicative ability also goes back in church history – to John Chrysostom, for example: "Commensurate with his zeal to address the need of the times with the will of God was John's ability to speak to the level of the listener in a way that he/she could relate to and benefit from" (Pless, "Seven Pulpit Paradigms", p. 199). Shadrack Wame preaches his theology and ethics in the colloquial dialect and artful diction of the local village storyteller, with no influence at all from a formal institutional theological training programme (which he never had).

dialect of a pastor'). The most commonly occurring type of figurative, or imagistic, language in Evangelist Wame's sermons is the *simile*, but there are also quite a few instances of *metaphor, hyperbole, irony, litotes* and *personification*. Examples of *metonymy, synecdoche, merismus* and *euphemism* also appear from time to time.[177]

The term 'idiomatic diction' includes *idioms* proper as well as all other rhetorical usages (in addition to the great many based on repetition, discussed earlier) that help to give the aural impression of natural, at times conversational or colloquial, speech,[178] for example, *ellipsis, asyndeton, aposiopesis, pleonasm, paraphrasis, parenthesis, antistrophe, communicatio, correction,* and *anacoluthon*.[179] Contemporary idiomacity includes the selective, contextually determined use of various 'English-isms,' that is, certain popular loanwords, both established ones (e.g., *buku, baibulo, batiza, botolo*) and those of more recent vintage (e.g., *kompyuta, diigri, dimokirasi*), calques or loan translations (e.g., *kwezani mikono* 'raise [your] arms [i.e., to vote]'; *tili pambuyo pa Yesu* 'we are behind [i.e., in support of] Jesus') and full or partial citations of complete utterance(s) that are probably familiar to most urban dwelling adults. The last type of borrowing, which manifests a distinct Malawianized accent, is often used for special effect, for example, to emphasize a certain point (*layifi ashulansi*, 'life insurance'; *iiti izi tuu leti!*, 'it is too late!'), or to depict a setting in which English would normally be used (*Wati izi yoa neemi?* 'What is your name?').

Professor Mitchell similarly stresses the importance of the Black American preacher's use of a local dialect and a natural, idiomatic speech style when

---

[177] At present my categorization of figures and idioms in the Chewa sermon corpus is very general and unsystematic. As the analysis continues, it should be possible (if deemed helpful at the time) to be more comprehensive and precise in identifying and classifying the various occurrences with the help of works such as Bullinger, *Figures of Speech Used in the Bible*, Lanham, *A Handlist of Rhetorical Terms*, and E.A. Nida et al., *Style and Discourse, With Special Reference to the Text of the Greek New Testament*, Cape Town: Bible Society of South Africa, 1983. The figurative inventory of the Chewa corpus is quite similar to that listed for the Ethiopian collection of Forslund (Forslund, *The Word of God in Ethiopian Tongues*, pp. 116f).
[178] "Idioms" may be defined as "combinations of two or more words which have a meaning which cannot be derived from the meaning of the component parts" (Nida et al., *Style and Discourse*, pp. 74f). Accordingly, they normally defy meaningful translation when rendered literally in another language.
[179] For classical definitions of these terms, see Bullinger, *Figures of Speech Used in the Bible*, pp. xix-xlvi.

proclaiming his sermon – that is, preaching in a familiar "soul language",[180] the genuine mother tongue of his people:

> ... the Black congregation responds to beauty of language – to the well-turned phrase. This does not mean complexity of structure. In fact, Black-culture preachers often use short, easily remembered sentences. But they use rhetorical flair. ... the impact of the lessons of faith is greatly enhanced by the natural poetry and music of gifted preachers. ... Real soul preaching demands rhetorical flair. ... Black preaching is the skillful use of poetic rhetoric.[181]

These words apply with equal relevance to the Chewa revivalists. Such speech fosters the immediate establishment of an *ethos* of interpersonal rapport, that is, in addition to increasing a sermon's overall emotive effect (*pathos*) and general intelligibility (i.e., pertaining to its *logos*). At all times, of course, preachers must not go too far and engage in linguistic acrobatics, which only serve to divert "attention from the focus of the sermon (if there be any) to themselves".[182]

In addition to idiomacity, there must also be a perceptible relevance with regard to the content that is being conveyed in a given sermon. This is as true for the figurative language that a preacher uses as it is for his literal discourse. As was noted under Evocative Description above, apt and artistic figures, simile and metaphor in particular, serve to render certain abstract or complex theological precepts and principles in a more conceptually accessible, life related and hence memorable manner. In short, each and every rhetorical device that is utilized in a sermon should ideally serve to reinforce either the righteous rebuke of God's law or the sweet comfort of his saving gospel.[183] The Scripture based preacher does not have to look far for an excellent model to follow in this regard:

---

[180] Mitchell, *Black Preaching*, p. 81.
[181] *Ibid.*, p. 96.
[182] *Ibid.* Forslund also notes the danger of what he terms "digression," that is, "turning the focus away from the topic of the sermon to the figures themselves" (Forslund, *The Word of God in Ethiopian Tongues*, p. 225). However, he goes on to point out the value of a concentration of figurative language: "A single figure of speech in isolation might deceive listeners in believing that it should be understood literally. The piling up of figures of speech makes it clear that the language is to be understood as imagery" (*ibid.*). Of course, a proper balance needs to be maintained in this respect in accordance with the particular audience concerned, the setting of the sermon being preached, and also its chief purpose.
[183] Cf. Thomas, *They Like to Never Quit Praisin' God*, p. 85.

Just as Jesus used familiar images to give clarity to his parables, the black preacher uses metaphor to build a biblical case for a contemporary circumstance by operating from the experience of his or her listeners. The preacher takes a biblical person or concept and uses it metaphorically to symbolize a struggle or joy in the lives of the present black Christians.[184]

As nearly all of the Wame sermon citations demonstrate, he is certainly an expert at conveying biblical truth in a way that captivates the imagination of his audience. He accomplishes this through the use of vivid imagery that is not only familiar in terms of their life setting and personal experiences, but is also quite novel or innovative as well – that is, stated in a picturesque form of expression that they probably have not heard before. Just as in the case of a skilled oral raconteur, Evangelist Wame has the linguistic ability to "employ words to paint mental pictures that appeal to our feeling and understanding."[185]

The following then are a few examples of idiomatic figuration, coupled with thematic (social/moral/spiritual) relevance, from the Wame corpus; they come from his sermon on unity (*umodzi*) in the Church, based on John 13:34-35 and 17:17-21 (SW13). Observe how repeated reference and allusion to the traditional (but still intensely current) practice of trapping witches comes to assume the status of a verbal symbol in the discourse, that is, "a concrete or familiar object (or action!) which is used in reference to, or as an explanation of, an abstract idea or a less familiar object or event"[186] – in this case, the unfortunately all too common manifestation of vicious, destructive rivalry and self-righteous pride in the Christian congregation.

> If you do not know one another [with your] hearts (*simudziwana mitima*), it's so easy to be grabbing (i.e., accusing) each other [as being] practitioners of witchcraft (*kugwirana maufiti*). By simply looking at [what you consider to be] the ugly face (*kungoona nkhopeyo kukuipira*) of your neighbour, you are displeased and say, "Hey, this fellow's a witch (*mfiti*)!" Right now as I am speaking here in this congregation, there's talk about grabbing witches, and pagan folk (*akunja*, 'outsiders') will say, "So these [are] the people of God,

---

[184] Blount, *Cultural Interpretation*, p. 81.
[185] Okpewho, *African Oral Literature*, p. 98.
[186] *Ibid.*, p. 101.

eh? Grabbing witches [is going on] in the congregation of God!" Say, is there any "victorious life" (*moyo wachigonjetso*, loan calque) here? How can those pagans know that we are the people of God?

To consider your fellow [guilty of what] you never saw – he's none other but the pastor! He's none other but a church elder! She's none other but a leader of the women's fellowship! Perhaps [his/her] ugly face displeases you (*kukuipirani nkhope*), could it be that, eh? Does an ugly face mean that this fellow must be a witch? Your companion [is] failing (i.e., you don't even give him a chance) to say, "No, as for me [witchcraft] 'medicine' (*mankhwala*) I have no knowledge of, and I was simply born (i.e., ever since I was born), even roots (*mizu*, i.e., protective/promotive charms) I have no knowledge of." [You reply], "Aah! don't deny it! You are a witch and that's it!" Grabbing witches – [if that sort of thing goes on] will the pagans really be able to realize that we are one? My children, the Lord Jesus says, "Love one another as I have loved you."

Let us [show] love [to] one another right here in this congregation by reproving one another of evil, yeees! [This is] love of great price, and [even] the disciples [of Christ], especially Peter, were not slow (i.e., litotes) to sin again and again – until [it reached a point where Christ had to] push him away saying, "Go away, Satan!" Later he (Peter) cooperates with him (Christ). [But then again Christ has to say], "Go away, Satan!" Later he (Peter) cooperates with him (Christ). My brothers, let us love one another by reproving one another of evil things – not by saying, "Let's see him, let's see him cut right off from this church! When hearing about something [bad that he's doing], let's just keep perfectly quiet (*duu!*, i.e., so he gets caught at it)!" Heeh! Instead of reproving one another – [you say], "[Set] the traps! [Set] the traps! Let's see him [cut off]! Let's see him [cut off]!" Instead of going to your fellow to reprove him [saying], "My friend, the things you are doing here will cause you to fall (*mugwa nazo*) in the congregation!" "My friend, the things you are doing here will cause you to throw away (*mutaya nawo*) your office!" "My friend, the things you are doing here [will cause your] Christianity to be lost!"

(The preceding is illustrated by a long anecdote that concludes as follows.) ... When the church elders see him (a fellow Christian with a weakness for beer) passing by, they rush to tell one another, "He's gone off [to the beer hall]!" "I'll get on ahead of him." [Another] says, "Wait for me!" So when that Christian passes by, the church elders [follow along] hiding behind [him]. Ehee! [They keep on] coming, hiding behind [him] saying, "Let's see him, let's see him (*timuonere*, i.e., to catch him in the act)!" [They keep on] coming, hiding behind [him], until they reach that bar (*bala*) there. [The unsuspecting "victim"] arrives, opens a beer, lifts it up, [and] begins to drink. [Immediately] one church elder comes in here, another comes in over there. Ehee! Now they're all moving quietly, sneaking up (*myamya!*), moving quietly, sneaking up. Then they all come upon him at once (*mwadzidzidzi!*). After that they start off with him – off to the pastor! Heeeh! [They are saying], "We've caught him, this drinker!" So should the pagans say that we love one another with this kind of love? Aah, with this kind of love, my brothers? [It's a] matter that causes sorrow – [this kind of] love that is deficient. We are not [showing] love [to] one another by [privately] reproving one another for evils [done], but instead [we are] setting traps for each other!

It is not very easy to follow the bare written text (translation) of such dynamic and idiomatic discourse, which is in effect a mini-drama in which the preacher himself vocally plays all the parts. Thus the text is often highly condensed, colloquial and communicative on the phonological level alone (e.g., through varied intonational patterns, paralinguistic overlays and pause placement). There is a great deal of information, emotion, and intention conveyed between the lines (and words), so to speak – implicit content that is clear to the listener who is right there on the scene, less evident to someone who must depend on a recording, and at times completely opaque to one who is limited to the words on a printed page (even with some of the implicit information indicated in brackets as above). Nevertheless, the manifold rhetorical force and the conceptual power of this sort of sermonizing surely shines through any media distortion to reveal a message that, with the Spirit's empowering, is able to pierce the hearts (*kulasa mitima*) of many receptors over and above those who constituted the original audience. It is to this very audience that we now direct our special attention to consider a final, generic, interpersonal technique in the Chewa preacher's fully stocked arsenal of rhetorical weapons.

Audience Involvement

This last category represents a composite function in the sense that a great diversity of devices is used in order to effect or realize it within a given sermon. Furthermore, in one way or another all of the techniques already discussed also contribute to the encouragement of receptor group involvement with the preacher as he presents his message (i.e., *pathos* and *ethos* in the service of *logos*). In keeping with a basic inductive approach and the familiar practice of traditional oral narrative performances, this religious communication event is to be (or at least seem to be) a joint, mutually participatory effort to better understand and experience the Scriptures – that is, a chosen pericope or a selection of texts – with reference to what this particular Word of God means for my life both now and, equally important (at least for the Chewa revivalists), in the hereafter. A powerful preachment of salvation *past*, effected during Christ's first coming, which is the basis for all believers' hope of a *future* salvation at his second coming, reinforces an encouraging experience of their *present* salvation and the Lord's comforting presence, no matter how difficult the circumstances they are living in:

> The sermon is experiential encounter, to the extent that the Bible is taking place in the midst of congregational life, and the people are included in the unfolding drama.[187]

Thus, "Black preaching has been shaped by interaction with the listeners"[188], that is, not only by the need to get the audience involved both cognitively and emotively in the actual sermonic event, but also by way of *anticipation* with reference to their particular spiritual needs as a given sermon is being prepared for its public preachment. "... if the people are to experience the sermon in delivery, then the preacher must experience it in preparation."[189] Several additional, more specific rhetorical methods for encouraging such enlivening audience participation are outlined below.[190] One of the most important ways of stimulating an active engagement on the part of listeners – a little homiletical dialogue as it were[191] – is by the use of

---

[187] Thomas, *They Like to Never Quit Praisin' God*, p. 46.
[188] Mitchell, *Black Preaching*, p. 100.
[189] Thomas, *They Like to Never Quit Praisin' God*, p. 63. The author elaborates upon this notion as follows: "Exegesis and rational inquiry are absolutely essential to quality preaching, but when exegesis is opened to include the emotive and intuitive, the preacher is able to generate images that shape and order experience. The effect of this is that the preacher comes off not as a distant scholar but as an eyewitness who has *experienced* the text-event and invites others to experience the same" (*ibid.*; original italics).
[190] The importance of this crucial factor in the process of preaching was noted already by Augustine: "[He] performed a radical restructuring of ancient rhetorical theory by changing the way in which the speaker and audience interrelate: instead of the ancient model of orator dominating the audience by his rhetoric, Augustine instituted a participatory model in which the teacher is a member of the audience in a dialogue" (Oberhelman, *Rhetoric and Homiletics*, p. 117) – an interaction that must of course be based upon and guided by the Scriptures. This is a relationship that all preachers – no matter what the language or culture – need to keep in mind.
[191] Similarly in the case of that ancient Christian model of effective preaching, John Chrysostom: "The

questions, both real and rhetorical. *Real*, audience directed questions (as opposed to those that are part of the biblical or another text, e.g., "How many are the days of your years?" – Gen 47:8, SW14) are usually not meant to be answered by them aloud at their point of occurrence in the sermon. Instead, each and every listener is expected to give an honest reply in the privacy of his/her own heart, e.g., "Mother (honorific form), how many are the days of the years of your life? Now before you die, how many days are left – how many years are left?" (SW14 – all the examples of questions in this section are taken from this single sermon). *Rhetorical* questions are not normally intended to elicit any information, as in the case of a real query. Rather, they usually have the purpose of emphasizing some type of assertion or response that should be obvious in the cotext of discourse in which it occurs. This device gives the audience an opportunity as it were to express this knowledge for themselves, often vocally, instead of having the speaker tell them directly. Frequently there is some additional attitude, implication, or emotion that is also conveyed, or connotated, by the interrogative form, e.g., "Now is there anyone here who at any time has kneeled down and prayed a prayer like this? Is there anyone?" ... "My brothers, what is it that fools us into [thinking that] we need not number the days of our life?" (with reference to Ps 39:4, the point of this obvious appeal to *pathos* being that they should definitely be engaged in such spiritual reckoning).

Another type of rhetorical question serves to highlight some particular compositional feature of the larger text, for instance, the introduction of a new topic or some aspect of the main theme, e.g., "What kind of people ought we to be as we enter upon this new year?" (at the onset of SW14); "How old did those ancestors of yours (Jacob's) get to be?" (a hypothetical direct question that begins a discussion of the comparatively longer ages of Isaac and Abraham). Some rhetorical queries function to foreground certain information in a negative way, that is, by drawing the listeners' attention to certain fact(s) that they probably do not know (nor could they be expected to), but which the preacher will now proceed to reveal for them, e.g., "But now these things that I [God] am telling him [Abraham] – [about] future generations coming [from him] – how is he going to know about them?"

---

sermon is often conceived of as a kind of dialogue with the hearers; the preacher is in touch with them, is quick to feel their mood and to respond to it. It is this that gives life to his preaching..." (S. Neill, *Chrysostom and his Message*, London (USPG): Lutterworth Press, 1962, p. 28).

(another hypothetical Q); "Now what year was Jacob born in?" (1836 BC according to Wame!). Questions of this nature may be extended and utilized to build a little *puzzle* or enigma into a sermon, one that draws the audience into its theme or hortatory purpose as the answer is gradually disclosed by the preacher on the basis of some Scripture passage(s), for example, how many types of "Pharisees" there are depicted in the gospels (SW44), or how many years you have left in this life (SW14):[192]

> Let us ask another question: How many are the days of the years of your life *(following the form of the old literal Chewa Bible)*? Jacob answers, "I am 130 years." "Well, [how many years] before you die?" He answers, "Seventeen years remain."[193] How did he know this? Today this very question we want to answer right here today. This question is among us today: Mother, this question is for you today. Father, this question is for you today. How old are you? What are you going to tell me? (There follows more questions of this kind for various listening groups.) ... I believe that you have all answered me: Some say, "I am 50 years old." Others say, "I am 30 years," others "19," others, "20," others, "Aah, 15." Am I lying? [No,] you've already answered me. Thanks a lot! But the question continues, "Well, before you die, how many years remain?" Who can answer me [that one]?

After this stimulating interrogative sequence, which leaves the final, climactic query with his hearers, Evangelist Wame proceeds to give a biblical reply to such questions (and doubts) about the future according to the exhortations of Psalms 39:4 and 90:12. Believers must seek to use wisely whatever time they have left, be it long or short, in the service of the Lord who will thereby remove all worries concerning what lies ahead.

An interactive rhetorical technique which is so common that at times it is either not fully appreciated or partially overdone is the *call-and-response*.

---

[192] This interrogative strategy seems to be similar in certain respects to one employed by Martin Luther: "Through mystification (raising genuinely perplexing questions, putting off the answers, heightening the perplexity), then through clarification (providing the satisfactory answer that is consistent with the argument, that resolves the dilemmas and coincides with scripture), Luther enacts an argument that builds trust between speaker and audience, trust which is predicated upon a theme of truth mined almost exclusively from God's written Word" (Leroux, "Perceiving Rhetorical Style", p. 29, original italics).

[193] Wame deduces this figure for his hypothetical query and reply from Gen 47: 9 and 28, coupled with the ages of Abraham and Isaac that he has already calculated in this sermon, working along in dialogue with the congregation.

When engaged in this mode of public dialogic style, either the preacher or his congregation (usually the former) will interject a word of encouragement or praise, e.g., *"Aleluya!"* and the other party will make an appropriate vocal response, e.g., *"Ameni!"* (this common correlative pair has of course been copied from certain Western evangelistic styles). Such an exchange, which may be repeated one or more times and accompanied by certain conventionalized gestures (e.g., standing up or waving hands), frequently occurs at some climactic point in the discourse where the preacher desires some positive *feedback* or wants to make sure that his listeners are following closely along and emotively engaged, or they, on the other hand, wish to assure him by way of anticipation that they are indeed with him.[194]

A less common variant is occasionally interjected by certain more expressive members of the congregation in reply to some important or forceful point that the preacher has just made, e.g., *zoona!* ('truly'), *ndithudi!* ('yes indeed'), or *basopo!* ('watch out'). This second type of exclamatory response, which tends to be spontaneous though it may also be uttered by way of anticipation, is usually inserted into the brief silence that is present when the preacher pauses, either to catch his breath, to mark the transition to a new topic, or to allow what he has just said to sink in. Mitchell notes this important African influence also in Black American preaching style:

> Black preaching is inherently dependent on call and response. African music and oral communication are characterized by considerable audience participation. The audience is deeply involved in the tale ... Even today, congregations of the Black masses feel cheated if no place for their response is provided. Black music is full of this antiphonal element as well.[195]

---

[194] Raboteau describes the purpose and setting of the call and response technique as follows: "The style of the folk sermon ... was built on a formulaic structure based on phrases, verses, and whole passages that the preacher knew by heart. Characterized by repetition, parallelisms, dramatic use of voice and gesture, and a whole range of oratorical devices, the sermon began with normal conversational prose, then built to a rhythmic cadence, regularly marked by exclamations of the congregation, and climaxed in a tonal chant accompanied by shouting, singing, and ecstatic behavior ... The dynamic pattern of call and response between preacher and people was vital to the progression of the sermon, and unless the spirit roused the congregation to move and shout, the sermon was essentially unsuccessful" (A. Raboteau, *Slave Religion: The "Invisible Institution" in the Antebellum South*, New York: Oxford University Press, 1978, pp. 236f). The Chewa revival sermons normally do not manifest such a climactic emotional display, but many of these same dramatic, audience-involving participatory features are present in abundance, certainly in the presentations of Evangelist Wame.

[195] Mitchell, *Black Preaching*, p. 31. The typical call-and-response exchange in the Chewa corpus is not

Similarly, while expressions such as "hallelujah!" or "amen!" may be Western (ultimately Hebrew!) in origin, the fact of their occurrence and interactive function in public speech is not. For example, the periodic, stereotyped audience response during the opening portion of certain types of traditional Chewa oral narrative (*nthano*), *tili tonse!* ('we are all [listening] together') is a most natural discourse feature.[196]

Another pair of effective audience involving measures, namely, *hymns* and prayers, may seem at first to be distinct types of discourse, but they are often so closely integrated into a given sermon that they can be considered to be part of it. Consider, for example, the following reference to a song that was sung earlier by a choir before the sermon (SW18):

> Those singers who are singing for us in the choir just sang a certain hymn called, "The salvation of my life can be removed by Satan." Now in those words we read from the book of Luke [6:46-49], the Lord Jesus was speaking with people like us. He was speaking with a congregation of people like us who follow Jesus, who daily see his wonderful works, who daily see his power. But Jesus turned around and asked them, "Why do you call me 'Lord, Lord' and do not do what I tell you?"

These songs, choruses, and hymns (at times accompanied by various musical instruments), when incorporated within a sermon, give members of the audience a chance to empathize with the preacher (*ethos*) and also to express their own emotions (*pathos*) during a sermon's delivery. Often Evangelist Wame will cite the number of the hymn he is about to sing, as it is found in the standard CCAP hymnal, to make sure that the congregation can participate. Such convenient hymns may also serve as a dramatic pause in the communication event as well as a direct or indirect means of introducing them to some important aspect of the sermon and its main theme or application. As in the case of the typical Black American sermon:

---

nearly as developed as it apparently is in the African-American tradition of such "participatory" sermonizing: "Black dialogue between congregation and preacher consists of the well-known cries 'Amen!' 'Praise the Lord!' 'Well!' 'Have Mercy!' 'Sho 'nough!' and a hundred other spontaneous audible responses. It also includes facial expressions, swaying bodies, nodding heads, raised hands, foot patting, shouting, tears, and (in recent years) hand clapping" (*ibid.*, p. 101). A number of the latter set of nonverbal reactions would also be found in the context of a Chewa sermon setting, especially one of the revivalist (*chitsitsimutso*) variety or camp meeting ([*msonkhano*] *wamisasa*) type.

[196] Cf. Chimombo, *Malawian Oral Literature*, p. 88.

> The great music of the church [whether a "classical" (Western-based) hymn, a traditional (African-based) spiritual, or a contemporary gospel chorus] naturally lends itself to the joyful reinforcement of the truth that has already been taught in the sermon. ... Bringing known music into the context of the present sermon celebration triggers past positive emotive experiences that aid the present celebration.[197]

Antiphonally sung songs were an integral part of many traditional folktales (*nthano*). At times this participation becomes extremely direct, as in the case of a hymn that is used as part of the very sermon text. In SW8, for example, a well-known chorus of rejoicing (*Ndadabwa ine!* 'I am amazed, I am!'), purportedly led by the recently resurrected youth from Nain (i.e., with Wame himself singing the lead), highlights his happy return into the village along with his mother and the company of former mourners (cf. Lk 7:11-17).

As for his *prayers*, Wame always begins his sermons with a petition or two plus a word of thanksgiving and praise that is relatively long and more general in nature, while he less frequently closes his delivery with a pointed appeal that is much shorter in length. In either case, he often makes reference to certain important issues that, depending on the placement, will be or have been brought up in the sermon. The following, for example, is the conclusion to sermon SW23:

> ... Let's take Jesus to be our friend. Man has no good [in this life]; the only good he has is Jesus. But if you delay, wasting time, doing the things that please some person – [what will happen]? The answer: He [that person] will just turn against you. The only good you have is Jesus. Doing that [becoming his friend] is what he came for. He wants to be your friend. Tell him what's on your heart (lit. 'neck') from today on. Aaaany trouble at all, if it comes today, kneel down [and pray], just like [speaking] to your close friend, not some "emperor" (*empala*)! He calls for your prayers, easily and softly. Then you will rejoice and be glad. Jeeesus wants to be your friend! How can you refuse? Let this question remain on your heart.
>
> "Lord, bless for us these words that we might receive Jesus as our Saviour. If we have not yet made Jesus our friend, let us make him our friend today. May we receive him, may he enter our hearts. He is

---

[197] Thomas, *They Like to Never Quit Praisin' God*, p. 100.

the only one who can make us happy in this life. May we not delay! Amen."

Some prayers are so elaborate that they almost become sermons in miniature, or prayed sermonettes. Evangelist Wame begins number SW29, for example (based on Prov 28:13, Acts 1:15-18, and 1Tim 5:24), with an extended prayer that pleads with sinners to repent, confess their sins, and accept the seeking love of Jesus. This petition opens with a powerful analogy which likens the love of Christ to the eager desire of a hunter looking for game. The point is then made by contrast. A hunter's search is intended to take a life, but Christ's search is aimed at saving life. The prayer continues with a little parable. A herdsman regularly puts his flock of goats in a protective corral at night. But some of the unruly ones keep breaking the gate open in order to spend their time at mischief outside. Finally, one night after this has happened, the herdsman returns to fasten the gate again. This time the goats are attacked by hyenas and rush to their corral for safety, only to find the gate securely fastened. Thus many so called Christians behave as unstable members of their churches. The only difference is that Jesus, the Good Shepherd, never locks the gate; the wild and wayward "goats" can always return to him for safety.

Wame's prayer concludes with an anecdote that personifies Christ's love and compares it to a person who sees someone walking along a path that leads to some grave danger. Love warns that person of the terrible things that lie ahead and tries everything possible – pointing, beckoning, calling – to get him to turn around and come back. But all too often Love's warning is ignored and even laughed at. In a final petition, Wame prays that the love of Christ might prevail and lead the lives of all those who are present. Such appeals indirectly (i.e., this is not, I think, a mere rhetorical device) serve to support the *ethos* of the preacher, who cares so much for his flock to pray so fervently on their behalf to the Lord – following his preeminent example in this regard.

Evangelist Wame also utilizes a public variation of the 'Nathan technique' to capture his audience (at least the guilty among those present) in their own self-satisfaction or sufficiency. This often takes the form of a theme-with-variation iterative sequence that builds to a humorous climax. Before his audience gets laughing too long or hard, however, Wame implicates them in the underlying accusation or admonition. Thus he asks them something like, "Why are *you* laughing now? Are you too not doing the same sort of thing?" This is followed by a characteristic call for personal repentance and a genuine amendment of one's hypocrisy and covertly sinful living.

To give a somewhat different example of this same ancient, audience incriminating rhetorical device (sermon SW7 on living as soldiers for Christ, Eph 6:10-17), Wame tells a little story about a boy who is sitting out in the bush on a small hill and sees a church elder passing by along the path. A little farther up this same path the lad spots a lion lying in wait. Without a word he rushes off to save himself while the elder continues walking to his death at the jaws of the lion. Later, at the man's funeral, the boy reveals that he had seen both the elder and the lion that day. When asked why he did not shout or say anything to warn the man, the boy simply replies, "I was too shy/ashamed!" (*Ndimachita manyazi!* i.e., out of respect for his honourable fellow Christian). The congregation immediately bursts out laughing at such foolishness, but Wame brings them up short by saying, "But is not this the very same thing that you do? Don't laugh now – it's you too [who are guilty]! That large lion is Satan. He wants to cause your companion to fall. But you just say, 'I'm too shy [to warn him].'"

In one memorable instance (SW1, based on 1Pet 1:24), Evangelist Wame applies the reverse of this incriminating Nathan technique. He implicates – or in this case, indirectly (ironically) accuses – himself in/of the crime of insulting his audience for bringing them the honest Word of God!

> These words [are] painful, my brothers, these words troubled me: How can I preach them? If these words were spoken by a human being, we would say [it's] an insult! But since it's God [who is speaking], for that reason they trouble my heart. The words say: "All people are like grass, and their glory like the flower of grass. Now the grass withers, and the flower falls off, but the Word of God remains -forever." These painful words, if a human being were to speak them, we'd say, "It's an insult!" Because there are elders present, respected due to their honour...now if somebody who comes from nowhere marches in (*tumba-tumba-tumba!*) and says, "You are all grass!" Are those nice words? "Why that's an insolent fellow!" [we'd say]. But the thing that troubles me is nothing else but [the fact that] the one who has spoken these words is God who made you to be grass! Indeed, I was afraid [that God would tell me], "Hey you, Wame, go tell those fellows that they are grass!" I said, "Eeeh!

Should I go tell them?" "Yes," he says, "go speak out!" Now I was troubled in my heart, "How can I go say [that]?" But because the one who began to speak [these words] is the Owner (*eni-ake*) who made you and says, "You are grass!" So [poor] me, what could I do? God has sent me, I can't do anything about it. God has sent me to tell you: He says, "You are grass!" No matter if it pains you – go ahead and take me to court, eeh! The one who began to speak [these words] is the Owner. I can't do anything about it – hallelujah! hallelujah! Amen! Amen!

Could a speaker ever get more emotively involved with his audience than that? He even actively plays their part in his dramatized little dialogue to press the present case home to their hearts.

Such apparent deflections or detours from the main line of an argument or exhortation are both natural and functional in the inductively shaped sermon. They are also a familiar device in the telling of traditional tales (*nthano*) and technically termed "*digressions*":[198]

> This is a device whereby the oral performer departs for a moment from the main line of the subject of a story or song either to address an object (or person) at the scene of performance or to comment on an issue which may be closely or remotely connected with the main subject. .... Internal digressions are generally useful for expatiating on a detail that the performer feels may not be immediately clear to the audience, or for throwing light on aspects of morality or social history.

At times such an aside may be inserted into the discourse to perform a phatic purpose, to retain, reestablish, or reinforce direct personal contact with the listening audience. Evangelist Wame is a master at this technique, which he utilizes so frequently and subtly that it is often difficult to tell that he is actually digressing from his main point at all. In the following elaboration on the rate of death in the world, his words serve to emphasize in the most concrete of numerical terms the inevitability of human mortality – hence the urgent need for Christians to "Get ready!" (SW30):

> But today I want to warn you – it's no time to be playing at your Christianity, no indeed. It's no time to be moving around practising

---

[198] Okpewho, *African Oral Literature*, pp. 96f; cf. Wendland, "Stylistic Form and Communicative Function", ch. 7.

witchcraft or smoking Indian hemp, not at all. These things are no good! Just listen to me: Someone has revealed the number of people who are dying day after day. He says "per second" (spoken in English) – "per second" now, the people who enter the grave in the whole wide world he says are 840 people *diii!* (thud!) – entering the grave – "every second" 840 people [become] grave-enterers. Now if you say "each and every minute" [that is] "840 times 60," we find out that there's "50,400 per minute" – people entering the grave every day – "50,400 per minute." Alright, let's figure it out "per hour" [that is] "times 60," and we find "3,024,000 per hour" – people who are entering the grave "every hour" – "every hour 3,024,000 per hour." Now let's figure it out "per day" [that is] "times 24" and we find 72,576,000 entering the grave. Yesterday 72,576,000 went. Also today 72,576,000 went. Tomorrow also on their way are 72,000,000. The day after that another journey [of the same number]. That's the number of those who are dying [while] we are still alive – a huge number are those who are dying. But you remain yet...

Finally, a preacher may also encourage his congregation to become engaged in a practical way with his sermon by assigning them, as it were, some *follow up activity* to carry out on the basis of what they have just heard. For example, in advising his listeners how to "hold on to their holiness" (*kusunga chiyero*) as Christians, Evangelist Wame tells them first of all to study their Bibles (SW19). A good way to get started in this essential spiritual exercise, he says, is to follow this simple plan: a) read the book of John in its entirety, verse by verse; b) then carry on with the New Testament, beginning with Matthew right through to Revelation; c) finally, do the same with the Old Testament, from Genesis to Malachi. The Bible is like a looking glass (*galasi*) for believers to help them see what needs to be put right in order to live a life of holiness (*moyo wachiyero*) before God. In a similar vein at the close of another sermon (SW11), Wame urges his congregation to go back home and reflect upon their reception of his (God's) words. There are five attitudes or activities, he says, which Satan uses to try and bring the message preached to nought and the listener to gahena, that is: poor attention, a lack of enthusiasm or commitment, listening with impudence ["I know all that!"], altering the sense and import of what was said, or blind unbelief. The only way to receive a blessing from the Word is to "hear and go do it!"

The Rhetoric of Inductive Discourse Organization

As has already been suggested (ch.2),[199] the typical Chewa revival sermon is organized quite differently from those that are composed according to a traditional Western homiletical model. The latter approach may be described in general terms as follows:

> ... a sermon's form is crafted on the basis of the assumption that the task of a sermon is to present to the hearers a clear elaboration of some important idea or thesis. ... The central idea of the sermon is divided into its essential parts, and these would become the major divisions, or points, of the sermon. These points are then further divided into subpoints and arranged according to some principle of internal logic (for example, moving from the lesser to the greater) to create the overall sermon design.[200]

A sermon organized according to such a *deductive* method (using this term in its wider, popular sense) thus begins with a central thesis, or theme, which is progressively and systematically broken down into supportive and/or contrastive arguments which are all explained, exemplified, and (hopefully) applied in turn to the hearer's situation. An *inductive* discourse, on the other hand, utilizes various examples, descriptions, types, precedents, proofs, citations, and case studies, real or fictitious, to illustrate and to progressively focus in on a particular thesis, claim, or conclusion, which may – but is less likely to – have one or more related subpoints.[201] In short, deduction relies upon a logical, step for step exposition to persuasively

---

[199] In this section I reiterate some of the key points that were considered earlier (ch 2) on the subject of inductive discourse due to the importance of this notion. A correct understanding of this traditionally-familiar, conceptual and compositional method is crucial for gaining an adequate grasp of the genius and practice of popular sermonizing in Chichewa. It is also important to be familiar with the essentials of this technique – and its principal counterpart, deduction – in order to be in a better position to assess its relevance and to evaluate its effectiveness (the potentials as well as the pitfalls) with respect to both the teaching of homiletics and also the implementation of Bible-based preaching in contemporary Africa (or anywhere else for that matter).

[200] Willimon and Lischer (eds.), *Concise Encyclopedia of Preaching*, p. 146.

[201] Koch and Felber argue that there are three principal types of inductive argument (A. Koch and S. B. Felber, *What Did You Say? A Guide to the Communication Skills* (Third Edition), Englewood Cliffs, NJ: Prentice-Hall, 1985, pp. 85-87). In the case of *generalization*, there are several tests for reliability, e.g., the relative quantity, typicality, and validity of the examples or evidence that is used. *Cause-effect* reasoning, that is, from the known to the unknown, on the other hand, becomes more persuasive if a control group or valid alternative instance is utilized as part of the proof. In the case of *analogical* reasoning, the various points of similarity must clearly outweigh the points of difference, more so with respect to quality than quantity.

argue for a given thesis or theme, whereas induction depends on analogous life related experience and familiar images to lead an audience into arriving at a certain common sense conclusion. Some theorists hold that "in a truly inductive sermon the listeners complete the thought, movement, and decision making within the sermon itself",[202] and that this active and essential completive role on the part of the audience is what differentiates induction from deduction. However, such a position is perhaps overstated and difficult to prove in any case one way or the other.

At any rate, we may roughly (in an over-simplified manner) characterize the organization of the *deductive* text as one that progresses from a general point (or points) to several specific ones, or from a thesis to its proof(s), by means of logical reasoning or some form of a topically subdivided, hierarchically arranged composition. The *inductive* text, on the other hand, is one that moves forward by means of topical recursion – from a number of specific instances to a general principle, from various pieces of evidence to the obvious conclusion – on the basis of a diverse but broadly interrelated set of illustrations. From this perspective then, we might classify the typical Chewa revivalist sermon as being primarily inductive in nature. The qualification *primarily* is necessary because most of these texts do start out, as in deduction, with some clearly set forth principal theme (a complete predication) or topic (simply a subject element). It is in how that central notion is further textually developed where the difference essentially lies, that is, relationally and synthetically (paradigmatically) in induction rather than by means of a deductive progression or analytical outline (i.e., syntagmatically). It is also characteristic of larger Chewa discourse construction to recycle itself. In other words, once the various interrelated examples have led listeners to a certain general truth or central theme, the process starts all over again with more illustrations leading to the same basic point and so on, any number of times – hence, *reiterated relational-induction*.

In either case, but especially with a discourse that is orally proclaimed, it is important to view the compositional organization of what is commonly judged to be a well-formed text both *organically* and *holistically*.[203] In other

---

[202] Willimon and Lischer (eds.), *Concise Encyclopedia of Preaching*, p. 149.
[203] While it may be possible to distinguish between text and discourse, with the first stressing the formal-semantic aspect of verbal composition and the latter its functional qualities, I do not maintain such a

words, the formation of a sermon should be regarded not as a static set of propositional facts set forth in some one dimensional syntagmatic arrangement, but rather as a *dynamic* "living" organism.[204] It is thus a body consisting of various members, or parts, having specific structural and functional properties and relations with respect to one another, to the unified piece in its entirety, and to the situational setting that is greater in scope and significance than the sum of its constituent segments. These sermonic components manifest (ideally) an incremental movement whereby one part or section builds upon or interacts with another to create an integrated total development, not only in the area of cognition (*logos*), but also in the associated pragmatic spheres of captivation, emotion and volition as well (*ethos* and *pathos*). The immediate impact and overall effect of the sermon is therefore a product of the listener's experience of the whole in all its diversity, based on the degree of one's sensory and psychological participation in the communication event, not simply the result of a mental grasp of the thematic outline or a list of the main points of the verbal text.

The inductive-relational style of Chewa sermonic composition tends to favour the use of *several* topically linked thematic passages from the Scriptures, often selected from both Testaments, which are referred to by exact citation, modified paraphrase, and/or indirect allusion. This key interlocking relationship, as perceived and fleshed out by the preacher, may be literal or figurative in nature, and the latter is either basically metaphoric (analogical) or metonymic (associative, e.g., cause-effect) in essence. Evangelist Wame in particular is fond of pairing a NT with an OT text from which he will choose a particular graphic image, key idea or common exhortation that can serve as a *thematic-imperative hook* or nucleus for the entire sermon, that is, to connect one biblical passage or secular example, story, allusion or illustration with another as the discourse unfolds. The principal subject is thus considered from different theological, moral, and socio-cultural perspectives as it is continuously recycled in various conceptual and literary forms throughout the text.

This skilful reiteration causes the *pragmatic* (persuasive) aspect of the rhetoric of this form of textual composition to become apparent. One point of view and denotative or connotative facet of the central thought (whether

---

distinction in this discussion.
[204] *Ibid*.

a theological principle or some ethical exhortation) is reflected off of another in a generative movement that gradually broadens and deepens the active listener's perception of the issue and his/her involvement with it in relation to his/her spiritual life.[205] The purely linear (hence somewhat misleading), diachronic arrangement of such a composition may be spatially depicted as shown below in the form of a main medial cylinder (the principal theme) around which revolves an expanding spiral of diverse but interrelated, mutually interacting expository, illustratory, and motivational segments. This hypothetical spiral represents the augmentative, centrally focused progression (i.e., having a distinct centripetal force) that creates the rhetorical effect of the discourse in its entirety by the time the "Amen!" (*ameni*) is reached. The revolving circle is viewed as slowly enlarging in order to suggest a cumulative action due to the fact that subsequent examples, illustrations, images, anecdotes, etc. inevitably build upon, reflect back on and resonate with those that have occurred (been situated) earlier in the discourse.

```
                                         t35
                           t20          t34 t36                    t52
              t9         t19 t21         t33  t37               t51 t53
     t2    t8  t10       t18  t22        t32  t38               t50     t54
  t1 t3    t7   t11      t17  t23        t31  t39               t49
  TC==>==>==>==>==>==>==>==>==>==>==>==>==>==>==>==>TC
     t4 t6      t12  t16        t24   t30           t40        t48
        t5         t13 t15      t25   t29           t41        t47
                     t14        t26 t28             t42        t46
                                 t27                t43 t45
                                                     t44
```

t	topic/type, i.e., Scripture or secular text, example, story, image, illustration, etc.
TC	thematic core around which all the topics revolve and which they reflect

This type of an iterative, relationally organized, inductive composition is well illustrated in a rather long Lenten sermon preached by Evangelist Wame at a teacher training school in Lilongwe, Malawi (SW32). Its the-

---

[205] As Althaus described one of Luther's typical sermons: "The whole is not undisciplined, but it is unregulated, uncalculated, alive, like a free-flowing stream" (cited in Meusner, *Luther the Preacher*, p. 57).

matic core (TC) is stated in the form of a twofold, audience implicative, rhetorical-real question: (a) "Why did Jesus have to die?" and [on the basis of the known answer to that query] (b) "How will you [individually now] respond to the sacrificial death of Jesus?" This central thread is shown as a broken double line to represent its virtual and often implicit reality within the discourse. The spiralling sequence of this text's major topical segments (t), which are related to each other both syntagmatically (=> greater measure of *progression*) and paradigmatically (=> greater degree of *concentration*) in an ever-widening circle of communicative sense and significance, is given in summary form below with reference to the individual items displayed within the preceding figure.[206]

t1 = biblical text: Blessed are the merciful (Mt 5:7)
t2 = biblical text: Jesus was crucified in our place and for sins he did not commit (Lk 23:39-43)
t3 = prayer: teach us to learn from the lesson of love that Christ displayed on the cross
t4 = thematic question (TC-a): Why did Jesus have to die on the cross?
t5 = dramatized biblical narrative retelling: God's creation of Adam and Eve and their fall into sin at the temptation of Satan (Gen 1-3)
t6 = traditional curse: play on the Chewa verb stem *-ona* "see" [death] (within [wi] segment t5)
t7 = extended play on words: based on the phrase "opening/closing of the eyes" (wi t5)
t8 = theological exposition: the result of Adam and Eve's sin is physical and spiritual death for all people
t9 = popular belief – a possible exception: little children are like angels in that they are [supposed to be] sinless
t10 = theological exposition: children are born sinners, cf. Ps 51:5, Rom 3:23

---

[206] The periodic reiteration of certain key topics, motifs, illustrations, exhortations, etc. in a typical inductive sermon would approximate the use of "core cliches" (or images) in African oral narrative performances as described by Scheub (H. Scheub, "The Technique of the Expansible Image in Xhosa *Ntsomi*-Performances", in B. Lindfors (ed.), *Forms of Folklore in Africa*, Austin: University of Texas Press, 1977). Thus one such repeated image set forms a patterned sequence that builds in familiarity, intensity and thematic-pragmatic implication as the discourse proceeds. A major strand of this nature is usually combined with others to form a bundle of significance that constitutes the sermon's essential message, which is apprehended more by participatory experience and emotive involvement than by logical deduction or cognitive conclusion.

t11 = local example: baby chicks fear a hawk by a strong natural instinct that they are born with (wi t10)
t12 = theological exposition: original sin is like this inherited instinct; thus children too need a Saviour from divine punishment for sin, cf. Exo 20:5
t13 = word study: the difference between sinfulness (*u-chimo*) and sin[s] (*ma-chimo*) (wi t12)
t14 = everyday image: a tree (sinfulness) and its branches (sins) plus a listing of illustrative instances (wi t13)
t15 = image extended: a stump and a new shoot which later matures and bears bad fruit (sins) because the stump itself was bad plus another listing of examples (wi t14)
t16 = popular sayings: self-righteous human objections to being considered a sinner in the eyes of God
t17 = theological exposition: overt sins are simply evidence of a sinful root (wi t13); the sin of Adam and Eve has indelibly affected all people, all of whom therefore need a Saviour from sin(fulness)
t18 = theological exposition: no sinful human being can pay for or satisfy his/her damning debt of sin
t19 = popular sayings: further objections to being considered a condemned sinner (cf. t16)
t20 = more examples: no one can pay the debt/price of sin, either for himself or for others (cf. t18)
t21 = allusion: a Chewa hymn, "No one among our brothers can die for us..."
t22 = everyday example: no person can be allowed to judge his (her) own case in court
t23 = theological exposition: the universal punishment for sin is hell (*gahena*)
t24 = popular sayings: objections to being found guilty of punishment in hell – they are all useless! There is a gradual shift to TC-b: What are *you* going to do now about Christ's death on the cross?
t25 = negative example: Judas is cursed for his betrayal of Christ (cf. Mt 26:23-25), but we are all under a similar curse (*tsoka*) because we daily betray Jesus with our sins!
t26 = theological exposition: concerning the image of God and how man differs from an animal – the goat!

t27 = theological exposition: all people are under the universal curse of sin/punishment (cf. t23)

t28 = everyday example: a dead person cannot be taken to court; therefore we must do something about our debt/sentence of sin during this lifetime, for we might die at any time (cf. t22)

t29 = theological exposition: no one can escape the final judgement and the eternal curse of punishment in gahena

t30 = problem posed: how to deal with this 'curse'? There are three ways, two of which are impossible: to be physically born again or to repent after you have died!

t31 = examples of human failure: includes students in the audience from the teacher training college where the sermon is being preached!

t32 = solution supplied: mankind needs a valid, perfect substitute to bear the curse – Who? – Christ!

t33 = graphic image: Jesus up in heaven watching the condemned souls go to hell

t34 = hypothetical dialogue in heaven: Jesus asks his Father for permission to become the complete sin substitute for all people

t35 = theological exposition: Christ was the only hope/possibility for us (based on 1Pet 1:18, 1Tim 2:5)

t36 = dramatic dialogue resumed: Jesus pleads with the Father, first for sinners (allusion to Isa 53), and later also for himself when he is bearing all sins – "Why have you forsaken me?!"

t37 = popular saying: God is merciful, therefore he won't punish sin (cf. Mt 5:7) – wrong!

t38 = hypothetical soliloquy (cf. t34, 36): Christ's speech reaches its emotive climax – on the tortuous cross

t39 = explanatory image: why God's mercy does not apply to sin – he demands one hundred percent perfection!

t40 = graphic picture (repeated): Christ sees lost souls on the way to hell and has mercy (cf. t33)

t41 = vivid imagery: Christ suffering on his undeserved cross – for me!

t42 = question raised: how do we know Christ really died? The blood from his side is proof positive! (cf. John 19:34-35)

t43 = dramatic biblical narrative retelling: John 19:31-35; allusion also back to Lk 23:39 and the two thieves on the cross – their legs were broken

t44 = leading question: Christ's legs were not broken – why? since he was holy and already dead!
t45 = theological exposition: Christ redeemed all people by his innocent, vicarious death on the cross
t46 = shocking image of application: those who refuse to repent are guilty of "breaking the legs" of Christ!
t47 = question raised: where did that blood from Christ's side come from? Normally blood does not flow from a corpse!
t48 = descriptive explanation: a popular lesson on the anatomy of the human heart; the blood came from a ruptured/broken heart (i.e., he was rejected by the Father for us)!
t49 = thematic question: What will *you* do now when confronted with the sacrificial death of Christ?
t50 = theological exposition: on the nature and effects of Christ's redemption (cf. t44)
t51 = graphic description (resumed): Christ's suffering on our behalf (cf. t41)
t52 = central appeal: repent and believe so that you may become righteous before a just but merciful God!
t53 = vivid warning with current examples: do not treat lightly the "bloody sweat" of the Lord on your behalf!
t54 = thematic question reiterated (TC-b based on TC-a): "we" (each and every listener) need to decide "what to do with Jesus?"!

An integrated spiralized (i.e., an incremental, cognitively instructive and emotively impactful) thematic development such as that described above[207] naturally becomes more complicated where two (rarely more) major themes are presented, usually in an A-B sequence. But since these individual strands are normally linked by means of an obvious contrast or a simple cause-effect relation, the problems of audience comprehension are not too greatly increased, especially for those who have been psychologically caught up in the performance.

---

[207] One may also note a gradually rising intensity of illustration in this sermon. In other words, some of the most vivid and emotively gripping imagery is saved for the close of the presentation, e.g., "breaking the legs" of Christ and the blood from his "broken heart."

It may be useful, in closing, also to distinguish between a *static* development in which the central theme remains more or less the same and a *dynamic* one (as illustrated above) in which the basic thematic notion is continuously expanded somewhat in its semantic complexity or augmented in its ethical implications. In either case, and when competently composed, we see that a notionally organized, inductive sermon is not really as loosely constructed as it may seem on the textual surface, that is, if evaluated only in topical or deductive terms. Instead, it evinces a subtle, less obvious, *interactive-participatory*, denotative-connotative, and structurally interlocking arrangement that is correspondingly geared to stimulate a fuller, more natural manner of cognitive, emotive and volitional engagement on the part of the audience concerned. Such an *affective* discourse is especially *effective* when presented to people who are already familiar experientially with this sort of intimate interaction with their situational environment and also with this particular method of synthetic textual organization on the basis of their ancient oral tradition of verbal art and didactic lore.[208] Three further illustrations of such inductively organized sermonic construction, as abundantly exemplified in the SW corpus, are presented in complete, translated form in the following chapter.

---

[208] This popular Chewa manner of discourse construction may be compared just for the sake of interest with the inventory of pre-Reformation sermons as catalogued by E.C. Kiessling (and cited in Neil Leroux, "Repetition, Progression and Persuasion in Scripture", *Neotestamentica* 29 (1995), p. 6). In addition to the standard *homily*, there was the complex category of scholastic sermons. The latter may be subdivided "into two families – *textual* (based directly on the text, like branches rising immediately from the roots) and *thematic* (based on a theme deduced from the text, like branches rising from a trunk, which in turn communicates with the roots). The former, textual, further consists of two more types – textual *pericope* (dealing with a scripture passage of some length) and textual verse (dealing only with a short verse); the latter, thematic, Kiessling says was far more common than the textual and can be divided into thematic *doctrinal* and thematic-*figurative* (emblematic)." It may be that this last type most closely resembles the popular Chewa sermon. However, instead of an "explication of key words (or themes derived from key words) [which] was a standard practice in the thematic sermon" (ibid., 23), we find in the Chewa corpus a manifold *illustration* of one (or perhaps two to three closely related) key word(s) or theme(s). Forslund reports that "a homily type of discourse, i.e., an informal exposition of a Bible text is generally practiced ... as a rhetorical devise [sic] to achieve amplification, in particular by repetition and the narrating of Bible texts" (Forslund, *The Word of God in Ethiopian Tongues*, p. 120). He later mentions "sermons with repetitive" elements that appear to be more similar to the average Chewa topic-iterative-relational structure outlined above (*ibid.*, p. 241), but does not attempt to analyze their distinctive manner of organization.

4. Induction in Detail: Wame in Action

Introduction to the Annotation

In this chapter, I present three representative sermons of Shadrack Wame as diverse illustrations of his dynamic rhetorical style and inductive manner of discourse organization. These are presented mainly in the form of a fairly literal English translation, with only selected key terms and expressions from the original Chichewa transcription given in parentheses and footnotes for reference. Ideally, the process should have been reversed, but the present, combined method (in favour of English) was chosen in view of space restrictions and in order to make these texts accessible to a wider readership for the purposes of exemplification and evaluation. To my knowledge, these are the first indigenous Chewa sermons of this popular revivalist genre to be made accessible in published form.

An assortment of analytical notes and comments is included as a more detailed record in the case of the first text (SW5). In particular, I have noted outstanding instances of the ten principal stylistic-rhetorical techniques (discussed in the preceding chapter) within the framework of an iterative, inductive-relational discourse development in general, along with any especially apparent appeal to the rhetorical species of logos (**L**, message focus: sense and significance), ethos (**E**, preacher focus: reliability, authority and credibility), or pathos (**P**, audience focus: emotion and volition). These annotative designations are indicated in parentheses within the translation, i.e., in addition to L, E, and P: **(1)** narrative preference, **(2)** personal exemplification, **(3)** traditional allusion, **(4)** dramatic delivery, **(5)** affective appeal, **(6)** evocative description, **(7)** strategic reiteration, **(8)** verbal intensification, **(9)** idiomatic figuration, **(10)** audience involvement. Naturally there is a considerable subjective element involved with such an analysis. It should also be pointed out that the selection is not nearly complete; certainly other items of interest could have been recorded. Therefore, readers are invited to carefully examine the evidence and come to their own conclusions. They are further encouraged to look for other instances of these same rhetorical techniques in the other two sermon examples, which are not analyzed in such detail.

A few observations are in order regarding my Chewa text transcriptions and English translations, especially with regard to the first sermon. The transcription was made as exactly as possible, i.e., including various types of repetition as well as performance errors and audience reactions, to the extent allowed by the relatively poor quality of the cassette recording made from a short wave radio.[209] Parentheses are utilized in the translation to record a number of the noteworthy (interesting, important, unusual, etc.) expressions that are found in the original Chewa text of the sermon. In addition, certain semantically significant implied information not lexically represented in the Chewa text is supplied in [brackets] within the English translation. Some prominent aspects of phonological marking (*pronunciatio*) are indicated as follows: vowel elongation [-vvv-]; loudness/stress [NNN]; a syntactic gap for the purpose of focus/emphasis, or a sudden, deliberate break/pause in speech, including anacoluthon [–]; a false start or hesitation [...]; and quickened tempo [___]. English sentences were determined on the basis of a combination of features in the original Chichewa sound record, for example: significant pause points, overall utterance intonation, emotive emphasis, conjunctive words and transitional expressions.[210] Explanatory

Mr Wame at Chawama RCZ in July 1994

---

[209] Okpewho offers some pertinent comments in this regard: "Oral literature is a living speech act .... In transcription, therefore, it should be accorded all the integrity and respect it enjoys in the familiar context of its expression .... [One must endeavor to] set down whatever the audio tape has captured that may be regarded as related in one way or another to the performance or to have affected the performers likewise. No comment should be considered trivial or treated as an 'aside'; the artist [i.e., preacher] may have heard it and been influenced by it in the development of the performance [i.e., his sermon]" (Okpewho, *African Oral Literature*, p. 348).

[210] While it would have been instructive and more accurate to lay the Chewa text and translation out in the form of line breaks, as in poetic verse, according to utterance units (breath groups), this was not possible due to space restrictions. For a useful discussion of the translation of African oral literature, see Okpewho, *African Oral Literature*, pp. 347-354 (cf. also Wendland, "Stylistic Form and Communicative Function", Appendix B).

footnotes are also supplied to make a brief comment at points where it seemed to be helpful.

"No Shortcuts to Heaven: Building Your House on Christ, the Rock" (SW5)[211]

We will read Matthew 7:21-24, 1 Corinthians 10:1-4, and will finish with Luke 9:23:[212]

Now here today we will begin with the first part: How does [Christian] sooooldiery begin (4)? Of the words [of Scripture] that we just read, we will focus (*tidzaima kwambiri*, lit., 'we will really stand') upon verse 24 – Matthew chapter 7, verse 24: "For this reason, eeeveryone who hears these words of mine and does them I will liken to a wise person who built his house upon bedrock. The rain fell and filled the rivers, and then the wind blew and beat against that house, but it did not fall because it was established upon that bedrock. Now everyone who hears these words of mine and does not do them is like a foolish person who built his house upon sand. Then the rain fell and filled the rivers, and the wind blew against that house, and it fell down. And its fall was very great indeed!"

How does Christianity begin (*chimayamba bwanji*)? Take a soldier [of Christ] – to begin his soldiery, how does he start out?[213] Now this question about soldiery in the army of God, this question may be expressed [like this], "How does Christianity begin?" (7, 10). Here, as we have read in

---

[211] The titles given at the head of each sermon are my own, simply for the purpose of identification.

[212] The three passages cited here are read from the old Protestant Chewa translation of the Bible called *Buku Lopatulika* ('Sacred Book'). An English translation of these is not provided. For an indirect rhetorical consideration of past and present Bible translation in Chichewa, see Wendland (Ernst R. Wendland, *Buku Loyera: An Introduction to the New Chichewa Translation of the Bible*, Blantyre: CLAIM, 1998). This sermon (SW5) was preached in 1992 at a revival meeting in Lusaka, Zambia, which featured the topic, "the army of the Lord," based on Eph 6:12. The present sermon is one of several that Evangelist Wame preached at this gathering, and it has as its general theme, "How does a soldier [of Christ] go about beginning his/her soldiery?" (*Kodi msilikali amayamba bwanji usilikali wake?*). To save space, I have omitted from the following translation Wame's initial remarks which serve to tie this sermon into the revival's overall theme.

[213] The Chewa generic word for person (*munthu*) as well as all personal pronouns are unmarked semantically with regard to gender, and could therefore be translated into English either as masculine and/or feminine, e.g., *iye* ('s/he'). I will simply follow convention and convenience and render these ambiguous – or inclusive – terms as masculine.

verse 24, the Lord Jesus did not mention any [particular] person. He says, "EEEVERY person who hears my words – and DOES them, I will liken him to someone who built his house upon bedrock. Then the rain fell__and the rivers rose__and beat upon that house.__But the house did not fall – because it was established on that foundation of STRONG and SOLID bedrock. But whoever hears these words and does NOT do them, SUUUCH a person I liken to someone who built his house upon saaand. Then the wind blew__the rivers rose__and the FALL – of that house was very great indeeeed" (1, 6, 7). Here he (Jesus) did not mention [anyone by name], he simply said – "a PERSON." He did not mention [a specific] person (7) because perhaps it is possible that – that "person" is right HERE (*ali pompano*) (10, **P**)! That peeerson [about] whom he says, "When he hears the Word of God, he does not do it."__He did not mention [him by name] (7). He merely said, "a person." It is possible [for the person] to be a mother__it is possible to be a father__it is possible to be a friend__it is possible to be a young girl (7, 2). He did NOT make [specific] mention at all (4, 8)!

Here these words reveal that we are [composed of] TWO groups present – those of us who are gathered here (10). There is a group of Christians who have built theeeir houses on bedrock, and there is another group of Christians who have built theeeir houses upon sand. So right here and now there are TWO groups present among us (7, 8, 10). So everyone must carefully look inside of himself [and ask], "AM I someone who built [my] house upon sand?__AM I someone who built [my] house on bedrock?" (2, 7, 10, **P**). EVERYone must carefully examine [himself] – right here we are [composed] of TWO groups! (5, 7, 8, 10).

So here now he says... to build a house upon sand... As we've already said – this group that has built its house upon sand – the house that he is taaaalking about, if we read in 1 Corinthians, chapter 3 – the house he is referring to – [is] we who have built upon the sand [and] others of us who have built upon bedrock – [that is] the house he is referring to.__You can see the THEME (lit., *mutu* 'head') of those words[214] – in 1 Corinthians,

---

[214] In this sentence Wame's "dramatic delivery" (4) gets him a bit ahead of himself, and while his overall meaning is clear, the syntax is rather twisted. Here he also introduces another key thematic passage (1Cor 3:9), one which he might have read at the sermon beginning along with 1Cor 10:1-4, but probably omitted for the sake of time.

chapter 3, verse 9.__[Here] we find these words: "CHRIIISTIANS are... they are the house of God, and Jesus Christ is the foundation of that house (L).ˮ[215] CHRISTIANS are the house of God, and the foundation of THAT HOUSE is Jesus Christ (7, 8). This very house is YOU, it is you! (8, 10). The house he is talking about is you (7).

Now there comes a question – as we have seen that we are [comprised of] TWO groups:__one group which has built a house upon sand__another group which has built a house upon bedrock, now – that very house is you all (7). As far as the CHRISTIAN life [is concerned], the Christian life – some have built upon bedrock, others have built upon sand (7, with parallel ordering). Now the question – why did this group build upon sand (10)?__The answer is – "A SHORTCUUUT (*chiduuule*)!" (4, 5, 8). Because a house built upon sand is not hard [to make] – even a foundation (*faundeshoni*, English loanword) – it's not difficult. You simply scoop it out with your hands, throw down some blocks (*zidina*), and build (6, L). The very same day you are able to finish [it]. A SHORTCUT is not difficult! (4, 8). That is why this group built upon sand – so it would finish FAST! (7, 8). Because to build upon bedrock is diiiifficult (4).__Some of you may have asked for a plot (*poloti*) [of ground for a farm, and], when they pointed to rocks (i.e., to rocky ground, *metonymy*, 9), you ran away (hyperbole, 9, P).__[You said], "I can't break up these rocks! [And] if I call for (hire) a tractor (*thalakitala*) so I might break up these rocks – [it would cost] too much money!" (2, 4).

Bedrock presents PROBLEMS__if you want to build a house upon it, you have to be STRONG.__It's no game, no sir! (*simasewero ayi*, 9). That's why he [Jesus] said, "He who builds his house upon sand is someone who wants a SHORTCUT.__Let [the house] be finished QUICKLY!" It's not difficult – to dig a foundation [there]. You simply scoop [it] out (*mumangofukula*) with your hands and throw in the blocks (hyperbole, 9 and 7) – a shortcut!__Let it be done quickly (*ithe msanga*)! That's why he built [his] house – upon sand. But say now, to build a house upon sand – to build a house upon sand, what does this mean (7, 10)? Just hear me out, you here who have built your houses upon sand (5, 10)!

---

[215] Wame's "quote" is actually a paraphrase of parts of verses 9 and 11, but the gist is certainly there. It is clear from the recording that he is citing the scriptures from memory (or in a contextualized manner) and is not reading any printed text at this point, or anywhere else in the sermon for that matter.

Do not forget the question: How does Christianity begin (7, 10)? Or HOW does [Christian] soldiery begin?__[It begins] with enlistment (*kulembedwa*). To build a house upon sand, that is to – [here's the] ANSWER (8)... [But first] let me ask a question: What do YOU say – to forsake sorcery (*nyanga*, lit., 'horn[s]', metonymy)[216] and to eat the [Lord's] Supper (*mgonero*), which is easier [to do] (2, 3, 6, 10)?[217] [To eat] the Supper, you say? How about forsaking sorcery, what about – (5, 10)? That's real bedrock, right? (Wame laughs.) RIGHT, that's no game (8, P)! (laugh) He (some hypothetical person) wants a shortcut, let [Christianity] be completed quickly (5)! [He says], "Let me first eat my Supper on the sand, OK (*eti*) (8)?" He simply throws his blocks [for building] down plop-plop-plop-plop! (*KHA-KHA KHA-KHAA!*, ideophone, 9). Let it [my house] be done quickly, right (5)? He-he-he-heeee (8)![218]

What do you say – for a person to forsake smoking (*fodya*, lit., 'tobacco', metonymy) or to give offerings [to church], which is more difficult? To forsake smoking, yaah – indeed yes, that's [building] on bedrock (7, 8)![219]__It's no game! He-hee!__What about for you to come here to CHURCH or to forsake adultery (*chigololo*), which is easier? – Why coming to church, of COOOURSE!__Forsaking adultery is [like building] on bedrock (*metaphor*, 9)!__That's no game at all (8)! Eeh! Hee! A shortcut!__Let things be done quickly (4)! Ehe-he-heee-hee! (E) EVERYONE who says he hears the Word of God [but] does not do it, I [Jesus] will liken to a person who has built his house upon sand.__WHAT causes him to build upon sand?__It's a shortcut.__Let things be done quickly (7)! HALLELUYA (4, 5, 8, 10)! (audience: "Amen!") What about for a person

---

[216] A "sorcerer" (*wanyanga* 'person of the horn') frequently makes use of an animal horn (i.e., for strength) in the preparation and application of his (typically a male) magical potions and powders.
[217] After this real-rhetorical question, some in the congregation reply "To eat the Supper" (*kudya mgonero*), which is of course the response that Wame wants for his follow-up query. The latter is replied to with an affirmation, "Yes!" (*Eeeh*).
[218] For a discussion on the difficulty of translating ideophones, see Okpewho, *African Oral Literature*, p. 352. The goal that "the translation should match the effectiveness of the original one to one" (*ibid.*) is commendable, but probably impossible to achieve in practice, especially in the case of such a dynamic stylistic feature and rhetorical technique. Similarly, the rendering of Wame's varied exclamations and laughter is obviously only a rough approximation.
[219] Here Wame continues with one of his characteristic flexible-frame patterns of recursion. The basic framework remains very similar in wording, but with each iteration a new key component is inserted into the focal slot. In this case there is a double, or correlative, slot, i.e., "forsake sorcery – eat the Supper," "forsake smoking – to give offerings," "attend church – forsake adultery," etc. (note the reversal in order for variety with the third example).

to forsake polygamy (*mitala*) or to be a church elder, which is easier? – YAH, to become a church elder!_To forsake polygamy is no game._It's [like building] upon bedrock! Ehe-hee-he-he! What about for a person – to forsake lying or to become a pastor, which is easier? Yes, becoming a pastor [is easier]._To forsake lying is no game._It's [like building] upon bedrock! Yes – a shortcut [is preferable]_Let things be done quickly! Hehee!_[To forsake lying] is no game – it's [like building] upon bedrock (4, 7, 8)! A shortcut [is preferable]._Let things be done quickly!

But HERE now when we read these words [from our Scripture texts], [we see that] THE OWNER (*mwini wake*) UP THERE IN HEAVEN (9) is refusing – saying, "As for these shortcuts, NO WAY(*ayiii*)!" For this reason he says, "EEEVERY person who wants to come after me, ONE (*wani*) – let him deny himself, TWO (*tuu*) – let him take up his cross, THREE (*filii*) – let him follow me!" There are THREEEE rungs [on a ladder] (*makwerero*) for us to arrive in (or: on the way to) heaven (6, L). The first rung – to deny oneseeeelf, rung two – to bear the cross, rung three – to follow JEEESUS – to follow Jesus (4, 7).[220] A SHORTCUT to heaven – there is NONE (*kulibe*). He [God] won't allow it – he won't allow it (8)!

Here on earth there is a path...if there's a LOOONG, winding path, we like [to find] a shortcut. [We say], "Let's cut over here, then we'll get there quickly!_If we wind alooong [following this path] up to the road, iih! we'll be too late!" (2, 4, 6, 8, L). Here in this world we like shortcuts so we can arrive quickly. But [the way] to heaven – he [God] has closed [it] – there's no shortcuts to get there quickly (5). When some people hear that the way to heaven is winding, they say, "Hey, let's take a shortcut here!" [But it's] imPOSSIBLE, impooossible (8)!

Those of us who have built our houses upon sand, when we hear that the way to heaven is winding, now [in looking for] a shortcut._let things be done quickly (10) – we simply cut the way [so] we will arrive quickly (9).

---

[220] Evangelist Wame is no synergist, as his other sermons clearly show. Like the Apostle James, he simply puts the emphasis in his preaching (remember most of these are revival sermons) upon a *living* faith, one that manifests itself in Christ-like works. In the present context, he is speaking about three types of Christian sanctified living, moving from the greatest (most committed) to the least. Similarly, "in Luther's context, 'preaching nothing except Christ' also meant something highly practical and contemporary – clarifying the place, function, and character of good works" (Meusner, *Luther the Preacher*, p. 21).

We just keep on sinning, but we also keep in mind – [that] if you pray (i.e., go to church, *metonymy*, 9) [it will be OK]. [Here's] a shortcut so we can get there [to heaven] QUICKLY (2, 5, **P**)! – Yes indeeeed (*eetu-eh!* 8)! It's better than just staying without [going to church]. [Besides], it isn't true that [all] those who go to church are righteous (2, 5). [So you say to yourself], "If I just stay [outside], without worshipping, then [when I die] they'll perform my funeral as if throwing away a [dead] DOG (6, 9)!_ They won't even sing for me!" (2, 4, 5, 6, 9).

If you wait until you abandon your beer-drinking (*mowa*, lit., 'beer'), iiih! you'll be too late [to fully enjoy yourself]! So we just keep on DRINKING BEEER, but we keep in mind – if you pray [it will be OK] (5, 6, 7).[221] [Here's] a shortcut, [let's] get there quickly! No way! (laugh) NO WAAAY! No way_ no way_ no WAAAY (7, 8, **P**)! If you wait until you get ready, you'll be too laaaate! [You say], "Aaaall those who go to church are other [than righteous] – some are drunkards_ others are polygamists_ others are liars_ others are adulterers – [so I may as well join them] (2)!" For if you wait to get ready and then begin going to church, [it may be too late], and surely they won't sing at your funeral. _They'll simply throw you away like a DOG (2, 5, 6, 9, **P**)! [You think], all your friends who are praying (worshipping) here, their character is just the same (sinful) (6, 7). So you may as well go on getting drunk, but remember [to go] to church_ to give offerings_ remember to – yeees, go to the [Lord's] Supper (5, 7, 9)! You may do whatever you want to, whatever helps (i.e., pleases) you (5, 9). Keep on getting drunk, but remember to pray (5, 6, 7)! [It's] a shortcut, let things be completed quickly! [But] the Owner of heaven has shut [the door] (9). He says, "Here alone there are no SHOOORTCUTS!_ There are no shortcuts! Down THERE [on earth] is where you'll find shortcuts._ Not here – not here! There are no shortcuts to heaven!" (4, 7, 8, **L**).

But FIRST OF ALL, if a person wants to go to heaven, he must deny himself (*adzikanize yekha*). To deny yourself – listen to me carefully now – it means to kneel DOOWN, eh, and confess your sins. When confessing there you tell Jesus, "As for me, lies – NO MORE – or deceiving myself! Fights

---

[221] Wame often displays the rhetorical focusing figure known as *enallage*, that is, a sudden shift in prononminal person, case, number, gender, etc. In this instance he moves unexpectedly from the second to the first person plural pronoun and then to a second person singular form.

– NO MORE (*toto*)! Slander (*miseche*) – NO MORE! Polygamy – NO MORE! Stealing – NO MORE (2, 5, 7)!" [That's] denyyyying yourself (8, **P**)! If you do that, you've set your foot down on the first step DOWN! PHAA! (ideophone), and you are on your way to heaven (6, 8).[222]

Kam'mwamba Anglican Parish: They received Jesus

How does Christianity begin? FIRST you must meet Jesus, and he will EN-LIIIST you as a SOLDIER. It is impossible for a soldier to start his soldiery (*usilikali*) without being enlisted (2, 7, 10). And a person who wants to become a PURE soldier – POWERFUL before God – FIRST he must meet Jesus.__He will enlist him into the soldiery (7, **L**). For this reason the Lord Jesus says, "If a person wants to come after me, FIRST he must deny himself.__Number two – let him bear his cross.__Number three – let him follow me (7)!"

Now after we have denied ourselves by saying, "NO MORE, no more! Tobacco – NO MORE! Lies – NO MORE!" (2, 4, 8, **P**), and Jesus has come and received us, and he has washed us with his blood and has given us the power of the Holy Spirit – when [all] this has happened, we've been enlisted (4)! Next, rung number (*nambala*) TWO – and that is to bear a cross (9). To bear a cross [means] to get ready for troooubles. When you have been converted (*mwatembenuka mtima* 'you have been turned in the heart'), SATAN (*Satana*) will not be happy. You will encounter all sorts of trials. Now you must realize that when you encounter all sorts of trials, you'll have to get ready for some PAAINS (*zowawa*, 'suffering, persecutions', *metonymy*) because of Christ (5, **P**). This is the "cross" that he's talking about.__The Lord Jesus says, "My children, do not be afraid.__Carry your cross. My power is also yours!" (2, 4). [He] means to say, "Do not fear troubles! The power that I used to defeat Satan – I did not

---

[222] "On the way" in the sense of discipleship – as in the key **passage, Luke 9:23-24** – not as a means of self-salvation.

remove when I went to heaven.__I have left it for you [to use]!" (5, 7). So then, the Lord Jesus did NOT take along to heaven (6) the power that he used to defeat Satan, he left it behind (7, L).

So when we receive Jesus, we are clothed with holiness (*tavala chiyero*, metaphor 6, 9)__[and] Satan is not happy.__He wants to cause that holiness to FAAALL (*kugweeetsa*, i.e., to fail, idiom, 4, 9). So get ready to struggle with that Satan until you fell him (5, 10)!__Just as Jesus felled Satan, so also that very same power he has given to us.__We will also fell him [Satan] by means of the POWERFUL authority [we have] from heaven (5)! When you do that in getting READY for troubles, you have carried your cross (L)!

Number three – [is] to follow Jesus. Following Jesus is the part about [Christian] worship. As soon as the iron [bell-bar] rings out *NGWEE-NGWEE! NGWEE-NGWEE!* (ideophone), you find yourselves going *LAAKHAA!* (ideophone) straight ahead down the right road on your way to wooorship (2, 6).__[That is] rung number THREE [on the ladder] – to follow Jesus. The part about worship – is rung number three (7). This rung – you will see only on Sundays when the iron bar rings (2). You will see a large group of people going along to worship.__If you see people going to worship – [that's] rung number three! So you too when you came here, you began [ladder] rung number three – to follow Jesus (10). If you go to all sorts of [Christian] gatherings (e.g., revival meetings), [that is] step number three – to follow Jesus (4, 7, L)!

Now the thing that makes me sad (*chikumvetsa chisoni*) [about] these words – [is that] we've JUMPED OVER (*talumpha*) the first rung (8)! That is, we've stepped down on rung number TWO and number THREE [only] (6). Some even have gone and jumped over number two – they step down only on rung number three *PHAA!* DOWN! (forcefully), to follow Jesus. But this person (you!) did not deny himself.__But this person did not get ready for troubles, now is that sort of soldiery poooossible (valid, 10)? Is it possible [such] soldiery (chiasmus, 8)?__Is it possible such soldiery? (7)__A LAAARGE group [of people] have JUMPED OVER rung number one! So the purpose of these words of mine [is] to plead with you (*ndikukugwirirani mwendo*, 'I am grabbing on to your leg', idiom, 9, E), to plead with you – *PHAA!* – go straight back (5, 6, 10)! You've jumped over [rung] number one – we shouldn't do that, not at all (8, **P**)! Whoever wishes to follow me, rung one – let him deny himself.__Number two – let him carry the cross.__Number three – let him follow me (7)!

Now this big shortcut – to jump up to rung number three... I'm trying to pull you by the jacket (*ndili kukukokani jeketi*) DOWN! so you may begin again with rung one – [or] to pull you by the dress (*deresi*) DOWN! so you might begin the first rung again, that is, to deny yourself (2, 4, 5, 6, 7, 10, **E**)! If that happens, then you are ready to be enlisted as a POWERFUL SOLDIER who will be able to serve the Lord (10). So my question is – will there be some day when you will kneel down (repent, 6) and DENY yourself (10)? May this question remain on your heart (*likhale pamtima panu*), may this question remain on your heart (4, 5, 7)! When that day arrives, when you have kneeled down and denied yourself, [may you confess], "Lord, I have arrived here at your feet. NO MORE slander for me! No more lies for me! No more fights for me! No more temper-tantrums (*kupsa mtima*, 'to be hot in the heart') for me (2, 4, 7, 8, **P**)!" [Tell me], WHO here has at any time kneeled down and denied himself (5, 10)? If you have never kneeled down and denied yourself, you are one of those who have stepped [up] to rung number three – to follow Jesus. Each and every Lord's Day, when that day arrives, that's it! (*basi!*) [you go off] running to church (8)!__[That's] rung number three.

Now the Owner up there in heaven refuses [to allow this], it is not Wame, no indeed (2, **E**)!__There's no shortcut to heaven, not at all! If someone thinks he can get there quickly by cutting out some of the rungs *LEELELE! THAA!* (i.e., swinging up in the air and then landing hard on the ground, ideophones) – right up to the third rung – so he might arrive quickly, it won't work there at all (*si kuno kumeneko ayi!* idiom) (9)! Because here on earth there are many crooked paths (*njira zokhotakhota*) [and shortcuts], he thinks that it's the same in heaven (6). On hearing that [the path to heaven] is crooked, he says, "[Let me take] a shortcut (4)!" Yes, he's off *ZII!* (ideophone) out of sight and on his way, with this in mind, just go and pray (worship) (6, 9)! __[But] there's no shortcut to heaven.__No, the Owner has refused [to allow it] (7, **L**)! There's no shortcut to heaven!

Now the question of all questions (*funso la mafunso onse*) [is this]: Have you ever knelt down and praaayed (i.e., in penitence) (10)? Those who have knelt down and prayed and received Jesus into their hearts, that means their Christianity is built upon bedrock (5, **P**). And his Christianity remains strong, and his Christianity remains fixed (7)! [If someone] curses it (*kuchitukwana*), it doesn't change (personification, 9). During hunger, it doesn't change. At [the time of] a funeral, [it doesn't change] – well, is it not [resting] upon bedrock (2)? Ehee (laugh)! And it does not become offended for just any reason (*wambawamba*, idiom) – well, is it not [resting] upon bedrock? And it does not complain for just any reason – well, is it not [resting] upon bedrock? (7) [If it] meets with troubles, [and] different kinds of trials, during strong pressure (*THINA!* ideophone) it remains quiet (*ZII!* ideophone) – well, is it not [resting] upon bedrock (7, 8, 9, **L**)?

Blessed are those whose HOUSE – whose CHRISTIAN LIFE – from the very BEGINNING is [built upon] Jesus (metaphor, 9). We have already read 1 Corinthians 10, verse 1... especially verse 4, which says – the people of Israel drank water coming out from bedrock. That bedrock, in case you didn't know it, was Jeeesus (9, 10, **L**). That mountain was the Lord Jesus (8, 9)! And a Christianity of that nature does not become eroded easily (*sichigomba wamba*, 6, 8). It does not easily become upset (*sichitengekatengeka*, personification). And even if it gets buffeted – by the wind he (Jesus) spoke of – that WIND (*mphepo*)... it remains unmoved – the WIND of slander, the WIND of lies, the WIND of cursing, the WIND of, you know, troubles of any sort (2, 5, 6, 7, **P**) – the BLOWING and BLOWING (*uwombedwaombedwa*) [of the] wind – it does NOT change at all. Since you built upon a real foundation, a proper one of bedrock, for that reason the house is very strong, it's very strong (10) – it's veeery strong (7, **L**)!

But those who built their house upon sand – who entered into Christianity (became a Christian) saying, "[Then] when I die, they'll sing songs in my honour (*akanandiimbire nyimbo*)!" (4, 5, 6) – [or] who entered into Christianity for OTHER purposes. There are many different reasons for entering into Christianity here. [Some] say, "A funeral without any singing [for you] is without hooonour (4)." [Some] come to Christianity so that they might find an honourable funeral [ceremony]. [Some] enter Christianity because – they want to find a family (*banja*, i.e., a marriage partner, metonymy). [Some] come to Christianity because their husband says, "If you don't become a Christian, [our] marriage is finished!" (4). [Some] come here to

BUY a maaarriage – that's right (8, 9)! [Some] become Christians because their wives say, "If you fail to pray [worship] regularly, it would be better to divorce me.__Let the marriage end!" (2, 4, 5, 7). [They] come to church to buy a MARRIAGE (i.e., find/keep a partner, idiom, 9, L/P)!

There are many reasons for coming here [to church]: Some come here to [see] their dear little girlfriend (*kachibwenzi kao*, 5). There are many reasons for coming here (7). [Some] enter the [women's] fellowship (*chigwirizano*) because [they say], "When we wear those white dresses, we receive special honour!" (4, 6). [Some] come here because of a [church] OFFICE (*mpando* 'chair' metonymy, 9), because of the pastorate, because of the eldership (*ukuluwampingo*), because of the choir (*kwaya*) – there are many different reasons (2, 7).__All those things are [building] upon sand (9, P).__The proof is when you meet with a DIIIFICULTY, your [women's] fellowship does not hesitate to become offended (personification, 9).__ Your eldership does not hesitate to become offended (9).[223] When the winds blow, ehee! hiiii! (8) – [the house] (metonymy, 9) has FAAALLEN! Its foundation was [built] upon SAAAND! [If someone] reviles you, you grumble about [it] – never to return to church at all (5, 8)! [If someone asks], "Say, why don't you come to church these days?" [You reply], "Aah, do you think those words that the secretary (*sekilatari*) of the [women's] fellowship spoke were very nice?__Those very words really offended me!__What am I supposed to do?__Are you not saying that I am the one who has destroyed the fellowship?" (2, 4, 5). Ah! he-heee! Did they build upon bedrock, this lot (9)? Hi-hiii! No indeed, they founded the fellowship upon SAND! The fellowship has fallen (8, P)!

Anyone who has built his house upon sand does NOT delay in taking offense.__"[So-and-so] was singing in the choir, [but] aah! he's become offended and left [the choir]!"__"As for the eldership, [so-and-so] does not come these days, he became offended!"__"This pastorship – I'll just leave the pastorate of this church (7, 9). There are many churches around.__I'll go join another one!" (2, 4).[224] All we can say is, "Eeh (yes), he built his

---

[223] These two idiomatic personifications obviously speak to the women and the men in the audience respectively. Wame is no respecter of persons!
[224] This is a set of hypothetical direct quotations supposedly uttered by an offended member, elder and even the pastor of a certain church. They are distinguished within the actual sermon by means of differing intonational patterns and vocal modulation.

house upon sand! Ehee! that house has FAAALLEN!" Ee-hee! (4, 8).
BLESSED are those who build their house upon BEEEDROOOCK (4, 5)!
Because when the WINDS blow, it won't be shifted even the least little bit
(8, **L**)!

But don't forget now – to build a house upon bedrock is no game (*simasewera*, litotes, 9). It's rocky – right there, you must not forget (7, 9)! Heeey!
It's no game to build upon bedrock – he-hee! It's rocky – – it's rocky! [It
is "hard"] for a person to kneel down, deny himself, invite Jesus to enter
into his heart, [and say] "NO MORE!" to such-and-such activities, that's
for sure (*eeeh!*) (2, 4, 5, **P**). But if you build [like that], eh-eh-eh! that
house is STROOONG (8)! Because [Jesus] says, "The wind blew_ the rivers rose_ and the house... they beat against that house._ But that house did
not fall, nor was it swept away (*sinakokoleka*, 6, **L**)."

But whoever builds upon sand... The WINDS blew – the winds of lies,
(cough) winds of trials, and they beat upon that house – on that Christianity
(personification of Christian, 9). And that Christianity had no peeeace._ It
had no peace._ And the end result was that it became offended and
FEEELL (*kugwa*) (2, 5, 6)! Haven't you ever heard [people talking like
this] – "Have you heard that church elder so-and-so FELL?" Falling means
that he had built upon sand. 'Say, have you heard that this girl who [used
to] sing in the choir fell?"_ "A-aaah! how did she fall?"_ "She built her
house upon sand (2, 4)!"[225] Ehe-hee! "Really, that lady who leads the singing in the [women's] fellowship, they say that she has fallen!"_ "A-ah! say,
what happened?"_ "They say that she stole someone else's husband (2,
4)!" All this falling that we are talking about, is it not that they built their
houses upon sand (7, 10, **P/L**)? The winds beat against it, and its fall was
very great indeed.

The rivers that he (Christ) is speaking about here – they may be [likened to]
those leading to hell (*gahena*)._ They [empty out] down into hell SPLASH!
(*UUU-PHUU!* ideophone) in the lake of fire (5, 6, 9)!_ Yes indeeed (*eeetueeh!* 8)! Now what have you built [your house] upon?_ Don't be so quick

---

[225] Sometimes it is difficult to differentiate the preacher, Wame's voice, from that of the hypothetical personages whom he portrays in his various little anecdotes. He becomes, as it were, a member of the congregation that he is preaching to and speaks as one of them – in a positive or negative (spiritual or carnal) manner as the situation applies.

to laugh so loudly (*usekatu*) (5, 10, **P**)! I have already said that right here now there are two groups (7, 10).__Some have built upon bedrock.__Others have built upon sand. Those who have built upon bedrock have knelt down and denied themselves (2). The ones [who built] on sand have simply leaped *UUULUU-THAA!* (ideophone) right over [the first rungs] – they are [depending] on baptism, on the [Lord's] Supper (2, 4, 5, 6, 9, 10)!__They say, "A shortcut – let things be done quickly!" (4, 7)__[But Jesus] refuses you, saying, "Here that sort of thing is out (*kuno ndiye ayi komweko!* 9)! He who wants to come after me must deny HIMSELF – that very first rung. NO LEEEAPING over it, not at all (4, 5, 10, **L**)!" If we have jumped over it, that means that we don't want to be strong soldiers. TODAY – let us kneel down, let us deny ourselves. Let us build our house upon bedrock – so that we may begin our soldiery right there NOW (10)! [Then] we will be STRONG soldiers, pure and faithful, who will be able to wage war – with SATAN, the enemy – the evil one (5, 9, **P**)!

Let us BEWARE – of the danger of shortcuts:__When we read Proverbs chapter 14, verse 12, we find the words, "There is a path that appears straaaight (right) to a man, but it ends up – as the path of death (*njira ya imfa*)" (9). Proverbs 14:12 – There is a path that appears to be straight to a woman, but it ends up as the path of death (7).[226] Have you ever read these words before (10)? Sometimes when a person is walking along on a journey...you see that, "Aah! this way – it is too long! Let's cut across here." (2, 4, 6).[227] When you spot a big road, beautiful and WIDE, you say, "That's the right way to go!" (2, 4, 6). But before you finish walking perhaps – one kilometre, you find out that you have arrived at a graveyard (*manda*, 5)!__You couldn't have seen (i.e., anticipated) anything like that (10)! "THIS BIG ROAD looked good but it ends up in a graveyard!" (4, 7). A path may look nice and straight, but its ending is a path to death (**P/L**)! Now it always happens that shortcuts – they give you big problems (hyperbole). Some of you can testify to [the truth of] this. SHORTCUTS – [when taking them] (i.e., especially at night) some get their clothes stolen

---

[226] Wame here repeats Proverbs 14:12 but substitutes the word "woman" (*mkazi*) for "man/male" (*mwamuna*) in the passage without explanation. He either expects his listeners to be following along in their Bibles or, more likely, to recognize this important rhetorical technique of contextualized paraphrasing.

[227] Notice the prominent pronominal *enallage* again in this utterance: "**a person**...you (sg)...we."

[by thieves], others get their suitcase stolen, others their money stolen. On the paths we're talking about here some are even killed (2, 5, 6)! You have seen [how] these shortcuts [end up] (10, **P**)!

TO HEAVEN there are no SHOORTCUTS, because a shortcut [can] cut off your LEEEG (3, 7)![228] It is better, if you want to travel, to follow the liiiight (*magetsi*, 'electricity', metonymy, 9). Paths [leading through] *malina* trees will not lead us to heaven, no indeed! (6, 8).[229] Some Christians have travelled the paths of the *malina* (metaphor, 9): [They say, for example], "We can keep on getting drunk if we just remember to pray (go to church)!" [It's] a shortcut – a path through the *malinas* (9)!__After two or three days (i.e., times, metonymy, 9) [of doing this] HE FALLS! Thugs have FELLED him (5, 6)! He wanted to take a shortcut! "A shortcut cuts off the leg," so spoke the elders (3, 7). Take care mother!__Take care father! (5)__Many fall into problems because of these shortcuts (10, **P**)!

A shortcut is not wanted in Christianity. [Some of us] we keep on sinning as long as we remember to pray [in church].__[But] there are no shortcuts in (to) heaven. And the warning is right here.__[On earth] we see examples of what happens. MANY have their money stolen.__Others enter a graveyard.__Some are killed – [that is] the danger of shortcuts (2, 5, 7, **L**)! It may seem like the path is genuine (i.e., it leads to your destination), but it ends up leading you into a GRAVEYARD (metaphor, 9)!__Now these ways that we are taking to the graveyard – you know that they are [really] leading you to hell (10)! Paths that look to be straight – they only end up leading you to a graaaveyard (7)!

HERE I am speaking here (*pano ndilikunena pano*) – about a Christianity that we build upon sand (cough) instead of fearing sin. It does not fear sin.__It fears getting cut off [from church] (personification, 9).[230] Christian-

---

[228] Here Wame introduces an alliterative proverb that nicely reinforces his point about shortcuts: *chidule chidula mwendo* ('a shortcut cuts off one's leg'). The use of 'shortcut' is itself figurative in nature, i.e., a personified metonym.

[229] The *malina* is a fast-growing, shady softwood tree that is grown for firewood on many private and public plantations in Malawi, especially surrounding urban areas. These dense m*alina* groves are known for their danger, especially at night, for those who walk through them, taking a shortcut to some destination.

[230] The word *cut-off* (*kudulidwa*) here, which refers to excommunication from a Christian congregation, features the same verb root (*-dula*) as shortcut (*chidule*) and is also used in the proverb cited earlier. It is highly likely that Wame intended this as a *pun* with both rhetorical as well as thematic implications.

ity built upon sand does not fear sin, but it fears being cut off (7). Because when it takes (gets involved with) that sin – when it takes that sin and goes along with it to do evil things (9), he (the sinner) embraces it – and hides it, looking out for the church elders (5, 6). What he fears here are the church elders, saying [to him/herself], "If they see me, they will remove me from the [women's] fellowship.__They will remove me from the eldership.__They will remove me from the pastorate.__They will remove me from the choir.__They will remove me from Christianity (the congregation, synecdoche)!" (2, 5, 6, 7, L/P). So he remains on the lookout. But over here he disappears and goes along, he goes along, hiding and looking out all the way, fearing the church elders – instead of the sin [he is committing] (6). Have you seen his secret (10)? Instead of fearing the sin – and getting rid of it, he loves that sin SO MUCH – so much so, that he hides it. Then he watches out for the church elders – he looks right and left (*uku ndi uku*, lit., 'here and here') (6). You (*enallage*) move in hiding, fearing another PERSON, a church elder or the pastor, [but] not fearing God who sees what you have hidden (5)! Christianity [built] upon SAAAND – it fears no sin. [But] it fears the church elders instead. He [the sinner] says, "[It's] a shortcut!" – so he can arrive quickly (7). [But that is] impossible, impooossible (4, 8, **P**)!

Mother – [here is] the question of all questions (10):[231] Have you – have you ever asked Jesus [anything] on your knees [in prayer] (2, 6)?__Have you ever denied yourself there? [That is] the first rung! If you have never denied yourself, [then] while you are receiving this lesson [of the sermon], let's begin by denying ourselves.__And after we have denied ourselves, let us be enrolled as a soldier (10, **P**). Tomorrow IF POSSIBLE [you can begin to be trained] – [that is], if you become a soldier now (5). After a Christian has received Jesus, he must be instructed (**L**). Blessed are those who – TODAY begin by falling on their knees.__Number two – carry the cross.__Number three – follow Jesus (6).

May the Lord bless these words for us so that they might lead us during this very gathering here. Ameen (10, **E**)! (Amen!)

---

[231] It seems a bit strange that Wame would conclude his sermon here with a vocative addressed only to the mothers (*amai*). It could be that the majority in his audience were women, but perhaps this is simply another rhetorical device, i.e., he mentions the group in his congregation that would be the *least* likely, humanly speaking, to be in need of observing his admonition to repent.

"Are You Ready to Go? Preparing for the Trip to Heaven" (SW37)[232]

The Word of God which is found – Psalm 50 – Psalm number 50... We will read at verse 9 – stopping [at] 12. Verse nine: "I will not take a cooow in (from) your house, nor a goooat from your stockade. For aaall living things in the bush are mine, and caaaattle on the hills – thousands. I know all the birds in the hills, and the wild animals (lit., 'animals of the bush') are with me. If I were huuungry, I wouldn't tell you, for the whooole earth is mine, even its very fullness."[233] Especially verse 12 – But as for you (presumably the addressee in the psalm, here individualized), "If I were hungry, I wouldn't tell yooou!" May the Lord bless the reading of these words of his. Aaamen!

Let us pray: In the sure knowledge that of ourselves we lack wisdom, for this reason we hurry (lit., 'run') to pray – since you ALONE can cause us to overcome__since you ALONE are the God (lit., 'owner' *mwini*) of righteousness__since you ALONE are the God of life__since you ALONE died, died for us. Lord, ooopen up our spiritual eyes (*maso auzimu*). Ooopen up our ears. May we receive WEALTH of the highest cost, which you, Lord, have brought us here. What you have already begun with us – yesterday – today – this morning – up to this moment__now continue! For you KNOW what we need. In your name, Jesus Christ, our living Saviour, we pray. Amen!

---

[232] This sermon was broadcast on TWR in April of 1997 with no information given as to where or when Evangelist Wame preached it. The text does indicate, however (see paragraph two), that this is one in a series of sermons that Wame probably preached over several days at some sort of Christian revival gathering. Note again that in the following two sermons I will not distinguish the various stylistic features as in the preceding example, and only the most prominent phonological features will be indicated in the translation.

[233] As might be expected from reading this literal, formal correspondence translation (from the old *Buku Lopatulika*), the listener is presented with a number of cultural problems in addition to the inevitable linguistic difficulties that render such a version rather hard to understand. Some of the most obvious instances include the following: In central Africa cattle are not kept in a person's house or somewhere up in the hill country as this translation suggests; the intended sense of God's "knowing the birds in the hills (or mountains)" is not clear at all, and what are the wild animals doing up in heaven "with him"? Moreover, it is culturally inappropriate for a rich person (like God) to inform a relative pauper (like a human being) that he is hungry as if he expected a meal from the latter. But in my experience (and based on the data at hand), such cases of conceptual interference and semantic opacity that arise from a literal Bible translation itself are only rarely, if ever, dealt with systematically by the preacher in his sermon.

The words which our God wants to speak to us at this time – [are] a warning.[234] [There is] a warning in verse 12. "If I were huuungry, I wouldn't tell yooou! For the WHOLE earth is miiine, and its fullness." These words reveal what God lacks up there in heaven. God, what he lacks...what he lacks up there in heeeaven – he lacks your life. He lacks your heart![235]

I asked a certain person the day before yesterday there in Salima, "How are you [this morning]?" (*Mwadzuka bwanji?*) He said, "Aah, I'm not very well at all (*ine sindinadzuke bwino*). I am not well in my whole body – the whole body is pounding in pain (*kuphwanya*, lit., 'breaking'). I think it must be malaria (*malungo*, lit., 'fever')." Then I said, "Nooo, you are saying too much there. Just say [this], 'We've received a letter (*kalata*) from home (lit., 'from the village'). He wants uuus!'[236] Eeehee-ee, hee (Wame laughs) – to speak in abbreviated form, hee, an abbreviation. Ehee-ii-hee, hoo! (laughter) AALL THE TIME THERE IN HEAVEN, what he (God) lacks – he lacks is you!" Then he (Wame's friend) says, "Aaaah! you're right – as for me, this is my letter from home." So if you go to the hospital and recover, it is like making this reply, "Aah, please wait for me a while – I'm coming."[237] But you will make that journey FOR SURE! (*mudzanyamuka ndithu!*) As for the way...to start off on the journey [may be caused by] an illness, but to [actually] arrive there requires JESUS![238] [So] say it by way of abbreviation, "I've received a letter from home" – because what God lacks (i.e., there in heaven) – he lacks yooouuu!

---

[234] The key term (a Wame-ism), warning (*chenjezo*), indicates that this is going to be one of his favourite types of sermons – a hortatory one that emphasizes reproof, admonition and encouragement (with much less attention being given to a text exposition of the Scriptures cited).

[235] Wame leads off with a conundrum of sorts, one that pits the biblical text that he has just read against his subsequent assertion: How can God lack the listener's "life/heart" if he is the owner of everything on earth? The point is of course that while God may control everything in this world, he cannot command a person to be saved and come live with him in heaven. In that sense then, he lacks (and desires) our presence there with him. Wame does not immediately or directly explain this little contradiction; he rather allows its meaning to be revealed during the course of this sermon.

[236] This is an idiomatic, euphemistic way of speaking about the proximity of death. When a person gets sick, it is like God sending a "letter" from "home" – from the "village" up in heaven – a reminder that this is the place where one really belongs; all one's true "relatives" are there.

[237] Wame is here extending the imagery and application of the original euphemistic expression even as he dramatizes it through the pertinent snatch of direct speech.

[238] Note the effective alliteration and assonance of this utterance: *pofuna kunyamuka ndi matendawa, koma pokafika kumeneko – pafunika Yesuuu*.

NOW we do read in the Word of God [about some] assurance (*chitsimikizo*) that God there in HEEAVEN lacks the life of [every] person. When the Lord Jesus came down here [to earth], we hear that – he thrashed the merchandise sellers in the temple (*kachisi*) – and that in there he overturned the[ir] tables and told them, "WHY do you consider the house of my Father a house of merchandise, a house of criminals? For this house is a house of prayer (*nyumba yopemphereramo*)." So he thrashed them and chased them all out, and he overturned the[ir] tables.[239]

Now let me reveal [something to you] (*pano tifuna tiulule*): The Lord Jesus was seeking – the heart (*mtima*) of Israel. It was lost, but it got lost in the church (*m'chalichi* the Temple, as a metonymic reference to the religious establishment).[240] Those tables he was overturning [shows that] he seeks the heart of a person. Those tables he was overturning [shows that] he seeks the heart of a person. So it is in heaven, God does not sleep night or day (*usiku ndi usana*) – seeking your heart, mother, that was lost – seeking your heart, mother, that was lost.[241] Night and daaay – God is seeeking your life, [that] you might go home since your home is not here [on earth]. Your home is in heaven. So heeere he reveals that – "When I [suddenly] cooome to your house, I will not take a cow since I myself am the one who gives you all these cows here. When I come, I won't take a goat – [from among] the goats that I myself gave you. I won't take any money – [from] the money that I myself gave you. I will not take a single thiiing – AAALL of it is already mine." But as for you – "If I were hungry, I wouldn't tell yooouu!"[242]

---

[239] Wame's use of this particular incident from the life of Christ is to prove that what God "lacks" he also cares enough about to go and make an active, even violent, search for. The story thus becomes a metaphor of Jesus' seeking the lost soul – he will leave no table unturned in this effort!

[240] What a profound, insightful irony Wame just briefly introduces here – but only in passing, for this is not the main point of his message at this juncture.

[241] The repetition here is of course for emphasis. It is much more effective as a rhetorical device in oral, as opposed to written, discourse. The reiterated mention of mother (*amai*, an honorific plural) may again be due to the fact that the majority in the congregational audience were women. Otherwise, one or another of the two parallel instances would have been replaced by fathers (*azibambo*).

[242] On the basis of this expression taken from Psalm 50: 12 (which acts like sort of a thematic refrain as well as a sectional closing motif), Wame once again stresses his central message: God is not in some way dependent upon our human offerings to him. These are mere outward tokens or religious symbols of our devotion to him – of our offering our lives to him in total trusting service. That is what God "lacks" in the sense of what he is looking for from believers. Our commitment ought to be as willing and automatic as the response of a host to a guest who has arrived at the home; the latter would have no need to ask for some food – indeed, it would be a great shame to (be forced to) do so. This climactic utterance also

Now the words, "If I WERE HUNGRY, I WOULDN'T TELL YOU!" mean that when a person dies down here – up there in HEAVEN a judicial asseeembly (*bwalooo*) takes place. There is a huge gaaathering (*chimsonkhanoooo*).[243] [There someone says], "We want someone to go and take the life of so-and-so." Then a disagreement arises. [Some say], "Nooo, just leave him (her) be. Perhaps he will repent of that witchcraft [that he's committing]." [Others respond], "So you say, but we want to go take him." "A-ah, nooo! you'll be making a mistake if you do that. We will take him [later] this year – [we'll give him] a FULL year (*chaka THII!*, ideophone)."[244] So the whole year goes by and you are still alive. [But] you [down] here you keep right on with all your bewitching (lit., 'you are in the middle of doing the witch's dance' – *uli mkati m'kutamba*), without realizing that the [heavenly] meeting already took place, [and] it adjourned [without coming to a decision on whether to 'take' you or not] (*msonkhano walepherekA*)! So you'd better get good and ready for the JOOOUURNEY (*ulendoooo womangamanga*, i.e., of death)! "As for you, if I (God) were hungry, I wouldn't tell yooouuu!"

Where they hold the meeting about my life (*msonkhano wa moyo wa ine*, i.e., the heavenly council concerning whether I should live or die), I am not preeesent. If I had known [that it were taking place], I would have prepared myseeeelf [to depart]. Perhaps the meeting will take place todaaay. Perhaps the meeting will take place tomoooorrow. My mother, when a person dies, in heaven there's no accident (*kulibe ngozi*).[245] HERE

---

stresses the fact that when God actually does decide to take your life, he will not inform you in advance. Therefore, a person should be ready to "depart" on this "journey" at any time.

[243] The implication of course (perhaps clearer in the oral than the written text) is that God's "heavenly council" meets to consider the case of a given individual *before* "s/he" (the Chewa third person pronoun may be either masculine or feminine) actually dies – or is "taken away" as the vivid imagery depicts it.

[244] This imaginary little dramatic dialogue, in which the preacher plays all the speakers, is humorous on the surface – but in a deadly serious sort of way, as Wame soon reveals. How could any listener who is living in sin not fail to be impressed that the judicial case being hypothetically debated actually concerns him/her? S/he had better make good use of this "time of grace" on earth!

[245] The socioculturally significant term, "accident" (*ngozi*), in this context refers to an unfortunate incident (from a human perspective), usually involving someone's death, that takes place suddenly or much sooner than was expected (in the case of someone dying). From a traditional African perspective, however, such a death would be no "accident", that is, in a Western sense. Rather, it would have been caused by witchcraft/sorcery (*ufiti*). Wame's point is that from God's perspective too, there are no such unexplainable "accidents" – everything takes place according to a divinely appointed schedule, which no human being can predict on the basis of his/her external circumstances or situation in life. This is another profound, albeit implicitly stated, theological insight. For the believer in Christ, there is no such thing as

ON EARTH we say, "There's been an acciiident!" But in heaven there are no aaaaccidents. They (i.e., the angels, etc.) know for sure that on such-and-such a day we go to take someone. Here as I am speaking, there are some of us whose [heavenly] meeting took place, but adjourned – three times, four times. Perhaps just last year they met, but they adjourned to give you a chance to repent, and you didn't even know [about it]. For this reason he (God) says, "As for you, if I were hungry, I wouldn't tell you!"

That [previous] year they met, they wanted to remove your life, [but] they adjourned the meeting [saying], "Let's allow him [to live] – maybe [his] witchcraft, maybe that lying – he will leave it![246] Maybe that beer [drinking], he'll leave it – YOOOUU don't know about such things. HEEERE [on earth] you are taken up with having a good time (*mwangotenga chimkondwa*). You are just pleasing yourself with eeearthly things. You merely follow the desires of your heart, WITHOUT realizing that [in] the meeting [up] theeere, they failed to reach an agreement (*alepherana*). Perhaps just this last year they met again – [and they said], "Ah nooo, let's just allooow him [to live]." But as for you [down] here, your days are running out! Perhaps this very year they have met again. There in heeeaven, there is no accident (i.e., with regard to time, place or person). HEEERE on earth is where we say, "There's been an accident!"

A heavenly accident (*ngozi yakumwamba*) takes place when a person is caught committing adultery (*akagwidwa ndi chigololo*). There in HEAVEN, the angels run [back and forth crying], "[There's been] an ACCIDENT, an accident, an accident!" – That's [what I mean by] a heavenly accident.[247] If a person is found in a drunken condition, the angels run about [crying], "[There's been] an ACCIDENT, an accident, an accident!" While you here decide to eat your fill [of life's pleasures] (*mukuti mukudyerera*), you are enjoying yourself – without realizing that in heaven an acci-

---

luck, fate, misfortune, or whatever, since "God works in all things for their good..." (Rom 8: 28).

[246] Wame here plays on two distinct, contextually-determined meanings of the verb *kusiya* – either "to leave" someone alone (i.e., to allow him/her to live), or "to leave" some bad habit or sinful practice.

[247] The fact that Wame earlier stated that there were no "accidents" which take place in heaven only serves to emphasize his claim now that accidents are indeed referred to or announced as having occurred (on earth). Such accidents occur on earth in the form of grave *sins* that threaten a person's spiritual life, e.g., persistent adultery or drunkenness, which are cited as socially prominent cases in point. Wame's dramatization of his imaginative perspective here – enhanced as always with realistic dialogue segments – has a powerful rhetorical effect on the listening audience, especially as an appeal to their emotions (*pathos*).

dent has occurred (lit., 'fallen', *kwagwa ngozi*). If a person is caught committing adultery, [up] there in heaven the angels run about [crying], "[There's been] an ACCIDENT, an accident, an accident!" – while you down here you keep on enjoying yourself (*mukuti mukusangalala*), without realizing that in heaven there an accident has occurred. If a person [happens to] die, in heaven it's no accideeeent._Here on earth is where we say, "There's been an accideeeent!" My mother, this greatly friiiigthens me!"²⁴⁸ (*chikundiopsaaaa!*) "As for you, if I (God) were hungry, I wouldn't tell you!"

The elders have this saying, "The death of a cockerel needs no counsel" (*imfa ya tambala ilibe upo*).²⁴⁹ Have you ever heard these words? Have you [heard them]? "The death of a cockerel needs no counsel." Listen to me very carefully now:

There was [once] a certain rooster.²⁵⁰ He went to the wetlands (*dambo*) – like over theeere – to find something to eat. Now when he reached a certain tree, he found that in that tree were some termites (*chiswe*), and when he saw those termites he started right in to eat [them]. Now he also encountered one of those large lizards with a big blue head – some call it a *gulo*. You know what I'm talking about, right? It's the kind that when it moves it shakes its head [up and down] like this – [we call it] the *gulo*.²⁵¹ And when he (rooster) found it – since IT TOO (the blue lizard) likes to eat those very same teeermites... So when he came up, the lizard said, "Eeh-eeh! What's up [Mr Rooster]?" Rooster replied, "[I've come] to share with you (*udzadya nawo*, lit., 'to eat with them')." [Lizard] responds, "Nooo, why not leave it (i.e., the termites) to me? MY FRIEND (*anzathu*), you've left maize bran (*gaga*) [at home where you live]. MY FRIEND, you've [got]

---

[248] Wame here suddenly shifts from his third-person presentation to address his congregation directly, especially the women ("my mother") and reveals the effect that his message thus far has on him (at least), if not on them. In this manner he often puts himself in the place of his listeners to demonstrate that he is not above or standing apart from them, but he is preaching to himself as well (an appeal to *ethos*).

[249] In other words, people in the village do not normally make plans to kill a cock – they may do so at any time when there's a cause for celebration, like when relatives or a visitor arrives at the homestead.

[250] Wame tells this story in the style of a traditional folktale (*nthano*), including its syntactic structure and intonational aspects such as utterance length and pause placement.

[251] Wame often includes asides like this to the audience to ensure that they are with him as he continues his account, the effect of which is greatly enhanced by their ability to imagine for themselves what is going on even as he narrates the various scenes and events.

rice [and] millet – so DON'T cheat me (*musatinyengerere*) heeere! I, your good friend (*anzathufe*), have just found these few termites (*kachisweka*).__I want to save a few for tomorrow so that perhaps I might begin [the day] with a good start (*mwina mmawa n'kudzaona poyambira*, i.e., a good breakfast!)."

He-heee! (laugh) The rooster says, "No, brother, just allow me to eat with yooouuu. If you knew the kind of millet [people] give us, you wouldn't talk like that – the riiice [too] that they give us, you wouldn't talk like that.[252] Yes, even the maize bran that they give us – you wouldn't talk like that!" He [lizard] says, "Nooo, DON'T FINISH everything off for me, MY FRIEND. When we [lizards] see a few termites like this, it's like we're dreaming (*timachita kuyesa kutulo*)! GO AWAAAY! Go somewhere else! My friend, you have left maize bran [back at your home].__My friiiend, you've left behind plenty of water which you drink in a basin (*zimadzi zomwera zam'beseni*). You've left rice behind." [So] they began to argue there.

Sadly the rooooster – he says, "Aah! My friend, IF YOU REALLY KNEW, you wouldn't speak such words. Just PERHAAPS the maize bran that you're talking about, I've already said farewell to (*ndatsazikana naye*).__Perhaps tomorrow I'll NEVER see it again after that (*sindingakamuonenso*). [Perhaps] I've said farewell to the rice. If yooouu only knew [the truth of what] the elders said, 'The death of a cockerel requires no counsel', (i.e., I can be killed at any time), you would not speak such words. OOOO-K, I'm goooing!" [So spoke the rooster] in a pitiful sort of way (*momvetsa chisoni*).

THEY DIDN'T KNOW THAT at that very time while they were arguing here, over there at the village some gueeeests arrived. "John!" "Yes, Master (*wawa*)." "Say – that rooster that I saw over here... Well, what are we going to do about these guests? There's nothing else at all that's available for the stew (*padziko panotu palibe ndiwo*, hyperbole)."[253] They did not

---

[252] It is Wame's ability to empathize with the diverse characters (whether human or animal) of his stories and anecdotes and to realistically "humanize" their interaction, especially via dialogue, that gives his sermons their special dramatic impact, interest, and appeal. And as the congregation is imaginatively "caught up" in such an account, the point of the main theological or ethical message is implicitly but indelibly being made.

[253] The "stew" (*ndiwo*) is what distinguishes any meal, that is, it is the variable element that accompa-

know that over there is a big aaaaargument! "The death of a cockerel requires no couuuunsel." "As for you, if I were hungry, I wouldn't tell you!"[254]

"Heh! Start looking for that rooooster!" [the master commands]. [But] the rooster is nowhere to be seen. "Aah," [the servant reports] "Daddy (*adadii*, 'my master'), I've looked all over – it cannot be seen." "Eeeh-eh, so what are we going to do about these guests? We can't waste any more time!" "Ha! Let's just wait a while. Perhaps it is coming." It is [indeed] coming [now], you children (*anaanu*),[255] travelling to his house (i.e., coop). Just as soon as he reached the doorway – haah! he met up with (*adakangokumana*) with the words [saying], "Heeey, if it isn't that rooster (*suuyu tambala uja*)!" [The rooster says to himself], "O-oooh (*a-aaaah?*), what in the world is going on here?"

Ah, you children, immediately the rooster flaps away in flight (*KWE-KWE! KWE-KWE!*, an ideophone depicting the action) – that's the roooster in fliiight, you children. Now what is happening there – how could it end (*zikutha-bwa?*), how could it end, how could it end (i.e., there's no doubt about the outcome)?! The chaser (i.e., servant) says, "[Let me get] a kniiiife on its throat (*pakhosi mpeniii*)!" Heee-heeeh (laugh)! "AS FOR YOOOU, if I were hungry, I wouldn't tell yooooouu!"

Eeeh-eeeh! You children, at last the rooster – caught! (*PHOO!*, ideophone). He's grabbed it! The rooster WEEPS as he says, "I told that friend of mine (i.e., the lizard) that perhaps the maize bran you're talking about, I will say farewell to it [today]. Let him hear [about it] (*amvetse*)!" So the rooster cried out, "SCREAM (*KWIIYOOO!*, an onomatopoetic ideophone)!" His friend [over there] pricks up his ears (*kuchera khutu*).

---

nies the central African "staff of life" – *nsima*, thick maize meal porridge. Meat for the stew, especially chicken, is reserved for special occasions or to receive a guest with the appropriate honor.

[254] Wame here juxtaposes his two key thematic (reiterated) utterances – the traditional Chewa proverb and the quote from Ps 50:12. In this subtle way he reminds his listeners that the little folktale he is telling them does have a spiritual point – one that is related to the sermon as a whole, and it is up to them to start looking for the connection, before he has to come right out and explain it.

[255] The apparent elided vocative "you children" (viz. *ana inu*) seems in its literal form to imitate a typical village folktale setting, as an older storyteller (e.g., a [grand]parent) addresses his/her audience to keep them actively involved in the telling. However, the term may have been conventionalized to function merely as an exclamation which conveys the (feigned) emotion of great worry or apprehension on the part of the speaker.

"SCREAM!" [again]. E-e-eeh! because of this, the lizard – what it did there as it was moving along, it says, "E-e-eeh! He (rooster) was telling [me] the truuuth! (laughter, also from the congregation) 'THE DEATH OF A COCKEREL REQUIRES NO PLAAAANING!' (Wame laughs.) 'THE DEATH OF A COCKEREL REQUIRES NO PLAAAANING!' Ee-eeh! ya! ya! (laugh) HE WAS TELLING ME THE TRUUUTH! 'THE DEATH OF A COCKEREL REQUIRES NO PLAAANING.' MY FRIEND IS GOOOONE (dead)!" Because of this, the lizard looked down to the ground in shame (*jojoli*, ideophone) as it said to itself, "E-e-e-eeh! (laugh) 'THE DEATH OF A COCKEREL REQUIRES NO PLAAANING!' MY FRIEND IS GOONE! MY FRIEND IS GOOOONE!" Heh! Heeeh![256]

My mother, SIINCE where they hold that [heavenly] meeting, NO ONE dwelling here on earth knows about – and you too know nothing about such things... [So] since you know nothing [about it], you'd better get ready for it. Perhaps TOMORROW you will set off on the journey to the village (i.e., you will pass away/die). PERHAPS TODAY you might set off – to the village. PERHAPS THE DAY AFTER TOMORROW you might set off – to the village. Perhaps when you leave THIS VERY PLAAACE, when you arrive there at your home, you might meet up with these very words: "SAY, ISN'T THIS THAT ROOSTER?!" [Someone tells you], "That friend of ours whom we were with at this gathering, yes indeed, they say she's dead (*ndithudi akuti m'maliro*)!" "A-aah! Tell me the truth now, you!" "Yes indeed, that woman who was singing the lead for the hymns, yes indeed, she's dead!" "Well, what happened?!" "Indeed, she met up with the words 'SAY, ISN'T THIS THAT ROOSTER?!'"[257] "A-aagh!" (exclamation of shock). BECAUSE THAT DAY IS NOT KNOWN, you'd better get yourself ready [for it]!

It may just happen that as you run away from (*kuthawa*, ironic hyperbole) this meeting, [all your] THOUGHTS are on a bottle of [local] gin (*kachasu*). [But] if God wants [to destroy] that bottle – SMASH! (*PHAA!*, ideophone) – as for you, you won't grab it at all! Perhaps you will just

---

[256] Wame almost seems exhausted here from the rigors and tension of the powerful tale that he has just told, and he exclaims his own relief now that it's over.

[257] Wame masterfully manufactures a metaphor from a key utterance of the tale he has just told: "Say, isn't this that rooster?!" – i.e., an unexpected/sudden death is about to occur. The rooster thus symbolizes everyone in the congregation (ironically mostly women in this case), and they should realize that any one of them could be "cut off" at any time and without any advance announcement (by God).

encounter the words, "SAAY, isn't this that rooster?!" (i.e., implying an imminent and immediate death) - and that bottle you won't [get a chance to] grab it at all. Such things are possible.

PERHAPS [your] FLIGHT away from this meeting [is] because [you want] to run after some dagga (*chamba*, i.e., Indian hemp, a narcotic plant that is smoked) - to run after [items of] sorcery (*nyanga*), adultery, to run after lies. [But] if God so DESIRES, right now, FOR SUUURE, it may be that you will never again grab any witchcraft! [Instead] you will just encounter the words, "SAAAY, isn't this that roooster?" - [and] death! (*maliro*, lit., 'a time of mourning,' i.e., a euphemistic metonym). Since that day you don't knooow - [the day] of going to the village/home - get yourself ready (*konzekeranitu*)!

Mother, get yourself ready. "The death of a cockerel requires no counsel." God is hungry for [your] heart (*ali ndi njala yakufuna mtimawo*, i.e., your repentance). He says, "When I come, I won't take any cows - [for] I was the one who gave you the cows. When I come - money, no - I was the one who gave it to you. When I come - goats, no - I was the one who gave them to you.[258] When I come - [your] automobile, no - I was the one who gave it to you. When I come - the maize mill (*chigayocho*), no - I was the one who gave it to you. The store, no - I was the one who gave it to you. When I come - MATHEMATICS (*samuyo*, lit., 'the sum,' i.e., a metonymic reference to mathematical ability), noo! - I was the one who gave it to you. When I cooome... BUT WHAT I LAAACK - I have a huuuunger (*njala*) TO REMOOOVE YOU, and bring you heeere [to heaven]. And "if I were hungry, I wouldn't tell yooouuu." "The death of a cockerel requires no coouuunsel!" Since I (Wame) don't know when [you will go] to the meeting, it would be better to get yourself reeeaady!

How about you, are you ready? Are you [really] ready? THE PURPOSE OF [this] MEEEETING [is that] we become ready. This getting ready [means] to receive Jesus as our Saviour - [he is] the way home to [our]

---

[258] Here we have another good example of Wame's characteristic iterative frame construction in which various specific items are mentioned, one being substituted after the other, in order to give an enhanced impression of the whole concept that is being spoken about - here, the various possessions that God provides us with in this life. Such a series often builds up to a climax and/or a sudden break in the pattern (both of which occur in this particular instance).

village (*njira ya kwathu kumudzi*). AT ANY TIME you can set off on this journey.__[Just see how] death is rushing about (*imfa mmene ikuthamangira*, i.e., the death rate is rising)!²⁵⁹

My brothers, let me just reveal a little something to you. Recently I myself was sick, and He (God) showed me how death was rushing about in the land. And what I saw as I was lying there (in a feverous sleep vision?) [makes me wonder] how we can remain alive down here [on earth]. Then I became AFRAAAID (*ndinachita mantha*) [and] up until the present time I don't understand it (i.e., what I saw in the vision).

[God] showed me some OLD, WRECKED, OUT-OF-DATE trains (*zimasitima zakutha zokalamba zakalekale*)...I have no idea how they could run – on the iron [tracks] – having such an ugly, but also a dreadful, appearance (*zopanda maonekedwe, komanso zoopsa*). [He also showed me some] OOLD, ugly, wrecked [and] out-of-date automobiles (*zimagalimoto*).__I have no idea how they could run. [He] also showed me some awful people (*ziwanthu*).__They [looked like] people who, when God made them, they got away from him (*zidampulumuka*) so he couldn't finish [the job on them]. THEY WERE LIKE – who is this person anyway?! (*okhala ngati munthu ndani ameneyu?*)²⁶⁰

Now as he was showing me [these things], he says, "Come, you will see how death is racing about [everywhere]." Those old trains were RAAACING about, and their speed (*sipidi*) was [the likes of which] I have never seen before. [They raced about] until they would crash together and get smashed to pieces – no hope of repair (*palibenso lipeyala*)! But then those ugly people – where they came from could not be seen – arrived to raise up [the trains] – right then and there, with a huge cloud of dust (*chifumbi PHAA!*, ideophone)!__And in no time at all (*kanthawi kang'onong'ono*) they were FULL UP with these ugly people – MANY

---

²⁵⁹ Wame now suddenly breaks off his train of thought to introduce a personal (ethos heightening) anecdote into the sermon – an illustration showing that he himself is not immune from an unexpected death, that he too must be ready to "depart."

²⁶⁰ Wame gives the impression here that the vision of what he saw was so terrible that he is at a loss for words to describe what he actually did see – of course leaving the rest up to the hearers' own imagination. Reference to the particularly ugly person here at the end is a specific localized stimulus to their thinking for special effect. The entire scene is like a fantastic, farcical imitation of what John saw in the visions recounted in the book of Revelation.

UUUUGLY PEOPLE, a MULTITUDE of people. He (God) says, "Look, Death is carrying them all to go dump them out – in hell (*gahena*)!__It goes to dump them – in the grave (*kumanda*)." So I saw some awful things [there] that I had never seen before – [like such] SPEEED! My, how fast these old trains traaaavelled!__And they are moving niiight and day – [raising] clouds of dust, clouds of dust (*fumbi lokhalokha*, an idiomatic metonym to describe any sort of rapid movement).

Then He says, "Come, let me show you the work to which I've sent you – the words which you are to preach." So I found myself at some train stops (*m'masiteji*) where people remain WAITING FOR those trains. So at [any] stop my job was to PREEACH the message (*yolalikira uthenga*, the gospel) – just preaching! But when one of those [big] old trains would arrive,[261] it would cover us with so much dust there that my companions (*anzanga*, i.e., those people whom I was with)... Where they would enter [the train] was unknown.__[And] where I would fall aside (? *ndikagwere*) was unknown.__I just found myself alone as [someone] says, "It (the train) started up – it's gone!" Until I began to wonder, "SO HOW DID IT HAPPEN TO LEAVE ME BEHIND? HOW IS IT THAT I AM STILL HERE?!" I could not UNDERSTAAAND [what was going on] AT AAALL (*wosamveetsaaa*)! A little later I found myself at [another] stop – with a HUUUGE crowd of people (*chiguuulu cha anthu*) – preaching the message [to them], preaching the message, preaching the message. A SHORT TIME LAATER, the old trains arrive from nowhere – those BIG, AAAWFUL, ugly ones! AT THAT VERY MOMENT dust [appeared] everywhere [as the trains] pick up [their passengers] – they're running night and day.__This is death!

So now according to how I see it, [the fact that we see] the sun rise until it sets – TRUUULY, [this is due solely to] the grace of God.[262] I don't know

---

[261] The Chichewa nominal (and concordial) marker *chi*- (pl. *zi*-) when prefixed to another noun may denote large size ('big') and/or connote disparagement ('old/ugly'). Since either, or all, these nuances would apply to the "trains" in question, it is likely that Wame did not intend to make any subtle distinction here.

[262] This utterance illustrates how concentrated and elliptical Wame's discourse can get at times, especially when he is excited and preaching rapidly. This naturally causes problems for both transcriber and translator alike – all the more so when the tape recording is not entirely clear. Thus there is always a certain measure of hypothetical interpretation (or just plain guessing!) that is involved, but I tried at all times to convey at most only the intended sense and basic implications of the recorded text (including the most prominent aspects of its phonological overlay), without altering or embellishing it in any way.

– how can these things be (*kaya zikutheka bwanji*)? But even we preachers are found preaching RIGHT IN THE VERY MIDDLE of these [mysterious] things. I don't know, how can it be that we are still alive?![263] Right up to the very present I have no answer [for this]. What I am telling you here, my brothers, concerns things that I have seen. It's POOOSSIBLE that your [heavenly] council has come to an end today (i.e., with a decision that you will die). Perhaps you [will] depart today. It's POOOSSIBLE that your council has come to an end. Perhaps you [will] depart tomorrow. Since you do not know [for sure when], get yourself ready. "The death of a cockerel requires no counsel." "AS FOR YOU, if I (God) were hungry, I wouldn't tell yooouu!"[264]

[Here is] the last part. The elders speak these words, "WHEN YOU PRACTICE WITCHCRAFT, YOU MUST LOOK TOWARDS THE LAKE (i.e., Lake Malawi, to the east), LEST THE DAWN ARISE UPON YOU" (i.e., while doing your dirty deeds – *ukatambatamba, umayang'aaana kunyanja, kungakuchere*).[265] Did you ever hear that song (i.e., the title or theme of some well-known traditional tune)? "WHEN YOU PRACTICE WITCHCRAFT, YOU MUST LOOK TOWARDS THE LAKE, LEST THE DAWN ARISE UPON YOU!" My home is near the lake, over there at Salima. So when it dawns, we see that it [first] gets

---

[263] I believe that what Wame is getting at is the tremendous mystery of the will, and even the election, of God. Why is it that we are allowed to live yet another day upon this earth? Indeed, we have no answer either – except simply to trust the grace of God, as Wame encourages his congregation. That is the passive side of the issue; the active side is what he stresses in this particular sermon, namely, to be prepared at any time to leave this life and depart for the heavenly "home." The wicked, however, urgently need to repent and get their life in order – lest they suddenly get picked up by one of those "terrible trains"!

[264] Like every good public speaker, in addition to characteristic pausal and intonational patterns, Wame utilizes certain distinctive discourse openers and closers to orally indicate the internal boundaries and progressive development of his message. One of the most obvious devices in this sermon is the repetition involving key thematic utterances, like the two "wise sayings" (one traditional, one biblical) that are once again combined here at the end of a major compositional unit. This is followed by an explicit reference to the fact that he has embarked upon the final stage of his sermon. Such verbal cues are a great help to the text transcriber and the translator as well.

[265] The verb *kutamba* ('to practice witchcraft') actually refers to a ritualistic, malevolent dance that night-witches are believed to perform as they are casting their noxious spell, normally at a grave(yard). Wame speaks freely about witchcraft (*ufiti*) and other occultic practices in his sermons. But he typically does so in a humorous, disparaging vein and often without magnifying such activities above other sins. By means of this strategy, he "defamiliarizes" the occult – brings its various aspects out in the open, so to speak – where they can be examined and rebuked as in the case of any other kind of wicked behavior. People who are caught up in such practices are thereby encouraged not to view witchcraft as the unforgivable sin, but to repent before God of this like any other evil and to leave it by the power of Christ.

reeed (*kumafiiira*) in the direction of the lake, then it gets white (*kuyera*) – the sun does. It is then that we know that the day is breaking outside (*kunja kuno kuli kucha*). So it is that WIIITCHCRAAAFT is fond of doing its dance [of bewitchment] (*ufiiiti umakoma utamba*) in the wee hours of the morning (*m'mabandakucha*), somewhere around four o'clock (*fol'oklooki*). That's when the witches like to dance. Am I telling lies? Those of you who are witches [in the congregation], am I here misrepresenting (lit., 'lying against') you? (laughter in the congregation!)[266] As if I were lying by saying... Isn't it a good [time] to bewitch at four o'clock – am I LYING? So [you think] I AM LYING?! (*ndikunama eti?*) Aa-aaah! So why are you looking down [in embarrassment]? (*bwanji kodi mukungozyolika?*) AAANSWER ME NOW! (laugh)

And so it is that since WITCHES have no watches (*zilibe maotchi*)... AAGH! Does a witch wear a watch? Say you witches, do you wear WATCHES? I know for sure that you are right here [in the audience]! (*ndikudziwatu mulipo pompano!*) DO YOU WEAR WATCHES?[267] And so it is that since they don't have watches, whenever they practice their witchcraft – dancing that dance [of theirs] (*kumavina guleyo*)[268] – so they must keep looking over there in the east, to see whether it's getting light.__They have to know whether the dawn is breaking. This is the meaning of that song – "When you practice witchcraft, you must look towards the lake, lest the dawn arise upon yoooouuu." So as they dance their dance, [they keep] looking to the east.__As they dance their dance, [they keep] looking to the east. They have to see whether it's getting liiiight. "E-eeh! we'd better

---

[266] Here we have another instance of effective topical defamiliarization of what is often treated as a taboo subject, certainly in a sermon. It would not be surprising, however, even among a group of Christians, to find some individuals who consider themselves to be witches (*mfiti*), whether the nocturnal, necrophagous kind or those who practice deliberate sorcery through magical means (for this distinction, see Wendland, "*Ufiti* – Foundation of an Indigenous Philosophy of Misfortune", pp. 209-243).

[267] It may seem, on reading the bare printed text (i.e., without actually hearing the dynamic recording, or better, being right there on the scene), that Wame is somewhat overdoing it in this section. But it is important to keep in mind that *time* – knowing the right time and being ready for a particular time – is an important aspect of this sermon's theme as it applies to Christian readiness to depart this life. In this case, the point is emphatically dramatized via a humorous antitype, namely, that society's supposed worst enemy – the witch – also needs to be very concerned about what time it is – or s/he too will be "lost"!

[268] The verb-noun phrase *kuvina gule* 'to dance a dance' refers either to the socially acceptable form of dancing (e.g., at a wedding) or to the ritual dancing ceremonies of the *nyau* male secret society. In this case, *kutamba* 'to dance a witch's spell' stands as the malicious antitype to both, but here it functions as the actual referent for the figurative usage of the former expression.

KNOOOCK OOOFF now! (*tiyeni tiwerukeeee!* i.e., as if the time of their "job shift" were over!) Let's get going!" Immediately UP-UP AND AWAY! (*PHAA!*, ideophone) [They] knock off [and] go away.

So it was that ONE DAY some witches went off to cast their spell (*zapita kokatamba*). And so it was that their witching was going so well (*kutamba kudakoma*) that they FORGOOOT to look to the east. You children, [the time] got to be SIX O'CLOOOCK (*sikisi kolokooo*) without their realizing it. It got to be SIIIX-thirty (*hafu sikisiii*) without their realizing it.__It got to be SEVEN without their realizing it.__[They were] strongly stomping the ground [doing their dance]! (*WA-WA-WA-WAA!*, ideophone) (Wame laughs). It got to be SEVEN THIRTY when [all of a sudden] they heard [a voice shouting], "[Look at those] WIIITCHES!" (*mfiiitizo!*) When they did like that (i.e., turned around), their eyes LIT UP! (*m'maso ngweee!*, ideophone).__It had already dawned! You children, when they tried to escape, SLAM! (*phii!*, ideophone, i.e., they got hit by some hurled weapons) – THEY (some people) GRAAABED THEM! He-heeh (laugh)! "WHEN YOU PRACTICE WIIITCHCRAFT, YOU MUST LOOK TOWARDS THE LAKE, LEST THE DAWN ARISE UPON YOOOUUUU!"

[I think] you know the meaning [of what I've said]: THOSE EVIL THINGS, as we are doing them – as we are drinking that BEER, as we are doing that WITCHCRAFT, [telling] lies, smoking DAGGA – [we need to] LOOOK AT THE WOORLD [and] where it is (lit., 'has arrived' – *kumayang'ana dziiiko pamene lafika*, i.e., "where it has come to" in terms of evil and its outcome). What time is it now? [We must] LOOOK at the world [and] where it is – which EVEN A RANK PAGAN (*ngakhale ndi mkunja yemwe*) knows that [the world's] time is finished (hyperbole)! IT'S NOT A TIME now to play at Christianity (*si nthawi yosolowetsa chikristu ino*)! IT'S NOT A TIME now to play at the ministry (*ubusa*)! IT'S NOT A TIME to play at eldership (*ukuluwampingo*)! IT'S NOT A TIME to play at the choir (*kwaya*)! IT'S NOT A TIME to play at preaching (*ulaliki*)! IT'S NOT A TIME TO PLAAAY AT A MEETING like this one! JUST LOOOK at the this world, and the season, and the time – where they stand (lit., 'are'). ANYONE can see (lit., 'know') that this world is... m-mmm! that this world is at an end (*kumapeto*).

THOSE WHO ARE NOT READY – if there are some things [preventing it] – they'd better get ready! The purpose of this [church] meeting iiiis GET REEEAADY! "WHEN YOU PRACTICE WITCHCRAFT, you must look towards the lake, lest the dawn arise upon you!" [Your] TIME is up (*nthawi yatha*)! But also [you have to] look where you came from, where you now are, [and] where you are going. But [you] also [have to] look at (i.e., consider) you own body – "Say, my good friend (*munthune*), how am I feeling?" – because you alone are able to know [this] for sure.[269] Perhaps you might say, "You children, when I die, do not think that I was never sick (i.e., that I never had an advance warning that death could come)." [You may say to yourself], "Say, my good friend, even though I am able to move about [OK],[270] there's something (i.e., a sickness, disease, defect, etc.) that's just lying in wait there [in my body] (*chinthu chidangoyala uko*). Now this very thing I just know that some day it's going to take me away (*chidzanditenga*, i.e., be the cause of my death)." So is this the time to be playing around with your Chriiiistianity (*n'kumachita masewera ndi chikristu*)?

You know [as you tell yourself], "This thing is most certainly going to take me!"__You know, "This very disease makes me sick every month, every month I'm sick – [I just know that] this disease is going to take me!" Then you see that after only two weeks, you're sick again – after three weeks you're sick again, the very same disease.__[You say], "Look here now, [after I die] don't start arguing about how I, your mother, died (*amai afa bwanji*) – [or] how I, your father, died![271] My friend, even though I've been

---

[69] Wame here applies the keynote of his parabolic witches' tale to his audience: Each and every person must take care to examine ("look towards") his/her own life – past, present, and future – including one's physical condition. This is all part of "getting ready" to meet the Lord, whenever He might call one "home."

[70] This saying may be a play off the idiomatic expression, *chimene chiyenda n'chachabechabe*, lit., 'the thing that is moving about (one's body) is completely useless,' i.e., the way a person moves about reveals that s/he is not well at all.

[71] While this might be an innocent query concerning the cause of a loved one's chronic illness, it could also be an allusion to the suspicions of witchcraft that arise in such instances. In other words, *who is the person* (witch/sorcerer) who has cast a spell on so-and-so to cause them such sickness? Thus Wame suggests that accusations of this nature are out of place; God is simply indicating to the sick person that s/he is about to be called "home." In this entire closing section, it is sometimes difficult to determine whether Wame's sermon *persona* is speaking to himself (or to a close family member) – or whether Wame is himself addressing the congregation. It could well be that this ambiguity is deliberate, another way of involving the present audience more directly in the psychological action that is evoked by his message.

mooooving about (i.e., living), I been troubled (lit., 'moving') with these things. Is this the time for me to be playing around with my Christianity (i.e., my faith-life)?!"

"WHEN YOU PRACTICE WIIIITCHCRAFT, YOU MUST LOOK TOWARDS THE LAKE, lest the dawn arise upon you." [Your] TIIME is up! The TIME when they will complete the [heavenly] meeting [concerning when I am to die] is unknown to me. My brothers (also "sisters"!), my brothers, "I WILL NOT TAKE ANY CAAATTLE from your hooouuse (i.e., homestead), for ALL OF THEM are mine. But as for YOOOUU, if I were hungry, I wouldn't tell yoouuu." "The death of a cockerel requires no cooouuunsel!" This is what is important for us – let's get ready [to die as a Christian]!"[272]

Let us close our eyes and pray._Let us close our eyes and pray._Let us close our eyes![273]

There's no other way that we can do (i.e., follow) than You, O LOOORD. INDEED I SEEEE that my TIIIIME [here on earth] is coming to an end, and at any day I can depart [on my journey]. Now since I do not know that day, I want to be prepared, ready to go. Lord, come – enter my heart! Lord, come – rule in my heart! Even though I depart todaaay, you are my way [to heaven]. Even though I depart tomorrow, or whether I depart the day after, or even next year, you are my way. JEEESUS, Son of God, I am calling you! Come, O come! IN THIS EVIL TIME, [I] DON'T WANT to be left without Jesus (*osasiyana ndi Yesu*), for death is rushing about [everywhere]. Diseases, diseases [everywhere]... Many people [are on] their

---

[272] Wame neatly rounds out his sermon by reiterating its key thematic motifs, both biblical and secular (folk wisdom), including the main message itself: Get ready to go to your God! Certainly if any listener does not leave this worship service with that theme firmly etched on his/her mind, it is not Wame's fault, for he has dramatically recycled it in a variety of rhetorically powerful ways via an inductive technique that arises from within the ancient tradition of Chichewa verbal declamatory and didactic art.

[273] There follows one of the longest prayers – actually two in combination – of the Wame sermonic corpus. In his various petitions he also further elaborates on the Christological and Christian implications and imperatives of what he has just preached about, thus making them part of the entire congregation's joint appeal to their merciful God. Thus Christians need not fear death's journey, because Christ has prepared their way to eternal life. In typical revivalist fashion, special attention is given (through the device of quoted direct speech) to those individuals in the audience who may feel that they need some special, personal assurance that this message is meant for them and that they must make a real commitment to act upon it, by the enabling power of Christ.

journey to the village (home).
Mother, perhaps you are saying, "Aah! please help me to pray (*ine thandizeniko kupemphera*)! Truly (*n'zoonadi*), I don't want to play any more games with my women's fellowship (*chigwirizano*), [with] my church leadership._I can really see this evil time. I don't want to play any more games (*ndi[sa]chitenso masewera*) with my choir, no more games with my ministry, no more games with the work to which the Lord has sent me._I don't want to play any more games in this evil time!" Just lift up your hand (*tangokwezani mkono wanu*), and I'll help you to pray – right at the very spot where you are sitting. AT THIS [EVIL] TIME, DON'T PLAAAAY with [your] salvation, for the TIME is running out! ANYBODY who sees how things are in this world must know that, "Ah-no, [surely] the earth is at an end (*dziko latha*)!" Raise your hand, let's help one another to pray._Thank you very much._May God bless you!

Mother, you alone are remaining behind (*mwatsala nokha*, i.e., are not responding to the call to repent)._Mister, you alone are remaining behind. Perhaps you don't know that this very day your [heavenly] council adjourned (*msonkhano wanu walephereka*, i.e., thus giving you another chance to repent). If you knew [for sure], you wouldn't be playing games. My brother (*mchimwene*), if you knew [for sure], you wouldn't be playing games. Let's close our eyes and pray. While your hands are still up in the air we will pray. [For] your own prayer, you can say [something like this]: "Come, Lord Jesus, enter into my heart. I really want to be ready [to depart]. It may just be that truly [I] am going to encounter these words, 'Say, isn't this that rooster?!' – but I am ready – by believing and receiving you, Jesus, as my Saviour."

Let us pray: In the name of Jesus Christ which has POWER (*mphamvu*) and authority (*ulamuliro*) – you who have been given ALL POOWER in heaven and on earth – look upon your people. THEY KNOW THAT OF THEMSELVES they are unable to reach heaven, not at all...OONLY [if] you, JEEESUS, enter their hearts. CAST DOWN THE POOOWER (*mugwetse mphamvu*) and the authority of Satan (*Satana*) so that you, Jesus, [rule as] king. For you yourself were the one who said, "You will receive power after the Holy Spirit (*mzimu woyera*) comes upon you – POWER that cannot retreat (or weaken, *siidzabwerera m'mbuyo*) – POWER that [will prevent] Satan [from] touching their bodies (i.e., to tempt to use as instru ments of sin) – POWER that [will prevent] them from giving a testimony to you (*kukuchitirani inu umboni*).

O Lord, take control of their life (*tengani ulamuliro wa moyo wao*).[274] TAKE their mouths. Take their hands, their eyes, their ears, their tongues, their legs – so that AAALL [of these members] can give a testimony to you, and so that all people everywhere may be assured that there is amazing POOOWER in you, Jesus. We have seen, Lord, these great things that you have done [for us]. Hear our crying. Hear our calling! Not [by] might, not [by] warfare, but [by] your Spirit...(we will prevail). In your name, Jesus Christ, our living Saviour, we pray – Ameen!

"Christian Offerings – Storing Up Treasures in Heaven!" (SW40)[275]

The Word of God [today] comes from three books. The fiiirst book – we will read from the book of Job, chapter 38 – Job chapter 38, we read from verse 1 – Job chapter 38. We read from verse 1. [Here is] the heading (*mau otsogolera*): "God appears to Job without rebuking him. But he reminds him of the surpassing greatness of God. Job humbles himself." Verse 1: "Then God answered Job in the whirlwind and said, 'Who is he who darkens advice, with words having no wisdom? Tie yourself up in the waist now as a male; let me ask you [so that] you might inform me. Where were you back then when I set in place the foundation of the world? Explain if you know [how to] perceive [something]. Who traced out its boundary, since you know? Who measured out its string? Its foundation was dug out of what? Or who set in place its cornerstone?"[276]

And we also go to Luke chapter 20 – the book of Luke chapter 20, and I will begin at verse 9. [The heading is]: "Parable of the people who tilled a garden of grapes." Verse 9: "And he (Jesus) began to speak to the people

---

[274] This particular utterance would seem to be a clear instance of a calque, that is, a direct loan translation of a common English (religious) expression.
[275] This is a sermon that Shadrack Wame preached in Lilongwe at the 105th anniversary celebration of the Zambezi Evangelical Church in Malawi (1997; no more precise information on the actual setting was given). It is the longest sermon in the entire Wame corpus, lasting over an hour and a quarter!
[276] Again the translation as it reads (sounds) is rather difficult to understand due to its literalness. Not only does it suggest that it was Job who was in the whirlwind, but it also reports that Job was trying to tie himself up in there.

this parable (lit., 'comparison,' *fanizo*): 'A person owned a garden of grapes (*munda wamphesa*),[277] and he lent it out to tillers, and he went to another land, and he spent a long time there. And at the season of fruit, he sent his slave to the gardeners [to ask them to] give him [some] fruit of that garden. The gardeners beat him and sent him back without giving him anything. And he again sent another slave, and he too they beat up, and mocked him, and sent him back without giving him anything. And he again sent another, the third, and he too they stabbed and threw him outside [the garden]. And the garden owner said, 'What will I do? And now (Wame adds this, *ndipo*) I will send my child,[278] whom I love very much. Perhaps they will show him some respect.' But those gardeners when they saw him [coming], they told one another, 'This is the owner who will inherit (lit., enter') the house.[279] Let's kill him so that the whole inheritance will be ours.' And so they threw him outside the garden and killed him. Now what should the garden owner do? He will arrive and will destroy those gardeners and give [the] garden to some others. And when they heard [this] they (who?) said,[280] 'Do not speak like that!'" – Verse 17: "But he (Jesus) looked at them carefully and said, 'What is this that was written, "The rock which the house-builders rejected, this very one became the cornerstone." And everyone who falls on this rock will be smashed; but he upon whom it falls, it will kill.' And the group of great ('high') priests kept trying to grab him with their hands at that very time. And they feared the people because they perceived that he spoke about them in this parable."

And let us finish up with the book of Psalms, number 116 – the book of Psalms number 116, verse 12: "WHAT shall I return to Jehovah (*Yehova*) because of AAALL his kindness which he has done for me?"

---

[277] Wame may have deliberately modified the literal Chewa text (*Buku Lopatulika*) in the interest of meaningfulness. The original wording reads: "A person *hoed* (*analima*) a garden of grapes," which like the NT Greek text (lit., 'he planted') does not make so much sense here since the "person" being referred to is clearly the garden's owner (cf. v. 13), who would have laborers to do the actual work.

[278] In the Chewa text it is ambiguous as to whether this 'child' (*mwana*) is male or female, as is the gender of the 'owner' him/herself. However, the assumption would be that males are meant.

[279] Wame adds the word *owner* (*mwini*) to the Chichewa Bible to make the implication clear(er) that the garden's "heir" is being referred to, though the concept is still difficult to grasp both linguistically and culturally (i.e., the notion of inheriting a plot of land or a farm), especially among the matrilineal, matrilocal Chewa people.

[280] The pronominal references in the literal *Buku Lopatulika* Bible text become very difficult to follow in this section, not only due to the lack of clear nominal antecedents but also because the third person, bound subject marker (prefix) on the verb is not distinguished as to singular or plural.

May the good LORD bless these words, and may honour be [given] to him for all time! Amen.

Greeetings to all of you in the name of our Lord Jesus Christ. We praise the Lord that he has favoured us in his HEART (*watikomera mtima*) [to allow] us to meet together again at [this] good time when we are celebrating (lit., 'remembering') in thiiis church – that we are 105 years old. Now while we are celebrating on a day like today – it's a very GREEEAT day... Say, for these 105 years what have we accomplished (lit., 'done')? The MESSAGE which God wants to speak to us is [about] the RESPONSIBILITY (*udindo*) of a Christian.

Let us close our eyes and pray: We have COME again to your roooyal throne, O God, knowing that YOU are our help who is always ever found (*thandizo lathu lopezekeratu*). And we know that when we come to YOU, everything we ask we will receive, for we have seen the GREAT THINGS that you have done for us when we prayed. But we have also seen GREAT THINGS for which we are at a loss (*tithedwa nzeru*) to thank you [properly]. And so THIS VERY LOOOVE OF YOURS has once again gathered us right here. Since you KNOW what we need, speak to us. Since you KNOW the very BOOOTTOM of our hearts, Lord, continue to bless us – just as you began to be with us that morning (i.e., when the meeting started), since we are a needy people at all times. OOOPEN our eyes to see the priceless TREASURE (*chuma chamtengo wapatali*) that you have brought for us. Lord, do not leave us alone. It is not [by] POWER, not [by] fighting [that we gain the victory], but [by] your Spirit. In your name, Lord Jesus, we pray. Ameen!

THE MESSAGE WE HAVE HERE is a waaaarning (*chenjeeezo*) – the RESPONSIBILITY of a Christian. When we receive JEEESUS, he gives us three things.[281] ONE – the forgiveness of sins [and] eternal life. Number TWO – he gives us a gift, the work of serving the Lord. Number THREE – he gives us people so that we might serve those [very] people. EEEVRY ONE of you who have received Jesus were given [these] three things. EEEVERY ONE of us has a responsibility in the Lord's church, because this is from God himself. But the thing that really pains me a lot (*chikundi-*

---

[281] These three divinely given gifts are obviously listed in their order of theological priority.

sautsa ine) [is the fact that] CHRIIISTIANS DO NOT KNOW that they have a responsibility in the church of the Lord. The work of God they simply leave to the pastors alone.

So it is that these Christians, instead of recognizing their responsibility, they quarrel with [their] pastors. [They say], "THIS PASTOR has destroyed the congregation!"[282] "THIS PASTOR [has caused] the congregation to be destroyed!"[283] "THIS PASTOR has come here just to 'eat' our money (*kudzangotidyera ndalama*)!" "THIS PASTOR is a corpse (*mtembo*, metaphor for an unproductive person), awaaay with him!" THE CHURCH HAS FAAAALLEN because of this pastor – because of this pastor!" [These are] INSULTING WOOORDS (*mau a mwanooo*) – if you ever spoke this way, don't do it again – pleeease! You are sinning against the PASTOR! Do not repeat [such] wiiicked words – [so] insulting!

A PASTOR, as a herdsman of sheep,[284] his work is to feed those sheep, to lead them to good pasture. A SICK ONE [he brings] to the veterinary clinic (*kuvetenale*) so that it can be given an injection of medicine (*adzailase mankhwala*)! Ehee-hee-hee! (Wame laughs as does the congregation.) Amen! (more laughter) The one with a broken leg [he must] make a splint for it. The one that cannot walk [he] carries upon his shoulders – the [whole] journey back to the village. That is the work of a pastor.

But in order for THOSE SHEEP TO REPRODUCE (*ziswane*), the question is – who produces sheep, the shepherd or the sheep – the one who produces its fellow (*amaswa mnzake*) is WHOOO? The one who produces its fellow is the sheep, right? – it's not the shepherd, right (*eti*)? That is why I said "insulting words" (i.e., referring to the hypothetical complaints spoken earlier). When a pastor comes, he does not produce sheep, but the sheep reproduce themselves – insults! (applause of approval from the congregation) Wicked words – wicked words![285]

---

[282] The Chewa word *mpingo* (pl. *mipingo*) can be translated either as "church" (people) or "congregation." In secular terms it refers to a large crowd/group of people, usually organized in some way.

[283] Wame here gives another one of his characteristic repeated frame utterances, in this case, one that highlights the various complaints that congregational members often unjustly level against their pastor.

[284] The Chichewa word for herdsman (*mbusa*, i.e., caring for cows, goats, sheep, etc.) is used to render the Christian term *pastor*, usually found as a plural of respect in direct address, *abusa*.

[285] Wame's point with this humorous example of course is that it is the members' job to be intensely involved in evangelism and church growth – even more so than the pastor, whose primary responsibility

Now [there are] some OOOOLD congregations [having only] thirty members – today I am revealing [to you] – the reason. Answer me this (*kodi inu*): what do they call a female barren sheep (*dzina lake amati chia* –)? A "barrenness" (*zinzii*, the congregation responds as well.) Well, what if it's a barren male, what is its name (*dzina lake nlota* –)? A "barren" (*mfuleni*), right? (*mfuu* – Wame here breaks into laughter, along with the congregation.)[286] Aleluuya! Today we're reveeeealing [everything]! An OOOOLD CONGREGATION [having only] 30 members, you children (*ananuu*) – WHY is that? [It's because] among the sheep of that congregation there are "barrennesses" and "barrens" that don't reproduce! PAAASTORS do not bear sheep, rather the sheep reproduce themselves! Don't ever talk like that again – don't ever talk like that again![287]

Right here as I am speaking, there are some [among you] who began their Christianity long ago (*chikristu mudachiyamba kale*) [but] there is not a SINGLE person whom they have witnessed to about Jesus – who came to know Jesus as his or her Saviour because of you. If it had been [the case] that [this] meeting would continue, we'd have said, "Tomorrow let us come back and EEACH one bring a person to whom we had witnessed so that s/he knows Jesus. And then that person would come right up here and testify [by saying],[288] "As for me, I recognize [who] JEEESUS [is] because of this person (*yaawa*, an honorific pronominal reference)." If I would say, "Bring him tomorrow," would you come with anybody? "Barrens" would not bring anyone tomorrow, not at all! (laughter) "Barrennesses" would not bring anyone tomorrow. (laughter) It is for this reason that the CHUUURCH is falling down (*uli kugwa pansi*).

---

is to care for the sheep that have already been gathered. The people listening had probably never heard the case for lay responsibility put in this novel way before. They should not be engaged in complaining about their pastor for the lack of progress (which Wame calls "insults" and "wicked words"), but rather be willing to commit themselves to doing something about the situation themselves.

[286] While certainly not pejorative, the specific terms that Wame uses here for "barren" animals were probably never heard by this congregation in a church service before—hence their enthusiastic reaction. Some perhaps anticipated where the preacher was taking them with this novel example.

[287] Wame again reproves church members who are always complaining about their pastor, but who do nothing, or very little, themselves to help the congregation to grow.

[288] The Chichewa words for 'witness' and 'testimony' are the same, i.e., *umboni*. Thus there is a little play on meanings here: X witnesses to Y about Jesus; Y, in turn, testifies to the congregation about the witness of X.

So what do YOU think – if EEEVERY Christian had [this] responsibility, we would say, let's have a competition (*mpikisano*) such that from January up until December EEEVERY ONE [of us] would bear witness [to Jesus]. But even if you don't know how to preach, could it truly be that from January to December he (pronominal *enallage*) could fail to attract a single person (*ndi mmodzi yemwe osamkopa*) – could not announce to him about Jesus [so that he might be] converted (*wosatembenuka mtima*, 'to be turned around in the heart')? Even though you do not know how to preach, could it truly be that [after] 12 months [you would not have] a single person – could this happen, could it happen (*zingatheke*)? EVEN THOUGH YOU DO NOT KNOW how to preach, but [look for] a single person until he has been fooound – perhaps two, three, five, maybe ten. If in that church there were thirty Christians, at the end of the year [there would be] sixty. After another year – sixty, [then] one hundred and twenty! YES, I'm revealing eeeverything (*ndiululaaa*) today – in that church of yours, if the church is falling, [it means that] there are too many "barrens" [and] "barrennesses"! Don't talk about [the pastor] again, not at all. So now the "barrennesses" [and] the "barrens" [who are] right here are looking down (in embarrassment, *zyooli*, ideophone). (laughter) They are right here (laughter) – [you must] look at me!²⁸⁹

ON THAT VERY DAY THAT YOU RECEIVED JEEESUS, you were given three things: [spiritual] LIIIIFE, a GIIIIFT (to serve the Lord with), and people who need to be witnessed to.²⁹⁰ You should know these things as of today. A PASTOR, as (if he is) a [good] pastor (*mbusa monga mbusa*) is performing his duties. He is giving (lit., 'feeding') you the Lord's Supper. He is preaching at [your] funerals. He you at the time of baptism. And in the midst [of all that work, he conducts] revival services (*zitsitsimutso*). A PASTOR, if he is a [good] one, visits [your] sick people –

---

²⁸⁹ Although the bare English transcription might suggest that Wame is being perhaps a bit too pugnacious or aggressive with his listeners in this section, the actual tape recording indicates that they heartily approved of his approach, as indicated by their various enthusiastic responses. This is another good example of his vigorous, interactive sermon technique: No member of the congregation sleeps – or even dozes – when Wame preaches (this was confirmed on videotape in the case of a sermon over an hour long).

²⁹⁰ Wame returns to the little "revelation" that he began his sermon with – namely, the fact that a believer "receives" three spiritual blessings when s/he by faith "receives" Jesus Christ. By this time, however, it is possible that the first two blessings might be understood in a purely physical way, i.e., life and (material) gifts (*mphatso*, the singular and plural forms of this Chewa noun are the same).

at the hospital [and] house to house. A PASTOR, if he is a [good] one, is fulfilling [his task of] feeding [his] sheep with the gospel.

But A PAAASTOR – what ought to happen, that is, as he keeps on feeding those sheeeep, he should milk them (*azikame mkaka*) so that he too can get faaaat (*anenepeee*), e-eh! Well, should you just get fat by yourselves? E-eeh! (laughter) So as he feeds those fat sheep, he should bring along a big bottle (*chibotolo*, i.e., to take some of their milk for himself!)... (laughter – Wame laughs too and has to pause). AALELUYAA! (Amen!) He must MIIILK [the sheep] so that he too can get fat! Hey, should you just get fat by yourselves? Should you get fat by yourselves? Do you know what is means to milk [the sheep]? [It is when] you give a little sugar (*kashuga*) to the pastor [saying], "Here, Pastor, use this to make some porridge for the children" – then he's received some MILK (*waakama pamenepo*)! (laughter) "Paaastor, here's a little bread (*kabuledi*)" – aah! [and so on] like that. "So [Pastor], what will you have?" – then he's received some MILK! "Pastor, here's a little shirt (*kashati aka*).[291] Perhaps if it's too tight, you can let me know – until it fits right. Well, we'd just like to thank [you] (i.e., for your pastoral services)" – then he's received some MILK! "Pastor, here's a little bicycle for you to use when you have to travel a long distance" – then he's received some MILK! "Pastor, here are the keys to [this] car" – then he's received some MILK! Allow him too to get FAAAAT! HE FEEEEDS [the flock], so let him receive some of the. miiilk!

But do you know what is really sad (*chomvetsa chisoni*)? There are some sheep who when the pastor is trying to get some milk – give him a boot BAAAAH! (ideophone, i.e., the sheep kicks him hard with a hind leg!) (laughter all around) [What a] BAAAD SHEEEP! (laughter) A bad sheep – a bad sheep! If it had been one of these "sheep" of ours – [one of these] goats, well then why not just sell it?![292] (laughter) [Or why not just]

---

[291] The various items mentioned here as being donated to the pastor (in an ascending series) are not really "small/little" in size or amount. The use of such diminutive forms is simply an idiomatic and honorific way of deflecting attention (or praise) from oneself as one presents a gift to someone, especially to a respected individual. The point too is that if every Christian plays his/her part, a pastor will be well supported through their cooperative efforts on his behalf.

[292] In central Africa, Malawi in particular, sheep are relatively rare; there is simply not enough good pastureland available. Thus the closest formal cultural equivalent is the goat (*mbuzi*), which is unfortunately not nearly the same either in social-functional terms or in popular connotation (i.e., male goats

SLAAAUGHTER (lit., 'kill') it?! – just go ahead and slaughter such a bad sheep! [It says], "The Pastor must get no milk!" If he tries to milk it – it boots him *BAAAH!* (it kicks him again). Aah, nooo! WHAT A BAAAD SHEEP! Say YOOOU, what kind of sheep are you? Are you a SHEEEEP that kicks [your] pastor with [both] legs (*mateki*)? This question – I want you to take it back home with you.

However, we pastors have to be caaareful here (i.e., in this matter). If a certain sheep is not fat enough, instead of squeezing out milk, you will squeeze out BLOOOOD (*mukama magazi*)! (laughter) ALELUUUYAAA! (Ameen!) A-ha-haa! (laughter) You will squeeze out BLOOOD! He-hee! (laughter) Instead of...[tending the flock], maaany pastors are chased away (*ali kuthamangitsidwa*)! When they are chased away [like that], we know that he was squeezing out blood! (more laughter all around) Ehee-hee! Because the GIIIFTS which Christians give us pastors vary according to (*zimasinthitsana*) the character (*khalidwe*) of the pastor. If a pastor has no character, he squeezes out blooood – he squeezes out blood. (The congregation claps.) [In] many congregations the pastors – [in] many congregations the church elders [do this]: when the congregation gives its offering, they simply "EAT" (*angokudya*, i.e., steal) that offering until the congregation becomes offended (*ukhumudwa*). Today I'm saying that you should not become offended. You are not giving to pastors.__You are not giving to church elders.__You are giving to God (*Mulungu*). As for THEEEM, if they EEEAT [the offerings], a curse (*tsoka*) is theirs!__They will have to look out for themselves (*akadzionera*) before the face of God (i.e., at his judgement; the congregation claps and cheers). This is because the GIIIFTS which we receive vary according to the character of the pastor. So it is that you have no character, then it's blood [that you'll be squeezing out]!

Let us not speak any more bad words [about each other], no more. SHEEEEP produce sheep just like themselves.__A PAAASTOR does not produce a sheep, not at all. EEEACH ONE of you (i.e., pastors and their people) has a responsibility. We "take" churches today like we take busses (*mabasi*). We just flop all over the seats (*kungokhalakhala m'mipando*) with our legs hanging down *KHOOBAA!* (an ideophone that depicts this action)

---

carry an undesirable sexual component of semantic significance). Through the use of this humorous illustration of ungrateful sheep (or goats), Wame is subtly making an implicit, preparatory linkage with Christ's parable of the wicked tenants (Luke 20) that is considered next.

in our seats. BUUUT the congregation gives him (i.e., the pastor) grief (*kusaukana naye*), just like we do in a bus. [The people say], "DRIIIVER, [give it] some more FIIIRE (*moooto*)! More fire! (laughter) Why [are we going so slowly], we want to arrive in good time, WEEE do! More FIIIRE, DRIIIVER!" [So they speak] as their legs are just hanging and swinging there *KHOOBAA!* (laughter) They are always quarrelling with their pastor [saying], "This pastor is a corpse.__He just came here to eat up [our] money!" But [as they say this] their legs are just hanging there limply *KHOOBAA!* There's nothing that you are doing to help that pastor.__You simply say, "MORE FIIIRE – more fire! Let's get [quickly] to heaven (*ulendo wakumwamba*)!" It's a shame (*kumvetsa chisoni*). (laughter)

THE CONGREGAAATION is like a BOOOAT – over there at the laaake. When we row (*tikamapalasa*) a BOOOAT, EEEVERYONE must take an oar (*chopalasira*). And a boat (i.e., a dugout canoe) like that travels with speed (*liwiro*).__It really races along, just as if it had an engine (*injini*).[293] But if we leave [just] one person out, that boooat doesn't move so fast. That's how it is with a congregation. EEEVERYONE has a responsibility. And if EEEVERYONE knew his (her) responsibility, our congregation would not fall down at all. But from this very day, EEEVERYONE of you knows that you have a responsibility in the church.__The work is not that of the pastor alone, not at all.

[Here's] a warning: THE WOORDS THAT we read here (i.e., from the Scriptures) [are] some TROUBLING WORDS, which are troubling me in my heart. HEERE we read in Luke chapter 20, especially beginning at verse 9 and ending at verse 18. HEERE we read the PAAARABLE of the gardeners (i.e., tenants). When the Lord JEESUS was preaching the good message (*uthenga wabwino*), and he presented this parable, he was with all [the people] along with his disciples.

And JEESUS stood up.__He says, "A certain man had a gaaarden (i.e., a plot of land).__He began a farming development scheme (*anatsekula esiteti*, lit. 'he opened up an estate').[294] For someone to begin such a farm (*esiteti*)

---

[293] Here is another easily visualizable scene that Wame utilizes from his own local setting, namely, the area of Salima, near Lake Malawi. Thus the audiences is able to imaginatively see one of his sermons, even as they hear it being preached. The point he is making is thereby also correspondingly reinforced.

[294] As is his custom, Wame here contextualizes the biblical (Lukan) account so that it harmonizes with a

is no game at all (*si masewero ayi*, i.e., a great deal of labour and expense is involved). Money was spent – [for] tractors (*mathalakitala*) to uproot trees – tractors for plowing up the soil, for making rows (i.e., furrows) – with labourers everywhere. MOONEY was spent – to buy hoes [and] new sickles. He spent a LOOOOT of wealth – right up until that FIELD (farm) was finished. So he prepared rows [for planting] and was waiting for the rain to fall so he could plant.__And AAALL his seed was ready (*leede*). As you know, [at such] an "estate" [you can] see maize, rice, groundnuts, millet – SEEED of every sort, it was all REEEADY! Then a message (lit., 'words') [calling] "O KIIING!" [arrived] just as the time for planting drew near and the rains were close by – ALL OF A SUDDEN (*MWADZIDZIDZI!*, ideophone) he set off on a journey. And [on] that journey he travelled to a country FAAAAAARR AWAAAY. And there where he went, he arrived when the time was already past finished (*nthawi yothaitha*), [so] he could not start (lit., 'open') another gaaarden. He could not start another "estate" since he arrived when the time was already past finished – [when] his colleagues (i.e., other farmers) had already finished plowing (and all).[295]

Since this king (or 'chief') was [so] good-hearted (*yabwino mtima*), HIS HEART pained him (i.e., before he left on his long journey). [He said to himself], "I have come from a country faaaar awaaay.__Just look, I suffered so much for that garden of mine, opening up an "estate," and spent a lot of [my] wealth [on it]. So now that I'm gone away, is this garden of mine going to be destroyed? Have I expended my strength for NOOOTHING (*pachabeee*)?!"

The king was deeply troubled at heart (*idavutika mkati mwamtima*). He said [to himself], "I cannot do otherwise.__Jealousy (*jelasi*, i.e., a bad attitude) is no good!" So he decided to call [his] people, "COOME HEEERE – let me give you this garden of mine. I put a great deal of effort into it

---

present-day rural setting in Malawi. In this case he conjures up the image of one of the large, well-run (and productive) agricultural farming schemes for which the country is well known in the region.

[295] The chiastic (A:B::B:A) semantic arrangement that is manifested in these last two sentences may be an oral, discourse-level signal that one narrative unit has come to an end while another is about to begin. It is interesting to observe all the local-color details and additional plot motivation that Wame supplies in his retelling of Christ's parable. The rhetorical purpose of course is the same as Christ's in the original event – namely, to draw the audience into the tale and encourage them to emotively identify with the good-hearted king/estate owner as the central crisis is evoked.

(*ndavutika nawoo*). But the TIME WAS RIGHT [for developing it] just as I was leaving. That my garden might [possibly] be destroyed, [you] gardeners, greatly troubles my heart. EEEVERY ONE of you come here so that I might apportion it out to you. Grow any type of crop that you might wish. Just let EEEVERY ONE of you farm. Those who want cotton, let them grow [it], [those who want] maize, let them grow [it], or perhaps it's rice, let them grow [it]. Let EEEVERY ONE of you grow [something], according to your wishes."

So I think that those people were happy because they found a garden already prepared for planting (lit., 'already opened up', *munda wotsekulatsekula*) – all the work was done alreeeady. All they had to do was to take their seed and go plaaant it. They rejoiced and JUMPED [for joy] (*nalumphalumpha*).

So the king went to that land FAAAR AWAAAY. Since he arrived there when the time [for planting] was over, he did not open up anoooother garden plot. And when the time of... for harvesting arrived, the time for eating [green] maize, the time when many other things have ripened, that king was seized with a great longing (*chifundo chidamugwira*) there in that far-off land. [He said], "I want some roasted MAAAAIZE!" A great looonging had SEEEIZED HIM. "I want a few toasted GROOOUNDNUTS!" A great looonging had SEEEIZED HIM. So he said, "I can do nothing else. I will send my SEEERVANT. He can go request a SIIINGLE cob of maize from those people to whom I left the gaaarden. [I have] A GREEEAT LOOONGING – I will ROOOAST [it]!"

So he summoned his servants (lit., 'slaves') and sent ooone of them. And when he arrived there, they welcomed him [saying], "E-eeh (exclamation of surprise), mister, what can we do for you? Is everything alright (*nkwabwino*)?" And he said, "Pardon me, great elders (*pepani, akuluakulu*, an honorific expression), I don't mean to be rude (*si chipongwe*, i.e., when I ask you this). [But] the king who gave you this gaaarden has sent meee to ask you to please give him [out of your] mercy a single maize cob to roooast [back] there."[296] [They replied], "WHAAAT (*chiaaani*) are you

---

[296] The key term mercy (*chifundo*) is the same Chewa word that was rendered as "great longing" above. Thus in order to satisfy the king's "longing," the tenants would have to show him a little "mercy," which is of course a great understatement because it was the king who had supplied them with

saying?!" [The servant repeated], "Just a single maize cob [by your] mercy so that he might roast [it]." "WHAAAT?!" Immediately after saying "what?" they said (i.e., before giving the servant another chance to reply), "Shut-up (*shat-apu!*)!²⁹⁷ [We're telling] youuu – you (i.e., the king) just eat away (i.e., enjoy yourself) while we have to trouble ourselves labouring for you here. STOOOMP HIM (*m'pondeeeni!*)! GRAAAAB HIM! (*m'gwireeeni!*)" Immediately they began to chaaase him.__[They caught him] and POOOW! (*PHAAA!*, ideophone), they beat him up. But [by] the grace of God (*chisomo cha Mulungu*)²⁹⁸ he escaped.

He arrived before the king, covered with dust – white *MBUU!* (ideophone) and said, "O King, I might have DIIIED [back there]!" "Why, what happened?" [The servant] replied, "They say that you are just eating awaaaay [here], a-aah!... they say, while they must trouble themseeeelves even to the point of suffering on account of their hoooeing. They say that we are simply eating away [here] while they are the ones who are being troubled with [all] the wooork!" The king did not BELIEEEVE [this, and said], "YOOOU are lying!__You are LYYYING!" THE KING DID NOT BELIEEEVE [his servant, and said], "I'm going to send your fellow [servant]!"

He sent a fellow [servant], and he too arrived [and said], "Pardon me, Masters (*mabwana*), I don't want to be rude, [but] the king who left you this garden has sent meee. He desires a single cob of maize for roasting, [by your] mercy!" "WHAAAT did you say?!" "A single maize cob..."

---

their prepared fields in the first place, all ready to plant. When the servant requests a "single ear of maize," this is another instance of depreciating or reducing the statement, here a request, as a verbal form of respect. In fact, the king wanted more than a single ear – but a reasonable amount, as deemed appropriate by the addressees. This is another instance of the subtle idiomatic nuances that permeate the many little internal dialogues of Wame's sermons. In his dramatic presentation of this exchange, he realistically plays all the speaking parts himself (normally only two, but sometimes more) with the diction and intonation that is natural for each role in the particular interpersonal situation that is being portrayed. At times, the dialogue is so thick that we find a quote within a quote, for example, at the end of the third paragraph down from this. There is also a lot of internal speech, when a character talks (aloud) to him/herself.

²⁹⁷ English borrowings and calques (loan translations) like this (*shatapu!*) punctuate Wame's dialogues, lending a touch of humor, emotion, emphasis and realism to what is being said.

²⁹⁸ The Chewa word *chisomo* was used in the old Bible to render 'grace,' but it really means 'good luck' or 'fair fortune' (a quality that is humanly derived or focused), which is not really the best way to express the original biblical concept. The new translation in Chichewa [Buku Loyera] uses a verbal expression, *kukomera mtima* 'to favor someone in heart' to convey this crucial notion.

"SHUT-UP! STOMP ON HIM!" They grabbed him by the neck and squeezed *PSII!* (ideophone). But fortunately (*mwamwai*) he escaaaaped. When he arrived before the king he was covered white with dust *MBU!* He said, "O King, I might have diiiied [back there]!" "WHY - WHAAAT [happened]?!" "They are saying that you are just eating [here], while they are troubled [there] with all the woooork. They even showed me the sores where their hoes cuuuut them (i.e., as they were hoeing with such great vigour).[299] I might have diiiied [there]!" But the king did not BELIEEEVE [him, and said], "YOU ARE LYYYING! YOU ARE LYYYING!" [The king continues, speaking now to a different servant], "You go, you the third one (*wa nambala filii*)!"

The third [servant] also went [there and said], "Pardon me, Masters, I don't mean to be rude, [but] the king THEEEERE who left you [this] garden has sent meeee." "So what are you saying! What are you saying! Don't let him speak!" They grabbed him by the neck *PSI!* [and said], "You are the ones eating [there] while we are [here] being troubled with work. SHUT UP!" Immediately they began to chaaaase him and they threw him oooout. He arrived back theeere [and said], "O KIIING, I MIGHT HAVE DIIIED!" "Why - what [happened]?!" "THEY ARE SAYING THAT YOU ARE JUST EEEATING [here], WHILE THEY ARE BEING TROUBLED WITH WOOORK!" [The king] replies, "A-ah! Nooo! Nooo! You are LYYYYING! YOU ARE LYYYYING!" The king did not believe him [and said], "I will send MY VERY OWN, MY VERY OWN, MY VERY OOOOWN (*wanga, wanga, wangaaaa*) son. Because they think that you are ROOOBERS - because this son of mine they KNOOOW... [Then] they will realize - they will know for sure - [saying] that, 'Eeh yeees! It's truuue! It's true, they were telling the truth! Isn't this his son who's coming up here?!' Yes, I'm going to send my son."

So the king sent his son. As soon as the son CAME INTO VIIIIEW (*atongotulukira*), AAAALL the tenants (*matenanti*) saaid, "Do you see that child coming theeere?" [Others] replied, "Yeees!" "He is the child (i.e., son) of that king. When the king dies, then this garden will belong to this very boy. What we can do now to get the garden is to kill the boy. Let's

---

[299] The servant appears to embellish his report at this point, perhaps to make an impression upon the king about his near escape from death. In any case, by the mournful sound of his voice (as mimicked by Wame), he must have been telling the truth!

just stab him *PHOO!* (ideophone), finish! (*bass!*) the garden will be ours! Do you see this garden, this fertile garden (*munda wachondee*) – do you see this garden, this garden of crops to harvest (*munda wadzinthu*)? Should this child take [all these things]? LET'S KIIILL HIM so that the garden becomes OOOOOURS!"

The son arriiived [and said], "Pardon me, great elders, I don't wish to be rude, [but] my father has sent meeee. He [only] desires a single cob of maize..." E-EEEH! He didn't even finish [speaking]! [They stabbed him] in the neck *PHOOOO!* The son cried out, "You've wounded me!" [They replied], "SHUT UP! You are the ones who are just eating while we are troubled [here] with all the work!" [They stabbed him again] *PHOOO!* – until they killed that BOOOY and threw [his corpse] out in the BUUUSH.[300]

Later the king heard the message [saying], "Your son has GONE AWAAAY (*wapitaaa*, a euphemism for death)!" My, but the king was suffering now in his heeeart (*idasauka mumtima mwakeeee*). [He exclaimed], "They've killed my son?!" "Yeeees (*eeeh*)!" "A-aaah! [have they gone so far as] to kill my son?!" "Yeees, they've kiiiilled the boy." Why did that king not believe [the report]? The first [servant] was cast out [of the garden], and he didn't believe it. The second [servant] was cast out, and he didn't believe it. The third [servant] was cast out, and he didn't believe it. Finally (*mpakana*) they killed his SOOON, AND HE DIDN'T BELIEVE IT! "[Have they gone so far as] to kill my son?!" They said, "Yes, the boy has gone away."

Why did he not believe it? There are three things...[301] "[On account of] a SIIINGLE COB of maize could they kill MY SON?! [On account of] a

---

[300] This would be the height of insulting behavior—not to give someone a proper burial. Even an alleged witch is (reluctantly) afforded that rite of passage, which is intended to promote unity in the community in such a time of crisis. In this case, however, the callus actions of these tenants demonstrate just how much they had alienated themselves from their longsuffering benefactor.

[301] It is not clear what this utterance refers to in the sermon, unless it is to the three main reasons why that killing should not have occurred: a) the garden belonged to the king; b) he requested an insignificant amount of its produce; and c) he had sent his most immediate and trustworthy representative, his own son, to deliver the message. At any rate, Wame now goes on to present what is apparently a poignant (and realistically jumbled) internal monologue as the king reviews these tragic events in his mind. He cannot bring himself to believe that the tenants whom he had been so good to could be so ungrateful, foolish, and cruel as to murder his only son – when all he had asked for was a cob of maize to roast for himself!

SIIINGLE COB of maize could they beat you up?! You are lying!__Get going you! A-aah! Who were those fellows? I myself picked them up (*ndidakachita kukawatola*, i.e., I gave them the chance to prosper), and now they begrudge me a single cob of maaaize?! You are lying!__Get going you! Hah! The garden is MIIINE, and yet they kill MY SON!__The garden is mine – for a single cob of maize?! You are lying!__Get going!" The king DID NOT BELIEEEVE IT! "[On account of] a single cob of maize?! Mmm, I don't belieeeve it. Who were those fellows?! I don't belieeeve it! The garden is MIIINE!__I DON'T BELIEEEVE IT!"

And when the king heard that his son was dead, he spoke these words, "If the king, the [garden] owner himself goes [there], what do you think he's going to doooo to those labourers?"[302] [There will be] A DISASTER, A DISASTER (*ngozi*)! And the final words that [Jesus] speaks is, "EEEVRY person who stumbles on this rock will be crushed, and he upon whom the rock falls will be KILLED!"

Those were the words that we read here.__Those were the words that we read. These words [may] puzzle us (*angotizungulira*). NOW I want to reveal [their meaning]:[303] That king is God. God is a rich kiiing, a kiiing who lacks nothing – that is God. That big garden is this here world. Those labourers are YOOOUU! The [king's] servants are pastors [and] evangelists. The [king's] son is Jesus. That is the [simple] meaning.

Now God did not exploit (*sanadyere*, lit., 'he did not feed upon it') the world. God DID NOT LEAVE the world after he had made some [leather] shoes (*nsapato*) – he simply left the animals. [It was up to] human wisdom to take the leather hides of those animals and to rub them soft (*nkumafufuta*) to make shoes for themselves – to exploit the earth['s resources]. God DID NOT LEAVE after he had made some sofas (*masofa*) – he left the trees. [It was up to] human wisdom to fell [the trees], to make planks and to construct sofas – such that when you sit on them, you sink dooown (i.e., in the cushions) – to exploit the earth. He-heeh! ALELUUYAA! (laughter)...to

---

[302] Wame now concludes his own elaboration of Christ's parable by making it coincide more or less with the Lukan account. There is a bit of confusion here, however, as the king's words are merged directly into those of Christ (cf. Luke 20: 15-16).
[303] Wame treats the parable as an allegory as he re-contextualizes it for a contemporary Malawian audience. No explanation of course was necessary in the original event: The Pharisees knew exactly what Christ meant to say by means of his barbed little story (cf. Luke 20: 19).

exploit the earth. God did not leave after he had made automobiles (*magalimoto*). [It was up to] human wisdom to go down DEEP in a mine (*mgodi*) and bring out COOOPPER (*koopaah*), yes, [and] GOOOLD (*golideee*) – and to construct metal ooobjects. Today we have [Mercedes] BENZES, [other types of] cars, Toyotas – [man is] exploiting the earth! God did not leave after he made iron roofing sheets (*malata*) – he left the rocks (i.e., iron ore). [People] melt these rooocks and construct iron roofing sheets – [to make] nice, big, beautiful houses – exploiting the earth. God did not leave after he had made bags of cement (*zimabeki za simenti*). He left the rocks [there]. [It was up to] human wisdom to go (i.e., dig) DOWN, SMASH [the rocks], grind [them] up and make cement.

Today you are sleeping in nice, big, beautiful houses. But now you are [sitting there] so quietly *CHEEETE!* (ideophone) (laughter) ALELUUUYA! (Amen!) You are exploiting the EEEARTH – exploiting the EEEARTH! God did not leave suits (*masuti*), dresses (*maderesi*) – just look now – umbrellas (*ma'abulera*). He just left cotton (*thonje*) – he just left cotton. [It's up to] human wisdom, that is, to plant that cotton. Riiight, [human] wisdom then to form cloth [and] suits. So when [a well-dressed gentleman] passes by here [you say], "What a respectable person (*abambo olemekezeka*)!" But [this is because] you are exploiting the land, ehe-hee! – exploiting the EEEARTH – exploiting the earth!

My brooothers, people become WEEEALTHY because of the sun. They become wealthy because of the SOOOIL! God did not leave after he had formed [cement] blocks [and] [burnt] bricks. Rather, [on account of] human wisdom [they learned how] to form bricks to make nice, big, strooong HOOOUSES (Wame laughs) – exploiting the earth. People get rich because of this soil. There are some big [farm] estates nearby here – there are some farms nearby here – and people become rich because of FAAAARMING! Just look at [all] the BIIG LOOORRIES (*zimaloleee*) – the BIIIG LOOORIES, EXPLOITING the earth['s wealth]! People get rich from the rain. People get rich from the sun – EXPLOITING the earth. They take a little piece of wood to poke in their teeth (*kutokonyera m'mano*, i.e., a toothpick!)[304] – exploiting the earth! (laughter and clapping) – exploiting the earth, hee!

---

[304] From the great, obvious examples to the absurd – like that of the little "toothpick" here – Wame is full of illustrations that evoke a continuous stream of scenes and settings to fully indigenize his message.

God just left [the earth] – he opened it up like a HUGE ESTATE (*chi-esiteti*), then he left it to make a journey to a distant country, up there in HEEEAVEN – giving [the earth] to you and to me as tenants. Ehee! My but how wealthy you are! (Wame laughs) You are wealthy – let me say it again, you are wealthy – to exploit the earth. It's a sad story. God did not leave bags of maize, he simply left maize seed. That was for you to plant – [and later to harvest] some 200 sacks, some 500 sacks, 2000 sacks – exploiting [the earth], yes! He did not leave bags of groundnuts, no. He left groundnut seed [for you to plant]. But you plant bags [and] bags (*zimabaki-zimabaki*)![305] We haul them away to the market – eh eh eh! He did not leave a huge head of cabbage (*chi-kabichi*), no – he simply left cabbage seed. But [on account of] human wisdom, you plant the seed, don't you? He-he-heeh! My but people are rich around here, ehee! – exploiting the earth! You even take a little piece of wood for poking around in the teeth – you've exploited the earth![306]

My brooothers, [this is] a paaainful matter (*nkhani yosautsa*) – a painful matter. HE DID NOT LEAVE drums [and] drums (*migolo-migolo*) of oil, no – noo! [On account of] human wisdom [people drilled] DEEEP DOWN to take paraffin (*palafini*) – exploiting the earth! [They drill] DEEEP DOWN to take petrol (*petulo*) – exploiting the earth, exploiting the earth! My brothers, the matter we have HERE IS VERY PAINFUL IN MY HEEEART! People are exploiting – the earth. TODAY GOD SENDS [HIS]

---

[305] Wame gives us another one of his picturesque figures of speech – a metonymy: the cause (planting) for the effect (harvesting). Here it is coupled with another emphatic English loanword, repeated to suggest a large number of "bags".

[306] Several things need to be kept in mind as one evaluates the written text (itself a translation, a pale reflection of the idiomatic original) of an inductive, Wame-style sermon. One is the great impact that a powerful, malleable human voice and the words of a gifted orator make upon an audience that is more attuned to the oral than the printed word. Thus the rhythmic repetition of a speaker like Wame is not considered to be boring or redundant. It is all part of the message – an essential element of the *pathos*-building technique of the rhetor. The actual information "load" may be relatively light, but the emotive burden that is being loaded upon the listeners is indeed heavy, and this makes the message have that much greater an impression upon the mind. There would not be many in this audience who would deny his charge that they too were among those who had in some way "exploited the earth" that God gave them, without giving much (if any) thought to the possibility that they might owe him something in an appropriate return – which Wame now goes on to apply to his "servants," those who proclaim his messages. Another thing to remember is that this audience has come prepared for a long sermon; thus they do not begin to get restless or start packing their books when Wame passes the half-hour point – or even the one hour mark! Wame too knows that he has the time to fully develop and emphasize – via reiteration – his key ideas.

SEEERVANTS - PREEEACHERS, PAAASTORS, PROOOPHETS [AND] THEY'VE COOOME TO YOOOUU. GOD WANTS TO MAKE SOME PROFIT (*phindu*) **FROM THE SOIL,** he wants to make some profit from [all] the houses that you've built - [for] he did not leave houses [on the earth]. You've exploited the land! [Now] he wants a [little] prooofit (i.e., from what God has given you as "tenants," or stewards). He wants some profit from the animals that he made. He wants some PROFIT from the trees he left [you here on earth]. He wants some PROFIT from the cotton he left [you]. He wants some PROFIT from the maize that he left [you]. He wants some PROFIT from the rocks (i.e., ores) that he left [you]. He wants some PROFIT from the paraffin that he left [you]. He wants some PROOOFIT! He has sent [his] PREACHERS, eeh!__He has sent [his] paaastors.__Now he wants some PROFIT - from AAAAALL that we have (i.e., that he has given us) - from all that we have.[307]

No person can work without [proper] waaages. [Take for example] even me myself here - God took me from the ground (*kudothi*) and formed me (*nandiumba*, i.e., like a clay pot) into becoming a human being (*munthu*). Out of respect you may call me "Wame,"[308] but God just calls me "ground." He knows that from this ground... "I will profit nothing from that.__Let me just leave it" (i.e., having formed it into a human being, to develop his/her God-given potential). What can we do to please God for giving us eeeeverything? Instead of honouring him, you cuuuurse him! This is what really PAAAINS God. He wants some PROOOFIT from the animals that you use to make your shoes from. He wants some profit from the trees.__He wants some profit from the sun.__He wants some profit from the rains [that] make you rich.__He wants some profit from the year (*chaka*, i.e., what you have "made" during the past year) [that] makes you rich.__He wants some profit from EEEVERYTHING that you have.

---

[307] In other words, as Wame puts the case in his metaphoric manner, when Christians take care of the needs of their pastors and preachers, they are only doing what is right and just. They are simply returning to God, the Creator, some of the "profit" from all of the resources on earth that he has provided them with - that they have "exploited" to the fullest (often without a thought about the Giver).

[308] Wame does not use the honorific form of address when referring to himself here (i.e., *aWame*), which most people in the congregation would undoubtedly have dignified him with. Instead, he uses the common form *Wame* - perhaps as an implicit rhetorical appeal to his own *ethos* as a speaker - that is, he does not exalt himself before his audience.

You were born naked (*amaliseche*), and you will also go (i.e., die) naked. Eeevery single thing that you have comes from God. I never heard of a child being born in a home having a baby blanket (*kotoni*, 'cotton' by metonymy, i.e., due to its soft texture) already in its hand, not at all. If there's a baby blanket in your home, that is some wealth [from God] – that is some wealth [from God]. EEVERY SINGLE THING that you possess is some wealth [from God]. Some of you may say, "[But] I'm just a poor person (*wosauka*)." What sort of "poorness" (*kusauka*) [are you talking about]? Simply figure out the total (*tachitani totolo*). Go ask your parents, when you were born – how much money was spent – for buying diapers (*matewera*), little blankets (*timabulangeti*), things to feed you – until they enrolled you in school (*mpakana kukuyimbitsani sukulu*) – until you reached the size (*saizi*, i.e., age) that you are here now. [Count up] the troubles that you met up with (i.e., and others had to help you out of), [all] the assistance that was spent (i.e., given to you), [all] the clothes you've been wearing, [all] the money that you've spent. When you have figured out the total, [you will come up with] THOOOUSANDS (*masauzande*) – thousands – thousands! So how can you say that you are impoverished (*amphawi*)?! Is it because you were not given CAASH (*kashi*), is that it?![309] You just keep on eating (*mumangodyeratu eti*) [but] still you want some cash, is that it?! (laughter) God wants some profit from EEEEVERYTHING that we have. There is no one who [can claim that he] is [too] poor, no. There is no one [too] poor. God wants some profit from EEEEVERY SINGLE THING that we have – from EEEVERTHING that he has given us. No one can work without [proper] wages (i.e., not even God!).

Now just liiisten to Malachi three, from verse 7 and ending up at 10: [God] says, "YOU HAVE ROOOBBED MEEE! Bring the teeenth part of ten portions to my house of prayer!" YOU HAVE ROOOBBED MEEE! I want some profit from MYYY work that I have worked. Now the profit [would be like this] – if you have TEEEN suits, then set aside (*patula*) one suit and offer it. He does not want (i.e., demand) a lot at all. Or if you have TEEEN cows, take one and offer it. He does not want a lot. Or [if you have] one Kwacha, take 10 Tambala and offer it. He does not want a lot. He does not want a lot. Or perhaps you have SO MAAANY cars,

---

[309] Wame argues his case for a more realistic approach to Christian stewardship in very concrete, irrefutable terms—beginning as it were from one's very beginning and God's blessings that begin there and then.

take some and offer them. He does not want a lot. Or perhaps you have soo maany chitenje cloths, take one and offer it. Or perhaps you have so many suits.__Perhaps you have so many shoes.__Perhaps you have so many chairs.__EEEVERY SINGLE THING THAT YOU HAVE! Perhaps you have so many bags of maize, [then offer] OOOONE bag – OOOONE bag [only]! HE DOES NOT WANT A LOOOT! [Just] ONE PART from the ten parts that you have profited – give that to God!__Give that to God!__Give that to God!

But my brothers, [here is] a matter that causes great sadness (*nkhani yomvetsa chisoni*): When the servants arrive – the pastors [and] preachers (i.e., evangelists)... So sorry (*pepani*) – the congregation becomes troubled. (An announcement is made at church:) "We would like every Christian to make an offering – starting from a [lay-] Christian, 10 Kwacha; the elders of the congregation, 20 Kwacha; the pastors, 30 Kwacha..." (Now here is a typical response): "Ha-ha-ha! Noo – not that (*izo ndiye ayi!*, 'no waay!' i.e., we refuse such a plan)! Noo – not that! You must speak some sense (lit., 'well') now (*umanene bwino*)! Can't you see that you have a job, while some of us are laid off (*ndife malova*)[310] – we have no work! For our food we have to depend on what others throw us (*amachita utiponyera*, i.e., gross exaggeration). Our houses, too, are rented (*ogula lendi*) – [we must pay for] water [and] firewood. So why do you specify a price (i.e., an amount to be offered)? Yes indeed, that church of yours (*mpingo wanuwo*) has become like any other BUSINEEESS (*wayamba nawo bizinesi*)! Heeey, just take a look at the pastor himself, how fat he is (*wangonenepa*)!__He's just eeeating up our money (i.e., offerings) – his big belly sticks out like thaaaat (*chimimba chili ukooo*)!" (much laughter) [By such talk] YOU'VE THROOOWN THE PROOPHETS OUTSIDE [the garden]!__YOU'VE THROWN THE SERVANTS [of God] OOOUTSIDE!__YOU'VE BEEEATEN THE SERVANTS!__ You've beaten the servants!

(Another lay person's response:) "Eeeeh! well I too am a poverty-stricken person also (*inenso ndine mphawinso*)![311] I also want some friends to help

---

[310] The Chewa term *malova*, from the English "loafers," does not necessarily have the same negative connotation, although it might – and thus the example is humorous because the speakers condemn themselves in their own words, so to speak (i.e., they are too lazy to get a job to earn some money to support the work of the church). Wame's language here is highly idiomatic, and the English rendering hardly does justice to its sense, let alone its dramatic significance in such an emotionally charged situation.

[311] The double enumerative suffix *-nso* (rendered 'too' and 'also') is deliberate: The speaker wishes to

me out (i.e., with an offering)! Eeh! I also am a poverty-stricken person! You'd better reconsider your 'prices' (*mitengo*, i.e., the proposed offering schedule)!" Right here and now as we speak the church is falling DOOOOWN FLAAAT! [It] lacks the [necessary] WEEEALTH (*chuma*, i.e., resources). [Church] OOOFFICES ARE BEING CLOSED – due to the lack of wealth. The church of God has been destroyed (i.e., hyperbole) due to the lack of wealth. Preachers of the gospel (lit., 'message') fail [to be supported] due to the lack of wealth!

(If someone/the pastor responds), "THE WORD OF GOD says, 'Give [your] offerings!'" (the people reply) "E-e-e-e-eeh! You'd better talk some sense here! Nowadays there are too many churches – [they are just like] businesses!" Then some people meet up with the "discounters" (*akachipseko*, i.e., cheaper churches!) who say, "Come to us here. We don't give oooofferings [in our church]!" (laughter) And so, you children (*ananu*), these people march straight off *NDUMBWINDUMBWI!* (ideophone, i.e., with the implication of ignorant action) [saying], "I have found a church where they don't give offerings!" (much laughter) [That's what it means] TO THROW THE PROPHETS OUT – [and] to beeeeat them! They are LEEEAVING without a thing. [This is] pure insolence (*mwano okhaokha*)!

When we act this way, God CANNOT UNDERSTAAAND IT at all! God cannot belieeeve it. When he considers your background (*bakigiraundi*, i.e., everything that he's done for you), and [sees that] now you are throwing stones at [his] pastors [and] prophets – you throw stones at [his] preachers, GOD SIMPLY CANNOT BELIEVE IT AT AAALL! Mother, God does not believe it! Father, God does not believe it! Son, God does not believe it! Daughter, God does not believe it! WHYYY NOOOT?! [God says,] "Who were THOSE PEEEOPLE (i.e., that they could now be so ungrateful)?! [All I wanted was] A SINGLE MAIZE COB, ah! And now THEY HAVE KILLED MY SOOON![312]

---

include himself among the complainers who do not wish to contribute any offerings for the support of their pastor/preacher. He thus indicts himself along with them in a misguided appeal to pathos.

[312] As is his usual practice, Wame effectively fuses the biblical story that he has just dramatized in contextualized form and the present application that he wishes to make of this particular message.

Right now as we speak, we are denying JEEESUS._We are BUUUSY (*bizee*) gathering WEEEALTH – while we throw STOOONES at Jesus – to KIIILL HIIIM! Is it your plan (*cholinga chanu*) to take over the whole world? Do you think that you are able to farm the whole world? [It's as if you] are saying, "Let's kill the son so that the garden becomes ours!" Can you farm the [whole] earth? [You would go so far as] to kill Jesus – the owner (*mwini wake*) of earth and heaven? You are so BUUUSY – gathering wealth. God cannot belieeeeve this._[He says to himself], "What kind of people were you (*anali yani iwo aja*, i.e., before he saved you through Christ)?!" God cannot belieeeve it._WHAT KIND OF PEOPLE WERE YOOOUU – in thoooose days before God brought JEEEESUS to youuu?[313] God cannot believe it – that you could even stone [his] prophets. Some of you, if you would testify to the truth of this (*muperekere umboni*), you would start weeping before you finish!

My brothers, I praise Jesus because before he came to take me (i.e., in conversion), I was in the mud (*ndidali kumatope*, i.e., of sin)._[There were] sores on my face (*mabalawa kumasoku*), scars because of [drinking too much] beer, scars because of fights.[314] I was EVEN CAUGHT BY SOME THIEVES at a beer [hall] (*kumowa*), where this arm was broken (i.e., in a fight with them). My brothers, if I were still there (i.e., in that sort of situation/life style), my life would be ALMOOOOST OVER (*udangotsala pang'oooonooo*)_It would be almost over! Before you'd fiiiinish [telling such a tale of woe], you would begin to weep![315] What can I repay to Jesus?_He was the one who PICKED ME UUUP!_He was the one who picked MEEE up! [So] when you deny JESUS, he cannot believe it. [He says], "What kind of people were they (i.e., before I found them)?!"

---

[313] This question (Just who were you?! *mudaali yani inu?*) is Wame's equivalent to the rhetorical question of the initial text he cited from Psalm 116:12: "What shall I return to the LORD for all his bounty to me?" (NRSV). It serves as a leitmotif throughout the second part of this sermon – a query that is similarly intended to highlight the blessings of God in one's life and the consequent obligation to show some concrete gratitude, in particular, by giving generous offerings in support of one's pastor.

[314] It is also Wame's custom to preach to himself as well as to his people. Following up on the preceding sentence, he proceeds to give his own testimony – that is, of the sinful life that he led before he became a Christian (cf. Appendix A). Such personal witness serves to enhance both the genuineness and the credibility of his message (i.e., *ethos*).

[315] Wame's voice begins to crack in this section – as if he himself were on the verge of breaking into tears. It is a powerful testimony of the Lord's gracious deliverance in his own life (cf. the Appendix).

Mother, WHO WERE YOUUU [that] you can now stone the prophets? MY BROTHER, WHO WERE YOU, when you were in [your] sins? Who were you when you were at the beer hall? Who were you when you were practising sorcery (*muli kunyanga*)? Who were you when you were a habitual liar (*muli kumabodza*, lit., 'when you were at lies')? Who were you when you were spreading slander (*muli kumisecheeee*, lit., 'when you were at slanders', idiom)? [Jesus] cannot believe it!__He cannot believe it!__And even you yourself are completely amazed (*muli kuthedwa nzeru*) that you are found here (i.e., at this Christian gathering), when you [too] were wronging Jesus. If you were to give your testimony here, you'd start weeping before you would finish! "Look (*taonani*)," you'd say, "If I were still THEERE, my life would be LOOOST!"

A-ah! At the end of it (*mapeto ake*, i.e., your testimony), you'd be crying. You ask, "[My life] would have been lost?" "Yes!" "You would have been like you had died (*mukadakhala mutafa*)?" "Yes!"[316] [Now] since along with [all] those sins there (i.e., in your former way of life) you left your mother [behind] – is she still ALIIIVE? You left behind your girlfriend (*achemwali*) there, while you are weeping here – say, is she ALRIIIGHT (i.e., spiritually)? [You say], "My father was left behind.__My mother was left behind.__My child was left behind.__My uncle was left behind."[317] Some of you are rejoicing happily (*mungoona ukondwerera*) here while YOUR MOTHER is weeping in HEELL (*kugahena*)! YOUR mother is not a Christian, no!__YOUR father is not a Christian, no!__YOUR child is not a Christian, no!__Your uncle is not a Christian, no! Here you just jump about [as they sing] the praise choruses (*m'makolasi*), when the purpose [of this meeting] must reach your mother so that SHE TOO can receive the good news. But here you are simply enjoying yourself, [saying], "Eeeh! [I have found] peace in Jesus!" – [while] your mother is going to hell!

I want to tell you here – who were you?__WHO WERE YOU before you arrived (i.e., through conversion) to take part [in singing] the choruses? WHO WERE YOU before you became a pastor? WHO WERE YOU

---

[316] The preacher here goes into a little dialogue, as it were, with a member of the listening congregation.

[317] Wame brings evangelism to a very personal level as he encourages each member of the congregation to think of any one of their close relatives who may have been "left behind" in an unconverted life, while believers are enjoying the blessings of the gospel during this special service of worship.

before you became a church elder? WHO WERE YOU before you became a preacher? [God was] the one who piiiicked you up. Now God cannot believe it that you would kill his son – that you would beat up his servants for no reason at all. Who were you anyway?!

Our offering[s] we exchange (*tisinthanitsa*) with what God did for us (i.e., our giving should match his great gifts to us – even if that is impossible to achieve). Just who was I (i.e., before I became a Christian)? If Jesus says, "I want 20 Kwacha," I will give 50 Kwacha – [for] who was I? [If he says], "I want 100 Kwacha," I will give 200 Kwacha – [for] who was I? [If he says], "I want 1000 Kwacha," I will give 2000 Kwacha – [for] who was I? When we begin to make our offerings, we exchange with what God HAS DONE FOR YOOOUU! [You may] TRY TO REPAY [the debt] BUT YOU CANNOT DO IT! THERE ARE SIMPLY TOO MANY GOOD THINGS that Jesus has done for you! And after you have given [all] those Kwachas, you can finish up with your very heart (*kuthatha ndi mtima*), but you will not be capable of it, no (i.e., of giving enough in return). [Remember] who you were. [This is] a matter that gives great sadness (i.e., that people, especially Christians, can show so much ingratitude by their lack of support). And God just cannot believe it.__He just cannot believe it!

WHO WERE YOU?! Just OOONE maize cob – [God] does not want (i.e., ask for) a LOOOT! Just OOONE part of ten parts! [He says], "Here you go and beat up the prophets [and] kill my SOOON.__But the garden is mine!" Yes, this world that you are exploiting is his, but you go ahead and kill his SOOON! JEEESUS cannot believe it.__God does not believe it. Just who were you?! My brothers, he just can't believe it!

[Point] number (*nambala*) two: Just WHO WERE YOU before you became educated (*musadaphunzire*, lit., 'before you learned/studied')? WHO WERE YOU, father?__Who were you, mother, before you got EEEDUCATED? God was the one who PICKED YOU UUUP! Now some of you were TROOOUBLED when you did your studies at school (*sukulu*). OORPHANS were educated by the government – [through a] BUUURSARY (*basaleee*). [Perhaps] your father died just when you were born.__The one who educated you is your mother [who earned money] by baking "we-love-life" [rolls] – "we-love-life" – "we-love-life" [rolls]![318] Today YOU HAVE BEEN EEEDUCATED – right up to the college level (*kupita kukoleji*).__[You have] a pile of degrees (*vimadigrii*) *THOO!* (ideophone). [So now] you are insolent (*mwayamba mwano*) [to God]! Just who were you?__Who were you?__WHO WEEERE YOOUU?! God cannot BELIEVE it!__He wants THAT WIIISDOM OF YOOOUURS! [He wants] you to HOOONOR HIM WITH IIIT! God does not belieeeve it (i.e., your refusal to use some of your education for his benefit).

Just who were YOOOUUU before you were eeeducaaated? Before you were educated, your parents troubled themselves to educate you! Some of you were orphans, and you were educated by the government.__Others were picked up (*anakutolani*, i.e., were helped out) by some merciful people (*anthu achifundo*). Now you have a JOOOOB – a HIGH-PAYING JOOOB (*nchito yapamwamba*, i.e., or one that is high-ranking). Today God is sending his servants [saying], "Go take some of the profit of [all] that education, [for] I EDUCATED HIM!" Instead [of repaying anything], you beat up [these] servants for no reason at all. E-eeeh! You just begin your businesses (*mabizinesi*) saying, "The offerings [will come] tomorrow!__The offerings [will come] tomorrow!" [But] who were you before you became educated? [This is] a very sad matter. Just who were you before you became educated? Moreover, to be educated through so much difficulty and to reach this point (*pointi*), if you yourself would sit down [and think about it], you too would be shocked (*mumathedwa nzeru*, i.e., regarding your lack of appreciation). [This is] indeed a very sad matter!

[Point] number two:[319] WHO WERE YOU before you got a joooob? THIS IS THE WAY IT WAS (*kumangoti*): [If you would] go here, [you'd be told], "No woooork (*m'kapita apa, palibe nchitoooo*)!" Go there, "No woooork!" Go heeere, "No woooork!" You children, how [much] you were afflicted (*kuzunzika*) as you went about looking for wooork! So you

---

[318] These rolls (*tizikonda-moyo*) are simple home-baked scones that are very filling, hence satisfying for one's "life". They also enable poorer folk to make a living—hence preserving their "lives"!

[319] We have already reached this "point" (see above). In the case of such a long sermon (with no printed text), it is not surprising that Wame gets a bit confused concerning his discourse divisions. However, this does not make a great deal of difference to his presentation, or to its inductive organization, which involves a continual incremental recycling (considerable repetition with variation and some addition) of his main ideas under the general theme of "Making an appropriate Christian response both to and with the many gifts that our gracious God has given us (*stewardship*)."

just went out and got a job that you didn't want – [like] digging ditches (*kumakakumba ngalande*) [saying], "What else can I do (*nanga titani*)?" [But] God in his grace felt sorry for you and picked you up. Say, those of you who dig ditches (i.e., among the audience), is there any one of you who does not know how to write? (Here is a hypothetical reply): "Aah, as for me, I *do* know how to write!" [This means that God] picked you up out of that DIIITCH! (laughter) Hah! Just who were you?!

So today this very same God has given you [the] wisdom (*nzeru*) [to obtain] some [job] promotions (*mapolomoshoni*) – one after the other (*usinjanasinjana*): this year – a promotion, next year – a promotion, the year after that – a promotion! [Until you reach the position of] GENERAL MAAANAGER (*ujenero manijalaaa*) – A VEEERY HIIIGH POSITION (*chimpaaaando chapamwamba*)! YOUR SALARY [is in the] THOOOUSANDS! (*ndalama masauzandeee!*) But when we consider the example of church (*tiyeni tibwere kichalichi*) – [and giving] an offering, [you reply], "Aaaah! [it's just] a little business (*kabizinesi*)! (i.e., therefore I need not give very much)!" A-a-ah! JUST WHO WERE YOU before you got that job of yours?! WHO WERE YOU before you got a job?! God was the one who PICKED YOOOUU UUUP! WHO WERE YOU before you reached the position of general manager?! WHO WERE YOU before you reached the position of personnel [manager] (*aperesonolo*)?! WHO WERE YOU before you reached the position of sargeant (*asajenti*)?! WHO WERE YOU before you reached the position of [office] messenger (*umisinjala*)?![320] (much laughter) THESE ARE THE THINGS that God just cannot believe! No, he cannot belieeeeve it!

[Point] number three:[321] WHO WERE YOU before you began your business? Wasn't it you who would go [to the market] to sell little [piles of]

---

[320] In this case Wame follows an order of *decreasing* rank/position, perhaps because most of his listeners would probably be members of a lower socio-economic class, and hence surprised perhaps to find that they too are included in this appeal to produce a more proportionate offering to the Lord. In the listing of the next paragraph, however, he moves from lower to higher types of "business." Perhaps this chiastic arrangement (i.e., up : down :: down : up) was deliberate; either way, it is a carefully measured rhetorical progression from one social pole to the other.

[321] This "new" point does not differ greatly from the preceding ones, but Wame does go on to emphasize the great poverty – or at least considerable financial pressure – that many pastors find themselves in due to the parsimony of their parishes. While the very poor are often quite faithful in their offerings – as exemplified in several of the anecdotes of this section – the more well-to-do frequently fail in their responsibilities in this regard and certainly could do more than they are.

charcoal (*timakala*) – with many patches (*zigamba*) sticking out *THOO!* (ideophone) all over your clothes? "Charcoal, charcoal!" [you'd call out] – as you sold along the alleys (lit., "lines", *m'malayinimu*, in your residential compound).__"Charcoal, charcoal!" – along the lines![322] Say, wasn't that you? Who were you [then]?! (Next are the tomato sellers): "Tomatoes, tomatoes, tomatoes!" – (selling) along the lines of houses! (Next are the leafy-vegetable sellers): "Leaves, leaves, leaves, leeaves!" [you would call out]. Who were you [then]?! [But] today God has blessed you with a big hawker's stand (*chihookala*) – all full up *THI!* (ideophone, i.e., with items for sale). After the hawker's stand, [God blessed you with] a big grocery shop (*chigolosale*) – all full up *THI!* Now it's a big store (*chisitolo*).__Eeeh! now a [transport] business – a car, all filled up *THI!*__[Next] a minibus (*minibasi*).__[Then] some lorries (*malole*)! A-ah?! He-heeh! [But] who were you [once upon a time]?! He-heeh! TODAY YOU ARE RIIICH!__And God sends [his] SERVAAANTS to go find some profit from AAAALLL the things you have.__BUT he does not want a great deal – just one part of ten parts.

But all you give him [in return] are insults (*mwano wokhawokha*) [saying], "These churches of yours are just businesses (i.e., in the business of making money). We are simply giving our money away to these pastors.__And can't you see that [this one] is already rich – with his big belly sticking way out there!" [Such talk] makes one very sad. If there's a pauper among paupers (*mphawi wa amphawi*) it is the pastor! You made him a PAUPER!__You caused him to leave his job so that he could serve you full-time (*fulu-tayimu*). So you are the very ones who are to FEED HIM (*kumudyetsa*, i.e., to ensure that he receives a liveable salary) [since] you made him leave his job. For him to have to go and find work on the side (*nchito yapadera*, i.e., so that he can support himself/his family) [will result in] his pastorate not operating properly (*ubusa wakenso sungayende bwino*) – things cannot be carried out in an orderly way (*sizingalongosoke*), not at all – not in the least little bit (*m'pang'onopang'ono pomwe*)!

---

[322] Wame evokes a typical street scene in a crowded housing compound: All of the (unlicensed) sellers, mainly women, are "lined up" (more or less) along the "line" of their duplicate houses, often with just a single commodity piled up or containered in roughly equal amounts, that is, in keeping with traditional African communal (non-individualistic/competitive) social standards. The charcoal-sellers would be some of the poorest of the lot due to the filth and low profit margin that is involved with such an occupation.

A pastor is the pauper of all paupers! A pastor does not receive money. The money that a pastor receives comes from lice (*nsabwe*) - lice from the neck - [from] the little towel (*katoweli*) of cloth of an elderly person (*nkhalamba*, undoubtedly a woman) - [from] a little handkerchief (*kahandikachifi*) like this one. When they [announce the offering and] say, "[Time for] THE OFFERING - [time for] the offering!" - a little old lady trembles (*kali kunjenjemera*) as she unties [her little handkerchief] to take 10 Tambala and throw it into the [offering] plate. [Meanwhile with the other hand] she is smashing the lice [in her handkerchief] - [one hand] smashing lice (*kuphwanyira*), [the other] throwing [a few coins] into the plate. When these little coins (*tindalama*) accumulate, then we call the pastor [saying], "Pastor, come receive [your pay] (*dzalandireni*)!" [But is it right that] one's salary comes from lice? Should a salary [really] come from lice?[323] Those of you who say, "We have made our pastor rich (*talemeretsa mbusa*)" - is it not true that you too want to become wealthy? Can a pastor really get rich on that 5 tambala coin of yours (i.e., which is no more than that given by a poor old woman)? Isn't it true that you too wish to become wealthy? Your words are insulting! Just who were you anyway, before you started up your business?! Today God HAS BLESSED YOU! You own big businesses - YOU OWN BIG BUSINESSES! You have bought MINIBUSES (*maminibasi*), CARS, LORRIES! You have constructed large houses - big plots (*zimapoloti*). WHO WERE YOU [before]?! If the Holy Spirit is in you, you will feel sorrow today!

What has God done wrong? God does not believe the way you talk back to him (*mukamamubwezera mawu*, i.e., all your excuses for not giving proportionate offerings). Who were you - before you took up FAARMING?! WHO WERE YOU before you opened up your estate?! WHO WERE YOU before you began to grow cotton?! WHO WERE YOU before you began to grow BURLEY TOBACCO (*barele*)?! Who were you before you began your farming - [growing your] vegetables (*mavejitabo*)?! Who were you

---

[323] Wame is by no means belittling the small offerings of the poor in a congregation. These offerings do accumulate and count considerably in the eyes of God, as graphically illustrated in the story of the rich man (European) and his gardener at the end of this sermon. His point - as emphasized by this picturesque, hyperbolic metonymy of the lice's offering - is that those **who have been abundantly blessed** by the Lord ought to give to his servants accordingly. The latter **must not depend on the** faithful offerings of little old women to support their pastor(s). It is a real shame that so **many relatively** wealthy Christians have been allowing their less-fortunate brothers and sisters to do **just that**!

before you began to grow groundnuts?!³²⁴ Who were you before you began to grow AAALLL THOSE CROOOPS that you are now farming?! Just who were you (once)?! Today God has blessed you because of your farming, and in such farming [activities] people become RIIICH – and so have you become rich! But [now] God wants some of the profit – [just] one part of AAAALL that you have. But today you are stoning the prophets. Just who were you?__Who were you?! It's a very sad affair.

WHO WERE YOU?! [Perhaps] you used to be sick every morning (*m'mawa mwadwala*) – sick every morning. Throughout your schooling you were troubled with continual sickness (*kudwaladwala*). But God brought you through (*adakupyoletsani*) ALL OF THAT! Today God has blessed you – while you continue to stone [his] prophets. Who were you?! As I speak here, there are some of you [listening] who are orphans – you have no mother.__You have no father, but God picked you up [and gave you] a big position (*chiudindo*). Some of you are great people in the country – [but] you were picked up [to that position] by God. Now God wants some PROFIT from AAAAALL the things he has done for you. But in place of that, you've thrown stones at [his] prophets. Just who were you?!

My brothers (and sisters!), [you went so far as] TO KILL MY SOOON! THESE WORDS are troubling God in his heart.__You want to steal [from him]. You stopped going TO CHUUURCH (*kuchalichi*) LOOONG AGOOO – you've never gone again! YOU STOOOPPED going to church looong ago. These words (i.e., 'who were you?!') – listen to me carefully now (*tandimvetsetsani*) my brothers – these words... Some of you here who have no church – these words... It makes no difference (*palibe kanthu*) if you have no church, but WHO WERE YOU before you got an education?! It is good to thank (*kumuthokoza*) God (i.e., in an overt, tangible manner).

There are some people who, when they see their glory (or great wealth, *ulemerero wao*, i.e., how well off they are in life), they possibly go to church [and say], "Pastor, here's a gift for you" – but he is a pagan man.³²⁵

---

³²⁴ This is another descending order of items – this time of cash crops, from the highest-paying produce (cotton) to the lowest (groundnuts). The majority of Malawians gain their livelihood from some sort of agricultural activity, whether as large farm owners, small garden growers, or ordinary day-laborers (tillers).

³²⁵ The term *mkunja*, (lit. 'one on the outside'), is usually used to refer to a pagan, an unbeliever, or a non-Christian. In this context the word may be understood as denoting someone who does not belong to

After seeing what he was [s/he says], "It makes no difference that I'm a pagan, but God has done great things for me!" Don't feel sorry for yourselves! Many people who offer gifts [to the church] [come from] pagan countries in Europe (*Yulope*) – they are not Christians – but on seeing what God has done for them, "Just who was I?!" [they say], and go on to give some money to thank God. "IT MAKES NO DIFFERENCE that I'm a pagan, but who was I [before God raised me up]?!"

If there are some of you pagans here – you don't belong to any church at all – but you feel sad today, just ask this question: Who were you before you became educated? Who were you before you began a business? Who were you before you took up farming? Who were you when you were sick all the time? TODAAAY you should feel SORRY, mister!__ You should feel sorry, lady! WHO WERE YOU, lady, before you were married? Who were you, mister, before you married? Who were you, lady, before you started up a business? If the Spirit of God is within you, you ought to feel sorry. If your husband had not picked you up [in marriage], you would not have this glory that you have now. You should be sorry! Who were you before you were married to Mr Banda (*aBanda*)? Who were you before you were married to Mr Phiri?[326] Who were you before you were married to Mr Jere? And you too, mister, just who were you before you married Mrs Phiri (*naPhiri*) – that hard-working wife of yours – that wife who has enriched you?[327] You have become wealthy because of that wife of yours.__ WHO WERE YOU [before you married her]?! This is a very sad business (i.e., the lack of gratitude that people tend to show towards their benefactors). If the Spirit of God dwells in you, then you ought to feel sorry! [These are] SORROWFUUULL WOOORDS! And God cannot believe it – "[that they would go so far as] to KILL MY SON – wanting to seize the land!" You stopped going to church long-long ago![328]

---

any particular Christian denomination since such a person is popularly thought of as a "pagan." However, it is likely that Wame really means a complete unbeliever here – another one of his hyperbolic examples – intended here to put each and every reluctant "Christian" (*mkristu*) giver to shame.

[326] Banda and Phiri are the two most common surnames (i.e., denoting macro-clans) among the Chewa people.

[327] Wame is no male-chauvinist preacher; in fact, he usually tends to hit the men harder in his sermons. This stands to reason because in general women tend to be stronger and more stable church members than men in central Africa, although they are not often given recognition and responsibility commensurate with their important congregational function.

[328] To refuse to go to church (as one sign of being an active Christian) is thus tantamount to killing Christ all over again because such a person thereby refuses to acknowledge the sovereignty of God in

For this reason [God says in] Job chapter 38, verses 1-6:[329] "Hey you (*Iwe!*), [I have this to say] since you have robbed me of [my] tithe (lit., 'one part of ten parts') and my house is falling down – but when I say, '[It's time for] AN OFFERING,' – all I get is insolence (*mwano wokhawokha*)! [Tell me]: were you there when I made the MAIZE that you now have become wealthy from? When I made the trees, were you there? When I made the animals [for] the shoes that you are wearing, were you there? When I made the ore (lit., 'rocks') [for] the money that is in your pocket, were you there? When I made the ROOOCKS – the silver, the gold, [the iron for] the big [Mercedes] Benz (*chibenzi*) that you are riding – were you there? Tell me, tell me – WERE YOU THEEERE?!"

[This is] A TOUGH QUEEESTION (*funso lovuta*) – A SAAADENING QUESTION (*funso losautsa*)! Lady, WERE YOU THEEERE when I made the cotton? WERE YOU THEEERE when I made the rocks? WERE YOU THEEERE when I made the paraffin? WERE YOU THEERE when I made the soil? WHERE YOU THERE when I made the sun – the rain? WERE YOOOUUU THEEERE? God cannot BELIEEEEVE it: "WHO WEEERE THOOOSE PEEEOPLE?!__[To go so far as] TO KIIILL MY SOOON – while the garden was MIIINE?!" If the Spirit of God is in you today, you should feel sorry.__[These are] sorrowful words! GIIIVE! GIIIVE! WHATEEEVER [you have]! Perhaps it's a chair, then give it! Perhaps it's a car, then give it! Perhaps it's some shoes, then give them! Perhaps it's some clothes, then give them! They can be sold at the church – they can do [God's] work! GIIIVE – a goat! GIIIVE WHATEEEVER you have! [Just] GIIIVE! You were born naked [and] you will also go [out] naked. Give [your offerings]! [These are] sorrowful words.__God cannot believe it (i.e., that his people need to be told this)! [These are] sorrowful words.__God cannot believe it!

The Word [of God] says, "When the owner [of that garden] comes, what will he do to those [malicious] workers?" When the MASTER comes, what

---

his/her life and the great sacrifice that his Son offered to redeem it. How can a grateful thanksgiving offering be given if a person does not even attend regular worship services?

[329] Wame proceeds to give his own, highly contextualized and sermon-specific rendering of this Scripture passage. He thus alters the reproof of God (to Job) to fit the point where he is at in this particular sermon as well as the central topic. In this case, it is a criticism of those Christians who refuse to recognize the Lord's mighty creative and provisionary works – works that extend to right up to the present time and to the individual lives of everyone who is present in the congregation.

will he do to those wooorkers? [It will be a] DISAAASTER (or misfortune, *ngoziii*)! [This] means that when Jesus comes and you continue to behave as you are behaving now (*mmene mukhalira inuyo*), HOOOOW are things going to end up (*kodi zidzatha bwanji*)? [It will be] a disaaaster! Now the Word of God says, "Everyone who falls upon THAT ROCK will be crushed, but whoever that rock falls upon will be killed." Here is the meaning: You who are offended by [the call to give] an offering [to the church] – that is, when Jesus calls for an offering, you become offended – you are [actually] becoming offended at (tripping upon) the [divine] Rock (*mwala*), because that rock is Jesus.[330] If you read the Word of God [in] 1 Corinthians 10, at verse 4, it says, "The people of Israel drank water coming out of a [large] rock (*thanthwe*) in the wilderness, and that rock was Jesus." [In] hymn [number] 102 we say (i.e., sing), "Within that rock that is split apart, let me hide myself completely (*thanthwe long'ambikatu ndibisale momwemo*)" – now that is Jesus!

If you are offended by [having to give] an offering, then you are like a person who is running, trips on a rock and falls *BAAA!* (ideophone). Will it turn out (lit., 'finish') well [for him]? If a person trips on a rock, does it turn out well? [No], he gets BAAADLY hurt (*amavulala mooipaaa*) – because [he's fallen] on a [big] rock! But if you fall on sand (*mchenga*), well, you simply brush off the dirt (i.e., sand). [But] on a rock it is bad! AAANYONE who trips on this Rock – meaning Jesus – he will GET HUUURT! DON'T TRIP ON AN OFFERING – YOU'LL GET HUUUURT! YOU HAVE FALLEN ON A [BIG] ROCK! But [the Word] also says that when that [big] Rock comes, it/he will grind him up [into flour] (*lidzamsinja*)[331] – meaning [that] at the [second] coming of the Lord Jesus, HE WILL FALL UPON YOU [and destroy you]! Things will not turn out well for you at all. Therefore, do not become offeeeended at [giving] an offering! Do not become offended at an offering!

[Now for my] FINAL WORDS – listen carefully: Matthew 6, verse 19 ending at 21, are words... This is what it says: "Store up (*dzikundikireni*)

---

[330] At this point Wame introduces a thematically significant play on words: The Chichewa verb *-khumudwa* can mean either trip over or, in an extended sense, become offended (or irritated) by some one or some thing.

[331] Here Wame adopts a more precise meaning of the original Greek verb λκυδω, that is, "grind to powder" (*-sinja*) instead of the general word as rendered in the old Chewa Bible, "to kill him (*-pha*).

wealth in heaven. DO NOT store up [wealth] on earth, where corrosion (*dzimbiri*) and moths (*njenjete*) destroy. STORE UP [wealth] in heaven. For where your heart is, there your wealth will also be.__Where your wealth is, there your heart will also be."[332] Let me repeat: "Store up wealth IN HEAVEN – NOT on earth where corrosion and moths destroy, but STORE UP [wealth] in heaven! For where your heart is, there your wealth will also be.__[And] WHERE YOUR WEALTH IS, there your heart will also be." What do [these words] reveal [to us]? Heeere they (or Jesus, the speaker) wish to reveal three things:

ONE (*wani*): GOD wants to know where a person's life rests (or sleeps, *moyo... umagona*, i.e., an idiom).[333] As for you (*inuyo*), if you don't earn (lit., 'find') any money, you cannot eat. These two travel together (*zikuyenda zonse*) – life and money. Without slapping down (*kugwetsa* – lit., 'causing X to fall') a tambala (i.e., some money – a hypobolic synecdoche),[334] it means you don't eat [anything]. Now God wants to know (i.e., test) this heart of yours (*mtima wanuwu*). And if HE SEES IT – that it's mixed together (*udaphatikizana*) with money, then God digs it (i.e., the heart!) up (*waufukulira*) saying, "Oh-oh-oh! This heart here – if I want to KNOW it, then I've got to GO THROUGH money!"[335] For this reason he says, "Please give me (*tandipatsanikoni*, a polite request form) a little 10 Tambaaala coin (*kateni tambala*) – [or] a little Kwacha note (*kawani kwachako*)!" This is not to say that God is a NEEDY person (*wosowa*). Some of you are speaking WIIICKED words.__You say, "God eats up (*amadya*, i.e., cheats us out of) [our] money! That's right! (*eeeeh!*)." [But] he does not eat it up at all.__I myself can testify to that. Does God really need anything? [I ask]. "Yeeess!" (i.e., the blasphemers among you may reply). [No], he doesn't lack a thing. All that money [you have]

---

[332] Wame gives his own unique paraphrase of this passage from Matthew: He excludes some elements (e.g., about the thieves) and reiterates others in poetic form (i.e., a chiasmus: heart-wealth=wealth-heart).

[333] This section features some very idiomatic Chichewa; thus my translation is only a dim reflection of the original in terms of rhetorical power and stylistic appeal.

[334] A tambala is a small coin of very little value, i.e., much less than one US cent. 100 tambala make up one Kwacha.

[335] This idiomatic Chewa expression is both alliterative and paronomastic: *mtima umenewu kuti ndiudziwe ndiudzere kundalama*. God effects this testing ("knowing") process by asking people to give to him what they (at least a majority of folks) may be tempted to desire or what they feel they need the most in this world, namely, money.

(*zindalamazo*) – God is the one who gave it to you! All those cars, mini-busses, suits [and] houses[336] – ALL THOSE THINGS God has given to you!

Now the shocking thing (*chodabwitsa*) is that some are saying that He (God) is begging for it again (*akupemphanso*). Isn't this a LIIIEE (*si bodza iliiii*)?! He is [simply] seeking a REEAASON (*chifukwaaaa*, i.e., to see what's in your heart). He is looking at your heart – to see where it LIIIEES. God is FEEEAARSOME (*woopsyaaa*, i.e., towards those who try to cheat him!). God cannot lack ten tambalaaaa. He completely surrounds [one's] heart (*wauzungulira mtima*, i.e., none of one's innermost thoughts escape him). He has seen that you are mixed up with money [and says], "For me to get to know this fellow, I've got to go through [his] money!" So he just asks for TEN TAMBALA and if you respond with insolence, he takes that little 10 tambala [coin] of yours (*kateni tambala kanuko*) and throws it away. He throws it saying, "I've heard those words of his. Just throw [his money] down – throw it away somewhere!"[337] (laughter) [So] these are the reasons (i.e., the evidence) that he's looking for. Thus some of you have LOOONG AGO been entered into [God's] record (*lekodi*).[338] Don't be surprised (*osadabwa*) – [do you think that] God eats up [your] money?! Don't be surprised – are these not reasons (i.e., enough to condemn you)?! All your wealth has been given to you by God, and so when he says, "I would like 10 Tambala,"... Eeh-he hee! There's a collision here (*pali ngozi apa*, i.e., between God's request and a person's impudent response). [These are] THE REASONS, ehee!

Some of you have been found out LOOONG-LONG AGO (*kalekaaaale*)! And long ago you've been entered into [God's] record book. He simply takes that little Kwacha of yours and throws it aside while he

---

[336] Wame hyperbolically uses the Chewa augmentative nominal prefix (*zi-*) on each of these items in the list (except for last, which prefers *ma-*).

[337] Wame speaks this utterance in English – for dramatic (and humorous) effect. As an aside, I might point out the fact that even after having preached for well over an hour by now, Wame's sermonic oratory shows no signs of diminishing – nor does it, to the very end. His voice remains loud and clear, with the same intonational malleability as before and keeping up his typical rapid-fire rate of delivery.

[338] The notion of the deeds of a sinful person, or the name of that person, being "recorded" in a book may be derived from OT passages such as Isaiah 30:8 or Jeremiah 25:13 due to the way in which these texts read in the literal Chichewa vernacular version. This idea is also promoted by the dramatic practice of a football (soccer) referee "booking" an offender – that is, writing into an official little book a player who has flagrantly violated the rules of the game. Soccer is of course the national sport of most countries in Africa.

takes those words that you are speaking [against him] and records them in a book. Right now as I am speaking EEEVERYTHING in that heart of yours is WIDE OPEN (*PAMBALAMBANDA!*, ideophone), completely visible (*pamtunda*)! Don't be surprised! For this reason he (or 'it', the Word) says, "Wherever your heart is, your wealth will be there too. But wherever your wealth is, there your heart will also be.

FIRST he wants evidence (*zifukwa*, lit., 'reasons/cases'). HE WANTS TO SEE DEEP DOWN in your heart – how do you praise him [there]? DEEP DOWN in your heart – how do you thank him [there]? RIGHT NOW I AM SAYING [that some of] you have looong ago been entered into the record book. That's the first thing [I want to say – in conclusion].

[Point] two: WHEREVER your wealth is, your heart will be right there. Here He (God) wants to reveal that where a person offers [his] offering (*amapereka chopereka*) is where [his] heart is.[339] If your heart is at (on) a BAR (*bala*, i.e., a beer hall), [then] you make your offering[s] at a bar. There is no person who offers nothing at all. THERE IS NO ONE who offers nothing – don't try to contradict thiiis (*musadzalankhul nsooo*)! EEEVERY ONE of you makes an offering, but your offering may be a BIIITTER ONE (*n'chowaaawa*, i.e., you may be forced to give it out of necessity or need)! You must offer an offering EEEVERY DAY! Without putting down a Tambala (i.e., some money), you don't eat. You offer/give [money] at the market.[340] Without putting [something] down, you don't eeeeaat. EEEEVERYONE must make an offering. At your homes can you point out (*mungandilozere*) something that you have that did not require some money (*chopanda ndalama*)? If someone gave you a present, where did he buy it? Where did he get it from? POINT OUT something that you have that did not require some money. Is there anything [like that] at your home?

---

[339] Again, it may be noted that I am using the masculine personal pronoun simply for convenience. The feminine could just as well be used (depending on the context) since the Chewa form is inclusive, that is, non gender-specific.

[340] Wame here plays upon two possible senses of the verb *-pereka*, namely, the sacred ('offer') versus the secular ('give'). The point is that people "offer/give" money on a daily basis for all sorts of things. His pointed question is: Just exactly how and where does God (and his work/workers) fit into the equation?

If you say, "Aaah! these churches today only want [our] money!" – then can you point out something there at home [that you obtained] without [paying any] money? Can this big congregation here (*chimpingo chachikulukulu chino*) fail to want (i.e., need) money, while you yourself have failed [to do without it]?! What is there at your home that did not require money? [Those are] insolent words! They cause [me] sadness. YOU WERE ENTERED looong ago into [God's] record book! EEEVERYONE makes an offering. If [your] BIG HEART (*chimtimacho*, i.e., a wicked one) is [fixed] on a BAR-GIRL (*bala-gelo*), then [your] OFFERING [goes] to a bar-girl! If your heart is on SORCERY (*nyanga*), then [your] OFFERING [goes] to that witchcraft. Wherever your heart is, your wealth will [also] be there. If your heart is at church (*kuchalichi*), then your OFFERING [will go] to church. There's no person who does not make an offering, not at all. EEEVERY ONE of you should see where he offers his offering!

[Here are my] final words (*mau omaliza*):[341] IF YOU OOOFFER [to God], there is a reward (*mphoto*) in heaven. In Europe (*yuropi*) there was a certain man... I'm telling you what [really] happened... This man was very wealthy. Now he had a garden boy (*galadeni boyi*) – a gardener (*gadenaa*) – someone who swept around the outside.[342] Now this gardener used to go to church and throw in [the offering basket] 2 Tambala – 5 Tambala – like the offerings that we are accustomed to give. But his master (*bwana*) used to just enjoy himself (*kumangokudya* – lit., 'he was just eating'). He had NO TIIIME AT ALL for (*analibe nazo nchito* – lit., 'he had no work with them') the things of God (*za Mulungu*) at all. Not even a single day did he ever go to church – he was simply enjoying himself. Heeeh! [enjoying the things] of this world!

Now death is blind (*imfa ndi yakhungu*) – it doesn't see anything (*simaona*). It suddenly arrived at (*idakangofikira*) that master and hit him *THIBU!* (ideophone) *WUU!* (ideophone) [he fell] DOWN (*pansi*)! [It struck him

---

[341] Wame lightens this final portion of his looong sermon and immediately recaptures the full attention of his audience by telling them the following fantastic, dialogic fable – one that dramatizes his main theme and thereby etches it upon the memory of everyone present.

[342] The redundancy here is rhetorical: It serves to focus on the foil of the following account while drawing the congregation emotively into the action. They realize now from the onset that the preacher's parable is going to set the wealthy master and his lowly servant into some sort of dramatic and thematic opposition.

again] *BAAA!* (another ideophone), and he died on the spot (*n'kumwalira*)![343] Now the angels came to escort him (*adakachingamira*), [and so] he thought, "[This is] a blessing (*m'madalitso*) [for me]!" Heee! (i.e., he was wrong!) The angels said, "MAAASTER (*bwanaa*, i.e., in mock respect)! Come over here.__We're going to give you your house." HAAA! [That fellow] was overjoyed (*aja chimwemwe chokachoka*). And they arrived at a building (*nyumba*, lit., 'house') of three stories (*fili sitoriis*). The master began to get happy now [saying to himself], "Yaa! here I am now, yaa! (*ndafika yaa!*)" – [thinking that] he had come along with the mastership (*kutengera ubwana*) that he had [enjoyed] down here [on earth]. He said, "Yaa! This must be my house!" [But] HE WAS SURPRISED (*anadzadabwa*) – as the angels passed by (*alikudutsa*) that building. So he got a bit upset (*adakhumudwa*, lit., 'he tripped/became offended') saying, "A-ah? Hey, why should we go anywhere else (*nanga tikupitanso kuti*)? I was thinking that this house was the place (*nyumbayo ndi imeneyi*)!" They replied, "No, we have not yet arrived at your house.__[But] we're almost there (*tatsala pang'ono*)!" He said, "Eeeh! so my house is going to be even higher than this one?!"

They kept on walking and they arrived at another [building] of three stories. He said, "Yaaa! this must be the one (*koma imeneyi*)!" He was surprised when that angel again passed on by. "Aaah! WHY SHOULD WE GO anywhere else?" [The angel] replied, "NOOO! We have not yet arrived at your house!" The master said, "Yaa! My but where that place of mine is, hee! There must be a real house indeed (*koma kumeneko ndiye kuli nyumba yangayo, hee! n'nyumbadi!*)!"

He was surprised in the end when they went and entered the buuush (*kutheeengo*) – in [dense] bush as if it were a graveyard (*kuthengoko kokhala ngati manda*)! And there was a house [that looked like] a big goat pen (*chikhola cha mbuzi*) – without any windows, without a door, with all four sides – all four sides – of its roof broken up (*chidasasukasasuka*, lit., unthatched). Now that aaangel and the big man (*mkuluyo*, i.e., sarcastically)...what I'm telling you is no folktale (*si mwambi*) – I saw these things

---

[343] This graphic narrative-dialogue portion is an outstanding instance of the Chewa master-storyteller's artistry. It (along with other Wame examples) ranks among the best I have recorded in over a quarter century of listening and collecting in both Zambia and Malawi (cf. Wendland, *Nthano za kwa Kawaza*; Wendland, "Stylistic Form and Communicative Function").

in a book. So they arrived at the entrance and [the angel] says, "We have arrived, master (*bwana*). This is your house!" "WHAAAT?!" "This is your house." "A-ah? This can't be (*sizingatheke*)! How can you give me a house like this?! [The angel] says, "Master, sorry [but] this is no insult at all (*si chipongwe ayi*). This is YOUR house!" So [the man] asked, "Well what about THAT HOUSE that we passed by along the way – the three-storied one – whose is that?" The answer (*yaaankho*) – he says, "This belongs to that [garden] boy (*boyi*) of yours." "ALLL-AH! (i.e., an exclamation of extreme disgust) How can you give THAT BOY OF MINE a house like that – a GAAARDENER (*gaaadenaa*) – and MEE you throw out in the bush here?!" [The angel] replies, "Sorry, master – but here we do not insuuuult one another (*sitimatukwana*)!" "WELL HOW CAN YOU GIVE A GARDENER A HOUSE LIKE THAT?!" The answer – he says, "He kept on sending us two tambala [coins] (i.e., small offerings), and we used [all] those two tambala [coins] to build a house for him [here]." (much laughter) ALLELUUUUYA! (Amen!) [The angels said], "Iiiih! Don't give us so much trouble (*musativutitse*)!" – they just threw him (*adangowaponya*) into the house, and he collapsed to the ground there. *THASA!* (ideophone). Immediately the angels left [him] and were gone *ZII!* (ideophone).

WHEN WE MAKE OFFERINGS, we should not say anything at all (*sitimanena ayi*) [in complaint]. The Word of God says, "STORE UP FOR YOURSELVES treasure in heaven." IN THE LAST DAYS LIKE THESE, THOSE WHO ARE WIIISE (*ochenjeeeraaa*) [act as if they are on] TRAAANSFER (*talansifaaa*, i.e., to a new job, location or managerial/political position). God gives us wealth (or possessions, *chuma*) – for three reasons (*magawo atatu*): ONE – we must eat (*tizidya*, i.e., take care of our basic needs, metonymy); TWO – we should help the poor (*anthu osauka*); THREE – [we use for doing] his work.[344] [All] THIS WEALTH – if we do not use it for these purposes, when Jesus comes, IT WILL BE LEFT THERE ROTTING (*chitsaaalaa choowola*)! As for you – you will arrive in HEELL (*kugaheena*)! But if you use it for the work of God, [you

---

[344] Wame here reminds listeners of his central theme with which he began this sermon, namely, the responsibility (*udindo*) of the Christian. He dealt with the need for personal evangelism – sharing the gift of the gospel – in the first portion, but he devoted the greatest amount of attention to the obligation of each and every Christian to use the resources that God has given him/her – whether much or little – to support the Lord's pastoral ministry in the world. To be sure, this is a **natural result** of a believer's faith, but as Wame emphasizes here at the end, it will also bring its **gracious reward in** the heavenly life to come.

will receive] A TRANSFER!_[You] cause [those things] to go on ahead (*kuthawitsa*) – [and] they will get there aheeeaaad of you (*zizitsogolaaaa*)! (laugher) O WIIIISE PEEEERSON, store up for yourself treasure IN HEEEEAAVEN! Storing up [means] to use the WEALTH of God (i.e., for his purposes). [Then] when Jesus comes, it won't be lost (or destroyed, *sizithedwa*)!

I was preaching somewhere else (*ndimalalikira kwina*) and said: For those of you who have received Jesus the world will not end (*dziko silidzakutherani ayi*).[345] For the Word of God (i.e., John 3:18) says, "The one WHO BELIEVES in him is not judged (*saweruzidwa*, i.e., condemned)._ [But] the one WHO DOES NOT BELIEVE is judged even now." If a person walks in the will of God, GOOOOD THINGS (*zokooooma*) begin for him right down here (*pansi pompano*). But if you get lost [and leave] the will of God, PUNISHMENT [begins] right down here. You who believe in Jesus – THE JESUS who is coming – you are a FREE [and] developed person (*mfulu ndi chitukuko*).[346] The development that people [of this world] want is that they eat well, are happy, and enjoy themselves. But OUR development [is] (ironically) that we get sick and die. But JEEESUS is coming with the development of [all] developments of this world (*chitukuko cha zitukuko za dziko lapansi*, i.e., a "development" that outdoes all of them put together here in this world). Because THE DEVELOPMENT OF JESUS [means] no more death, no more famine, no more sickness! YOU WHO HAVE RECEIVED JESUS – the Jesus who is coming – you are [truly] a free [and] developed person.

WHAT IS GOING TO HAPPEN TO YOU is that the world (i.e., life) will not end for you, but there'll be a transfer – to leave [one] development (i.e., new spiritual life in Christ) and enter [another] DEVEELOPMENT (i.e., eternal life with Christ – *kuchoka m'chitukuko kulowa m'chitukukooo*)! HALELUUUYAA! To go and enter [that] DEVELOPMEENT! _To eat with them (*kudya nawo*, i.e., to enjoy [life] with

---

[345] Wame employs a rather subtle figure (metonymy) here, namely, "world" in the sense of "life." As he goes on to point out, believers will be "transferred" out of this temporal life of troubles and pain and into an eternal life of heavenly joy in a new "world" when Jesus comes again.

[346] Wame here uses the well-known abstract noun *chitukuko* ('development', commonly used to refer to socio-economic progress in a nation) as a unique metonym to refer to a "developed" person, that is, someone who is made complete (that is, fully "developed") in the eyes of God by his/her faith in Christ.

fellow believers)³⁴⁷ everywhere (*ponseponse*) – to eat with them down here ON EARTH – to eat with them IN HEEEAAVEN! I want you to be wise people.__The TIME is up (i.e., no more delaying)! He (or she) who wants his wealth to reach heaven – [to make] a TRANSFER – must use it for the work of God.__It will go on ahead [of him/her] (*chitsogola*). [The angels] might say, "Look (*taonani*), your 'boy' (i.e., menial worker) was sending [his] tambalas here.__[And] those TAMBALAS we were using to build a house for him (*timamumangitsira nyumba*). Well (*nanga*), did you send us anythiiing?!" The masters (bosses) will simply stand there *CHETE!* (ideophone) with nothing to say.

THE OFFERINGS THAT YOU GIVE – you are offering [them] to God.__You aren't throwing [them] away, not at all. WHATEEEVER you can give to the work of God has its reward in heaven. You ought to know this today. GIIIVE – giiive – give (*perekani*)! May the Lord bless us [all] (*Ambuye atidalitse*)! Aamen! (Ameeeen!)

---

³⁴⁷ Meal fellowship ranks very highly among the cultural value of the Bantu peoples. It demonstrates unity, harmony, solidarity, friendship, reconciliation, peace, and many other key social attitudes and qualities (see Healey and Sybertz, *Towards and African Narrative Theology*, ch. 6). Thus biblical imagery in this respect strikes a very responsive local chord (e.g., Luke 13: 29; 14: 15-24; 15: 25-32).

5. Summary and Assessment: Induction – Some Pros and Cons

Strong on Contextual Exemplification (Exhortation), Weak on Textual Exposition (Instruction)[348]

As has been shown in the preceding two chapters, an overall inductive-relational, topically recursive, dynamically integrated mode of discourse development establishes the rhetorical framework of the typical Chewa revivalistic type sermon in a contemporary sociocultural setting. Within this larger cumulative and climactic structural movement, ten overlapping stylistic techniques have been illustrated, those that have a special impact and appeal within a contextualized oral-aural medium of communication, where the gift of good *pronunciatio* to stimulate *logos* (message content), *ethos* (preacher credibility) and *pathos* (emotive interaction) is greatly appreciated. These features of course vary in the extent of their textual realization and effectiveness from one preacher to the next. But when and where manifested, they normally operate in close conjunction with one another – namely, three that pertain to the wider fabric of *generic preference*: narrative predominance, personal exemplification and traditional allusion; three that pertain to the *mode of presentation*: dramatic delivery, affective appeal and evocative description; three that pertain to the level of *micro-stylistic technique*: strategic reiteration, verbal intensification and idiomatic figuration; while all of the preceding serve to reinforce and to complement several more specific devices aimed at encouraging a participatory *audience involvement*.

This is a spontaneous, personally interactive, dialogic sort of rhetoric that encourages an active mental, verbal and even physical participation on the part of the listening audience with respect to their sensory, imaginative, emotional, volitional and intuitive faculties in addition to accessing the cognitive dimension of message transmission. Thus while considerable attention is devoted to the content of the biblical message and its contemporary application, the necessary psychological or experiential engagement of

---

[348] Martin Luther felt that "a sermon is comprised of teaching and exhortation (*Lehre* and *Ermahnung*). ...Teaching lays out for the people what is true [on the basis of Scripture]; exhortation encourages them to believe it and live it" (Meusner, *Luther the Preacher*, p. 25).

the audience with this Scriptural *logos* is encouraged through a strong appeal to their individual and collective recollection, imagination and feelings (*pathos*) along with an effort to assure them that the preacher is himself one of them (*ethos*) in terms of interests, needs, values, aspirations and spiritual problems in this life.[349]

The affinity of many sermons in the Chewa evangelistic-revivalist corpus to those that are typical of the African-American homiletical tradition has been noted on a number of occasions in this monograph. It is clear that this type of listener orientated preaching performance, which has many features in common also with the various types of indigenous African oral literature, differs considerably from a traditional Western sermonic production:

> Generally speaking, Black preaching is probably as varied in structure as White preaching, except that more Black sermons are apt to consist of one single Bible narrative (with or without extended comments on the side). Thus the percentage of classical or traditional sermons – with text, exposition, the inevitable trinity of points or applications, and climax – would be somewhat lower in the Black total. In addition, Black preaching, even when there are such "points," tends not to sound so carefully organized [*i.e., "telegraphed" in the text by means of devices such as enumeration and explicit transitions*]. The force of the message does not hinge so much on logical persuasion of the sort in which the preacher scores points in an essay or debate. Thus when Black preachers are more persuasive, they are apt to seem more to plead out of passion than to argue out of logic. They seek to guide the listeners in an experience, rather than to overwhelm them with intellectual evidence, even though they may use it well.[350]

But whereas various methods have been devised to evaluate the relative quality of the traditional Western sermon (largely deductively oriented, analytical criteria), there does not seem to be a corresponding number of means available to measure or assess the comparative *level of excellence* of the inductive sermonic composition in terms of features such as structural organization, exegetical fidelity, theological depth, practical (life related)

---

[349] Again it needs to be emphasized that the empowering, purifying and guiding operation of the Holy Spirit must be presupposed as the divine *sine qua non* in this entire discussion of stylistic technique and rhetorical effect with respect to any human audience.
[350] Mitchell, *Black Preaching*, p. 114.

relevance, pragmatic impact and esthetic appeal.[351] Clearly not all inductive sermons are created equal – but what is it that differentiates a better from a worse instance of the genre, how or on what basis is one to determine this and who should carry out the task of assessment?

It may seem out of place for a Westerner to attempt such an evaluation, but the following observations are offered as a place to begin the debate from the point of view of a participant-observer who has been studying (and practising) this subject for a considerable time, along with the invaluable advice and assistance of trained mother tongue Chewa pastors and lay preachers. Such an *etic*, or ethnic outsider's, perspective, if guided by competent *emic* (insider) input, may provide a valid, if imperfect, initial framework that may be complemented, corrected and perfected by the considered opinion of national scholars.[352]

What then are some of the pros and cons of the popular Chewa iterative-inductive homiletical approach? The benefits have, I think, been sufficiently outlined and illustrated in the preceding discussion. This particular rhetorical style, when employed to communicate a solid, biblically based message, has been used by God to work many significant, revival oriented mini movements in south central Africa, both evangelistic and edificational in nature, within and without the ecclesiastical circle of established church denominations and groupings. I believe that in particular these dynamic sermons have served to provide their addressees, including the thousands of weekly radio listeners, with some potent and captivating, strongly life related, Scriptural weapons for defending themselves against a powerful panoply of antagonistic forces, which are perceived as being the varied manifestations of Satan and sin in their society. As noted earlier, these

---

[351] Professor Frank Thomas, however, has made a good beginning with regard to the various "celebratory" aspects of preaching, for example, the "principles of celebrative design" (Thomas, *They Like to Never Quit Praisin' God*, pp. 43-48), "the preaching worksheet" (*ibid.*, pp. 74-80), and "the guidelines of celebration" (*ibid.*, pp. 90-98), namely, "avoidance of new concepts, contagious [emotional] conviction [preacher => congregation], affirmative [general] themes, focus on the [main sermon] theme, and [climactic] timing of impact" (*ibid.*, p. 90).

[352] Chichewa tradition offers a proverb that seems appropriate to the present situation: *mlendo ayenda ndi lumo lakuthwa* "the stranger/traveler moves about with a sharp razor" [i.e., with which he may "cut through" certain local disputes and controversies if so called upon]. Healey and Sybertz offer some pertinent comments on this issue and cite the following "African" proverb: "*It is the visitor who can point out where your roof leaks*" (Healy and Sybertz, *Towards and African Narrative Theology*, p. 14, italics as in the original text).

strongly contextualized hortatory messages directed against the various manifestations of latent (but still very potent!) traditional religion – such as, witchcraft, sorcery, spiritism, superstitions and magical practice – contrast markedly with the sermons that are typically preached in many formal (Protestant) worship services today.[353]

However, there is one major drawback as I see it, that is, assuming that the several other evaluative criteria listed below have been satisfied. This concerns mainly the *quantity* of exegesis and related instruction that is normally manifested in any given sermon. I have found the overall *quality* of exegesis generally to be rather limited but acceptable,[354] at least in the Wame corpus and taking into consideration the widespread lack of basic scholarly resources available to most of these preachers (e.g., Scripture commentaries, dictionaries, lexicons, study Bibles and Bible studies) in English, let alone corresponding texts written in the Chichewa language. The practical deficiency in their competency with respect to the biblical languages must also be considered. But the chief problem appears to be the absence of a sufficient amount of sustained, in depth *interpretation* with regard to the original (vernacular) text of Scripture, whether this happens to be applied in a localized or a periodic manner within the sermon and with reference to its specific historical, ecological, political and sociocultural context.

Thus most instances of a direct exegesis or exposition of a biblical pericope, though usually quite insightful and informative, tend to be very restricted in both scope and extent with respect to concrete (objective) facts as well as consequential (subjective) imperatives. At its worst, barring an outright misinterpretation of the text, an encounter with the original hermeneutical horizon takes the form of a partial consideration of only a relatively small portion of the keynote passage. This typically serves as merely a support for, or an illustration of, the main theme chosen for the sermon, or as a convenient springboard for an immediate, present day application, for example, with regard to some pressing, problem related exhortation or

---

[353] Cf. Ross, "Preaching in Mainstream Christian Churches in Malawi", pp. 90-94.
[354] Not unexpectedly, the greatest amount of exegetical difficulty seems to present itself in prophetic, especially eschatological, passages – for example, to cite one recent sermon, where the scene of Ezekiel ch. 39 is interpretively set completely within the framework of an apocalyptic, millennial (post-tribulation) world scenario.

admonition. Dierks calls attention to a related potential problem in this connection:

> By the existentialisation of the biblical text African sermons have an enthralling effect, since hearers identify existentially with Biblical events. The sermon does not remain a mere talk on a past occurrence but becomes an existential moment of decision for the congregation before God. However *African extentialisation runs the risk of dehistoricising biblical events.*[355]

While one must beware of probing too deeply or confidently into the psychology of an African "sermon experience" (especially on the part of a foreign observer), this danger must certainly be considered as a real possibility and countered by a greater measure of significant, clearly differentiated biblical background information related to the text at hand.

Thus, the crucial issue of widespread ignorance about the Scriptures and what they have to say in their own contextual setting (historical, sociocultural, geographical, etc.) is not being adequately addressed. It could be argued that one should not expect to find a great deal of interpretive exposition and instruction in an evangelistic or revivalistic sermon – that too much background information of such a nature is only distracting and irrelevant. However, there is a definite minimal critical mass that ought to be present to initiate and sustain a genuine, Spirit led, spiritual reaction and to serve as the divinely fixed foundation upon which all contemporary religious discourse, including so called local theologies, must necessarily be constructed. This would include a significantly greater emphasis upon and elucidation of the complete and interconnected divine story of salvation as recorded in both the Old as well as the New Testament, the unfamiliar accounts along with the old stand-bys.[356]

Although directed toward preaching in a completely different sociocultural setting, the observation by T.G. Long with regard to Western

---

[355] Dierks, Review of Rainer Albrecht, p. 140, italics added.
[356] With respect to his Ethiopian corpus, Forslund makes the seemingly contradictory observation: "Themes dealing with the duties and responsibilities of Christians are stressed more than themes on salvation. ... The exhortations which have an immediate bearing on Christian life are in many cases related to the spiritual sphere rather than to daily life" (Forslund, *The Word of God in Ethiopian Tongues*, p. 149). The second characterization in particular would not be typical of sermons of the Chewa revivalist preachers.

Christianity would seem to apply equally well to the current homiletical scene in central Africa:

> What is underplayed, of course, in the more recent understandings of sermon form [*and its concrete realization, or preachment*] is exactly what was emphasized in the traditional models: ideational content and didactic purpose. Ironically, the future may hold a renaissance of traditional sermon form as the pulpit increasingly faces a church unaware of its tradition and woefully lacking in knowledge of the basic content of the faith.[357]

Now in the African context we would not be dealing with a *renaissance* so much as a *discovery* of a greater measure of more *expository*, or educative, text centred preaching – not of the alien deductive-analytical variety, but moulded to fit within the framework of a more listener friendly, recursive-relational, inductive model as has been proposed in chapters 2 and 3. To that end, the following tentative evaluative and corrective criteria are proposed for consideration. With respect to any sermon then, one might critically interrogate its construction with rhetorically oriented queries such as these pertaining to structure, source, significance and style (they are merely suggestive of the types of question that need to be asked):

a) *Structure*: How tightly in terms of cohesion (form) and coherence (meaning) is the illustrative spiral wound around its medial thematic core? Do any of these outer topical segments seem to veer off course, or do entire loops appear to be extended too far from the conceptual (biblically based) nucleus? Is the central Scriptural focus ever lost or significantly blurred during the unfolding progression of the sermonic discourse? Does one illustration, image, citation, example or case study move smoothly to the next, or are there some jarring disjunctions and detours within the overall flow? Is there a strong, unified impression of the principal (theological, religious) theme and its rhetorical-pragmatic (didactic, hortatory, admonitory) purpose at the end of the discourse?

b) *Source*: How closely connected are the major theme(s) and all related illustrations, etc., to the main Scriptural texts that are cited during the course of the sermon? Are the latter mere decorative props (fillers), or do

---

[357] This is cited in Willimon and Lischer (eds.), *Concise Encyclopedia of Preaching*, p. 151; the words in italics are mine.

they play a significant role in the overall construction of the discourse? Do thematic Bible pericopes tend to be more law oriented or gospel centred in nature – is there a potential imbalance here? Does the practical relationship between these two basic types of text appear to be clearly demonstrated? Is there an over-emphasis upon personal sin and sanctification as opposed to divine action and enabling involvement? How clearly and coherently is the basic biblical plan of salvation presented? Do the various Scripture passages complement one another or do they lead the listeners off on topical tangents not closely related to the main theme? Are difficult terms and concepts in the vernacular version clearly explained? Is there a proper textual apportionment among the compositional components of biblical exposition, homiletical illustration, rhetorical elaboration, contemporary application and spiritual motivation (celebration)? Does the amount of explanation, interpretation and instruction pertaining to the original text reach the critical mass stage, that is, sufficient to support the amount of exhortation and admonition that is manifested in the sermon?

c) *Significance*: How does the sermon being preached measure up in terms of situational relevance, that is, with respect to the degree of processing effort required to understand its essential message in comparison with the number of valid (biblically based) contextual effects that listeners derive from it in their current circumstantial setting?[358] What is the level of local, experiential and life related contextualization that is exhibited by the sermon's message? How efficiently (subtly, appropriately, proportionately, etc.) is such material introduced and interrelated in the discourse? Is there a danger that the content and intent of the cited Scripture texts have been over-contextualized (transculturized), that is, unduly modified or even distorted in favor of an indigenous worldview, value system, religious framework and way of life? Has the sermon's main rhetorical (persuasive) and inspirational, or spiritual, purpose been achieved in relation to its primary audience and setting of proclamation? If not, what has gone wrong, and what may be done to set things right?

d) *Style*: How effectively is the sermon's message conveyed stylistically in the receptor language (Chichewa), especially with regard to naturalness on the level of both the macro- as well as the micro-structure of discourse

---

[358] E. A. Gutt, *Relevance Theory: A Guide to Successful Communication in Translation*, Dallas: Summer Institute of Linguistics, 1992, p. 24f.

formation? Is there any danger of the stylistic form overshadowing the discourse content during the presentation? To what extent has an appeal to both *pathos* and *ethos* been utilized to reinforce the primary theological *logos* content being proclaimed as well as its practical, life related implications? Is there any imbalance or exaggeration with regard to the level of *pathos* or *ethos* that is evoked in the text, that is, in relation to *logos*? In other words, does the preacher play to his audience or seem to magnify himself at the expense of the biblical text? Or does the elaborate nature of the rhetorical strategy itself somehow deflect attention from the central theme in any way? How has the oral-aural dimension of communication been accommodated, and actually capitalized upon and promoted during the process of both verbal and also non-verbal transmission? Does the sermon cater for the ear as well as the mind's eye of individual and collective imagination in order to facilitate an immediate application of the essential message of Scripture to the heart as well as the mind of the audience?

Conclusion: Five Proposals

We may note the following major implications of the present preliminary study concerning the nature, composition and effects of contemporary popular sermonody in (south central) Africa. These pertain in particular to the rhetorical power (form) and related spiritual power (content and function) of this sort of a sermon style, which constitutes the primary focus of the religious desires and needs of the people that it is intended to serve:[359]

a) The teaching of *homiletics* in seminaries, theological colleges, Bible schools and TEE (Theological Education by Extension) programs needs to be contextualized to a much greater degree in the effort to develop and encourage a more indigenous, *African model* of sermon construction. The results of the present study would seem to indicate that the potential value of a recursive-relational, emotive-experiential, inductive method must be

---

[359] On the crucial notion of power in relation to a central African world-view and traditional religious beliefs, see Wendland 1990, "Traditional Central African Religion", pp. 83-87; Wendland, "*Ufiti* – Foundation of an Indigenous Philosophy of Misfortune", pp. 214-219. I must continue to specify the location of this study and hence also to circumscribe the observations and conclusions that are based upon it lest it be assumed that they are meant to be applied to every region in Africa. My results may or may not be valid or supportive in relation to similar research being carried out elsewhere on the continent. There is thus a great need to encourage and coordinate these different homiletical investigations (cf. the Preface to this volume).

more fully investigated in this regard. However, this should be complemented by a more fully applied, text-oriented approach in order to provide greater instruction in the Word for both the preachers themselves (through their formal training) and the congregations that they serve (through their Scripture centered preaching).

To this end I would like to propose the wider use of what might be termed an "integrated homily" type of sermon. As in the case of the classical homily (cf. chapter 2), a presentation of this nature would be based upon a sustained verse-by-verse unfolding of the sense and significance of key concepts of the biblical text in relation to its original context on the one hand and an appropriate central theme on the other. This progressive exposition would in turn be continually and extensively illustrated and applied by inductive means (including the use of parallel and associated Scripture passages) throughout the development of the discourse as a whole, as shown schematically on the diagram below:[360]

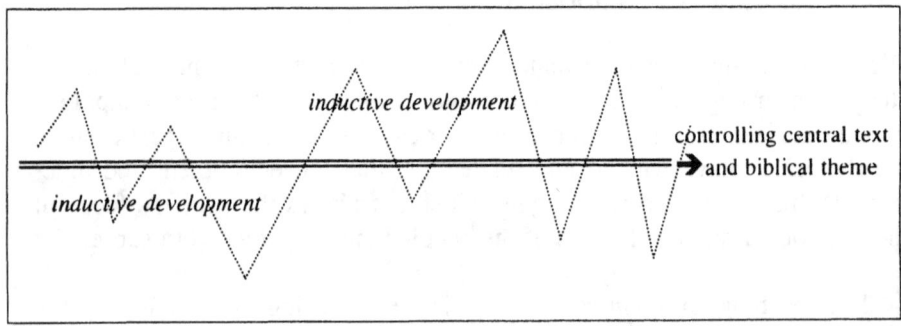

Perhaps the use of a more inductively oriented technique might prove helpful too in the practical teaching of sermon preparation and presentation. Such instruction could be carried out, for example by means of case studies

---

[360] The homiletical method that I am proposing here essentially originates with Martin Luther (and no doubt others as well), as described by Meusner (Meusner, *Luther the Preacher*, p. 47): "The aim of the sermon is therefore to help hearers understand the *text*, not just a religious truth. ...Its method is to take a given segment of Scripture, find the key thought within it, and make that unmistakably clear. The text is to control the sermon. ...A homily usually moves verse by verse, without tying the whole together. Luther insisted on finding the *Sinnmitte*, the heart of the text. That heart, that *Kern* or kernel is to save the preacher from getting lost in details. Every story has a *Herzpunkt* which the preacher must find and return to again and again. ...The main point of a sermon is to be so clear in the preacher's mind that it controls everything that is said."

(i.e., studying vernacular sermon exemplars, both good and bad), the joint class critique of recognized outstanding instances, a greater level of instructor-student dialogue, the tape (with or without video) recording and later critical (but non-confrontational) discussion of student sermons, involving actual congregational audiences in the assessment and promotion of various methods and styles of preaching, and so forth.[361]

One primary goal of such an exercise in indigenization would be to develop a flexible, situation sensitive set of receptor centred diagnostic criteria (along the lines of those proposed above, but more emic in nature) for evaluating the relative *quality* of such predominantly inductive productions and their communicative effectiveness in comparison with either a purely deductive or a mixed approach. However, the critical problem of a general lack of sustained biblical exegesis and exposition also needs to be honestly addressed. In what way(s) might inductively oriented preachers naturally incorporate a greater amount of basic Scripture study into their sermons, that is, without detracting from their popular style of presentation? Are students being given an adequate foundation in biblical studies to enable them to effectively bridge the hermeneutical gap between the original text and its present day context – that is, to competently deal with a passage exegetically? If not, what types of courses would help most to remedy the situation from an indigenous, national perspective?

b) The results of this and similar studies of effective oral discourse in the Bantu vernaculars may be cautiously and carefully applied to the production of needed *written* materials in the language – Bible translation, for example, or the development of various kinds of Christian *literature* (educational/instructional booklets, tracts, Bible studies, etc.). In other words, one would seek to encourage the use of a more familiar inductive method in terms of stylistic form and rhetorical technique in order to achieve greater naturalness (idiomacity), impact (dynamicity), appropriateness

---

[361] Cf. Wendland, "The Case for a 'Case-Study'". Augustine, who argued that rhetorical eloquence cannot be separated from biblical truth, was of the opinion that "this eloquence should be gained not in school (although such training is fine for youths), but simply from reading the scriptures and the works of good Christian writers and from listening to accomplished preachers" (Oberhelman, *Rhetoric and Homiletics*, p. 116). In his colorful way, John Chrysostom also argued that "...as we likewise have to roast the gold drawn from Apostolic mines, not by casting it into the furnace, but by depositing it in the thoughts of your souls; not by lighting an earthly flame, but kindling the fire of the Spirit, let us collect the little particles with diligence" (cited in Pless, "Seven Pulpit Paradigms", p. 193).

(relevancy) and appeal (attractiveness/beauty) in the diverse texts that are being produced.[362] Which oral-aural compositional devices would continue to be natural, and which would sound unnatural or artificial, when transformed into the medium of the printed word (e.g., use of the ideophone, exclamations, syntactic anacolutha, word order variations, etc.)? What may be done to produce a more reader friendly text – that is, one which is not only easier but also more meaningful to actually read (through the application of various text formatting and typographical techniques)? In this connection, one would also need to investigate the crucial economic factor – that is, how much more costly would it be to publish literature of this nature, for example, due to the greater level of redundancy, illustration, and format modification that would have to be incorporated into any given text or lesson?

c) The employment of an iterative, inductive-relational style should also be studied with regard to other mass media methods, such as cassette recording, video production and television. To what extent is a *transmediatization* of the message possible, or even to be encouraged, not only with respect to biblical-religious content, but also in terms of stylistic form and rhetorical strategy?[363] While such a ready cross media transfer of this method might be simply assumed, it should really be thoroughly previewed and audience tested first in view of the particular characteristics of the specific medium concerned. Video communication of course adds a whole new dimension to the process of message transmission, and therefore its effect on the composition of the message cannot be simply taken for granted, e.g., with respect

---

[362] In their attempt to use the Scriptures as their primary model in sermonizing, Augustine and his colleagues faced a formidable barrier – namely, the woodenly literal nature of the various translations that were currently available in the Latin language. Thus in contrast to the dynamic, masterful style that is everywhere evident in the original (Hebrew and Greek) text, Augustine had to make do with a "Bible, which, unfortunately, existed in Latin versions of such clumsy, illiterate, even incomprehensible grammar and syntax that some Christian intellectuals cringed when approaching the text" (Oberhelman, *Rhetoric and Homiletics*, p. 115). His contemporary, Jerome, forged ahead and did something about this lack by rendering a completely new translation. This masterful work was "prepared for the people as a whole, from which fact it gained the name *vulgatus*, and is known today as the Vulgate" (E. A. Nida, *God's Word in Man's Language*, New York: Harper and Row, 1952, p. 81). The sermons of the popular Chewa revivalists serve as a valuable resource for developing key theological terms and religious expressions that may be utilized in a popular-language Bible translation as well as in meaningful (non-jargonized) Christian literature even today (cf. Wendland, *Buku Loyera*).
[363] Cf. T.E. Boomershine, "A Transmediatization Theory of Biblical Translation", *Bulletin: United Bible Societies* 170/171 (1994), New York: United Bible Societies.

to overall discourse organization on the one hand and the variegated nuances of idiomatic verbal diction on the other.

In this connection, detailed *research* into the relative effectiveness of the various mass media productions needs to be carried out and continually re-evaluated in view of current and probable future developments, not only technologically, but also with respect to the overall socio-economic situation of the target population. Despite initial predictions of the imminent demise of the radio, for example, it certainly is not dead yet, not even in the West where it has experienced a surprising renaissance in recent years (e.g., talk shows, panel discussions and phone in dialogues to complement the ever-popular musical programs). I am of the opinion that as far as the next decade and south central Africa is concerned, the audio (radio/cassette) medium holds the greatest potential for improving the communicative capacity and consumer outreach of a biblically based, contextually sensitive Christian message.[364]

d) These Chewa revivalist sermons should serve as valuable sources and instances of grass roots *theological reflection* because they are usually preached outside the confines of formal, mainline worship services (where

---

[364] For an earlier study of mine on the significant communicative possibilities of the audio (radio) medium, see Wendland, "Stylistic Form and Communicative Function", pp. 87-110. The potential outreach of radio has been considerably magnified in recent years due to the establishment of a number of local Christian stations in south-central Africa (that is, in addition to the large, regional transmissions of *TransWorld Radio*), e.g., *Radio Christian Voice*, which in addition to its normal FM programming, also broadcasts in short-wave. My assessment has been more recently been supported by the mass-media research of Spitulnik: "The linguistic significance of radio in Zambia is substantial because it is the most widely consumed medium in the country, it is a primary site for exposure to English, and it is the only widespread mass communication form that uses Zambian languages" (Spitulnik, "The Social Circulation of Media Discourse and the Mediation of Communities", p. 165). Surveys have indicated that 63% of Zambia's total population listen in to the radio "daily or almost daily" (ibid., p. 183). Spitulnik concludes that "radio is a source and reference point for phrases and tropes which circulate across communities ... they are part of what can be termed a society's (or a subculture's) 'public words.' ... Many of the popular phrases inspired by radio broadcasting have a distinctive kind of symbolic value because of their association with the medium, which is itself a site of innovation, word play, and colorful drama. ... As a far-reaching, ongoing, public communication form...radio broadcasting has the potential to magnify, and even create, this 'socially charged life' of certain linguistic forms" (ibid., pp. 166, 170, 182). The implications for popular radio preaching should be obvious, though further research is needed to substantiate this supposed impact with regard to current religious vocabulary and idiom. For example, preachers who either prepare their sermons directly for radio broadcast or who know that their sermons will be recorded and later broadcast will want to make sure that the graphic, potentially catching and memorable expressions that they use do in fact accurately reflect basic biblical truths and imperatives (cf. point [d] above).

the theology tends to be kept more ecclesiastically party line in nature), to people who may not be regular church goers and by evangelists who may not have experienced a formal seminary or Bible college training (e.g., Shadrack Wame himself). Their particular hermeneutical approach to the Scriptures (e.g., what they tend to find interesting, significant, problematic and preach-worthy) and their concrete manner of contextualizing the Word for their audiences will certainly prove to be instructive to theologians, teachers and theological students alike.

Some form of classificatory *catalogue* of these homiletical images, illustrations, insights and implications ought to be prepared for the purpose of analysis within one language culture group and then compared with similar studies made elsewhere on the continent. Most (if not all) of the Chewa popular preachers are oral communicators alone (i.e., they do not contribute to theological journals, church magazines, etc.), and hence their sermons (theology) are accessible and analyzable only through some type of recording, whether audio or video.[365] Their concerns, perspectives, methods and proposed solutions with regard to key theological and moral issues need to be more fully investigated and made available (published) for future analysis, evaluation, inspiration and application by national religious scholars and other members of the clergy.

e) This study has shown that the ancient gospel communication method of *preaching* (cf. Acts 2) is definitely *not passe*, at least not with reference to its current use in south central Africa. Although the publicly preached sermon may be a Western importation as far as its genre is concerned (having no real indigenous Bantu equivalent), it does not seem to be regarded as an undesirable or ineffective imposition. On the contrary, the *sermon* has been enthusiastically adopted in one format or another by virtually all Christian church bodies, including the so called African Independent Churches (AICs), whose preachers exhibit some of the longest, most colorful instances of this didactic, hortatory, Christian verbal art form.

---

[365] This crucial indigenous resource needs to be discussed more extensively, for example, in the otherwise thorough work of Healey and Sybertz – that is, in relation to methodological issues concerning the development of "an African narrative theology of inculturation" (Healey and Sybertz, *Towards an African Narrative Theology*, ch. 1).

Furthermore, the fear of public speaking (on the part of men) is not nearly the problem that it is in the West which has no comparable institution to the still dynamic oral tradition of Africa (hence proportionately fewer potential lay preachers available for Christian witness). Similarly, in the West (outside of the long standing African-American tradition) we see a general decline in the influence and impact of the listening audience upon the sermon (hence also the preacher) since the prevailing media of the modern age generally encourage listener passivity, silent visualization, personal individualism and a lack of participation or interaction, either with the source of the message or with fellow receptors. Perhaps there is something significant here that Africa could teach the West with regard to the crucial importance of the *spoken* word (in its essential bonding role) when proclaiming the living Word for the "teaching, rebuking, correcting and training" of the *communal* fellowship of believers in Jesus Christ (2Tim 3:16, NIV). The vital sermon event is not intended to be a mere intellectual exercise. Rather, it should function to captivate the entire sensory and psychological capacity of the congregation present, one that is fully engaged in the performance, not as isolated individuals, but as mutually participating members of a dynamic community of faith and life.

I would therefore conclude that public preaching, when carried out along the experience oriented but text based, inductive-relational lines suggested earlier, is a very effective means of reaching the masses with a relatively complete representation of the emotive and volitional aspects of the message of Scripture. However, as also noted, such a programme needs to be carried out with a greater emphasis being laid upon a more substantial *cognitive* foundation, that is, fundamental textual exposition. This is to accomplish the goal of helping people overcome their general *lack of knowledge* of the Bible (in its details as well as its dynamics) and their consequent fear of the various forces of imminent evil in their hearts and lives – malevolent powers that have already been completely defeated by the cross and resurrection of Jesus Christ (Eph 1:19-23). As the apostle John emphasizes in his first epistle, a true "knowledge" of God and his Son, Jesus Christ is able to generate by his Spirit the "perfect love that casts out all fear" (4:18; cf. 2:21,27;3:18-19;4:1-3;5:2-3,20).

In order to follow up on the above applications, **however,** and also to provide a satisfactory basis for future **research, we need** to encourage the gathering of an adequate corpus of sermon texts – collected in various Bantu vernaculars as well as in local English – in print as an unsatisfactory minimum, but ideally recorded in audio and, if possible, also video form. These examples must all be accurately transcribed, translated, annotated (including structural, rhetorical-stylistic, as well as performance and sociocultural contextual data, and studied with regard to form, content, function and (where available also) audience reaction. A collection of such concrete case studies – ideally analyzed and evaluated by national scholars and sermon practitioners – will enable us to refine, correct, supplement, and apply the results of the present minimal investigation.[366] This will in turn give us a much clearer picture of the rhetorical potency and potential of the Holy Scriptures as they are being preached and taught via different communications media against the diverse powers of darkness – internal and external, social and spiritual, personal and institutional, intellectual and experiential, traditional and modern – that trouble the everyday world of the public majority in (south central) Africa. Can the light of the gospel of Jesus Christ not be communicated with an even larger measure of luminance – that is, with more completeness, comprehension, and conviction – through the use of more indigenous African models, materials and methods? The heart grabbing sermons of Shadrack Wame can surely set us off in the right direction and spur us on in this determined search for greater homiletical energy, effectiveness and relevance.

---

[366] After his book-length study of Ethiopian sermons, Forslund too proposes that "others investigate how rhetorical studies can contribute to a better understanding of the preaching in [non-Western] churches" (Forslund, *The Word of God in Ethiopian Tongues*, p. 247). Such research may in turn perform a contrastive and corrective role by drawing attention to what it is that makes much Western-style deductive sermonizing so dead (spiritually), dry (stylistically), and dormant (in terms of significance) for many African audiences – notwithstanding the clear emphasis upon the saving Scriptures that they may indeed manifest.

APPENDIX A

"My Testimony" by Shadrack Wame[367]

Mr and Mrs Wame

Beloved of God, greetings in the most gracious and wonderful name of our Lord Jesus Christ.

I want to tell you how I came to know the Lord and received him as my personal Saviour and of what he is doing in my daily life up to now.

My name is Shadrack Jonas Wame and I was born on 21st October, 1940 in Amwanzalamba Village, Traditional Authority Ndindi, Salima District. I was born in a Christian family, and my parents and I are still Christians in a Presbyterian Church (Church of Central African Presbyterian).

I started attending Catechism lessons in 1960 and was baptized in April, 1962. When I was baptized, I took life easy because I thought I had achieved all what a man is supposed to achieve in a Christian life. I thought I had received eternal life. I did not know that Christianity is in two parts:

1. Christianity that is outside the heart and soul which can be seen with human eyes.

2. Christianity that affects the soul which leads to forgiveness of sins and eternal life.

The first part of Christian life has steps a man has to fulfil, i.e. taking Holy Communion, giving offerings, church positions, membership, etc. This is merely a religious part whereby we thank the Lord for all the good things he has done for us, but it never saves a man. But when we serve the Lord

---

[367] The following text is an exact duplication of a written document that was given to me by Evangelist Wame on April 10, 1998 (Good Friday). It is reproduced here with his kind permission. Incidentally, it indicates that Mr Wame's competence in English is considerably greater than he admits to, no doubt in the interest of humility.

honestly, he shall give us a gift in addition to the grace which we received when we accepted him to be our Saviour.

The second part of Christianity is that of the soul which is in the hands of the Almighty God and is therefore only possible with Him alone. This is the type of Christianity that changes the heart of a person and therefore leads to eternal life. This is what the Lord Jesus Christ talked about in a discussion with Nicodemus (John 3:1-10). These two types of Christianity combine together to make a person acceptable before God.

I was a religious man for six years from 1962 to 1967, but I lacked the soul-affecting Christianity. I was lost in worldly things, among which four were main ones as follows:

1. I wanted to get rich and therefore went to a witchdoctor who later came to my house to make money for me amounting to MK 10,000 (ten thousand Malawi Kwacha). During the money-making process, a lot of things took place which would require more paper to write on. Then I was invited to visit his home so as to give me instructions on how to keep the wealth. I used to go to the witchdoctor's home only during the night. The Bible says, "Whosoever committeth sin is the slave of sin." I was truly a slave of sin.

When I arrived at the witchdoctor's home, I was taken to the graveyard where I talked to the spirits of the ancestors, who instructed me not to use the money before taking some medicine so as to use the money carefully. The witchdoctor demanded a deposit (fee) of MK 48.00 (forty-eight Malawi Kwacha), whilst the normal fee was MK 300.00 (three hundred Malawi Kwacha).

2. I was a tobacco smoker.

3. I liked dances.

4. I used to put on magic charms to enable me to know those practising witchcraft, and I really knew them. I also had a bad temper.[368]

---

[368] Note for those who do not live in a local setting: The four "worldly things" that Mr Wame describes here are not unusual for the times; most young men – even Christians – indulge in these same vices, and probably add another, namely, a great deal of extra-marital sexual activity.

All these things came to an end in November 1967 at 6:00 p.m. when I had organized a dance at my house in Blantyre City.[369] The dance was intended to run throughout the night, but gramophone needles needed replacement with some new ones. So I left my house for the nearest shop to buy some. On my way back I was hit by a motor car, and I fainted. While in that state, I found myself going to the heavenly throne of God the Almighty. As I was approaching, I saw all the bad things I did while here on earth, and I knew there was nothing good for me before God.

When I was hit, I did not feel any pain at all because death does not pain, but sickness does. So when we are in this world, we should not fear death, but rather we should be afraid of our destination. Just as good as when God called Adam in the Garden of Eden, the man said he was afraid because he was naked. He was afraid to appear before God in his nakedness. As I was nearing God's throne, there was a cool breeze which, upon reaching me, returned me back to normal life. It is at that time when I realized that I was surrounded by many people and policemen who took me to the hospital where I was admitted for 4 (four) days.

During the night of the day I was discharged from the hospital, I heard the voice of the Lord in a vision saying, "TOO MANY EVIL THINGS" and I knew the accident was a punishment from God for the evil things I had done. At that moment I confessed my sins to the Lord and I asked for his forgiveness, which He did. The other night I had a vision of the Lord Jesus Christ who came to teach me the perfect Christian life. Shortly afterwards I woke up and recorded everything in a notebook. When I had slept, the Lord came to me again to continue His teaching, and I recorded the event again, and this happened four times. That night the Lord was with me from 9:00 p.m. to 4:00 a.m. the following morning.

When the Lord appeared to me for the fourth time, I saw a vision of heavy wind, which dropped letters from heaven followed by numerous fish (*chambo*), the tilapia type. Then I saw an angel from God who came to sort out the letters until the one addressed to me was found. The message in this letter read, "*This is your Glory from now onwards.*" Lastly, in the same vision I was made to carry a basket full of Bibles.

---

[369] No specific day is mentioned in the text at this point.

The meaning of all these were:

1. The letter indicated my salvation.
2. The basket full of Bibles indicated my work for the Lord.
3. The fish indicated people to whom I would witness.

This happened on 29th January, 1968, and from that time I have four note books in which I record the Lord's teachings. I never went to a Bible School, neither did I go to any Bible College. I am not against anyone going to these institutions though, because I know that this is where one adds up knowledge and wisdom to the revelations we receive at the time we receive Jesus Christ in our hearts as our personal Saviour.

One other night I saw a white hand with a measure like a ball-point pen. Then I heard a voice telling me that time was gone, with a finger pointing at the point of the pen indicating that [the] time left was as short as the pen's point. The voice further said [that] I had gathered wealth in the very last days, and there was very little time left for me to spend it. Where, therefore, could I use it (James 5:3)? When I woke up the next day, these words were like a hammer in my heart. Thereafter and during the daytime I saw the Lord Jesus coming to whip me because of the money the witchdoctor had made for me. I cried bitterly, and when people saw me crying, they thought I was mad, not knowing that it was the power of the Lord Jesus Christ.

I did not have [the] peace of mind until I returned the money back to the witchdoctor, and I also witnessed to him that if he did not repent, God would destroy him because he had nothing good before God.

When I came back home, an angel of the Lord appeared to me at night and took me to a big house full of God's glory. The angel opened the door and showed me heavenly treasures. I was then asked whether or not I ever read Matthew 6:19, and if I did, I was asked to quote the verse. I answered affirmatively and said, "Lay not up [for] yourselves treasures on earth, where moth and rust doth corrupt, and where thieves break through and steal (verse 20). But lay up for yourselves treasures in heaven, where neither moth nor rust doth corrupt, and where thieves do not break through and steal."

The angel told me that from that date my treasure was that which I saw, and he asked why I was wasting my time on earthly treasures. Now I have so much heavenly treasures that I am sharing to various people in various places.

While I was in my house another day, I also heard the voice of the Lord telling me to throw away the magic charms I had because that was a beast. It was very difficult for me to throw it away wholeheartedly because each time I threw it away, I took it back again. There was conflict within my heart; so many questions cropped up in my mind. I thought that if I did throw away the charms, I could be bewitched. This really shows that when one wants to repent, there is such a strong conflict within the heart - so much that if one is not decided, it is very difficult to repent from [a] sinful life.

I finally threw the charms away wholeheartedly, and an angel of the Lord came that night and woke me up. I then realized that the door of my house was open, and [I] did not know who had opened it. The angel asked me to look to the doorway, and to my surprise I saw a lion going out of my house. I was told that the lion was the magic charm I threw away. I was assured that by keeping the charms, I tamed that lion, and therefore whosoever keeps sin in his heart, he or she tames a beast which will appear on the last day.

While sleeping in my house one night, an angel came to me and showed me a very big white cloth and asked me to observe it more closely to see what was to happen to the cloth. I then saw smoke coming from the cloth which dirtened the whole cloth. The angel then explained that the white cloth indicated how one's heart should be, but when one starts smoking, the heart becomes dirty, and the Holy Spirit cannot dwell in such a heart. I then realized that smoking is sin and stopped smoking immediately.

At the time I was hit by a motor car and whilst unconscious, I heard a voice and then was shown the sin of dances. Right away I sold the gramophone I had and warned the buyer to be very careful not to use it for similar types of dances [that] I used to organize.

The buyer ignored my warning and started to use it for the dances he organized. Not long did he do this and he was also hit by a motor car. He then sold it to another man who used it for the same purpose, and he was also hit by a motor car.

After washing away my sins mentioned above, the Lord blessed me with the following:

1. Grocery shop

2. Instead of trusting magic charms to know those practising witchcraft, an angel of the Lord comes to tell me what would happen to me before hand.

3. Instead of the gramophone, I now have a good record player which I use for spiritual music.

When God removes sin, He fills one's life with very good things. My evangelism ministry started when an angel of the Lord appeared to me in a vision and took me in spirit to a football pitch-like area surrounded by all the churches in the world. The angel asked whether or not I knew why I was placed at the centre of the churches. I was told [that] this was because I had a very big task in these churches. In all the churches, the angel said, one thing was missing in them. I was therefore told to go to all the churches, starting with my own, regardless of the differences in their practices.

Upon hearing this, I was very surprised and I could not imagine what this one thing is. The angel then instructed me not to preach against the church traditions or religion. Both of these are being followed very well, but one thing [is] missed – JESUS. That reminded me of Martha who cried unto Jesus, "Lord, if thou hadst been here, my brother may not have died" (John 11:21). Martha knew that wherever Jesus is, there is peace – no mourning. There was death in Martha's home because Jesus was not there. This also means that whenever there is no Jesus in a family, there is always mourning in the heart, quarrelling, fighting, etc. A church which does not have Jesus is mourning everyday.

The Lord told me to preach Jesus wherever I go and Him alone. Since I had this vision, I have been invited to minister to various churches. Indeed, the vision had opened the doors in the churches. Since 1967 till now, I have never organized a meeting on my own but have ever since been invited by various churches here in Malawi, colleges, secondary and primary schools, villages, individuals in their homes (house to house), fellowship groups, and do preach in open air meetings in places like market squares.

Out of 24 (twenty-four) districts in Malawi, I have visited 21 (twenty-one) districts. I have not yet visited the remaining 3 (three) because of pressure of God's work. In the district visited I have helped people in many ways, and some people invite me for personal spiritual needs.

The Lord blessed me with the following gifts: teaching, knowledge, healing, revival, encouraging and evangelism through letters. The Lord shows me everything that I meet in my ministry and all the blessings before hand. Not only does the Lord show me this, but also my weakness after the ministry, which I later rectify.

In this ministry I just commit my life to the Lord and as such I don't get paid. I was once employed by the government as a gardener taking care of the flowers for 17 years. Since I met the Lord, I have been going to various places using my own money, and when it was evident there was too much work, I decided to fully commit my life to the Lord and thus retired in 1980.

After my retirement, I went back home where I asked the Lord how I would be supported in this ministry. The Lord showed me the hawker business where I could get transport money.[370] The Lord is still blessing me so much that I now have a grocery shop from where I get money for my transport and other needs.

I did not go further in my education because my parents were so poor that they could not afford to pay for my school fees. I paid fees on my own by getting employed in one year and the following year going to school. So I was on and off from school. I only attended up to standard 4 at a primary school.

---

[370] A hawker is a person who sells various small items out of a little portable stand or a more permanent shop. Obviously, this is not a very high-paying business.

I am a Chewa by tribe, and I can read English but not speak fluently. Nevertheless, I understand many things in English.

I praise and thank the Lord who died for me on Calvary and shed His precious blood for me, a sinner, and put me [as] a Watchman to preach. I do not have anything to give the Lord in return other than to commit myself so that the Lord can receive honour for everything He did for me (2 Timothy 2:2).

Yours in the Lord Jesus Christ,

Shadrack Jonas Wame
P.O. Box 242
Salima, Malawi

B. Further Comments By aWame on Preaching[371]

Four Characteristics of a Good Gospel Preacher

1. He must first be *born again* by a regenerative act of God (like Nicodemus, John 3). Every human being, including the preacher, is like the embryo of an egg: he must be born twice. The first birth occurs in the form of the egg itself. But obviously that is not enough for true life; God must break that hard outer shell so that the person can emerge and live and grow in the image of God to reach his (her) full potential.

2. He must *grow spiritually* (*mwauzimu*) by continually reading and studying the Word of God. His aim is to learn the "deep things" of Scripture so that he can feed his flock sufficiently and in a fitting manner. The pastor's business is not to see visions or work miracles but to communicate God's "wisdom" (1Cor 2).

---

[371] The following is a selective summary of a two-hour interview that I had with Evangelist Wame (in Chichewa) on 13 April 1998 in Lusaka (Kamwala). In my questions, I tried to focus upon his God-given gift of preaching the gospel: How does he go about it, especially in terms of method and preparation, both mental and spiritual? But I really did not have to lead him in this interview, for Mr Wame had already prepared in advance much of what he wanted to say on the subject before I arrived, for example, the "four characteristics of a good preacher" with which he began.

3. He must carefully *study man*, who is the one receiving the divine message. The preacher cannot assume that he knows his people simply because he is a fellow human being. "People are difficult" (*munthu ndi wovuta*), i.e., in the sense that they are naturally resistant to God's Word and ways, and yet they are also as spiritually fragile as the mantle of a gas lamp. Therefore, the pastor has to diligently investigate all their customs, thoughts and behaviours (*miyambo, maganizo, makhalidwe*) so that he can better prepare his sermons to meet their needs and weaknesses. Often the best way to do this is simply by visiting the people on a regular basis so that he can get to really know them.

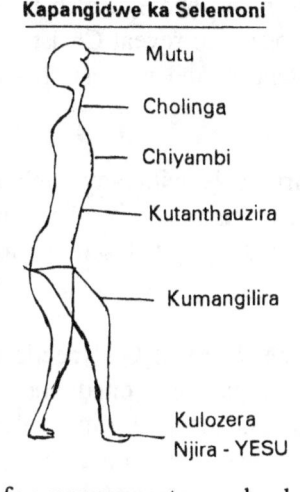

4. He must learn *how to catch* (*-gwira*) people with the gospel. The main point here is for young pastors who have just graduated from the seminary or some theological college to make every effort to transform all their religious theory into practice so that they will not fail in the field, where their real "test" will come. They have to learn how to imitate a skilled hunter (*mlenje*) who fully knows the individual characteristics of his weapon(s), the various types of game that he will be hunting, where he must strike each type for the best results and the method of stalking each one so as to outsmart it. One of the main things for the preacher to keep in mind in this regard is to "lower his knowledge" (*kutsitsa nzeru*) so that he does not preach over their heads and hence completely miss their hearts with his message.

The Making of a Good Sermon (*Kapangidwe ka Selemoni*)

There are six parts involved in the process of composing a sermon; they correspond to the human body, beginning with the head and moving down:[372]

---

[2] Mr Wame had drawn a little diagram for me according to which he illustrated these six points.

1. Head = the foundation (*maziko*): This is the text (passage/s) from the Bible on which the sermon is to be based. Every proper sermon starts here, not with all sorts of stories about personal experiences.

2. Neck = the aim (*cholinga*): Here we have the main theme, which leads people into the sermon proper. The primary purpose is to reveal Christ and to magnify Him. One must also capture their attention and interest so that they are prepared to listen further.

3. Heart = the beginning (*chiyambi*): This part deals with any biblical background information that is needed (e.g., history) so that the congregation can properly understand the text in its original setting and circumstances.

4. Abdomen = interpretation (*kutanthauzira*): The Word of God needs to be clearly explained on the basis of the various passages cited and in relation to the closest corresponding meaning (places, titles, customs, roles, etc.) that is apparent in the present day lives and experience of the congregation.

5. Thighs = conviction (*kumangirira*): The people's sinful way of life in contrast to God's will needs to be exposed and rebuked so that they can sincerely repent of all their wickedness. Here the law of God is used to show people what they ought to be doing as his servants, but how they have failed in this respect.

6. Feet = direction to Christ (*kulozera kwa Yesu*): After being convicted of their sin, people need to be shown what to do. They must also be empowered by the Word and pointed in the direction they must travel in life so that they can best serve the Saviour who did so much for them and left them an example to follow.

Dealing with Witchcraft (*Ufiti*)

Having conquered the power of witchcraft and magic in his own life, Wame is not afraid to tackle this controversial occult subject in his sermons. He offers the following three pieces of advice for those who are troubled by such manifestations of Satan in their lives:[373]

1. Acknowledge the superior power of Christ. His power is supreme, for he is the "master of all witches" (*mfiti ya mafiti onse,* lit. 'the witch of all witches'!). This vital fact is demonstrated in that he can do anything that they can (e.g., pass through solid walls) - and more (e.g., be present everywhere in the world at once). He also created the very items of nature that witches use in their spells (e.g., parts of a tree). Christ has already defeated Satan, and he dwells with his protective powers within each and every believer (1 John 4:4).

2. Make use of the mighty God-given weapon that we have - the Bible. Satan will always run away from the Word of God (Mt 4:1-11) since it is the sword of the Spirit for conquering all the evil spirits and forces that come to attack us (Eph 6:10-17).

3. Do not give Satan a chance or reason (*chifukwa*) to get into your life by allowing some unrepentant sin to dwell within your heart. Such wickedness can only grow and lead to spiritual death (James 1:13-15). It is like a "landing strip" that invites witches (demons) to "fly in" and enter your life-space. So first repent of that sin so that you can be ready to do battle with the devil and his evil forces (witches, sorcerers, evil spirits, bad magic).

Miscellaneous Comments

There were several other interesting observations that came out of our discussion about preaching and related topics:

Evangelist Wame has adopted a unique strategy of *continuous preparation* for preaching. During the time of his daily Bible readings (which he emphasizes is an essential practice for any preacher of the gospel), he often happens upon an interesting passage or pericope which, on further

---

[373] Immediately after the interview with me, Evangelist Wame was scheduled to go and visit a member of the local congregation where he had preached to help that person (and his family) combat the power of witchcraft which was threatening to ruin their lives. This was on his day off - after preaching six times in three days (all different sermons, including a funeral) for an average of an hour at a time! Rev Wame appeared to be genuinely happy to go anywhere at anytime and do anything if it would further the cause of Christ and defeat the power of Satan.

reflection, inspires a sermon outline in his mind. He writes this outline down on a piece of paper and files it in the appropriate place in his Bible (*Buku Lopatulika*). His personal copy is full of these slips of paper, and he says that there are hundreds filed away back at home. He is thus prepared to preach a particular sermon at any time or place (cf. 1Pet 3:15) with a ready outline at hand, needing only to be "contextualised" and fleshed out according to the specific audience, setting and situation concerned.

Evangelist Wame does the same sort of thing in the case of all the illustrations, examples and analogies that continually vivify and color his sermons. He is a careful observer of nature and everyday life, he says. Anything that seems especially noteworthy, interesting or unusual he records on a piece a paper for possible future use in a sermon. He refers to certain of these insights as being "visions" (*masomphenya*) from God (or Christ), and in the sense that all true spiritual wisdom has a divine origin, this is true. Such experiences are distinct, however, from the serious "revelations" (*zivumbulutso*) that he also receives from God (Christ) or an angel, but which normally occur during a realistically vivid dream at night. How does he know for sure that all these revelations, etc. come from God and not Satan? In answer to this (my question), Wame replies, "My 'level' (*levulo*), or standard of measurement, is always Jesus Christ!" Anything that will help him to reveal Christ more forcefully and clearly to people, he believes, originates with God, not man or the devil. He is the only Saviour and the one way to eternal life in heaven (John 20:30-31). This is the predominant focus of Rev Wame's entire ministry.

Along these same lines, Evangelist Wame feels that the greatest threat to contemporary Christianity in Malawi (and Africa in general) is a crippling "ignorance" (*umbuli*) of the Scriptures. Most Christians, he complains, really do not know anything substantial about what is contained in their Bibles – that is, beyond what is said in the familiar texts and basic Sunday School lessons. They tend to know the specific doctrines and regulations of their church much better, but cannot relate these to the teachings of the Word of God. They do not perceive the "big plan," namely, the story of salvation as it is unfolded in sequence throughout the Bible – from Genesis to Revelation. And the saddest thing, Wame stresses, is their lack of understanding of who Jesus Christ really is (true God), and why he became a human being (true Man) to save the world from their sin and a future damnation in hell. The full gospel message, therefore, has become the foundation of Rev Wame's ministry and the vital core of every sermon that he preaches. Such a burning desire is immediately apparent to anyone who speaks to this modern-day "prophet" of the Lord or who has the privilege of hearing (especially in person!) one of his dynamic, revivalistic, Christ-centered sermons. It is a truly "heart-grabbing" experience!

APPENDIX B

I have recorded below the Chichewa transcriptions of the three Wame sermons that were presented in translated and annotated form in chapter 4. However, the typographical conventions employed there in order to highlight certain of the phonological aspects of Wame's rhetoric are not used here so that the actual words of the text are easier to distinguish. The correspondence between the transcription and its translation is not always exact because of the poor quality of the cassette recordings in some places and due to the fact that these were carried out as separate exercises with almost a half year's interval in between. This transcription was made as exact, lexically speaking, as possible – given the combined hearing abilities of two pairs of ears. Therefore, apparent grammatical or other speech "errors" were left uncorrected so as to provide the closest possible approximation of Wame's sermonic "dialect." Naturally, when a preacher is speaking rapidly and with strong emotion, he is not usually concerned about reproducing the "standard" form of the language.

Obviously, these Chichewa transcriptions do not give a fully accurate reflection of Evangelist Wame's preaching art and technique since they lack the essential dimension of sound. Thus all of the emotive, connotative and oratorical meaning that is conveyed by the skilled human voice is still missing. But for those who are able to read and appreciate the Chichewa language, these texts will undoubtedly be more "meaningful" in a complete sense than the English translations that were discussed earlier.

Palibe Chidule Kupita Kumwamba (SW5)

Tidzawerenga Mateyu 7:21, 1 Akorinto 10:1-4; tidzamaliza ndi Luka 7:23:

[Muone mau awa m'Buku Lopatulika.]

Ndiye pano lero tidzayambira chigawo choyamba: Kodi usilikali uyamba bwanji? Mwa mau amene aja tawerengawa tidzaima kwambiri pa vesi ya 24 – Mateyu chaputala cha 7, vesi ya 24: "Chifukwa chake chimenechi, yense amene akamva mau anga amenewa ndikuwachita ndidzamfanizira ndi munthu wochenjera amene anamanga nyumba yake pa thanthwe. Inagwa mvula nidzala mitsinje, ndipo zinaomba mphepo, zinagunda pa nyumbapo, koma siinagwa chifukwa inakhazikika pathanthwepo. Ndipo yense amene akamva mau anga amenewa ndi kusawachita adzafanizidwa ndi munthu wopusa yemwe anamanga nyumba yake pa mchenga. Ndipo kunagwa mvula nidzala mitsinje, ndipo zinaomba mphepo, zinagunda pa nyumbayo, ndipo inagwa. Ndi kugwa kwake kunali kwakukulu ndithu!" Chikhristu chimayamba bwanji? Monga msilikali, kuti ayambe usilikali, amayamba bwanji? Tsono funso - usilikali wonsewu wa nkhondo ya Mulungu, funso apa nlakuti, kodi Chikhristu chimayamba bwanji? Pano monga tawerenga pa vesi ya 24, Ambuye Yesu sadatchulepo munthu. Akuti munthu yense wakumva mau anga nawachita ndidzafanizira ndi munthu amene anamanga nyumba yake pa thanthwe. Ndipo mvula inagwa, mitsinje inadzala nigunda pa nyumbayo, koma nyumbayo siinagwe popeza inakhazikika pa maziko a thanthwe lolimba ndi lamphamvu. Koma amene amati akamva mauwa osawachita, ameneyo ndidzafanizira ndi munthu amene anamanga nyumba yake pa mchenga. Ndipo mphepo zinaomba, mitsinje inadzala, ndipo kugwa kwake kwa nyumbayo kunali kwakukulu ndithu. Pano sanatchule, anangoti "munthu." Sanatchule munthu. Mwina nkutheka munthuyo ali pompano. Munthu amene amati akamva mau a Mulungu osawachita sadatchule. Angoti munthuyo. Nkutheka kukhala amai. Nkutheka kukhala abambo. Nkutheka kukhala achimwene. Nkutheka kukhala mtsikana. Sanatchule ayi.

Pano mau amenewa akuulula kuti tilipo magulu awiri pamene takhala pano. Pali magulu a Akhristu amene amanga nyumba yao pa thanthwe, ndiye pali gulu linanso la Akhristu amanga nyumba yao pa mchenga. Panotu tilipo magulu awiri. Tsono aliyense adziyang'anitsitse mwa iye yekha - kodi ndine ndinamanga nyumba pa mchenga? Kodi ndine n'namanga nyumba pa thanthwe? Aliyense adziyang'anitsitse - tilipo pano a magulu awiri.

Tsopano pano akuti tikamanga nyumba yathu pa mchenga, monga tanena kale, gulu limeneli lamanga nyumba pa mchengadi - nyumba akunenayo, tikawerenga pa wani Akorinto chaputala cha thrii - nyumba imene akunena tamanga pa mchengayo, ena tamanga pa thanthwe - nyumba akunenayo mutu wake wa mauwo, wani Akorinto chaputala cha thrii, pa vesi ya nayini pali mau akuti Akhristu ali nyumba ya Mulungu, ndipo Yesu Khristu ali maziko a nyumbayo. Akhristu ali nyumba ya Mulungu, ndipo Yesu ali maziko a nyumbayo. Nyumba imeneyo ndi inuyo - ndi inuyo.

Tsopano funso likubwera, monga taona kuti tilipo magulu awiri – gulu lina lamanga nyumba pa mchenga, gulu lina lamanga nyumba pa thanthwe. Tsopano nyumbayo ndi inuyo. Moyo wa chikhristuwo – ena anamanga pa thanthwe, ena anamanga pa mchenga. Tsopano funso: Chifukwa chiani gulu ili lamanga pamchenga? Yankho lake ndi lachidule. Chifukwa nyumba yomanga pa mchenga siimavuta – olo faundeshoni siimavuta. Mungofukula ndi manja nkumaponya zidina nkumamanga. Lero lomwe mukhoza kumaliza – chidule sichivuta. Nchifukwa chake gulu ili lidamanga nyumba pa mchenga, ithe msanga. Chifukwa umanga nyumba pa thanthwe nkovuta. Enanu mudakapempha poloti, adakulozerani ku miyala, mudathawako. "Sindingathe kuphwanya miyala imeneyi! Kuti ndikaitane thalakitala, chikaphwanye miyala imeneyi, n'ndalama zambiri."

Pa thanthwe nkovuta kuti umange nyumba. Pafunika kulimbika, si masewero ayi! Nchifukwa chake pano akunena kuti uyu anamanga nyumba pa mchengayo ndi kufuna nyumbayo ithe msanga. Sipamavuta pokumba faundeshoni, komaso mumangofukula ndi manja nkumangoponya zidina. Chidule – athe msanga! Nchifukwa chake anamanga nyumba pa mchenga. Kodi nanga kumanga nyumba pa mchenga kumatanthauza chiani? Mvetsetsani amene mwamanga nyumba yanu pa mchenga!

Musaiwale funso: Chikhristu chimayamba bwanji? Monga msilikali amayamba bwanji? Ndi kulembedwa. Kumanga nyumba pa mchenga, ndiye kuti yankho... ndifunse funso: Kodi inu kusiya nyanga ndi kuti ukadye mgonero, chapafupi ndi chiti? (Mgonero.) Mgonero eti? (Eeee!) Kuti usiye nyanga bwanji? Mpathanthwe eti? (Eeee!) Ee, si masewero ayi. (kuseka) Afuna chidule, chithe msanga. Ndifuna ndiyambe ndadya nao mgonero mpamchenga eti? Kumangoponya kha-kha, kha-kha! Ithe msanga eti? (kuseka)

Kodi inu nuti usiye fodya nkuti uzipereka zopereka, chapatali nchiani? Kusiya fodya – eee, ndithu ee, mpathanthwe – si masewero! Ndi kuti uzibwera kuno ku tchalitchi ndi kusiya zigololo, chapafupi nchiani? kubwera ku tchalitchi inu. Kuti usiye chigololo mpathanthwe, si masewero ayi. (kuseka) Chidule – zithe msanga! (kuseka) Yense amene amati akamva mau a Mulungu osawachita, ndidzawafanizira ndi munthu amene wamanga nyumba yake pa mchenga. Nchiani chim'mangitsa pa mchenga? Ndi chidule, ithe msanga! Aleluya! (Ameni!) Ndi kuti munthu usiye mitala ndi kuti ukhale mkuluwampingo, chapafupi nchiani? Eee, ukhala mkuluwampingo – kuti usiye mitala si masewero, mpathanthwe! (kuseka) Ndi kuti munthu usiye mabodza ndi kuti ukhale mbusa, chapafupi nchiani? Ee, kukhala mbusa. Kuti usiye bodza simasewero, mpathanthwe. Chidule kuti zithe msanga!

Koma pano mmene tawerengera mauwa mwini wake kumwambako ali kukaniza zachidulezi – "Aayi!" Ndi chifukwa chake akuti, "Munthu aliyense amene afuna kudza kwa ine – wani, adzikanize yekha; thuu, asenze mtanda; thrii, anditsate." Pali makwerero atatu kuti tikafike kumwamba. Khwerero loyamba – kudzikaniza, khwerero lachiwiri – kusenza mtanda, khwerero lachitatu – kutsata Yesu. Chidule kumwamba kulibe. Alukaniza, alukaniza.

Pa dziko lapansi pamakhala njira – njira ija ikakhala yaitali yozungulira, timakonda njira yachidule. Tingodzera apa ndiye tafika msanga. Kuti tikazungulire mpakana ku mseu – "Iih! tichedwa!" Pa dziko lapansi timakonda njira zachidule kuti tikafike msanga. Koma kumwamba adatseka, kulibe njira zachidule zokafika msangazo. Pakungokumva kuti njira ya kumwamba ndi yokhotakhota, ndiye ali, "Tiye, tikangodulira apa!" Osatheka, osatheka!

Amene tamanga nyumba pa mchenga, pakungomva kuti njira ya kumwamba ndi yokhotakhota, tsono – chidule, zithe msanga, ndiye kungodula njirayo, tikafike msanga! Kuchimwaku – tizichimwa, koma umakumbuka umakapemphera – chidule, tikafike msanga! Eetu, ee! Kusiyana nkumangokhala. Si kuti amene ali kutchalitchiko ndi olungama. Inuyo mukati muzingokhala, koma osakapembedza – maliro anu akachita utaya ngati galu, sakayimbira!

Mkadikira kuti musiye mowa, iiih! muchedwa. Kumwaku – tizimwa, koma umakumbuka umakapemphera. Ati, chidule – akafike msanga. Kulibe (kuseka)! Kulibe, hee, kulibe, kulibe! Mukadikira kuti mukonzeke, ayi, muchedwa. "Onsewa ali kutchalitchiku, ena nga kumwa, ena ali ndi mitala, ena nga mabodza, ena nga zigololo." Kuti inuyo muchite kuti mukonzetse, ndipo mkayambe tchalitchi – ndithu, maliro anu sakayimbira. Akachita utaya ngati galu. Onse anzanu ali kupempherawa – khalidwe lao ndi limeneli. Tere inuyo kumwako, muzimwa, koma muzikumbuka nako ku tchalitchi. Kumakumbuka nako zopereka, kumakumbuka nako...indee,

255

kumapita ku mgonero. Kuti muzingokhaliratu, sizikuthandizani. Kumwaku, tizimwa, koma umakumbuka kepemphera. Chidule, zithe msanga! Eni ake kumwamba atseka. Akuti, "Kuno kokha kulibe chidule! Pansi pompano mpamene pakhala zidule – kuno, ayi! Kulibe zidule kumwamba!"
Koma choyambayamba munthu akafuna kupita kumwamba, adzikanize yekha. Kudzikaniza wekha – mundimvetsetse – ndiko kugwada pansi ndikuulula machimo ako. Poululapo, kumuuza Yesu kuti, "Ine bodza, toto! Ndikudzikaniza! Ndewu, toto! Miseche, toto! Mitala, toto! Kuba, toto!" Kudzikaniza. Mukateropo, mwaponda khwerero loyamba phaaa! Ndiye kuti muli pa ulendo wopita kumwamba.

Chikhristu chimayamba bwanji? Poyambayamba ukumane ndi Yesu, akulembe monga msilikali. Sizingatheke msilikali kukayamba usilikali asanalembedwe. Na munthu amene afuna kukhala msilikali wangwiro, wamphamvu pamaso pa Mulungu, choyambayamba akumane ndi Yesu, amulembe usilikali. Ndi chifukwa chake Ambuye Yesu akuti, "Ngati munthu afuna kudza pambuyo panga, choyamba adzikanize yekha, nambala thuu, asenze mtanda, nambala thrii, anditsate ine!"

Tsono tikadzikaniza zakuti, "Toto, toto – mafodya, toto! Mabodza, toto!" Ndipo Ambuye Yesu amabwera ndikutilandira, ndipo iyeyo amatisambitsa ndi mwazi wake, natipatsa mphamvu ya Mzimu Woyera. Zikatero, talembedwa! Tsopano khwerero lanambala thuu ndiye kusenza mtanda ndikukonzekera zovuta. Pamene mwatembenuka mtima, Satana sadzakondwa. Mudzakumana ndi mayesero osiyanasiyana. Konzekerani kulandira zowawa chifukwa cha Khristu – ndiye mtanda akunenawu. Ambuye Yesu akunena kuti, "Ana anga, musaope. Senzani mtanda wanu. Mphamvu za ine nzanunso!" Kutanthauza kuti musaope zovuta. Mphamvu zimene anagonjetsera Satana sanatenge, anazisiya.

Pamene ifeyo tamlandira Yesu, tavala chiyero. Satana samakondwa, amafuna kugwetsa chiyerochi. Tsopano inu konzekerani kulimbana naye Satanayo kuti mpakana mutamgwetsa. Monga Yesu anamgwetsa Satana, mphamvu yomwe ija adatipatsanso, ndipo tidzamgwetsanso ndi ulamuliro wamphamvu wochokera kumwamba. Mukateroko – kukonzekera zovuta – mwasenza mtanda!

Nambala thrii – kumtsatira Yesu. Kutsatira Yesu ndiye gawo la chipembedzo. Chitsulo chitangolira kuti ngwee-ngwee! ngwee-ngwee! ndiye mukapeza kuchita kuti laakaa! ndi mumseu momwemu kupita ukapembedza. Khwerero la nambala thrii, kutsatira Yesu. Gawo la chipembedzo ndi khwerero la nambala thrii. Khwerero limeneli mudzaliona Lamulungu lokhalokha chikangolira chitsulo. Mudzaona chigulu cha anthu chikupita kokapembedza. Ngati mumaona chigulu cha anthu kokapembedza – khwerero la nambala thrii! Tere inuyo uyamba kumene mwayamba kubwera kunoku ndi khwerero la nambala thrii – kutsatira Yesu. Ngati mumapita m'misonkhano yosiyanasiyana, khwerero la nambala thrii – kutsatira Yesu!

Tsopano chimene chikumvetsa chisoni mau awa – khwerero loyamba lija talumpha. Ndiye takaponda khwerero nambala thuu ndi la nambala thrii. Tere ngakhale ufuna kukhala msilikali, kungoponda khwerero la nambala thrii, phaaa! – kutsatira Yesu. Koma munthuyo sanadzikanize, komanso munthuyo sanakonzekere zovuta – kodi usilikaliwo utheka? Koma munthuyo sanadzikanize, komanso munthuyo sanakonzekere zovuta – kodi usilikaliwo utheka? Eti, utheka usilikali, utheka usilikali?! Chigulu chachikulu chalumpha khwerero loyamba. Tere cholinga cha mauwa ndikukugwirani mwendo, phaa! Bwerera, mwalumpha loyamba – sitero iyayi! "Ofuna utsatira ine – khwerero loyamba, adzikanize yekha; nambala thuu, asenze mtanda; nambala thrii, anditsate."

Tsono chinthu chachikulu chokaponda khwerero nambala thrii...tere ndikamba pamodzi ndilikukukokani jeketi phaa! – pansi, muyambirenso khwerero loyamba! Kukoka deresi pansi, uyambirenso khwerero loyamba – ndiko kudzikaniza. Zikafika pamenepo ndiye kuti inuyo mwalembedwa usilikali wamphamvu, amene tikhoza kumtumikira Ambuye. Tsono funso langa ndi lakuti, kodi lilipo tsiku lina lake mudagwada pansi modzikaniza? Funso limeneli likhale pamtima panu. Funso limeneli likhale pamtima panu: "Ambuye, ndafika ine pamapazi anu. Toto ine miseche! Toto ine mabodza! Toto ine ndewu! Toto ine kupsa mtima!" Ndani apa amene tsiku lina lake adagwada pansi nadzikaniza? Ngati simunagwade pansi nudzikaniza, ndinu mmodzi amene mwaponda khwerero la nambala thrii – kumtsata Yesu. Tsiku ndi tsiku Lamulungu lililonse likangokwana tsiku limenelo, basi kuthamangira ku tchalitchi – khwerero nambala thrii!

Tsopano eni ake akumwamba alukaniza – si Wame, a-a-ah! Kumwamba kulibe chidule ayi. Ati akafike msanga udutsa makwerero enawo, ali thaa! Ati akafike msanga. Si kuno kumeneko ayi! Popeza njira za pansi ndi zokhotakhota, ayesa nkumwamba komwe. Pomva kuti ndi yokhotakhota, ali, "Chidule, ee!" Umangoti zii! ulendo umakumbuka ukapemphera. Kulibe chidule kumwamba, ayi. Akana pano eni ake, kulibe chidule kumwamba.

Tsono funso la mafunso onse: Kodi mudagwapo pansi, nupemphera? Tsono amene adagwada pansi napemphera namulandira Yesu, mkati mwa mitima yao ndiye kuti chikhristu chao adamanga pa thanthwe. Ndipo chikhristu chake chimakhala cholimba, ndipo chikhristu chake chimakhala chokhazikika. Kuchitukwana, sichisintha. Pa njala, sichisintha – pa maliro. Nanga sichili pa thanthwe?! Ehee! Ndipo sakhumudwa wambawamba – nanga sichili pa thanthwe? Ndipo sadandaula wambawamba – nanga sichili pa thanthwe? Kukumana ndi zovuta, mayesero osiyanasiyana – thima lili zii! Nanga sichili pa thanthwe?

Ndi odala amene nyumbayo – moyo wachikhristuwo – choyambayamba masiku akewo ndiye Khristu. Tawerenga kale wani Akorinto teni, vesi wani... makamaka vesi folo. Akuti, "Aisraeli anamwa madzi otuluka m'thanthwe." Thanthwelo ngati simulidziwa ndi Yesu – phirilo ndi Ambuye Yesu. Ndipo chikhristu cha mtundu umenewu sichikugwa wambawamba. Sichitengeka-tengeka. Ndipo ngakhale chitagundidwa mphepo akunena ija – ndi mphepo, mbiri zomangokusinjirira, mphepo za mabodza, mphepo zokutukwana, mphepo zokusinjirira, mphepo kaya za mavuto a mtundu wanji. Uwombedwaombedwa mphepo, sumasintha ayi, popeza unamanga pa maziko enieni oyenera a thanthwe. Popeza nyumbayo ndi yolimba kwambiri, ndi yolimba kwambiri!

Koma amene anamanga nyumba yake pa mchenga – amene adalowa chikhristu kuti, "Ntakafa, akanandiimbire nyimbo!" – amene adalowa chifukwa cha zolinga zina. Pali zolinga zosiyanasiyana zimene tilowera chikhristu. Akuti maliro osaimbira alibe ulemu. Kubwera kuchikhristu kuti akapeze maliro aulemu. Kulowa chikhristu kuti apeze banja. Kubwera ku chikhristu chifukwa choti amuna akuti, "Mukapanda kulowa chikhristu, ukwati ukutha!" Kubwera kuno kudzagula ukwati. Inde, kubwera ku chikhristu chifukwa akazi anena kuti, "Naa mukapanda umakapemphera, nkwabwino mukangondisiya, ukwati ukutha!" Kubwera ku tchalitchi kudzagula ukwati!

Pali zifukwa zosiyanasiyana zimene tili kubwerera kuno. Ena kubwera kuno, kuli kachibwenzi kao. Pali zifukwa zosiyanasiyana kubwera kuno. Ukalowa chigwirizano chifukwa choti, "Tikavala zovala zoyera zija, timakhala ndi ulemu wina wapadera." Kubwera kuno chifukwa cha mpando, chifukwa cha ubusa, chifukwa cha ukuluwampingo, chifukwa cha khwaya – pali zifukwa zosiyanasiyana! Zimenezi mpamchenga. Chitsimikizo chake – ukakumana ndi vuto, chigwirizanocho sichichedwa ukhumudwa. Ukuluwampingo sumachedwa ukhumudwa. Zaomba mphepo, ehee – iih! yagwa! Maziko ake anali pa mchenga! Kungokutukwana, wanyanyala, wosabweranso ku tchalitchi. "Kodi masiku ano inu bwanji simubwera ku tchalitchi?" "Ah, ngati mau aja adandilankhulira asekilitali ku chigwirizano ndi mau abwino aja? Andikhumudwitsa, ndiye nkazichitani? Nanga simukuti ine ndine ndili kuononga chigwirizano?!" Ah! he-heee! adamanga pa thanthwe awa? Hi-hiii! adamanga chigwirizano pa mchenga. Chagwa chigwirizano!

Amene adamanga nyumba yake pa mchenga sachedwa ukhumudwa. Khwaya – "Anali kuimba m'khwaya – ah! anakhumudwa, adasiya." Ukuluwampingo – "Sabweranso masiku ano, adakhumudwa!" Ubusa umene – "Ndingowasiyira ubusa umene. Matchalitchi ndi ambiri, ndikalowa kwina kwake!" Timangoti, "Eeeh! adamanga nyumba pa mchenga! Ehee! nyumba ija yagwa!" Ee-hee! Odala amene amanga nyumba yake pa thanthwe. Chifukwa mphepo zikaomba, sizidzasinthika ngakhale m'pang'ono pomwe!

Koma tsono musaiwale kufuna kumanga pa thanthwe – si masewero, m'pamwala! Pamenepo ndiye musaiwale! Ehee, si masewero kufuna kumanga pa thanthwe, m'pamwala, m'pamwala. Kuti munthu ugwade pansi, udzikanize, nkumuitana Yesu alowe mu mtima – toto zakutizakuti! Eeh, koma tsono ukangomanga, e-e-eh! nyumbayo ndi yolimba. Chifukwa akuti, "Inaomba mphepo, nidzala mitsinje, ndipo zinagunda pa nyumbayo. Siinagwe, ndiponso siinakokololeka!"

Koma amene anamanga nyumba pa mchenga – zinaomba mphepo, mphepo za mabodza, mphepo za mayesero, ndipo zinagunda pa nyumbayo – pachikhristupo. Ndipo chikhristucho chinasowa mtendere. Chikhristucho chitasowa mtendere, mapeto ake nkukhumudwa ndi kugwa. Ngati mumamva kuti, "Kodi mwamva akuluampingo aujenitu agwa?" Kugwa, ndiye kuti anamanga pa mchenga. "Inu, mwamva kodi mtsikana uja amaimba khwayayu anagwa?!" "A-ah! anagwa bwanji?" "Adamanga nyumba pa mchenga." Ehe-hee! "Amai aja ndithu amatsogolera nyimbo m'chigwirizano, akuti anagwa." "A-ah! inu, chachitika nchiani?!" "Akuti adakalanda mwamuna wa mwini wake." Kugwa kumene timati adagwako, nanga si nyumba ya pa mchenga? Zidaomba zimphepo, ndipo kugwa kwake kunali kwakukulu!

Mtsinje ali kunenawotu nkutheka kukhala ku gahena – ukagwera ku gahena uuu-phu! ku nyanja yamoto! Eeetu-eh, inu ndiye mwamanga pati? M'samangoona usekatu! Ndanena kale kuti panotu pali magulu awiri: Ena amanga pa thanthwe, ena amanga pa mchenga. Gulu limene linamanga pa thanthwe lidagwada pansi nkudzikaniza. La pa mchenga langolumpha uuuluu-thaa! – ali pa ubatizo, pa mgonero. Ati, "Chidule – zithe msanga!" Akukukanizani, akuti, "Kuno ndiye ayi komweko! Naa uyu afuna kubwera kumbuyo panga adzikanize yekha – khwerero loyamba ilo, osalumpha ayi!" Ngati tinalumpha, ndiye sitifuna ife tikhale asilikali amphamvu. Lero tiyeni tigwade pansi, tidzikanize. Timange nyumba yathu pa thanthwe kuti pamenepo tsopano ndi pamene payambire usilikali wathu. Tidzakhala asilikali amphamvu, angwiro, okhulupirika, amene tidzakhoza kumenyana nkhondo ndi Satana, mdaniyo woipayo.

Tiyeni tipenyetsetse kuopsa kwake kwa njira yachidule: Tikawerenga Miyambo, chaputala cha 14, vesi 12, pali mau akuti, "Ilipo njira yooneka kwa mwamuna ngati yoongoka, koma matsiriziro ake njira ya imfa." Miyambo 14:12 – "Ilipo njira yooneka kwa mkazi ngati yoongoka, koma matsiriziro ake njira ya imfa." Mudawerengapo mau amenewa eti? Nthawi zina zake munthu akamayenda pa ulendo zomwe ndanenazi... udaona kuti, "Aah! njirayi yatalika! Tiye tingodzera apa." Pakuchiona chimseu chokongola, chotakata bwino, umati, "Ndiyo njira imeneyi!" Koma usanayende pafupifupi kapena wani kilomita, mukangopeza mwakatulukira kumanda! Sukadaona chomwecho. "Sitidazione zimenezi?! Chinjira chooneka bwino, koma chokatulukira ku manda!" Njira yooneka ngati yoongoka, koma matsiriziro ake njira ya imfa! Tsono nthawi zonse njira zachidule ndi zovuta kwambiri. Enanu mundiperekera umboni kuti njira zachidule – ena awavula zovala, ena awalanda chikwama, ena awalanda ndalama. Pamene tikunena pano, ena aphedwa! Mwaziona njira zachidule!

Kumwamba kulibe chidule chifukwa njira m'chidule chimadula mwendo. Nkwabwino ukafuna kuyenda, tsata ku magetsi. Njira ya m'malayinazi sitikafika kumwamba, ehee! Enatu chikhristu chidayenda njira za m'malayina. "Kumwaku tizimwa malinga ukumbuka umakapemphera!" Chidule – njira za m'malayina, masiku awiri, atatu, wagwa! Akugwetsa achifwamba. Amafuna uchite chidule. Chidule chimadula mwendo, akuluakulu amatero. Samalani amai, samalani abambo – njira zachidule, ambiri agwa nazo m'mavuto!

Chidule sichifunika pa chikhristu. Kuchimwa, tizichimwa malingana kukumbuka kupemphera. Kulibe kumwamba zimenezo! Ndipo njira zoterezi pansi pano, taona zitsanzo: Ambiri awalanda ndalama, ena alowa m'manda, ena aphedwa – kuopsa kwake kwa njira zachidule! Pamaoneka ngati njira yeniyeni, mapeto ake ukatulukira kumanda. Tsono njira imene tatenga ifeyi – kumanda kwake mwakudziwa ukatulukira ku gahena! Njira yooneka ngati yoongoka, mapeto ake kukatulukira kumanda!

Pamene ndili kunena pano chikhristu chimene tamanga pa mchengachi m'malo moopa tchimo – sichiopa tchimo. Chimaopa kudulidwa. Chikhristu chomanga pa mchenga sichiopa tchimo, koma chimaopa kudulidwa. Chifukwa chikatenga tchimolo – tchimo lija akalitenga kuti alupita nalo kukachita zoipa, amalifungatira ndi kulibisa, ndiye nkumayang'ana akuluampingo. Chimene akuopa pamenepa, akuopa akuluampingo kuti, "Akandiona, andichotsa m'chigwirizano. Andichotsa mu ukuluwampingo. Andichotsa mu ubusa. Andichotsa m'khwaya. Andichotsa m'chikhristu!" Ndiye amasuzumira, koma uku wakuphathira. Ndiye akamapita, amapita akubisala nkumasuzumira, kuopa akuluampingo m'malo mwakuti akadaopa tchimolo. Mwachiona chinsinsi chake? M'malo moti akadaopa tchimo, alitaye tchimo, ndiye akulikonda kwambiri mpakana kulibisa. Ndiye nkumayang'ana akuluampingo nkumayang'ana uku ndi uku. Iwe uyenda mobisala, ukuopa munthu, mkuluwampingo kapena mbusa, osaopa Mulungu amene akuona zimene wabisazo. Chikhristu cha pa mchenga sichiopa tchimo, chimaopa akuluampingo. Ati, "Chidule!" – akafike msanga. Osatheka! Osatheka!

Amai, funso la mafunso onse: Kodi inuyo mudamuuzapo Yesu pa maondo? Kodi mudadzikanizapo? Khwerero loyamba! Ngati musadadzikanize, pamene mukutenga maphunziro awa, tiyambe kudzikaniza. Ndipo titadzikaniza, tilembedwe monga msilikali. Mawa ngati nkutheka msilikali tsopano, ayambe kuphunzitsidwa. Pamene mkhristu walandira Yesu, ayenera kuphunzitsidwa. Odala amene lero adzayamba kugwa m'maondo – nambala thuu, kusenza mtanda – nambala thrii, kutsatira Yesu.

Ambuye adalitse mau amenewa kuti atitsogolera pa msonkhano umenewu – Ameni! (Ameni!)

Kukonzekera Ulendo Wopita Kumwamba (SW37)

Mau a Mulungu amene akupezeka m'Masalimo fifite, Masalimo nambala fifite... Tidzawerenga pa vesi ya naini kulekeza thwelofu. Vesi naini: "Sindidzatenga ng'ombe m'nyumba mwako, kapena mbuzi m'makola mwako. Pakuti zamoyo zonse za kuthengo ndi zanga, ndi ng'ombe za pa mapiri zikwi. Ndidziwa mbalame zonse za m'mapiri, ndipo nyama zakuthengo zili ndi ine. Ndikamva njala, sindidzakuuza, pakuti dziko lonse ndi langa, ndi kudzala kwake komwe." Makamaka pa vesi thwelofu – "Koma naa iweyo – ndikamva njala, sindikuuza." Ambuye adalitse kuwerenga kwa mau ake amenewa. Ameni!

Tipemphere: Pakutsimikiza kuti mwa ife tokha mulibe nzeru, nchifukwa chake timathamangira kupemphera, popeza ndinu nokha mungatipambanitse – popeza ndinu nokha muli mwini chilungamo – popeza ndinu nokha muli mwini moyo – popeza ndinu nokha mudafa, kutifera ife. Ambuye, tsegulani maso athu auzimu. Tsegulani makutu athu. Tilandire chuma cha mtengo wapatali chimene Ambuye mwatitengera pano. Chimene mwayamba nafe kale – dzulo lija, lero ku m'mawa, kufikira tsopano – ndipo pitirizani, popeza inu mudziwa chosowa chathu. M'dzina la inu, Yesu Khristu, mpulumutsi wathu wamoyo, tikupemphani. Ameni.

Mau amene Mulungu wathu afuna kulankhula nafe nthawi ino – chenjezo! Chenjezo pa vesi ya thwelofu: "Nditamva njala, sindikuuza, pakuti dziko lonse ndi langa, ndi kudzala kwake komwe." Mau awa ali kuulula chimene Mulungu ali kuchisowa kumwambako. Mulunguyo, chimene ali kusowa kumwambako – amasowa moyo wanuwo. Amasowa mtima wanuwo!

Wina wake ntafunsa dzana lija ku Salimako, "Mwadzuka bwanji?" Akuti, "Aah! ine sindinadzuke bwino. M'thupi muno sindili bwino – thupi lonse kuphwanya! Ndidziwa kuti amenewa ndi malungo." Ndiye ndinati, "Iiyaayi! mwatalikitsa kunenako! Mungonena kuti, 'Talandira kalata ya kumudzi – akutifuna!' Eehee-ee! (kuseka) kunena mwachidule, hee, kunena kwachidule. Ehee-ii-hee, hoo! (kuseka) Nthawi zonse kumwambako, chimene akusowa – akusowa inuyo!" Ndiye akuti, "Aaaah! mwatero! Ine ndi kalatatu imeneyi ya kumudzi!" Tere m'tapita ku chipatala muchira, ndiye kuti mwayankha kuti, "Aah, bandiyembekezani, ndikubwera." Koma mudzanyamuka ndithu! Njira yake pofuna unyamuka ndi matendawa, koma pokafika kumeneko, pafunika Yesu! Kunena mwachidule, "Ndalandira kalata ya kumudzi" – popeza chimene Mulungu amasowa, amasowa inuyo!"

Tsopano timawerenga m'mau a Mulungu chitsimikizo chakuti Mulungu kumwambako asowa moyo wa munthu. Ambuye Yesu atabwera pansi pano, timamva kuti adakwapula ogulitsa malonda m'kachisi, ndipo akuti m'menemo anagubuduza magome, nawalankhulira, "Bwanji mwayesa m'nyumba ya Atate anga nyumba ya malonda – nyumba ya achifwamba. Popeza nyumbayi ndi nyumba yopemphereramo!" Ndipo anawakwapula, nawathamangitsa onse, ndipo akuti anagubuduza magome.

Pano tifuna tiulule: Ambuye Yesu uja anali kufuna mtima wa Israeli. Utataika, koma udatayikira m'tchalitchi! Magome amagubuduza aja nufuna mtima wa munthu. Magome amagubuduza aja kufuna moyo wa munthu. Tere kumwambako Mulungu sagona usiku ndi usana kufuna mtima wanuwo amai udatayika – ufuna moyo wanuwo amai udatayika. Usiku ndi usana Mulungu ali kuufuna moyo wanuwo, uzimka kwanu. Popeza kuno si kwanu – kwanu ndi kumwamba! Ndiye pano ali kuulula, nditangobwera kunyumba kwako, sindidzatenga ng'ombe, popeza ng'ombezi ndikupatsa ndine. Ndikabwera, sindidzatenga mbuzi – mbuzinso n'dakupatsa ndine. Sindidzatenga ndalama – ndalamazo n'dakupatsa ndine. Sindidzatenga chilichonse – zonse ndi zanga kale. Koma, "Naa iweyo – nkamva njala, sinkuuza!"

Tsono mau akuti "Ndikamva njala, sinkuuza" – kutanthauza kuti pomwalira munthu pansi pano, kumwambako kumakhala bwalo – kumakhala chimsonkhano. "Timafuna ena apite, akatenge moyo wa auje." Ndiye pamakhala mkangano – "Iyayi, tamsiyani! Mwina mwake kapena nkulapa nyanga zija!" Nkutero, "Ai, timati timtenge!" "A-ah! mulakwa mukatero.

Timtenge chaka chino – chaka thii!" Chatha, mudakali ndi moyo – iweyo kuno uli mkati kutamba, osadziwa kuti msonkhano anakumana, walephera! Ulendo womangamanga! "Naa iweyo – nkamva njala, sinkuuza!"

Kumene apangira msonkhano wa moyo wa ine, ine kulibe. Ndikanadziwa, ndikanakonzekeratu! Mwina mwake msonkhano ungathe lero, mwina mwake msonkhano ukutha mawa. Mai wanga, pomwalira munthu – kumwambako kulibe ngozi. Pansi pano timati, "Kwachitika ngozi!" Koma kumwamba kulibe ngozi. Adadziwikatu kuti tsiku lakuti tilukatenga wanthu. Pamene ndikunena pano, enafe msonkhanowo walephereka katatu, kanayi. Mwina chaka chatha icho adakumana – udalephereka kukupatsani mpata kuti mulape. Inuyo simuzidziwa! Nchifukwa chake akuti, "Naa iweyo – ntamva njala, sinkuuza!"

Chaka chatha icho anakumana – achotse moyo wanuwo – msonkhano unalephereka. "Tiyambe tawasiya – kapena nyanga, kapena mabodza aja nkusiya. Kapena mowa uja nkusiya." Inuyo simuzidziwa! Kuno mwangotenga chimkondwa, mwangokondweretsedwa ndi za dziko. Mwangochita zokhumba za mtima wanu – osadziwa kuti msonkhano uko alepherana. Mwina chaka chatha chomwechi anakumananso. "Iyayi, tiyambe tamusiya" – inuyo kuno masiku ali kutha. Mwina chaka chomwe chino anakumananso. Kumwambako kulibe ngozi. Pansi pano ndiye timati, "Kwachitika ngozi!"

Ngozi ya kumwamba ndiko kuti munthu akagwidwa ndi chigololo – kumwambako angelo amathamanga, "Ngozi, ngozi, ngozi, ngozi!" Ndiye ngozi ya kumwamba. Munthu akapezeka ataledzera, angelo amathamanga, "Ngozi, ngozi, ngozi!" Pamene inu kuno mukuti mukudyerera nkusangalala, osadziwa kumwamba kuti kwagwa ngozi. Munthu akagwidwa ndi chigololo, kumwambako angelo amathamanga, "Ngozi, ngozi, ngozi!" Pamene inu pansi pano mukuti mukusangalala, osadziwa kuti kumwambako kwagwa ngozi. Munthu akamwalira, kumwamba kulibe ngozi – pansi pano ndiye timati "ngozi!" Mai wanga, chikundiopsa! "Naa iweyo – nkamva njala, sinkuuza!"

Akuluakulu amati, "Imfa ya tambala ilibe upo." Mudamvapo mau amenewa? Mudamvapo?! Imfa ya tambala ilibe upo. Tandimvetsetsani:

Padali tambala wina wake. Adapita kudambo – ngati uuko – kunka naadya. Ndiye adakafika pamtengo. Pamtengopo padali chiswe, ndipo atachiona chiswecho, adayamba kudya nthawi yomweyo. Ndipo adapeza chibuluzi chija cha mutu wa buluu – ena timati gulo. Mwamdziwa eti? Uja amati akayenda nkumapanga chonchi – mutuwu kuvina gulo. Ndiye atampeza – popeza nayenso kudya kwake nchiswe chomwecho... Ndiye atafika, gulo akuti, "Ee-eeh! chikatere aTambala?" Akuti, "Basi, udzadya nawo!" Akuti, "Iyayi! Tisiyireni! Anzathu, mwasiya gaga. Anzathu, mwasiya mpunga – mapira! Pano musatinyengerereni anzathufe. Titapeza kachisweka, kena tisungako kuti mwina mawa nkudzaona poyambira!"

He-hee! (kuseka) tambala akuti, "Yayi, ndileke, mbale, ndidye nawo. Mukadadziwa kuti mapirawo amene amatipatsira, simukadalankhula. Mpungawo chimene amatipatsira, simukadalankhula. Inde, gagayo chimene amatipatsira, simukadalankhula!" Akuti, "Iyayi, musatimalizire, anzanufe! Tikaona kachisweka, timachita kuyesa kutulo! Chokani, kazipitani, anzathu! Mwasiya gaga, anzathu! Mwasiya zimadzi zomwera za m'beseni! Mwasiya mpunga!" Kuyamba ukangana pamenepo.

Omvetsa chisoni aTambala akuti, "Aah! mnzanga, ukadadziwa, sukadalankhula mau amenewa. Mwina mwake gaga unena iweyo ndatsazikana naye – mwina mawatu ine sindingakamuonenso. Mpungawo ndatsazikana nawo. Ukadadziwa iwe! Akuluakulu adati, 'Imfa ya tambala ilibe upo!' Simukadalankhula mau amenewa. Chabwino, ndapita!" – momvetsa chisoni.

Osadziwa kuti nthawi imene amakanganayi, kumudziko kwabwera alendo. "Joni!" "Wawa!" "Kodi tambala uja nnamuona anali apa?" "Inde." "Nanga alendowa tatani? Padziko panotu palibe ndiwo!" Osadziwa kuti kuja – mkangano! Imfa ya tambala ilibe upo. "Naa iweyo – nkamva njala, sinkuuza!"

"Heh! funafunani tambala!" Tambala saoneka. "Ah, aDadi, ndafunafunatu, sakuoneka!" "Ee-eeh! nanga alendowa tatani?! Nthawinso yatha!" "Ha, tingoyembekeza, mwina abwera." Akubwera ananu – ulendo wa kunyumba. Chokangotulukira pakhomo – haa! adakangokumana ndi mau ongoti, "Suyu tambala uja!" "Aaa-aaah! kodi padziko pano panali nkhani yanji?!"

Ah, **ananu**, nthawi yomweyo kwe-kwe! kwe-kwe! kwe-kwe! – pothawa **ananu tambala**! Zija achita zikutha bwa-? zikutha bwa-? zikutha bwa-? Wothamangitsa akuti, "Pakhosi mpeni!" Hee-heeh! (kuseka) "Naa iweyo – nkamva njala, sinkuuza!"

Eh-eh-eeh! ananu, aTambala kenaka phoo! wagwira! Polira aTambala, "Mnzanga uja n'namuuza kuti mwina gaga wanenayo m'wotsazikana naye! Amvetse!" Ndiye tambala amati akati kwiiyoo! – mnzake uja kutchera **khutu** kwiiyoo! E-e-eh! nchifukwa chake buluzi chimati chikayenda – chikayenda kuti, "E-e-eeh! amanena zoona! (kuseka) Imfa ya tambala ilibe upo! Wapita mnzanga!" Ndi chifukwa chake chibuluzi chija chimati chikati jojoli! "E-e-e-e-eh! imfa ya tambala ilibe upo. Wapita mnzanga – wapita mnzanga!" Hee-hee! (kuseka)

Mai wanga, popeza kumene apangira msonkhano – onse okhala pa dziko lapansi sakudziwa – ndipo inuyo simuzidziwa. Popeza simudziwa, konzekeranitu! Mwina mawa munganyamuke wa ku mudzi. Mwina lero munganyamuke wa ku mudzi. Mwina mkuja munganyamuke wa ku mudzi. Mwina pochoka pano pokafika kunyumbako, mwina mukukangokumana ndi mau, "Si uyu tambala uja?!" "Anzathu aja tinali nawo pa msonkhano, ndithudi, akuti m'maliro!" "A-aah! tanenani bwino inu!" "Ndithu, amai aja amatsogolera nyimbowa – eeh, ndithu, m'maliro!" "Chachitika nchiani?" "Ndithu, anangokumana ndi mau akuti, 'Suyu tambala uja?!'" A-a-ah! Popeza tsikulo silidziwika, konzekeranitu!

Mwina nkutheka kuthawa pamsonkhano pano, maganizo ali pa botolo la kachasu. Mulungu atangofuna botolo phaaa! inunso simungakaligwire! Mwina m'kukangokumana ndi mau akuti, "Suyu tambala uja?!" – botolo lomwelonso osaligwira! Nkutheka zimenezo!

Mwina ndi kuthawa pa msonkhano chifukwa cha kuthamangira chamba – kuthamangira nyanga, zigololo – kuthamangira mabodza. Mulungu atangofuna pano, zedi mwina nyangayo simungakagwirenso. Mutangokumana ndi mau akuti, "Suyu tambala uja?!" Maliro! Popeza tsikulo simulidziwa lopita kumudzi, konzekeranitu!

Amai, konzekeranitu! Imfa ya tambala ilibe upo. Mulungu ali ndi njala **yakufuna mtimawo**. Akuti, "Ndikabwera ine, sinditenga ng'ombe. Ng'ombezo n'dakupatsa ndi ine. Ndikabwera ine, ndalamazo ayi, n'dakupatsa ndine. Ndikabwera ine, mbuzizo ayi, n'dakupatsa ndine. Ndikabwera ine, galimotoyo ayi, n'dakupatsa ndine. Ndikabwera ine, chigayocho ayi, n'dakupatsa ndine. Sitoloyo ayi, n'dakupatsa ndine. Ndikabwera ine, samuyo ayi, n'dakupatsa ndine. Ndikabwera ine – koma chimene ndisowa ine – ndili ndi njala yakuchotsa – kubwera kuno. Ndipo nditamva njala, sinkuuza." Imfa ya tambala ilibe upo. Popeza kumene kupita msonkhano, sindikudziwa. Nkwabwino kungokonzekeranitu!

Mwakonzeka inu? Mwakonzeka? Cholinga cha msonkhano, tikhale okonzeka. Kukonzekerako ndiko kumulandira Yesu monga mpulumutsi wathu – njira ya kwathu ku mudzi. Nthawi iliyonse mukhoza kunyamuka – imfa m'mene ikuthamangira.

Abale anga, ndingokuululani pang'ono. Ndinadwala ine pakatipo. Ndipo akadandionetsa imfa m'mene ikuthamangira ku dziko. Ndi zimene ndinaonera m'mene munali kugonamo. Sindili kumvetsa kuti ifeyo tizipezeka ndi moyo pansi pano. Ndipo ndinachita mantha – mpakana pano sindikumvetsa.

Adandionetsa zimasitima zakutha, zokalamba, zakalekale, zopanda maonekedwe, komanso zoopsa. Komanso zimagalimoto zakutha, zopanda maonekedwe, zokalamba, zakalekale – kaya zikutheka bwanji kuyenda. Ndi kundionetsanso ziwanthu zokhala ngati anthu okhala ngati Mulunguyo amazipanga, ndiye zidampulumuka, sadamalize – okhala ngati munthu ndani ameneyu!

Tsono adakali kundionetsa akuti, "Bwera, udzaone imfa m'mene ikuthamangira!" Zimasitima zimenezo zili kuthamanga, ndipo sipidi yake sindidaione – mpakana kumagundana ndi kuphwanyika, palibenso lipeyala! Koma kumene kuchokere ziwanthu zija, zosaoneka bwino, kudzadzutsa, nthawi yomweyo chifumbi phaaa! Kanthawi kang'onong'ono chapakira ziwanthu – ziwanthu, unyinji wa wanthu! Akuti, "Taona yanyamula imfa onse. Ikupita ukatulayi ku gahena – ikupita ukatulayi kumanda." Ndipo ndinaona zoopsa, sindidaone – sipidi! Zimasitima zimenezi ndipo zinathamanga, ndipo zili kuyenda usiku ndi usana. Ndipo m'fumbi lokhalokha, fumbi lokhalokha!

Ndiye akuti, "Bwera, udzaone ntchito imene ndakutumayi – mau amene mumalalikira." Ndiye ineyo ndimapezeka m'masiteji m'mene anthu amakhala kudikira zimasitima zimenezo. Ndiye pasitejipo ineyo, ntchito yanga inali yolalikira uthenga – kulalikira. Koma chikangofika, fumbi limene atithire pamenepo, anzangawo kumene alowe, nkosadziwika. Kumene naine ndikagwere nkosadziwika – kungopezeka ndili ndekha. Akuti, "Chanyamuka, chapita!" Mpakana ine kumadabwa – nanga ine chandisiya bwanji? Ineyo ndikupezeka pano bwanji? Wosamvetsetsa kanthawi kang'onong'ono, ndakapezekanşo pa siteji, ndipo chigulu cha wanthu – kulalikira uthenga, kulalikira uthenga. Kanthawi kang'onong'ono kumene zibwerere zimasitimazo – zoopsa, zosaoneka bwino. Nthawi yomweyo fumbi lokha kudzanyamula. Ali, "Zikuthamanga usiku ndi usana. Imeneyo ndiyo imfa!"

Tsono ndi m'mene ndinaoneramo, dzuwalo likatuluka mpakana ukalowa, zedi, ndi chisomo cha Mulungu. Kaya zikutheka bwanji? Komanso ngakhale ifeyo olalikira tikupezeka kuti tikulalikira mkatikati mwa zimenezo, kaya zikutheka bwanji kumapezeka ndi moyo? Mpakana pano sindili kupeza yankho. Mau ndikunena pano, abale anga, ndikukuuzani zimene ndinaziona. Nkutheka lero msonkhano wanu watha, mwina lero munyamuka. Nkutheka msonkhano wanu watha, mwina mawa munyamuka. Popeza simudziwa, konzekeranitu. Imfa ya tambala ilibe upo. "Naa iweyo – nkamva njala, sindikuuza!"

Chigawo chomaliza: Akuluakulu amanena mau akuti, "Ukatambatamba, umayang'ana ku nyanja, kungakuchere." Mudaimvapo nyimbo imeneyi? "Ukatambatamba, umayang'ana kunyanja, kungakuchere." Ine kwathu ndi ku nyanja, ku Salima uku. Ndiye kukamacha, timaonera kunyanjako – kumafiira, kuyera – dzuwa limenelo. Ndipo timadziwa kuti, "Kunja kuno kuli kucha!" Ndiye tsopano akuti ufiti umakoma kutamba m'matandakucha cha mafoo okloko. Ndi kumene kumakoma mfiti kutamba. Ndikunama? Amene muli mfiti, ndikukunyengezerani? (kuseka) Monga ndikunama kuti, si kukoma kutamba foo okloko – ndikunama? Ndikunama eti?! Ah-aaah! Bwanji kodi mukungozyolika? Tandiyankhani! Ehee-hee! (kuseka)

Ndiye kuti popeza mfitizo zilibe mawochi – aah! mfiti ili ndi wochi?! Inu amfiti, muli ndi mawochi? Ndikudziwatu mulipo pompano. Muli ndi mawochi? Ndiye kuti popeza zilibe mawochi, ndiye zimati zikamatamba – kumavina guleyo – zimayang'ana kum'mawaku, aone ngati kuli kuyera, adziwe kuti kunja kuli kucha. Ndiye tanthauzo la nyimboyi, "Ukatambatamba, umayang'ana ku nyanja, kungakuchere." Ndiye akamavina guleyo, kumayang'ana kum'mawaku - akamavina guleyo, kumayang'ana kum'mawaku. Akangowona kuti kuli kuyera, "Eeh! tiyeni tiweruke, tizipita!" Nthawi yomweyo phaaa! kuweruka, kumapita.

Ndiye kuti tsiku lina mfiti zina zapita kokatamba. Ndiye kuti kutamba kudakoma mpakana kuiwala kuyang'ana kum'mawa. Ananu, imakwanira sikisi koloko, osazidziwa. Imakwanira hafu sikisi, osazidziwa. Imakwanira seveni, osazidziwa - kuli wa-wa-wa-waa! He-heee! (kuseka) Imakwanira hafu seveni, adangomva, "Mfiitizo!" Pamene amadzatero, m'maso ngweee! Kunja kwacha! Ananu, kuti azithawa phiii! nagwira! Ehee-heee! Ukatambatamba, ukamayang'ana kunyanja, kungakuchere!

Mwadziwa tanthauzo lake: Zoipazo tikamachita - mowawo tikamamwa, nyangazo tikamachita, mabodzawo, chambacho tikamasuta - kumayang'ana dziko pamene lafika! Ndi nthawi yanji ino? Kumayang'ana dziko pamene lafika - limene ngakhale ndi mkunja yemwe akudziwa kuti nthawi yatha! Si nthawi yosoweretsa chikhristu ino. Si nthawi yosoweretsa ubusa ino. Si nthawi yosoweretsa ukuluwampingo. Si nthawi yosoweretsa khwaya. Si nthawi yosowera ndi ulaliki. Si nthawi yosowera pa msonkhano ngati uno. Taonani, dzikoli nyengo ndi nthawi pamene zafika! Aliyense akudziwa kuti dzikoli - mmmmh! m'dziko lino nkumapeto!

Amene ali osakonzeka ngati panali zina, akonzeretu! Cholinga cha msonkhano - konzekani! Ukatambatamba, umaonera kunyanja, kungakuchere - nthawi yatha! Komanso kumaona kumene wachokera, pamene ulili, kumene uli kupita. Komanso kumaona m'thupi mwako, "Kodi munthune ndikudzimva bwanji?" Chifukwa umadziwa ndithu wekha. Mwina nkumanena, "Ana inu, ine nkadzamwalira, musaganize kuti sindinadwale." "Munthune, ngakhale ndili kuyenda, chinthu chidangoyala uku. Tere chimenechi ndikuchidziwa kuti chidzanditenga ndithu!" Kodi nthawi imeneyi nkumachita masewera ndi chikhristu?

Ukudziwa kuti, "Chinthu chimenechi chidzanditenga ndithu!" Mukudziwa kuti matenda amenewa - mungoti, "Pa mwezi kudwala, mwezi kudwala - ine, adzan'tenga matenda omwewa!" Mungoti - pakapita nthawi pang'ono mwadwalanso, "Milungu itatu ndadwalanso, matenda ndiye pano, m'sadzakangane kuti, 'Amai afa bwanji?' 'Abambo afa bwanji?' Munthune ndakhala ndikuyenda, ndikuyenda nazo. Kodi nthawi imeneyi ndikusewera ndi chikhristu?"

Ukatambatamba, umayang'ana ku nyanja, kungakuchere – nthawi yatha! Nthawi imene azimaliza msonkhano wanga, ine sindiidziwa. Abale anga, abale anga, "Sindidzatenga ng'ombe m'nyumba mwako popeza zonse ndi zanga. Koma iweyo, ndikamva njala, sindikuuza!" Imfa ya tambala ilibe upo. Chofunika ife, tiyeni tikonzekeretu!

Titseke m'maso, tipemphere – titseke m'maso, tipemphere – titseke m'maso:

Palibe njira ina imene tingachite koposa, Ambuye. Ndikuona nthawidi yatha, koma ndikhoza kunyamuka tsiku lili lonse. Popeza tsikulo sindilidziwa, ndifuna ine ndikhale okonzekeratu. Ambuye, bwerani, mulowe mumtima mwanga. Ambuye, bwerani, mulamulire mumtima mwanga. Kaya ndinyamuka lero, njira yanga ndi inuyo. Kaya ndinyamuka mawa, kaya ndinyamuka mkuja, kaya m'chaka cha mawa – njira yanga ndi inuyo. Yesu, Mwana wa Mulungu, ndikuitanani! Bwerani, bwerani! Nthawi yoipa ino osasiyana ndi Yesu, popeza imfa ili kuthamanga. Matenda, matenda – wanthu ambiri – ulendo wa kumudzi!

Amai, mwina nkutero kuti, "Aah, ine thandizeniko kupemphera. Zoonadi, sindifunanso kuti ndichitenso masewera ndi chigwirizano changa – ukuluwampingo wanga. Ndiionadi nthawi yoipa ino. Sindifuna kuchita masewera ndi khwaya yanga – masewera ndi utumiki wanga – masewera ndi ntchito yanga imene Ambuye andituma. Sindifuna kuchita masewera nthawi yoipa ino!" Tangokwezani mkono wanu, ndikuthandizeni kupemphera – pamalo pano pamene mwakhalapo. Ndi nthawi ino osasewera ndi chipulumutso, popeza nthawi yatha. Aliyense pakuona dziko ndi m'mene zinthu zilili, aliyense akudziwa kuti, "Ah-yai, dziko latha! Takwezani mkono wanu, tithandizane upemphera. Zikomo kwambiri, Ambuye akudalitseni!

Amai, mwatsala nokha – abambo, mwatsala nokha. Mwinanso inu simukudziwa kuti lero lenilenilo msonkhano wanu walephereka. Mukadadziwa inuyo, simukadachita masewera. Mchimwene, mukadadziwa inuyo, simukadachita masewera. Titseke m'maso, tipemphere: Muli chikwezereni mkono wanuyo, tidzapemphera. Pemphero lanu inuyo mungonena kuti,

"Ambuye Yesu, bwerani, mulowe mumtima mwanga. Ndifuna ndikhale okonzekeratu. Mwina nkuthekadi tsono kukangokumana ndi mau akuti, 'Suyu tambala uja!' Koma ndili wokonzeka pakukukhulupirirani ndi kukulandirani Yesu monga mpulumutsi wanga!"

Tipemphere: Tsono inu mulikumvetsera nthawi ino, ndikupemphani kuti mupemphere nao ngati uthengawu wakukhudzani:

M'dzina la Yesu Khristu limene lili ndi mphamvu ndi ulamuliro, amene mphamvu zonse zidapatsidwa kwa inu kumwamba ndi dziko lapansi. Taonani anthu anu. Adziwa kuti mwa iwo okha sangakafike kumwamba ayi – pokhapokha inu Yesu mulowe m'mitima yao. Mugwetse mphamvu ndi ulamuliro wa Satana kuti inu Yesu mukhale mfumu. Popeza ndinu nokha mudanena, "Mudzalandira mphamvu, Mzimu Woyera atadza pa inu" – mphamvu imene siidzabwera m'mbuyo – mphamvu imene Satana sadzakhudzanso matupi ao – mphamvu imene sadzaopa kukuchitirani umboni.

Ambuye, tengani ulamuliro wa moyo wao. Tengani pakamwa pao. Tengani manja ao, maso ao, makutu ao, lilime lao, miyendo yao – kuti zonse zikakuchitireni inu umboni ndi kuti anthu onse kuli konse akatsimikize muli mphamvu yodabwitsa mwa inu, Yesu. Takuona zazikulu zimene Ambuye mwachitirazi. Imvani kulira kwao. Imvani kufuula kwao. Si mphamvu, si nkhondo, koma m'Mzimu wanu! M'dzina la Yesu Khristu, mpulumutsi wathu wamoyo, tikupemphani. Ameni! (Ameni.)

Udindo wa Mkhristu (SW40)

Mau a Mulungu achokera kumabuku atatu: Buku loyamba, tiwerenga kuchokera m'buku la Yobu, chaputala 38 – Yobu chaputala 38, tiwerenga kuyambira vesi ya wani. Yobu chaputala 38, tiwerenga kuyambira vesi ya wani. Mau otsogolera: "Mulungu aonekera kwa Yobu wosamtsutsa. Koma anamkumbutsa za ukulu wopambana wa Mulungu. Yobe adzichepetsapo." Vesi ya wani: "Pamenepo Yehova anayankha Yobu m'kamvuluvulu, nati, 'Ndani uyu udetsa uphungu ndi mau opanda nzeru? Udzimangire m'chiuno tsono ngati m'mwamuna. Ndikufunsa, undidziwitse. Unali kuti muja ndinaika maziko a dziko lapansi? Fotokoza ngati udziwa kuzindikira. Analemba malire ache ndani popeza udziwa? Anayesapo chingwe chake ndani?

Maziko ake anakumbidwa pa chiani? Kapena anaikapo ndani mwala wake wapangodya?'"

Ndipo tipitenso ku Luka chaputala 20 – buku la Luka chaputala 20. Ndipo tidzayambira pa vesi ya naini: "Fanizo la anthu olima m'munda wa mphesa." Vesi ya naini: "Ndipo iye anayamba kunena kwa anthu fanizo ili: Munthu anali ndi munda wa mphesa, naukongoletsa kwa olima munda, nanka ku dziko lina, nagonerako nthawi yaikulu. Ndipo pa nyengo ya chipatso anawatumiza akapolo ake kwa olima munda kuti ampatseko chipatso cha m'mundamo. Olimawo anampanda, nambweza osampatsa kanthu. Ndipo anamtumizanso kapolo wina, ndipo iyenso anampanda, namchitira chipongwe, nambweza osampatsa kanthu. Ndipo anamtumizanso wina wachitatu, ndipo iyenso anamulasa namtaya kunja. Ndipo mwini mundayo anati, 'Ndidzachita chiani? Ndipo ndidzatuma mwana wanga amene ndimkonda kwambiri. Kapena adzamchitira iye ulemu.' Koma olima mundawo pamene adamuona, anauzana wina ndi mnzake, nati, 'Uyu ndiye mwini wolowa m'nyumba. Tiyeni timuphe kuti cholowa chonse chikhale chathu.' Ndipo anamponya kunja kwa mundawo, namupha. Pamenepo mwini munda ayenera kuchita chiani? Iye adzafika, nadzaononga olima munda aja, nadzapatsa munda kwa ena. Ndipo pamene iwo anamva, anati, 'Musamatero ayi!'" Vesi ya 17: "Koma iya anawapenyetsetsa iwo, nati, 'Nchiani ichi chinalembedwa? Mwala umene adauyesa omanga nyumba womwewo unakhala mutu wapangodya. Ndipo yense wakugwa pa mwala uwu, adzaphwanyika. Koma iye amene udzamgwere, udzamtswanya.' Ndipo gulu la ansembe akulu anafunafuna kumugwira ndi manja nthawi yomweyo. Ndipo anaopa anthu pakuti anazindikira kuti ananenera iwo fanizo limeneli."

Ndipo titsirize ndi buku la Salimo 116 – buku la Masalimo nambala 116, vesi ya 12: "Ndidzabwezera Yehova chiani chifukwa cha zokoma zake zonse anandichitira?"

Ambuye wabwino akadalitse mau awa, ndipo kwa iye kukhale ulemu nthawi zonse. Ameni! (Ameni!)

Kwa inu nonse m'dzina la Ambuye wathu Yesu Khristu – mooni! Tiyamikira Ambuye kuti watikomera mtima, takumananso nthawi yabwino pamene tikumbukira mu mpingo uno – kuti takhala zaka 105. Tsopano pamene tikumbukira monga tsiku lalero ndi tsiku lalikulu kwambiri. Kodi pa zaka 105 tachitapo chiani? Uthenga umene Mulungu afuna kulankhula nafe ndi Udindo wa Mkhristu.

Titseke m'maso, tipemphere: Tafikanso ku mpando wanu wachifumu, Mulungu wathu, pakudziwa kuti inu ndi thandizo lathu lopezekeratu. Ndipo tikafika kwa inu, timadziwa kuti chili chonse chimene tidzachifuna, tidzachilandira – popeza taona zazikulu zimene mwatichitira pamene tinakupemphani. Komanso taona zazikulu zimene tithedwa nzeru kuti tikuthokozeni. Ndipo chikondi chanu chomwecho chatisonkhanitsanso pompano. Popeza mudziwa chosowa chathu, lankhula nafeni. Popeza mudziwa pansi pa mitima yathu, Ambuye, pitirirani kutidalitsa. Monga mwayamba nafe kale, m'mawa uja, popeza ife ndife anthu osowa nthawi zonse. Tsekulani maso athu, tichione chuma cha mtengo wapatali chimene mwatitengera. Ambuye, musatisiye tokha. Si mphamvu, si nkhondo, koma m'Mzimu wanu. M'dzina la inu, Yesu Khristu, tapempha. Ameni!

Uthenga uli pano ndi chenjezo – udindo wa mkhristu. Pamene talandira Yesu, amatipatsa zinthu zitatu: Wani – chikhululukiro cha machimo, moyo wosatha. Nambala thuu – amatipatsa mphatso, ntchito tikamtumikire Ambuyeyo. Nambala thrii – amatipatsa anthu kuti anthuwo tiwatumikire. Aliyense wa inu amene atalandira Yesu, adapatsidwa zinthu zitatu. Aliyense wa ife ali ndi udindo mu mpingo wa Ambuye, popeza ichi ndi chochokera kwa Mulungu mwini wake. Koma chimene chikundisautsa ine – akhristu sali kudziwa kuti ali ndi udindo mu mpingo wa Ambuye. Ntchito ya Mulungu angosiyira abusa okha.

Ndiye akhristuwo, m'malo moti azindikire udindo wao, amakalipitsana ndi azibusa. "Mbusa ameneyu waononga mpingo!" "Mbusa ameneyu, mpingo wao waononogeka!" "Mbusa ameneyu anabwera pano kudzangotidyera ndalama!" "Mbusa ameneyu alibe Mzimu!" "Mbusa ameneyu ndi mtembo – achoke pano!" "Mpingo wagwa chifukwa cha mbusa ameneyu – chifukwa cha mbusa ameneyu!" Mau a mwano! Ngati mudalankhulapo, musadzalankhulenso, choonde! Mumchimwira mbusa. Musadzabwerezenso mau oipa – amwano!

Mbusa, monga mbusa wa nkhosa, ntchito yake ndi kudyetsa nkhosazo – uzilondolera ku msipu wabwino. Yodwalayo ku vetenale, adzailase mankhwala.

Ehee-hee-hee! (kuseka) Ameeni! Ulendo... Yothoka mwendo kumachiritsidwa. Yolephera kuyenda kuisenzera pa mapewa – ulendo kumudzi. Ndiyo ntchito ya mbusa imeneyo!

Koma kuti nkhosazo ziswane – funso: Kodi amene amaswa nkhosa – mbusa ndi nkhosa – amaswa mnzake ndani? Amaswa mnzake ndi nkhosa eti? Osati mbusa eti? Nchifukwa chake ndati "mau a mwano." Akadza mbusa, sakuswa nkhosa, koma nkhosazo zimaswana zokha. Mwano! (kuseka ndi kuomba m'manja) Mau oipa – mau oipa!

Tsopano mipingo yakalekale – mamembala thati (30)! Lero ndiulule chifukwa chake. Kodi inu, nkhosa yosabala yaikazi, dzina lake amati nchia-? Dzidzi – timati dzidzi. Nanga itakhala yaimuna yosabala, dzina lake nlota-? Mfuleni, eti? Mfu... hee-heeeya! (kuseka kwakukulu) Aleluya! (Ameni!) Lero tiulula! Mpingo wakalekale – mamembala, ananu, thati okha – chifukwa chiani? Nkhosazo mumpingo muli zadzidzi ndi zimifuleni zosabala! Mbusa sakuswa nkhosa, koma nkhosazo zimaswana zokha. Musadzalankhulenso – musadzalankhulenso!

Pamene ndili kunena pano, mulipo ena pano chikhristu mudachiyamba kale – palibe m'modzi amene mudamchitira umboni za Yesu – amene adadziwa Yesu monga mpulumutsi wake chifukwa cha inu! Moti msonkhanowu udapitirira, tikadati mawa tibwerenso aliyense, akatenge munthu amene adamchitira umboni kuti adziwe Yesu. Ndipo munthuyo adzaimirire pano, adzaperekere umboni kuti iwe... kuti, "Ndizimdziwa Yesu chifukwa cha awa!" Nditati mubwere naye mawa, mukabwera naye munthu? Mifuleni siikabwera ndi munthu mawa ayi! (kuseka) Adzidzi sakabwera ndi munthu mawa! (kuseka) Ndi chifukwa chake mpingo uli kugwa pansi!

Inu muganiza mkhristu aliyense akanakhala ndi udindo – tatiyeni titati tichite mpikisano kuti kuyambira Janyuale mpakana Disemba, aliyense akachitire umboni. Koma ngakhale sudziwa kulalikira – koma ndi zoonadi, Janyuale mpakana Disemba angalephereke ndi m'modzi yemwe, osamkopa, osamlalikirira za Yesu, osatembenuka mtima? Ngakhale inuyo simudziwa kulalikira, koma zoonadi, twelfu manzi wopanda ndi m'modzi yemwe – zingatheke, zingatheke?! Ngakhale utakhala kuti sudziwa ulalikira, koma m'modzi yekha mpakana atapezeka – mwina awiri, atatu, fayifi, mwina teni! Ngati mumpingomu munali akhristu thati (30), pamene chizitha chaka

– sikisite (60). Pakutha chaka chinacho sikisite – handredi twente (120). Eeeh, ndaulula lero! Mumpingo mwanu mwanu muja, ngati mpingo ukugwa pansi, mwachuluka timafuleni, zadzidzi! Musadzalankhulenso, ayi! Tere adzidziwo – amifuleni ili pompano ikungoti zyooli! Ili pompano! (kuseka) Mundiyang'ane!

Tsiku lija mudalandira Yesu, mudapatsidwa zinthu zitatu: moyo, mphatso, ndi anthu ofunika uwachitira umboni. Muzidziwe zimenezi kuyambira lero! Mbusa, monga mbusa, ali kukwanitsa ntchito yake – ali kukudyetsani mgonero, pa maliro afunika kulalikira, pa ubatizo akubatizani, zitsitsimutso mkati. Mbusa, monga mbusa, pa matenda akuyenderani ku chipatala, nyumba ndi nyumba. Monga mbusa, ali kukwana kuzidyetsa nkhosa zake uthenga wabwino.

Koma mbusa – chimene chiyenera kuchitika, aziti akadyetsadyetsa nkhosazo, ndiye azikama mkaka kuti nayenso anenepe. E-eh! nanga mungonenepa nokha?! Heeh! (kuseka) Aziti akazidyetsa nkhosa zonenepa, ndiye atenge chibotolo, ehee! ango... (kuseka) Aleluyaaah! (Ameni!) Akameko mkaka, nayenso anenepe! Heeh, muzingonenepa nokha?! Muzinenepa nokha?! Mwakudziwa kukama mkaka? Kashuga kaja m'mapatsa mbusa, "Abusa, muchitire phala ndi ana." Wakama pamenepo! (kuseka) "Abusa, kabuledi aka!" Aah! choncho nanga muzitani – wakama pamenepo! "Abusa, kashati aka. Mwina kakathina, mudzandiuza kakatakwana. Ayi, tingothokoza!" Wakama pamenepo! "Abusa, kanjinga aka, muziyendera mtunda, watalika!" Wakama pamenepo! "Abusa, galimoto – makiyi ndi awa." Wakama pamenepo! Nayenso anenepe! Akadyetsa, nayenso akame mkaka!

Koma chomvetsa chisoni mwachidziwa? Pali nkhosa zina zikuti mbusa akati akame mkaka – theeki baaa! Aaah-haa! (kuseka ndi kululutira) Nkhosa yoipa! (kululutira) Nkhosa yoipa – nkhosa yoipa! Kukanakhala nkhosa zathuzi – mbuzizi – bwanji kukangogulitsa nanga?! (kuseka) Kupha, ah! kungokupha nkhosa yoipa! Mbusa asakame? Akati akame – theeki baaa! Aagh! iyayi! Nkosa yoipa! Kodi inuyo, ndinu nkhosa ya mtundu wanji? Kodi ndi nkhosa imene ikumenya mateki mbusa? Funso limeneli, mupite nalo ku nyumba.

Komanso abusa tichenjezeko! Nkhosayo ngati siinenepa, m'malo mokama mkaka, mukama magazi! E-e-eeh! (kuseka) Aleluya! (Ameni!) A-ha-haa! (kuseka) Kukama magazi! (kuseka) He-he-hee! M'malo mwake, azibusa ambiri ali kuthamangitsidwa. Atangothamangitsidwa, timangodziwa kuti wakama magazi! (kuseka) Ehee-hee! Chifukwa mphatso zimene amatipatsa akhristu azibusa zimasinthitsana ndi khalidwe la mbusa. Ngati mbusa alibe khalidwe, akama magazi – akama magazi! (kuomba m'manja) Mipingo yambiri, azibusa... mipingo yambiri, azikulu a mipingo – mpingo ukangopereka chopereka, iwo angokudya choperekacho mpakana mpingo ukhumudwa. Lero ndinene kuti musamakhumudwe. Simupereka kwa mbusa, simupereka kwa akuluampingo – mumapereka kwa Mulungu! Koma iwo, ngati akudya, tsoka ndi lao! Akangodzionera wokha pamaso pa Mulungu! (kuomba m'manja ndi kufuula) Chifukwa mphatso zimene tikulandira zimasinthitsana ndi khalidwe la mbusa. Ndiye ngati ulibe khalidwe, ndikuti magazi!

Mau oyipa – tisadzanenenso ayi! Nkhosa zimaswana nkhosa zokha. Mbusa sakuswa nkhosa ayi. Aliyense wa inu ali ndi udindo. Mipingo lero taitenga ngati mabasi – kungokhalakhala m'mipando, miyendo ili khobaaah! pa mpando. Komanso saukana yekha mpingo monga m'mene tichitira m'basi. "Dalaiva, mooto! mooto!" (kuseka) "Bwanji – tifuna tifike nthawi yabwino ifee! Motooo, adalaiva!" Miyendo ili khobaah! (kuseka) Kumangokangana ndi abusa, ayi. "Mbusa ameneyu ndi mtembo. Adangobwera pano udzadya ndalama!" Koma miyendo ili khobaah! Palibe chimene mukumuthandiza mbusayo. Muli, "Moto! moto! – ulendo wa kumwamba!" Nkumvetsa chisoni! (kuseka)

Mpingo uli ngati bwato kunyanjako. Bwato tikamapalasa, aliyense amatenga chopalasira. Ndipo bwato wotere umayenda ndi liwiro. Umathamanga kwambiri, ndiye ngati uli ndi injini. Koma ngati tisiyira munthu m'modzi m'bwatomo, suthamanga kwambiri. Ndi m'mene ulili mpingo. Aliyense ali ndi udindo. Ndipo aliyense atadziwa udindo wake, mpingo wathu sukadagwa pansi ayi. Koma kuyambira lero aliyense wa inu mudziwe kuti muli ndi udindo mu mpingo. Ntchitoyi si ya abusa okha ayi!

Chenjezo: Mau amene tawerenga pano – mau osautsa amene ali kundisautsa mumtima mwanga. Pano tawerengapo pa Luka chaputala twente, makamaka kuyambira vesi ya naini kulekeza eitini. Pano tawerengapo fanizo la olima munda. Pamene Ambuye Yesu amalalikira uthenga wabwino, ndipo adapereka fanizo limeneli, ali pamodzi ndi akuphunzira ake.

Ndipo Yesu anaimirira, akuti, "Munthu wina wake anali ndi munda – anatsekula esiteti. Pofuna kutsekula esiteti, simasewera ayi. Ndalama zidatayika. Mathalakitala kuzula mitengo – mathalakitala kutipula, kupanga mizera – anchito mkati. Ndalama zidatayika – kugula makasu, zikwanje zatsopano. Adataya chuma chochuluka kwambiri! Ndipo mpakana mundawo udatha. Ndipo adapanga mizera, nayembekezera kuti mvula ikagwa, akabzale. Ndipo mbewu zoonse afese zinali leede, mongo esiteti – kuona chimanga, kuona mpunga, kuona mtedza, kuona mapiri, mbewu ya mtundu uliwonse – zinali leede! Ndipo mau akuti mfumuyo – nthawi yobzala itangoyandikira kuti tsopano mvula ili pafupi, mwadzidzidzi adanyamuka ulendo. Ndipo ulendowo, adapita ku dziko lalitaaali. Ndipo kumeneko atapita, adakafika nthawi yothaitha. Sadakatsekulenso wina munda – sanakatsekulenso ina esiteti popeza adafika nthawi yothaitha, ena anzao atatha kale kulima.

Popeza mfumuyi idali yabwino mtima, mtima wake unampweteka. "Ndili kuchoka kupita ku dziko lakutaaali. Taonani munda wanga – n'nasauka nawo, kutsekula esiteti! N'nataya chuma chochuluka. Kodi – tsopano ndikuchoka – kodi munda umenewu ungowonongeka? Nditaye mphamvu yanga pachabe?!"

Mfumu idavutika mkati mwamtima. Akuti, "Sindingachitire mwina. Jelasi si labwino!" Ndipo akuti adaitana anthu, "Bwerani kuno! Ndikupatseni munda wangawu. Ndavutika nawo, koma nthawi yakwana – ndili kuchoka! Kuti munda umenewu uwononogeke, olimalima, mtima wanga ukuvutika! Yeense wa inu bwerani – ndikugawireni. Mulime mbewu zina m'mene mungafunire. Aliyense alime! Ofuna thonje, alime! Chimanga, alime! Kaya ndi mpunga, alime! Aliyense wa inu alime monga m'mene ali kufunira."

Ndipo ndidziwa kuti anthu aja anakondwa chifukwa anapeza munda wotsekulatsekula, ntchito yonse itatha kale. Iwo adangotenga mbewu ukabzala. Anasangalala, nalumphalumpha.

Ndipo mfumuyo inapita ku dziko lija lakutaali. Popeza kumeneko adakafika nthawi yakutha, mfumuyo siidakatsekulanso munda. Ndipo itafika nthawi yokolola – nthawi yakudya chimanga – nthawi dzinthu zonse zacha bwino – akuti mfumuyo kudziko lakutalilooo, chifundo chidamugwira. "Ndifuna chimanga chowotcha!" Chifundo chidamugwira. "Ndifuna kamtedza kokazinga!" Chifundo chidamugwira. Ndipo akuti, "Sindingachitire mwina. Ndituma akapolo anga, apite." Anthu aja tinawasiyira munda, akangopempha chimanga chimodzi – chifundo – ndidzawotche!"

Ndipo akuti akapolowo anawatuma, ndipo anapita kapolo wina. Ndipo atakafika, anamulandiradi, "E-eeh! Bambo, tikuthandizeni chiani? Nkwabwino?" Ndipo akuti, "Pepani akuluakulu, si chipongwe. Mfumu ija idakupatsani munda yandituma ine. Akuti muipatseko chimanga chimodzi – chifundo – akawotche." "Ukuti chiani?! Chimanga chimodzi – chifundo – akawotche, nchiani?!" Nthawi yomweyo akuti, "Chiani?! Shatapu! Inu, ndiye amangokudya – ife ndiye tizikhala timavutika m'kukugwirirani ntchito! M'pondeni! M'gwireni!" Nthawi yomweyo adamuthamangitsa – phaaa! Adampanda, koma chisomo cha Mulungu, mpakana adapulumuka.

Adakafika pamaso pa mfumu ali mbuu! kutuwa. Akuti, "Mfumu, nkadafa ine!" "Nchiani?!" Akuti, "Ati inuyo ndiye omangokudya – aah, akuti iwowo avutika okha, mpakana kusauka ndi kulima. Akuti ifeyo ndiye omangokudya, iwo ndiwo ovutika nkugwira ntchito!" Mfumu ija siidakhulupirire. "Ukunama iwe – uli kunama!" Mfumu siinakhulupirire, "Ndimtuma mnzakoyo!"

Adamtumanso mnzake. Nayenso anakafika. "Pepani mabwana, si chipongwe. Mfumu ija idakusiyirani munda yandituma. Akufuna chimanga chimodzi chowotcha – chifundo!" "Chiani?!" "Chimanga chimodzi." "Shatapu! M'pondeni!" Pakhosi psii! Mwamwai anapulumuka. Pamene anakafika pamaso ali mbuu! kutuwa. Akuti, "Mfumu, nkadafa ineee!" "Nchiaani?!" Akuti, "Ati inuyo ndiye omangokudya, iwowo ndiye omavutika m'kugwira ntchito. Mpakana kundionetsa mabala pamene khasu lidawatema. Nkadafa ineee!" Koma amfumu sadakhulupirire. "Ukunama iweee – uli kunama iwee! Pita iwe wa nambala thrii!"

Adapitanso wanambala thrii. "Pepani mabwana, si chipongwe. Mfumu ija idakusiyirani munda yandituma..." Ndiye, "Ukuti chiani – ukuti chiani?!"

Amvekere asadalankhule – pakhosi psii! "Inu ndiye omangokudya, ife ndiye omavutika nkugwira ntchito. Shatapu!" Nthawi yomweyo adamuthamangitsa, namtaya kunja. Atakafika ukooo, "Mfumu, ndikadafa ineee!" "Chiani?!" Akuti, "Ati inuyo ndiye omangokudya, iwowo ndiwo omavutika nkugwira ntchito." Akuti, "Aah! Iyayi-iyayi! ukunama iwe! Ulikunama iweee!" Mfumu siidakhulupirire. "Ndimtuma mwana wanga, wangawanga! Popeza inuyo akukuyesani mbala – popeza mwana wangayu amamudziwa! Akakazindikira, akadziwadi kuti, 'Eeh, zoonadi-zoonadi! Akunena zoona – si mwana wao uyu wabwera panoyu?!' Ndimtuma mwana wanga!"

Ndipo mfumuyo inatuma mwana wake. Mwanayo atangotulukira, ooonse matenanti akuti, "Mukumuona mwana akubwera apoyo?" Akuti, "Eee!" "Mwana ameneyo ndiye wa amfumu aja! Mwana ameneyu, amfumu aja akadzamwalira, ndiye kuti munda uno udzakhala wake. Chimene tipange ife kuti mundawu ukhale wathu – tiphe mwanayo! Tikangoti phooo! basi, munda udzakhala wathu – m'mene mukuonera munda umenewu, munda wa choonde – m'mene mukuonera munda umenewu, munda wa dzinthu! Ndiye adzatengenso mwana ameneyu?! Tiyeni tiphe kuti mundawu ukhale wathuuu!"

Mwana uja atafika, "Pepani akuluakulu, si chipongwe. Atate andituma, akufuna chimanga chimodzi..." E-eeeh! asadamalize, pakhosi phooo! Ali mwanayo, "Mundipweteka!" "Shatapu! Inu ndiye omangokudya, ife ndiye omavutika m'kugwira ntchito!" Phooo! mpakana mwanayo adapha, nkukataya kuthengooo! Mpakana mfumu inamva uthenga, akuti, "Mwana wanu wapitaaa!"

Akuti mfumu idasauka mumtima mwake! "Aniphera mwana?" "Eeeh!" "A-aagh! mpakana uniphera mwana?" "Eeeeh, mwana uja aphaaa!" Nchifukwa chiani mfumu siidakhulupirire? Woyamba adamtaya, osakhulupirira. Wachiwiri adamtaya, osakhulupirira. Wachitatu adamtaya, osakhulupirira. Mpakana kumuphera mwanaaa, osakhulupirira! "Mpakana kundiphera mwana?!" Akuti, "Eeeh, mwana wapita!" Chifukwa chiani siidakhulupirire?

Pali zinthu zitatu... "Chimanga chimodzi ndiye nkundiphera mwana?! Chimanga chimodzi, mpakana nkukupandani? Mukunama inu – tapita! A-ah, adali yani iwo aja? Ndidakachita kukawatola ineyo, mpakana andimane chimanga chimodzi. Uli kunama iwe! Pita ndiwe! Aaah! munda uli wanga, mpakana kundiphera mwana! Munda uli wanga - chimanga chimodzi! Mmmm, sindili kukhulupirira! Munda uli wanga - sindikhulupiriraaa!"

Ndipo mfumu itamva kuti mwana wafa, akuti idanena mau akuti, "Kodi akangopita mfumuyo mwini wakeyo, anthu antchitowo akawataniiii?!" Ngozi! Ngozi! Ndiye mau omaliza anena kuti, "Aliyense amene adzakhumudwa pa mwala uwu, adzaphwanyika. Ndiye amene mwalawo udzamgwera, udzamuphaaa!"

Ndiwo mau amene tawerenga pano - mau amene tawerenga pano. Mau amenewa angotizungulira. Pano ndifuna ndiulule: Mfumu ijatu ndiye Mulungu. Mfumu yolemera, mfumu yosasowa kanthu ndi Mulungu. Chimunda chija ndi dziko lapansi. Antchito aja ndi inuyo. Akapolo aja ndi azibusa, azilaliki. Mwana uja ndi Yesu. Ndiye tanthauzo lake.

Tsopano dziko lapansi, Mulungu sanadyere dziko lapansi. Mulungu sadasiye atapanga nsapato, adangosiya nyama. Nzeru za wanthu, nyamazo - chikopacho nkumafufuta kumapangira nsapato - kulidyera dziko lapansi! Mulungu sadasiye atapanga masofa, adasiya mitengo. Nzeru za wanthu zikuigwetsa kumapala matabwa nkumapanga masofa - choti ukakhala, umachita kulowa pansi - kulidyera dziko lapansi! Ehee! Aleluyaaa! (kuseka) Kulidyera dziko lapansi! Mulungu sadasiye atapanga magalimoto. Nzeru za wanthu zikupita pansi pa mgodi ukatulutsa koopa - eee, golide - ndi kupanga zitsulo. Lero kuli zimabenzi, zimagalimoto, zimatoyota - kulidyera dziko lapansi! Mulungu sadasiye atapanga malata, iye adaasiya miyala. Ali kuisungunula miyala imeneyo nkupanga zimalata - zinyumba zabwinozabwino zochita ukongola - kulidyera dziko lapansi! Mulungu sadasiye atapanga zimabaki za simenti, iye andangosiya zimiyala. Nzeru za wanthu, akupita pansi ukaphwanya ndi kugaya ndi kupanga simenti. Lero mukugona m'zinyumba zabwinozabwino zokongola!

Koma ndiye muli cheete! Ehe-heee! (kuseka) Aleluyaaa! (Ameeeni!) Mukulidyera dziko lapansi - kulidyera dziko lapansi. Mulungu sadasiye masuti, maderesi - taonani maabuleza! - iye adangosiya thonje, anasiya thonje. Nzeru za wanthu ati mpakana umakabzala ati thonjelo. Eee, nzeru ati mpakana nkumaumba zinsalu, masuti. Akamabwera apo abambo olemekezeka, koma ndiye mulidyera dziko - ehee-heee! - kulidyera dziko lapansi - kulidyera dziko lapansi!

Abale anga, anthu alemera chifukwa cha dzuwa. Alemera chifukwa cha nthaka. Mulungu sadasiye ataumba zidina, -zinjerwa. Koma nzeru za wanthu ati mpakana umaumba zinjerwa kumamanga zimanyumba zolimba zabwino - ehee! kulidyera dziko lapansi! Nthâka imeneyi anthu alemera nayo! Kuli maesiteti kunja kuno - kuli mafamu kunja kuno. Ndipo anthu alemera chifukwa cha ulimi. Taona zimalolee, zimalolee - kulidyera dziko lapansi! Mvulayi anthu alemera nayo. Dzuwali anthu alemera nalo - kulidyera dziko lapansi! Kuchita kumatenga kamtengo kumatonyera m'mano - kulidyera dziko lapansi! Ehee-heee! (kuseka ndi kululutira) Kulidyera dziko lapansi!

Mulungu adangosiya, iye adangotsekula ngati chi-esiteti - dziko lapansi - nachisiya, uleendo wa ku dziko lakutali kumwamba - kukupatsani inuyo ndi ine ngati matenanti. Ehee-hee! koma ndiye mwalemera, he-he-heeeh! Mwalemera, tikutero, mwalemera - ulidyera dziko lapansi! Nkhani yomvetsa chisoni! Mulungu sadasiye matumba a chimanga, adangosiya mbewu ya chimanga. Mpakana inu mbewuyo mumakabzala - zimatumba, ena 200, ena 500, 2000 matumba - ulidyera, yeeh! Iye sadasiye matumba a mtedza, koma inu mwakabzala zimabagizimabagi! Tikapita kumsikako, eheh-eh! sadasiye chikabichi ayi, adangosiya mbewu ya kabichi. Koma nzeru za wanthu, umakafesa ati! (kuseka) - ulidyera dziko lapansi! Umachita utenga kamtengo kutokonyera m'mano - mwalidyera dziko lapansi!

Abale anga, nkhani yosautsa - nkhani yosautsa! Sadasiye mafuta migolomigolo, ayi, ayi! Nzeru za anthu ati mpakana paaansi ukatenga palafini - kulidyera dziko lapansi! Pansi ukatenga petulo - kulidyera dziko lapansi, kulidyera dziko lapansi! Abale anga, nkhani ili pano ndi yosautsa mumtima mwanga! Anthu akulidyera dziko. Lero Mulunguyo - Mulunguyo watuma akapolo - alaliki, azibusa, aneneri. Afika kwa inuyo. Mulungu akufuna phindu la nthaka. Akufuna phindu la nyumba zimene mwamanga. Iye sadasiye nyumba - mwalidyera dziko! Iye akufuna phindu la nyama zimene adapanga. Akufuna phindu mitengo adaisiya. Akufuna phindu thonje limene adalisiya. Akufuna phindu chimanga chimene adachisiya. Akufuna phindu miyala yake imene adaisiya. Akufuna phindu palafini amene adamusiya.

Akufuna phinduuu! Watuma alaliki, eeh! Watuma azibusa – afuna phindu la zooonse zimene tili nazo – zoonse zimene tili nazo! Palibe munthu amene angagwire ntchito yopanda malipiro. Ngakhale ndi ineyo Mulungu adanitenga ku dothi, nandiumba nkumati ndi "munthu." Pondilemekeza inuyo mumati "Wame," koma Mulunguyo amangoti "dothi." Dothilo kumadziwa kuti, "Apa sindipindula – ndimasiya!" Tidzamkondweretsa nchiani Mulungu – kutipatsa zonse? M'malo momulemekeza, m'kumamtukwana. Chimenechi Mulungu chamusautsa. Akufuna phindu la nyama zimene mwapangira nsapato. Akufuna phindu la mitengo. Akufuna phindu la dzuwa. Akufuna phindu la mvula mwalemera. Akufuna phindu la chaka mwalemera. Akufuna phindu la zooonse zimene muli nazo!

Mudabadwa amaliseche, mudzapitanso amaliseche. Chili chonse chimene muli nacho ndi chochokera kwa Mulungu. Sindidamvapo kuti m'nyumbamo mwabadwa mwana, wangobadwa m'katoni kumanja ayi. Ngati kunyumba kwanu kuli katoni, ndi chuma chimenecho – ndi chuma chimenecho. Chili choonse chimene muli nacho ndi chuma chimenecho. Enanu m'mati, "Ine ndine wosauka!" Kusauka kwanji?! Tachitani totolo: Muwafunse makolo. Mutangobadwa, ndalama zimene zidatayika – zogula matewera, timabulangeti, zokudyetsani, mpakana kukuyimbitsani sukulu, mpakana mwafika sayizi imene muli nayoyi. Zovuta zimene mwakumana nazo, thandizo limene lidatayika, zovala zimene mukuvala, ndalama zimene mwataya. Mutachita totolo – masauzande-masauzande-masauzande! Tsono mukuti ndinu amphawi?! Nchifukwa chakuti sadakupatseni kashi eti?! Ehe-heee! (kuseka) Mumangodyeratu eti? Inu mumafuna kashi eti? Hee-heee! (kuseka) Mulungu afuna phindu la zooonse zimene tili nazo. Palibe osauka ayi – palibe osauka! Chili chooonse chimene tili nacho, Mulungu afuna phindu – ndi zooonse zimene iyeyo adatipatsa. Palibe amene angagwire ntchito yopanda malipiro!

Koma tandimvetsetsani, Malaki thrii, pa vesi ya seveni kulekeza teni akuti, "Mwandilanda! Bwera naloni gawo limodzi la magawo khumi ku nyumba yanga yopempherera." Mwandilandaaa! Ndikufuna phindu la ntchito yanga imene ndidaigwira. Koma phindu lakelo – ngati uli ndi masuti teni, patula suti imodzi, ukapereke. Sakufuna zambiri ayi! Kaya uli ndi ng'ombe teni, tenga ng'ombe imodzi, ukapereka. Safuna zambiri! Kaya wani kwacha, tenga teni tambala, ukapereke. Sakufuna zambiri - safuna zambiri! Kaya muli ndi magalimoto angati, tengani ina, mukapereke. Sakufuna zambiri! Kaya muli ndi zitenje zingati, tengani china, mukapereke. Kaya muli ndi masuti angati, kaya muli ndi nsapato zingati, kaya muli ndi mipando ingati. Chili chooonse chimene muli nacho! Kaya ndi matumba a chimanga angati - thumba limodzi, thumba limodziiii! Salikufuna zambiri! Gawo limodzi mwa magawo khumi zimene inuyo mwapindula, mumpatse Mulungu - mumpatse Mulungu - mumpatse Mulungu!

Koma abale anga, nkhani yomvetsa chisoni: Akapolowo akafika - azibusa, azilaliki - "Pepani, mpingo wavutika. Timafunitsitsa kuti mkhristu aliyense apereke, kuyambira pa mkhristu teni kwacha, akuluampingo twente kwacha, azibusa thati kwacha..." Aha-haah! "Izo ndiye ayiii! Izo ndiye ayiii! Umanene bwinotu! Waona kuti iweyo uli pa ntchito, ife enafe ndife maloova, ntchito tilibe. Ndipo kudya kumene amachita utiponyera. Manyumbanso ogula lendi - madzi - nkhuni. Bwanji mungonena mtengo?! Eeh, mpingo wanuwo wayamba nawo biiizinesi! Eeh, mumuona ndi mbusa yemweyo wangonenepa. Ndalama zathu zija akungokudya - chimimba chili ukooo!" Eheee! (kuseka) Wataya kunja aneneriwooo! Wataya kunja akapolo - kuwapanda akapolo, kuwapanda akapolo!

"Eeh, ineyonso ndine mphawinso. Ndifunanso anzanga ondithandiza! Eeh, ineyonso ndine mphawi - umanena bwino mitengo yanuyo!" Pamene tikunena pano, mpingo uli kugwa paaansi - kusowa chuma! Maofeesi atsekedwa - kusowa chuma! Mpingo wa Mulungu waonongeka - kusowa chuma. Olalikira uthenga kulephera - kusowa chuma!

Mau a Mulungu akuti, "Perekani!" "E-e-e-eeh! umanena bwino! Masiku ano mipingo yangochuluka mabizinesi. Ndiye kukakumana ndi akatchipitseko, akuti, "Bwera kwathu kuno - sitipereka ife zopereka!" He-hee-hee! (kuseka) Ndiyetu, ananu, tumbwi-tumbwi! ndithu - ulendo! Akuti, "Ndapeza mpingo wosapereka zopereka!" Hee-heee! (kuseka) Kuwataya kunja aneneri - kuwapanda! Ali kuchoka popanda kanthu - mwano okhaokha!

Pamene tikutero Mulungu sali kumvetsetsa, ayi. Mulungu sali kukhulupirira. Akaganiza bakigiraundi yanu kuti mpakana inu kumaponya miyala azibusa, aneneri - muponya miyala azilaliki - Mulungu sakhulupirira koonse. Amai, Mulungu sakhulupirira! Abambo, Mulungu sakhulupirira! Mnyamata, Mulungu sakhulupirira! Mtsikana, Mulungu sakhulupirira! Chifukwa chiani? Adali yani iwo aja?! Chimanga chimodzi? Aah! mpakana kundiphera mwana!

Pamene tinena pano, tili kumkana Yesu! Tili bizee kusonkhanitsa chumachooo – Yesuyo nkumamponya miyala, kumuphaaa! Cholinga chanu, mufuna dziko mutenge. Mungalilime dziko lapansi inu?! Ati, "Tiyeni tiphe mwanayo, munda uno ukhale wathu!" Mungalilime dziko lapansi?! Mpakana kumupha Yesu, mwini wake wa dziko lapansi ndi kumwamba! Muli biizee – kusonkhanitsa chuma! Mulungu, zimenezi sakhulupirira. Anali yani iwo aja?! Mulungu sakhulupirira. Mudaali yaaani inuuu – Mulungu, masiku aja akadalibe kukutolani Yesu?! Mulungu sakhulupirira – mpakana kuwaponya miyala aneneri! Enanu kuti muperekere umboni, simumaliza – muzilira!

Abale anga, ndiyamika Yesu amene akananditenga ndidali ku matope ine – mabalawa kumasoku, zipsera za mowa, zipsera za ndewu! Ndidagwidwa ndi mbala ine ku mowa, mkonowu udathyoka uwu! Abale anga, ndikadakhala kuti ndinali komweko, moyo wanga udangotsala pang'onooo – udangotsala pang'ono! Musadamalize kuyamba kulira! Ndibwezera chiani Yesu? Adakachita kunditola ineee – adakanditola ineee! Pamene muli kukaniza, Yesu sakhulupirira. Adali yani awa?!

Amai, mudali yani inu kuti muponye miyala aneneri? Mchimwene, udali yani iwe uli ku machimo? Udali yani uli ku mowa? Mudali yani muli ku nyanga? Mudali yani muli ku mabodza? Mudali yani muli ku zigololo? Mudali yani muli ku misechee? Sakhulupirira, sakhulupirira, ndipo muli kuthedwa nzeru kuti muzipezeka pano! Muli kumulakwira Yesu! Kuti muperekere umboni, simumaliza – mulira! Taonani, mukuti, "Ndikadakhala kuti ndinali komweko, moyo wanga ukadatayika!"

Ah-aah! mapeto ake, muli kulira mukuti ukadatayika! Eeh, mukadakhala mutafa! Eeh, popeza kumachimoko mudasiya amai. Kodi iwowo ali moyo? Mudasiya achemwali, kujaku m'nali kuliraku – kodi ali bwino? Abambo adatsala, amai adatsala, mwana wanga adatsala, amalume adatsala. Enanu mungoona ukondwerera apa, mai anu ali kulira ku gahena! Mai wanu sali akhristu ayi – bambo wanu sakhristu ayi – mwana wanu si mkhristu ayi –

amalume anu si mkhristu ayi. Pano mungolumpha m'makolasi, chomwe cholinga chake chikafike kwa amai anu, nawonso alandire uthenga wabwino. Koma pano mungokondwerera, "Eeh, mtendere mwa Yesu!" - mai ali kupita ku gahena!

Ndikufuna kukuuzani pano, mudaali yani inu? Mudali yani musadafike poimba makolasi?! Mudaali yani kuti mukhale mbusa inu?! Mudaali yani kuti mukhale akuluampingo?! Mudaali yani kuti mukhale alaliki? Adakachita ukutolaniii! Sakhulupirira Mulungu kuti inu mpakana m'kuphera mwana - mpakana nkuwapanda akapolowo opanda kanthu! Mudaali yani inu?!

Chopereka timasinthanitsa ndi zimene Mulungu adakuchitirani. Ndidaali yani ine?! Yesu akati, "Ndikufuna twente kwacha," ndipereka fifite kwacha - ndidaali yani ine?! "Ndifuna wani handredi kwacha," ine ndingopereka thuu handredi kwacha - ndidaali yani ine?! Tikayamba kupereka, timasinthanitsa ndi zimene Mulungu adakuchitira. Kufuna kubwezera, koma sungakwanitse! Zachuluka zokoma zimene Yesu alikutichitira! Utangopereka makwachawo, kuthatha ndi mtima - koma sitingakwanitse ayi. Mudaali yani inu?! Nkhani yomvetsa chisoni. Ndipo Mulungu sakhulupirira ayi, Mulungu sakhulupirira!

Mudaali yani inuuu?! Chimanga chimodzi - safuna zambiri! "Gawo limodzi la magawo khumi, ndiye m'kundipandira aneneri, kuphera mwana, komanso munda uli wanga?!" Dziko lapansi mulikulidyererali ndi lake, koma mpakana kumuphera mwana! Yesu sakhulupirira ayi - Mulungu sakhulupirira! Mudaali yani inu?! Abale anga, sakhulupirira!

Nambala thuu: Mudaali yani musadaphunzire? Mudaali yani, abambo - mudaali yani, amai, musadaphunzire?! Mulungu adachita ukakutolani, ndipo enanu maphunziro a sukulu ndi mwavutika. Ana amasiye lidakuphunzitsani ndi boma - basalee! Bambo wanu adangomwalira mutangobadwa. Anali kukuphunzitsani amai anu, kumaphika tizikonda moyo, tizikonda moyo. Lero mwaphunzira mpakana kupita ku koleji - vimadigrii thoo! Mwayamba mwano! Mudaali yani inu?! Mudaali yani inu?! Mudaali yani inu?! Mulungu sali kukhulupirira. Amafuna zanuzoo, mumlemekeze nazooo! Sali kukhulupirira Mulungu.

Mudaali yani musadaphunzireee?! Musadaphunzire, makolo adavutika kuti akakuphunzitseni. Enanu ndi amasiye – mudaphunzitsidwa ndi boma. Ena anthu achifundo kuchita kukutolani. Lero muli pa ntchito – eeeh, ntchito yapamwambaaa! Lero Mulungu watuma akapolo, "Kalandire phindu la maphunziro aja ndidamphunzitsa." M'malo mwake kuwapanda akapolo opanda kanthu! Ee-eeh! mwangoyamba mabizinesi, mungoti, "M'mawa zopereka – m'mawa zopereka!" Mudaali yani inu musadaphunzire?! Nkhani yomvetsa chisoni kwambiri! Mudaali yani musadaphunzire – ndipotu kuphunzira movutika, kumafika pa poyinti imeneyi?! Nokha mutakhala pansi, inunso umathedwa nzeru! Nkhani yomvetsa chisoni kwambiri!

Nambala thuu: Mudaali yani inuyo musadayambe ntchito? Kumangoti m'kapita apa, "Palibe ntchito!" Mupite apa, "Palibe ntchito!" Mupite apa, "Palibe ntchito!" Ananu, kuzunzika kunka mufuna ntchito. Mudakangolowa ntchito imene simumaifuna, kumakakumba m'ngalande – "Nanga titani?!" Chisomo cha Mulungu, atamva chisoni chanu mpakana kukutolani. Kodi inu mukumba ngalandenu, palibe uyu amadziwa kulemba pano?! (kuseka) "Aah, ineyo ndimadziwa kulemba ineyo!" – nkukukatola ku ngalande, ehee-heee! (kuseka) Ha! mudaali yani inu?!

Lero mpakana Mulungu yemweyo wakupatsani nzeru – mapolomoshoni! Omachita usinjanasinjana – chaka chino polomoshoni, chaka cha mawa polomoshoni – chaka cha mkuja polomoshoni! Mpakana ujenero-manijala – chimpando chapamwamba – ndalama masauzande! "Tiyeni tibwere ku tchalitchi!" "Chopereka – aagh! nkabisinezi!" A-a-aah! mudaali yani musadayambe ntchito inu?! Mudaali yani musadayambe ntchito? Mulungu adachita ukutolani! Mudaali yani musadafike pa ujenero-manijala?! Mudaali yani musadafike aperesonolo?! Mudaali yani musadafike pa asajenti?! Mudaali yani musadafike pa umesinjala?! Ehe-heee! (kuseka) Iih-aah! Eee-eeeh! Mulungu, zimenezi sakhulupirira ayi, sakhulupirira!

Nambala thrii: Mudaali yani musadayambe bisinezi?! Si inu uja m'manka mugulitsa timakala inu – zigamba zili thoo! Eeh! "Makala-makala!" – m'malayinimu. "Makala-makala!" – m'malayinimu. Si inuyo inu?! Mudaali yani inu?! "Tomato-tomato-tomato!" – m'malayinimu. "Masamba-masamba-masamba-masamba!" Mudaali yani inu?! Lero Mulungu wakudalitsani chihookala – thiii! Pambuyo pa hookala, chigolosale phiii! Nanga m'chisitolo? Eeh! Bisinezi! Galimoto thiii! Minibasi, malole – aaah!

(kuseka) Mudali yani inu?! Ehee-heee! (kuseka) Lero mwalemeraaa, ndipo Mulungu watuma akapolo, akapeze phindu la zooonse zimene muli nazo. Komanso safuna zambiri - gawo limodzi la magawo khumi.

Koma mwano okhaokha! "Matchalitchi anuwo angoyamba mabisinezi. Ndalama timangopatsa abusazi. Simuli kumuona walemeranso - chimimba chili ukoo!" Nkumvetsa chisoni! Ngati kuli mphawi wa amphawi onse, ndi mbusa! Mbusa ndi mphawi! Mudamusiyitsa ntchito zake kuti akhale fulutayimu kwa inu. Ndipo ndinu nomwe amene muyenera kumudyetsa - mudamsiyitsa ntchito! Kuti iyeyu azigwira ntchito yapadera, ubusa wakenso sungayende bwino. Sizingalongosoke ayi mpang'onong'ono pomwe!

Mbusa ndi mphawi wa amphawi onse! Mbusa salandira ndalama. Ndalama imene amalandira mbusa yochoka pa nsabwe - nsabwe za m'khosi - nsabwe zake za nkhalamba! Kahandikachifi ngati aka - akati, "Choperekachopereka!" kankhalamba kali kunjenjemera nkumasula teni tambala, aponye m'mbale. Tsonotu nkumaphwanyira tinsabwe - kuphwanyira tinsabwe, kuponya m'mbale! Tindalama timeneto tikachuluka, ndiye nkumaitana abusa, "Abusa, bwerani, dzalandireni!" Malipiro amachoka pa nsabwe?! Malipiro amachoka pa nsabwe?! Ngati inuyo mukuti, "Talemeretsa mbusa," inuyo ndiye simukufuna kulemerako? Mbusa angalemere ndi kafayifi tambala kanuko?! Inuyo ndiye simukufuna kulemerako?! Mmau a mwano! Mudaali yani inu musadayambe bizinesi? Lero Mùlungu wakudalitsani, muli ndi mabizinesi akuluakulu, muli ndi mabizinesi akuluakulu! Mwagula maminibasi, magalimoto, malole. Mwamanga zimanyumba, zimapoloti. Mudaali yani?! Ngati Mzimu wa Mulungu ali pa inu, mudzimvere chisoni lero!

Walakwa chiani Mulungu? Mulungu sakhulupirira, mukamamubwezera mau. Mudaali yani musadayambe ulimi? Mudaali yani musadatsegule esiteti? Mudaali yani musadayambe kulima thonje? Mudaali yani musadayambe kulima barele? Mudaali yani musadayambe kulima ulimi - mavejitabo? Mudaali yani inu musadayambe kulima mtedza? Mudaali yani musadayambe kulima mbewu zija mukulima zija? Mudaali yani?! Lero Mulungu wakudalitsani chifukwa cha ulimi, ndipo mu ulimiwo anthu alemera, ndipo mwalemera. Koma Mulungu akufuna phindu - gawo limodzi la zoonse zimene muli nazo. Koma lero kuwaponya miyala aneneri - mudaali yani! Mudaali yani?! Nkhani yomvetsa chisoni!

Mudaali yani inu? Mmangoti m'mawa mwadwala, m'mawa mwadwala - sukulu yochita kuvutikira kudwaladwala. Koma Mulungu adakupyoletsani monsemo. Lero Mulungu wakudalitsani muli kuponya miyala aneneri! Mudaali yani inu?! Pamene ndikunena pano, enanu ndinu amasiye - amai mulibe, abambo mulibe - koma Mulungu adakutolani mpakana chiudindo. Enanu ndinu akuluakulu a dziko - kuchita kutoledwa ndi Mulungu! Koma Mulunguyo akufuna phindu la zooonse zimene adachita. Koma mmalo mwake kuwaponya miyala aneneri! Mudaali yani inu?!

Abale anga, "Mpakana kundiphera mwana!" Mau amene Mulungu ali kumusautsa mumtima mwake, mufuna kulanda. Ku tchalitchi mudasiya kalekale, simupitanso. Ku tchalitchi mudasiya kalekaale. Mau amenewa, tandimvetseta abale anga, mau amenewa - mulipo ena pano mulibe matchalitchi. Mau amenewa, palibe kanthu mulibe tchalitchi, koma mudaali yani musadaphunzire? Ndi bwino kumuthokoza Mulungu!

Alipo anthu ena akangowona ulemerero wao, zimatheka kupita ku tchalitchi, "Abusa, mphatso ndi imeneyi!" - ndikulandira, koma ndi mkunja. Kuona mmene adalili, "Palibe kanthu ndine mkunja, koma Mulungu wandichitira zazikulu!" Osadzimvera chisoni. Ambiri amene akupereka mphatso m'maiko akunja ku Yurope. Si kuti ndi akhristu okhaokha, koma kuona zimene Mulungu wachitira, "Ndidaali yani ine?!" Mpakana umapereka ndalama kumthokoza Mulungu. "Palibe kanthu ndine mkunja, koma ndidaali yani ine?!"

Ngati mulipo pano akunja, mulibe ndi mpingo womwe, koma mudzimvere chisoni lero, mudzifunse funso limeneli: Mudaali yani musadaphunzire? Mudaali yani musadayambe bizinesi? Mudaali yani inuyo musadayambe ulimi? Mudaali yani inuyo mumangodwaladwala? Lero mudzimvere chisoni, abambo - mudzimvere chisoni, amai! Mudaali yani, amai, musadakwatiwe? Mudaali yani, abambo, musadakwatire? Mudaali yani, amai, musadayambe bizinesi? Mudaali yani, amai, musadayambe bizinesi? Ngati Mzimu wa Mulungu uli mwa inuyo, mudzimvere chisoni! Pakadapanda amuna kukutolani inu, si bwenzi muli ndi ulemerero umene muli nawowu. Kumadzimvera chisoni! Mudaali yani mukadapanda ukwatiwa ndi aBanda inu? Mudaali yani mukadapanda ukwatiwa ndi aPhiri? Mudaali yani mukadapanda kukwatiwa ndi aJere inu? Inunso abambo, mudaali yani mkadapanda kukwatira naPhiri, mkazi wa zintchito?

288

Mkazi wakulemeretsani! Mwapeza chuma chifukwa cha mkazi amene uja! Mudaali yani inu?! Nkhani yomvetsa chisoni kwambiri! Ngati Mzimu wa Mulungu ali mwa inu, mudzimvere chisoni! Maaawu osautsa, ndipo Mulungu sakhulupirira! "Mpakana kundiphera mwana kufuna kulanda dziko!" Ku tchalitchi mudasiya kalekale.

Nchifukwa chake Yobu thati-eeti, wani tu sikisi akuti, "Iwe, popeza wandilanda ine gawo limodzi la magawo khumi, ndipo nyumba yanga ili kugwa... Ndikati, "Chopereka," mwano okhaokha! Kodi iweyo, chimanga chimene walemera nachocho – pamene ndikapanga, udalipo? Pamene ndimapanga mitengo, udalipo? Pamene ndimapanga nyama – nsapato wavalazo – udalipo? Pamene ine ndimapanga miyala – ndalama zili m'thumbazo – udalipo? Pamene ine ndimapanga miyala – siliva, golide, chibenzi wakweracho – udalipooo?! Tandiuza, tandiuza – udalipooo?!

Funso lovuta, aaah! Funso losautsa! Amai, kodi mudaalipo pamene amapanga thonje? Mudaalipo pamene amapanga miyala? Mudaalipo pamene amapanga palafini? Mudaalipo pamene amapanga nthaka? Mudaalipo pamene amapanga dzuwa? Mvula? Mudaalipooooo?! Mulungu sakhulupiriraaaa! "Adali yani iwo aja? Mpakana undiphera mwana – munda uli wanga!" Ngati Mzimu wa Mulungu uli mwa inu lero, mudzimvere chisoni! Mau osautsa! Perekaaaani, perekani chili chonse! Kaya ndi mpando, perekani! Kaya ndi galimoto, perekani! Kaya ndi nsapato, perekani! Kaya ndi zovala, perekani! Ku mpingo zigulitsidwa, zikagwira ntchito yake. Perekani mbuzi, perekani chili chooonse chimene muli nacho! Perekaaani! Munabadwa wamaliseche, mudzapitanso amaliseche. Perekani! – mau osautsa, Mulungu sakhulupirira. Perekani! – mau osautsa, Mulungu sakhulupirira.

Mau akuti, "Kodi atangobwera eni akewo, adzawatani antchitowo?" Bwanayo atabwera, adzawatani antchitowooo?! Ngoziii! Kutanthauza kuti – kodi Yesu akabwera muli chikhalireni mmene mukhalira inumo, kodi zidzatha bwanji? Ngooziii! Tsono Mau a Mulungu akuti, "Aliyense akugwa pa mwalawo, adzaphwanyika. Amene mwalawo udzamgwera, udzamupha!" Tanthauzo lake ndi ili: Amene mukhumudwa ndi chopereka – pamene Yesu aitanitsa chopereka mukhumudwa – mwakhumudwa pamwala, popeza mwalawo ndi Yesu! Mukawerenge Mau a Mulungu wani Akorinto teni-folo, akuti, "Aisraeli adamwa madzi otuluka m'thanthwe m'chipululu, ndipo thanthwelo ndiye Yesu." Nyimbo 102 tikuti, "Thanthwe long'ambikatu, ndibisale momwemo!" – ndiye Yesu.

Mukakhumudwa pa chopereka, muli ngati munthu amene amathamanga pa mwala, ndiye wakhumudwa – pansi baaa! Zikutha bwino? Munthu akakhumudwa pa mwala, zikutha bwino? Amavulala moipa! – chifukwa ndi pa thanthwe. Koma utagwa pa mchenga, ayi, umangosasa dothi. Pa mwala mpoipa! Aliyense amene akhumudwa pa mwala uwu – amanena Yesu – adzavulalaaa! Musakhumudwe pa chopereka – muvulaaala! Mwagwa pa thanthwe! Komanso akuti thanthwelo pobwera lidzamsinja – kutanthauza, kubwera kwa Ambuye Yesu, adzakugwerani! Zinthu sizidzatha bwino, ayi. Chotero, musakhumudwe pa chopereka – musakhumudwe pa chopereka!

Mau omaliza, mundimvetse! Mateyo sikisi, naintini kulekeza pa twente wani – pali mau, mau ake ndi awa: Akuti, "Dzikundikireni chuma kumwamba. Musadzikundikire ku dziko kumene dzimbiri ndi njenjete zimaononga. Koma dzikundikireni kumwamba. Popeza komwe kuli mtima wako, chuma chako chidzakhala komweko. Kumene kuli chuma chako, mtima wako udzakhala komweko." Ndibwerezanso, "Dzikundikireni chuma mmwamba, osati pa dziko kumene dzimbiri ndi njenjete zimaononga. Koma dzikundikireni kumwamba. Popeza komwe kuli mtima wako, chuma chako chidzakhala komweko. Kumene kuli chuma chako, mtima wako udzakhala komweko." Afuna kuulala chiani? Pano afuna kuulula zinthu zitatu:

Wani: Mulungu akufunafuna moyo wa munthu, audziwe pamene udagona. Inuyo, kupanda kupeza ndalama, simudya. Zikuyenda zonse, moyo ndi ndalama. Kupanda kugwetsa tambala, ndikuti simudya. Tsopano Mulunguyu akufuna kudziwa mtima wanuwu. Ndiye wauona kuti udaphatikizana ndi ndalama, ndiye Mulungu waufukulira. Akuti, "Oh-oh-oh! mtima umenewu, kuti ndiudziwe, ndiudzere ku ndalama." Nchifukwa chake akuti, "Tandipatsanikoni kateni tambala, kawani kwachako." Kuteroko si kuti Mulungu ndi osowa. Enanu mumanena mau oipa. Mukuti, "Mulunguyo amadya ndalama?" "Eeeh!" Sakudyadi! Inenso nkuchitirani umboni. Mukuti, "Mulungu amasowa?" "Eeeh!" Sasowadi! Zindalamazo wakupatsani ndi Mulungu. Zimagalimoto, zimaminibasi, zimasuti, manyumba – zoonsezo wakupatsani ndi Mulungu!

290

Tsono chodabwitsa nchakuti, ati, Akupemphanso!" Si bodza iliiii?! Ali kufuna chifukwaaa! Ali kuona mtima wanuyo pamene umagonaaaa! Mulungu ndi woopsa. Mulungu sangasowe teni tambala! Wauzungulira mtima, waona kuti udagwirizana ndi ndalama. "Bambo amenewa, kuti ndiwadziwe, ndiwadzere kundalamako." Ndiye akangoti, "Teni tambala!" - inu ndi kumalankhula zamwano. Akutenga kateni tambala kanuko ndi kukataya! Iye akukataya, "Throo iti dauni - throo iti samiwheya!" Zifukwa izi ali kuzifunazi! Tere enanu mudalowa kalekale mu lekoodi. Osadabwa, Mulungu amadya ndalama?! Osadabwa, si zifukwa izi?! Chuma chanu chonsecho wakupatsani ndi Mulungu. Ndiye angati, "Ndili kufuna teni tambala..." Eeeh-he hee! (kuseka) Pali ngozi apa - zifukwaaa! Eheee!

Enanu mwapezeka kalekaaale! Mudalowa kalekale mu lekodi. Iye amangotenga kakwacha kanuko nkutayirani uko - iye akutenga mukulankhulazo, akulowetsa m'buku! Pamene ndikunena pano, mtima wanuwo - zooonse zili pambalambanda! pamtunda. Osadabwa! Eeh-hehee! (kuseka) Nchifukwa chake akuti, "Kumene kudzakhala mtima wako, chuma chako chidzakhala komweko. Koma kumene kuli chuma chako, mtima wako udzakhala komweko."

Poyamba, afuna zifukwa, awone pansi pa mtima wanu. Mumuyamikira bwanji? Paansi pa mtima wanu mumuthokoza bwanji? Pano ndinena pano mudalowa kalekaaale mu lekodi - choyamba chimenecho!

Kachiwiri: kumene kuli chuma chako, mtima wako udzakhala komweko. Pamenepo akufuna kuulula kuti kumene munthu amapereka chopereka, nkumene kuli mtima wake. Mtima ukakhala ku bala, chopereka ukapereka ku bala! Palibe amene sapereka ayi! Palibe amene sapereka - musadzalankhulenso! Aliyense wa inu mupereka chopereka. Koma chopereka chanu nchowaawa! Mupereka tsiku lililoonse. Kupanda kugwetsa tambala, simudya! Mukukapereka ku msika. Kupanda ugwetsa, simudyaaa! Aliyeeense akupereka. Kunyumba kwanu, mungandilozere chimene muli nacho chopanda ndalama? Ngati wina anakupatsani mphatso, iyeyo adakagula kuti? Adakaitenga kuti? Mundilozere chimene muli nacho chopanda ndalama! Chilipo kunyumba kwanu?

Mukamanena kuti, "Aaah, mipingo ya masiku anoyi **ingofuna ndalama!**" - inuyo ndiye kunyumba kwanu mungandilozere chopanda ndalama?!

291

"Chimpingo chikulukulu chino chingaleke kufuna ndalama?!" - apo sukanika inuyo. Nchiani kunyumba kwanu chimene muli nacho chopanda ndalama. Mau amwano - nkumvetsa chisoni! Mudalembedwa kaaale mu lekodi! Aliyense apereka! Chimtimacho chikakhala ku mabalagelo, chopereka kwa balagelo! Mtimawo ukakhala ku nyanga, chopereka kunyanga! Komwe kuli mtima wako, chuma chako chidzakhala komweko. Mtima ukakhala ku tchalitchi, chopereka ku tchalitchi. Palibe amene sapereka ayi. Yeeense wa inu awone kumene amapereka chopereka!

Mau omaliza: Mukapereka, kuli mphoto kumwamba. Ku Yuropi kunali bambo wina wake - ndikuuzani zomwe zidachitika. Bamboyu anali wolemera kwambiri. Ndiye anali ndi galadeni boyi - gadena - wosesa panja. Ndiye gadena ameneyu anali kupita ku tchalitchi nkumaponya kathuu tambala - kafaifi tambala - monga zopereka timapereka. Koma bwanayo nkumangokudya. Za Mulungu analibe nazo ntchito ngakhale tsiku limodzi lomwe kupita ku tchalitchi. Kumangokudya - heee, dziko lapansi!

Imfa ndi yakhungu - siimaona. Idakangofikira pa abwanawo - thibuu! wu! - pansi baaa! Kumwalira! Ndiye adakachingamira angelo, iwo nkumati mmadalitso. Ehee! Angelo akuti, "Bwana, tiyeni kuno, tikakupatseni nyumba yanu!" Haa! aja chimwemwe chokhachoka! Ndiye adakafika pa nyumba ya fili sitoli. Abwana anayamba kukondwa. Akuti, "Yaah! ndafika, yaah!" - kutengera ubwana umene anali nawo pansi pano. Akuti, "Yaah! imeneyi ndiyo nyumba yanga!" Anadzadabwa angelo alikudutsa pa nyumba ija. Ndiye adakhumudwa kuti, "A-aah! nanga tikupitanso kuti?! Ndimayesa nyumbayo ndi imeneyi!" Akuti, "Ayi, kunyumba kwanu sitinafike. Tatsala pang'ono." Akuti, "Eee, ndiye kuti nyumba yake ndi yapamwamba kuposa iyi!"

Ali kupita, anafikanso pa ina - fili sitoli. Akuti, "Yaah! koma imeneyi!" Anadzadabwa ndi mngelo uja adutsanso. "Aaaah, nanga tili kupitanso kuti?!" Akuti, "Ayi, sitidafike ku nyumba yanu." Bwana akuti, "Yaah! koma kumeneko ndiye kuli nyumba yangayo - heee! mnyumbadi!"

Anadabwa pomaliza ali kukalowera ku thengo - kuthengoko kokhala ngati ku manda! Ndiye kudali nyumba ngati kuti nchikhola cha mbuzi - chopanda mawindo, chopanda chitseko. Chidengachi, mbali inayi, mbali inayi chidasusukasusuka. Ndiye angelowo ndi mkuluyo - ndikukuuzanizi si mwambi, ndadaziona ine kuchokera m'buku. Ndiye anakafika pa khomo paja ndiye akuti, "Tafikatu, bwana. Nyumba yanu ndi imeneyi!" "Chiani?!" "Nyumba yanu ndi imeneyi." "A-ah! sizingatheke! M'ngandipatse nyumba imeneyi?!" Ali, "Bwana, pepani, si chipongwe ayi. Nyumba yanu ndi imeneyi." Ndiye adafunsa akuti, "Nanga nyumba ija timaidutsa m'njira fili sitoli imene ija ndi ya yani?" Yankho akuti, "Ndi ya boyi wanu uja!" "Aaa-la! boyi wa ine mungampatse nyumba ngati imene ija – gaadena?! Ine m'ndiponya kuthengo ngati kuno?!" Akuti, "Pepani, bwana – kuno sitimatukwanaaaa." "Chifukwa chiani gaadena mwamupatsa nyumba ngati imene ija?!" Yankho ndi lakuti, "Amatitumizira mathuu tambala, ndiye mathuu tambalawo timawamangira nyumbaaa!" (kuseka) Aleluyaaaa! (Ameeeni!) "Iiih! musativutitse!" Adangokuwaponya thasaa! m'nyumbamo! Nthawi yomweyo angelo aja zii! adapita.

Pamene tipereka, sitilikutenga ayi. Mau a Mulungu akuti, "Dziunjikireni chuma kumwamba." Masiku otsiriza ngati ano, ochenjeraaa – thalansifaa! Mulungu amatipasta chuma m'magawo atatu: Wani – tizidya, thuu – tithandize anthu osauka, thrii – pa ntchito yake! Chuma chimenecho ngati suchigwiritsira ntchito imeneyo, Yesu akabwera, chitsalaaa choowolaa! Inunso kukafikira ku gahena! Koma mukachigwiritsira ntchito ya Mulungu – thalansifaa! Kuthawitsa, zizitsogolaaaa! Ehee-he! Wochenjeraaa, dzikundikireni chuma mmwambaaa! Kukundika kwake nkuchigwiritsa chumacho ntchito ya Mulungu. Yesu akabwera, sichithedwa!

Ndimalalikira kwina ndi kuti, amene mwalandira Yesu, dziko silidzakutherani ayi. Popeza Mau a Mulungu akuti, "Okhulupirira iye saweruzidwa. Osakhulupirira iye nkuweruzidwa ngakhale tsopano!" Munthu ukayenda m'chifuniro cha Mulungu, zokoooma zimayambira pansi pompano. Koma ukatayika m'chifuniro cha Mulungu, chilango chili pansi pompano. Inu amene mwakhulupirira Yesu, Yesu ali kubwerayo, ndi mfulu ndi chitukuko. Chitukuko chimafuna anthu azidya bwino, azikondwa, azisangalala. Koma chitukuko chathuchi, timadwala ndi kumafa. Koma Yesu akubwera ndi chitukuko cha zitukuko za dziko lapansi. Popeza chitukuko cha Yesu, kulibe kufa – kulibe njala – kulibe matenda! Amene mwalandira Yeesu, Yesu akubwerayo, ndi mfulu ndi chitukuko.

Chimene chidzachitika kwa inu, dziko silili kutherani. Koma ndi thalansifaa – kuchoka m'chitukuko nkulowa m'chitukuko. Haleluuyaa! Kukalowa m'chitukuko, kudya nawo ponseponse - pansi pano kudya nawo, kumwamba kudya nawo! Ndifuna mukhale anthu ochenjera. Nthawi yatha! Uyu akufuna kuti chuma chake chikafike kumwamba - thalansifaa! - kuchigwiritsa ntchito ya Mulungu, chitsogola! Akuti, "Taonani, boyi wanu amatitumizira kuno matambala. Matambala 'amenewo timamumangitsira nyumba. Nanga inu mudatitumiziraaa?!" Mabwana kungoti cheete!

Zopereka zimene mupereka, mupereka kwa Mulungu - simuli kutaya ayi! Chili choonse chimene mungapereke ku ntchito ya Mulungu chili ndi mphoto kumwamba. Mudziwe zimenezi lero! Perekani - perekani - perekani! Ambuye atidalitse, ameeni! (Ameeni!)

BIBLIOGRAPHY

Adams, J.E., *Preaching with Purpose*, Grand Rapids: Zondervan, 1982.

Albrecht, R., *Eine Trommel allein singt kein Lied: Predigt als dialogisches Geschehen in einer Kultur der Oralitaet. Untersuchung zu Inhalt und Struktur evangelischer Predigt in Nordwest-Tanzania*, Erlangen: Verlag der Ev.-Luth. Mission, 1996.

Blount, B.K., *Cultural Interpretation: Reorienting New Testament Criticism*, Minneapolis: Fortress Press, 1995.

Boomershine, T.E., "A Transmediatization Theory of Biblical Translation", *Bulletin: United Bible Societies* 170/171 (1994), pp. 49-57.

Burkle, H., "Patterns of Sermons from Various Parts of Africa", in D.B. Barrett (ed.), *African Initiatives in Religion*, Nairobi: East African Publishing House, 1971, pp. 222-231.

Bullinger, E.W., *Figures of Speech Used in the Bible, Explained and Illustrated*, Grand Rapids: Baker Book House, 1898 (reprinted 1968).

Chimombo, Steve, *Malawian Oral Literature: The Aesthetics of Indigenous Arts*, Zomba: University of Malawi Centre for Social Research, 1988.

Craddock, F., *Preaching*, Nashville: Abingdon, 1985.

Davis, G.L., *I Got the Word in Me and I Can Sing It, You Know: A Study of the Performed African-American Sermon*, Philadelphia: University of Pennsylvania Press, 1985.

Dierks, F.A., "Review of Rainer Albrecht," 1996, *Missionalia* 27:1 (1999), pp. 139f.

Fogelin, R.J., *Understanding Arguments: An Introduction to Informal Logic* (Third Edition), New York: Harcourt, Brace, and Jovanovich, 1987.

Forslund, E., *The Word of God in Ethiopian Tongues: Rhetorical Features in the Preaching of the Ethiopian Evangelical Church Mekane Yesus*, Uppsala: International Tryck, 1993.

Gutt, E.A., *Relevance Theory: A Guide to Successful Communication in Translation*, Dallas: Summer Institute of Linguistics, 1992.

Healey, J. and D. Sybertz, *Towards an African Narrative Theology*, Nairobi: Paulines Publications Africa, 1996.

Jones, D.L., "The Sermon as 'Art' of Resistance: A Comparative Analysis of the Rhetorics [sic] of the African-American Slave Preacher and the Preacher to the Hebrews", *Semeia* 79 (1997), pp. 11-26.

Kennedy, G.A., *New Testament Interpretation Through Rhetorical Criticism*, Chapel Hill: North Carolina Press, 1984.

Kennedy, G.A. (translator/ed.), *Aristotle On Rhetoric: A Theory of Civic Discourse*, Oxford: Oxford University Press, 1991.
Kennedy, G.A., *Comparative Rhetoric: An Historical and Cross Cultural Introduction*, Oxford: Oxford University Press, 1998.
Kerr, H.T., *Preaching in the Early Church*, New York: Fleming H. Revell, 1942.
Kings, G., "Proverbial, Intrinsic, and Dynamic Authorities: A Case Study on Scripture and Mission in the Dioceses of Mount Kenya East and Kirinyaga", *Missiology* XXIV:4 (1996), pp. 491-501.
Koch, A. and S.B. Felber, *What Did You Say? A Guide to the Communication Skills* (Third Edition), Englewood Cliffs, NJ: Prentice-Hall, 1985.
Kumakanga, S.L., *Nzeru za Kale* [Ancient Wisdom], Lusaka, Zambia: Longmans, 1949.
Lanham, R.A., *A Handlist of Rhetorical Terms: A Guide for Students of English Literature*, Berkeley: University of California Press, 1969.
Leroux, Neil R., "Perceiving Rhetorical Style: Toward a Framework for Criticism", *Rhetorical Society Quarterly* 22:4 (1992), pp. 29-41.
Leroux, Neil R., "Repetition, Progression and Persuasion in Scripture", *Neotestamentica* 29, pp. 1-25.
Lewis R.L. and G. Lewis, *Inductive Preaching: Helping People Listen*, Westchester, IL: Crossway Books, 1983.
Mack, B.L., *Rhetoric and the New Testament: Guides to Biblical Scholarship*, Minneapolis: Fortress Press, 1990.
Mbiti, J.S., *Bible and Theology in African Christianity*, Nairobi: Oxford University Press, 1986.
Meusner, F.W., *Luther the Preacher*, Minneapolis: Augsburg Publishing House, 1983.
Mijoga, Hillary P.B., *Separate but Same Gospel: Preaching in African Instituted Churches*, Blantyre, Malawi: CLAIM, 2000.
Mitchell, H.H., *Black Preaching: The Recovery of a Powerful Art*, Nashville: Abingdon Press, 1990.
Mitchell, H.H., "African-American Preaching", in W.H. Willimon and R. Lischer (eds.), *Concise Encyclopedia of Preaching*, Louisville, KY: Westminster John Knox Press, 1995, pp. 2-9.
Murphy, N.C., *Reasoning and Rhetoric in Religion*, Valley Forge, PA: Trinity Press International, 1994.
Mvula, E.S.T., "Four Songs from Malawi", *Kalulu* 3 (1982), pp. 62-64.

Neill, S., *Chrysostom and his Message*, London (United Society for Christian Literature): Lutterworth Press, 1962.

Ngulube, N.M.J., *Some Aspects of Growing Up in Zambia*, Lusaka: Kenneth Kaunda Foundation, 1989.

Nida, E.A., *God's Word in Man's Language*, New York: Harper and Row, 1952.

Nida, E.A., J.P. Louw, A.H. Snyman, J.V.W. Cronje, *Style and Discourse, With Special Reference to the Text of the Greek New Testament*, Cape Town: Bible Society of South Africa, 1983.

Oberhelman, S.M., *Rhetoric and Homiletics in Fourth-Century Christian Literature: Prose Rhythm, Oratorical Style, and Preaching in the Works of Ambrose, Jerome, and Augustine* (American Classical Sudies 26), Atlanta: Scholars Press, 1991.

Okpewho, I., *African Oral Literature*, Bloomington, IN: Indiana UP, 1992.

Ong, W.J., *Orality and Literacy: The Technologizing of the Word*, London: Methuen, 1982.

Pless, J., "Seven Pulpit Paradigms from the Prince of Preachers: John Chrysostom", *Wisconsin Lutheran Quarterly* 95/3 (1998), pp. 191-209.

Preminger, A. and T.V.F. Brogan (eds.), *The New Princeton Encyclopedia of Poetry and Poetics*, Princeton, NJ: Princeton University Press, 1993.

Roboteau, A., *Slave Religion: The "Invisible Institution" in the Antebellum South*, New York: Oxford University Press, 1978.

Ross, Kenneth R., "Preaching in Mainstream Christian Churches in Malawi: A Survey and Analysis", in *Gospel Ferment in Malawi: Theological Essays*, Gweru: Mambo Press, 1995, pp. 81-106, Kachere Book No. 2.

Scheub, H., *The Xhosa Ntsomi*, Oxford: Clarendon Press, 1975.

Scheub, H., "The Technique of the Expansible Image in Xhosa Ntsomi-Performances", in B. Lindfors (ed.), *Forms of Folklore in Africa*, Austin: University of Texas Press, 1977.

Schoffeleers, Matthew, *Religion and the Dramatisation of Life: Spirit Beliefs and Rituals in Southern and Central Malawi*, Blantyre: CLAIM, 1997, Kachere Monograph No. 5.

Shaw, R.D., *Transculturation: The Cultural Factor in Translation and Other Communication Tasks*, Pasadena: William Carey Library, 1988.

Shorter, A., "Form and Content in the African Sermon: An Experiment", *AFER*? (1969 (?)), pp. 265-279.

Siegert, F., "Mass Communication and Prose Rhythm in Luke-Acts", in S.E. Porter and T.H. Olbricht (eds.), *Rhetoric and the New Testament: Essays from the 1992 Heidelberg Conference*, Sheffield: Sheffield Academic Press, 1993, pp. 42-58.

Skjevesland, O., "Tracing the Dimensions of Homiletics", in A. Tangberg (ed.), *Text and Theology: Essays in Honor of Prof. Dr. Theol. Magne Saebo*, Oslo: Verbum, 1994, pp. 276-293.

Spencer, J.M., "Folk Preaching (African-American)", in W.H. Willimon and R. Lischer (eds.), *Concise Encyclopedia of Preaching*, Lousiville, KY: Westminster John Knox Press, 1995, pp. 142f.

Spitulnik, D., "The Social Circulation of Media Discourse and the Mediation of Communities", *Journal of Linguistic Anthropology* 6(2), 1997, pp. 161-187.

Thomas, F.A., *They Like to Never Quit Praisin' God: The Role of Celebration in Preaching*, Cleveland: United Church Press, 1997.

Trible, P., *Rhetorical Criticism: Context, Method, and the Book of Jonah*, Minneapolis: Fortress Press, 1994.

Thuren, L., *Argument and Theology in 1 Peter: The Origins of Christian Paraenesis*, Sheffield: Sheffield Academic Press, 1995.

Wendland, E.H., *Preach the Word: A Study in Homiletics*, Lusaka: The Lutheran Press, 1988.

Wendland, Ernst R., "Lexcial Recycling in Chewa Discourse", in R. Rhodes (ed.), *Working Papers of the Summer Institute of Linguistics* XI, Grand Forks, ND: Summer Institute of Linguistics, 1975, pp. 28-92.

Wendland, Ernst R., *Nthano za kwa Kawaza* (Tales from Kawaza-land), Lusaka: Zambia Language Group, 1976.

Wendland, Ernst R., "Stylistic Form and Communicative Function in the Nyanja Radio Narratives of Julius Chongo", PhD, University of Wisconsin, 1980, Ann Arbor: University Microfilms International.

Wendland, Ernst R. *The Cultural Factor in Bible Translation: A Study of Communicating the Word of God in a Central-African Cultural Context*, London and New York: United Bible Societies, 1987.

Wendland, Ernst R., "Traditional Central African Religion", in P.C. Stine and E.R. Wendland (eds.), *Bridging the Gap: African Traditional Religion and Bible Translation*, New York: United Bible Societies, 1990, pp. 1-129.

Wendland, Ernst R., "*Ufiti* – Foundation of an Indigenous Philosophy of Misfortune: The Socioreligious Implications of Witchcraft and Sorcery in a Central African Setting", in M.L. Lynn and D.O. Moberg (eds.),

Research in the Social Scientific Study of Religion, Vol. 4 (1992), Greenwich, CT: JAI Press, pp. 209-243.

Wendland, Ernst R., "Finding Some Lost Aspects of Meaning in Christ's Parables of the Lost – and Found (Luke 15)", *Trinity Journal* 17NS (1996), pp. 19-65.

Wendland, Ernst R., *Buku Loyera - An Introduction to the New Chichewa Bible Translation,* Blantyre: CLAIM, 1998.

Wendland, Ernst R., "The Case for a 'Case-Study' Approach to Theological Education in Africa", *Africa Journal of Evangelical Theology,* 1998b.

Willimon, W.H. and R. Lischer (eds.), *Concise Encyclopedia of Preaching,* Louisville, KY: Westminster John Knox Press, 1995.

Index

affections (emotions) 104, 109
affective **appeal** 14, **81**, 98, 104, 109, 123, 149, 225, 104n
African Independent Church(es) 51, 237
African Traditional Religion (ATR) 52, 89, 97, 299, 89n
alliteration 102, 168
allusion 14, 56, 81, 93-95, 110, 122, 142, 146f, 149, 225, 82n, 94n, 96n, 182n
Ambrose 298, 23n, 24n, 32n, 99n, 124n
anacoluthon 122, 125, 151
analogy 35, 49, 56f, 61, 136, 27n, 52n, 111n
analysis 9, 13, 15, 17, 27f, 32f, 66, 75, 77, 80, 83, 130, 237, 296, 298, 12n, 15n, 18n, 26n, 27n, 28n, 32n, 83n, 117n, 125n
ancestral spirits 19, 115
anecdote(s) 74, 89, 91, 128, 136, 143, 163, 173, 177, 210
anticipation 99, 106, 130, 133
antithesis (opposition) 46, 57, 28n, 124n
application (of sermon) 17, 31, 39, 49, 52, 55, 60, 62, 65f, 68, 71, 74, 76, 78, 84, 91, 95, 100, 110, 113f, 124, 134, 147, 225f, 228, 231f, 235, 237f, 72n
argument, argumentation 26, 29, 31, 35, 53f, 116, 138, 299, 27n, 50n, 132n, 140n
Aristotle 26f, 297, 27n, 29n, 33n
artistry 41n, 221n
assonance 102, 101n, 168n
attribution 122
audience 13f, 27, 31, 34f, 39, 41, 43, 46, 48f, 53-76, 81-109, 110-180, 220, 225-232, 12n, 14n, 27n, 30n, 55n, 67n, 72n, 81n, 82n, 85n
audience involvement 14, 81, 104, 129, 149, 225
augmentation, augmentative 84, 107, 121, 123, 143, 218,
Augustine 29, 228, 29n, 32n, 81n, 99n, 124n, 130n, 234n, 235n
back-shift 123
Bible 10f, 23f, 25, 35, 51f, 56, 59, 62, 66, 73, 77, 78, 83, 111, 130, 132, 139, 226, 228, 231f, 234, 237, 241-243, 250f, 296, 13n, 16n, 17n
biography 55, 61, 89
Black American (African-American) 72, 105, 125, 133f, 18n, 22n, 55n, 84n, 87n, 101n
borrowing(s) 125, 94n, 196n
call-and-response 132f
calque 125, 128, 185, 196n
case-study 300, 39n, 65n, 234n
celebration, celebratory 13, 63, 72-74, 93, 96, 105, 107, 112, 135, 231, 299, 22n, 29n, 65n, 67n, 70n, 74n, 87n, 99n, 101n, 172n, 185n, 227n
chiasm, chiastic 159, 217, 117n, 122n, 194n, 210n
Chichewa, Chewa (NB--footnote #1, Preface) 11-17, 33, 81, 111, 120, 149f, 228, 231, 253, 300, 12n, 32n, 37n, 41n, 101n, 120n, 124n, 140n, 149n, 152n, 178n, 183n, 186n, 189n
chreia (commonplaces, sayings) 34
Christ 18, 20-22, 24, 30, 34f, 37f, 46f, 52f, 56f, 59f, 62f, 65, 68, 77, 83, 85-91, 99, 102, 106, 109f, 112, 114, 127f, 130, 136, **146f, 157**
Christianity **8, 18, 23**, 44, 53, 89, 95,

301

97, 109, 128, 139, 152, 155, 158, 161, 163, 165f, 181, 189, 229, 240
Chrysostom 91, 298, 29n, 81n, 91n, 96n, 101n, 105n, 124n, 130n, 131n
classical (Greco-Roman) rhetoric 15, 17, 26, 31f, 34, 135, 226, 233, 298, 17n, 24n, 26n, 28n, 31n, 32n, 100n, 180n
climax, climactic 35, 43, 47, 53-55, 60, 72, 78, 100, 106, 107f, 118, 121, 136, 147, 226, 65n, 101n, 112n, 133n
citation 24, 35, 91, 125, 127, 140, 142, 230, 118n
cognitive, cognition 34, 49, 51f, 72, 79, 114f, 130, 142, 148, 225, 238, 99n, 101n, 144n, 214n
colloquial 49, 125, 129, 124n
communal 8, 52, 75, 82, 238, 65n, 211n,
communication 27, 32, 37, 40, 44, 52, 59, 62-64, 70, 88, 95, 102, 106, 130, 133f, 142, 225, 232, 235
complication 72, 74, 79, 105, 70n, 87n
concentration 14, 111, 123, 144, 20n, 126n
condensation, condensed 122f, 129
connotation, connotative double check
context (verbal, situational) 9, 15, 18f, 25, 28, 41, 44, 50, 58, 62, 65f, 68, 70, 76f, 79, 85f, 94, 103, 114f, 125n, 225n
contextualize, contextualization 103, 225, 228, 231f, 65n, 154n, 164n, 194n, 199n, 205n, 215n
contrast, contrastive focus 35, 46, 48, 50, 57, 61, 67, 69, 71, 96, 99, 101, 106, 111, 113, 121f, 136, 140, 148, 228
credibility 27, 29, 35, 88, 102, 149, 225, 55n, 206n

culture 19, 32, 36, 44, 68, 75, 126, 237, 17n, 20n, 28n, 48n, 130n, 236n
deductive, deduction 15, 28, 31, 35f, 38, 44, 48, 50f, 62, 64, 67-76, 141, 148, 226, 230, 234, 31n, 50n,
defamiliarization 117
deliberative 29-31
delivery, dramatic delivery 6, 14, 28, 31-33, 40, 62, 64, 74, 79, 81, 98, 104, 123, 130, 134f, 149, 225, 33n, 81n, 153, 218n
demon(s), demonic 19, 21, 88, 92, 106, 115, 250, 114n, 149n, 172n,
description 6, 12-15, 33, 52, 69, 79, 81, 98, 106, 109, 111, 114f, 117, 126, 140, 147, 149, 225, 20n, 27n, 97n, 99n, 101n, 114n
development 10, 15, 31, 34, 36, 40, 43, 46, 49, 51, 54, 60, 73f, 76, 78, 81-83, 93f, 103, 103, 105, 120f, 142, 148, 149, 194, 223, 225, 233f, 236, 61n, 83n, 101n, 121n, 151n, 179n, 223n, 237n
dialogue(s), dialogic 35, 58, 61, 69, 88, 102, 104, 114, 130, 133, 138, 146f, 225, 234, 236, 17n, 59n, 65n, 102n, 130n-132n, ʾ134n, 170n, 171n, 173n, 196n, 107n , 220n, 221n
diction 82, 124f, 228, 236, 27n, 33n, 124n, 168n, 196n
didactic 42, 44, 63, 88, 97, 148, 230, 237, 63n, 183n
digression (aside) 116, 138, 82n, 126n
diminutive 191
direct speech (discourse) 49, 59, 61, 168, 183,
discourse organization 6, 115, 140, 149, 236
dispositio (discourse arrangement) 26, 31-33
drama, dramatic 6, 14, 16, 39-41, 54, 55, 63, 69, 81, 83, 85, 96, 98, 99, 100-

101, 102, 104f, 111, 121, 123, 129f, 134, 147, 149, 225, 99n, 102n, 114n, 133n, 153n, 170n, 173n, 196n, 204n, 218n, 220n, 236n
dramatize, dramatization 4, 35, 57, 87, 90, 102f, 106f, 110, 122, 138, 145, 33n, 168n, 171n, 180n, 205n, 220n,
dream(s) 92f, 251
dynamic, dynamics 12, 15, 20, 26, 33, 35f, 41, 52, 59, 88, 98, 100, 107, 129, 142, 148, 149, 227, 238, 252, 297, 16n, 99n, 133n, 155n, 180n, 235n
effect (impact and appeal) 85
elaboration (descriptive) 84, 102, 123, 138, 140, 199n
elision, elide 174n
ellipsis 56, 125
elocutio (stylistic composition) 13, 31f
elongation 99, 122, 151
embellishment, embellish 35, 111, 178n, 197n
emic 227, 234, 20n
empathy, empathize 86, 134, 173n
emphasis, emphatic 151, 229, 231, 238, 18n, 23n, 28n, 82n, 83n, 95n, 101n, 116n, 117n, 156n, 169n, 196n, 201n, 239n,
enthymeme(s) 31
enunciation 32, 69, 101
epideictic 29f, 30n, 31n
etic 20, 20n
ethos 27, 28f, 32, 34, 54, 70, 81, 88f, 92, 95, 102, 104, 122, 124, 126, 130, 134, 136, 142, 149, 225f, 232, 28n, 29n, 55n, 88n, 101n, 172n, 177n, 202n, 206n
euphony, euphonous 102
evangelism, evangelistic 9, 10, 14, 16-23, 38, 40, 44, 64, 133, 226f, 229, 245, 246, 81n, 207n, 222n
evocation, evocative 6, 14, 2, 35, 65, 81, *85, 98, 100, 104f, 107, 109, 111, 113-115, 121, 126, 149, 225, 114n
exclamation(s) 43, 60, 93, 121-123, 175, 195, 222, 235, 133n, 155n, 174n
exegesis 25, 66, 72, 228, 234, 65n, 116n, 130n
exhortation 29f, 36, 45, 49, 51, 54, 68, 79f, 74, 76, 78, 84, 100, 107, 111, 114, 121, 132, 138, 142f, 225, 228, 231, 31n, 144n, 225n, 229n
exigence (rhetorical situation) 28, 88
experience, experiential 4, 8, 19, 20, 33, 34f, 39, 42-43, 49, 51-53, 55f, 65, 68-71, 74, 76, 79, 83, 86, 88f, 91-93, 96f, 103, 105, 107, 110f, 114f, 127, 130, 135, 141f, 226, 229, 236-38, 249, 251f
exposition, expository 7, 25, 35f, 54, 65, 67f, 71, 74, 76, 114, 141, 143, 145-147, 225f, 228-234, 238, 81n, 149n, 168n,
figuration, figurative language 6, 14, 56, 81, 89, 115, 124-127, 142, 149, 225, 111n, 114n, 125n, 126n, 149n, 165n, 180n
figure of speech 56, 57, 126
focus (of text, textual) 14, 26f, 31, 35, 51, 54, 64, 71, 76f, 90, 93f, 102, 109, 111, 114, 126, 140, 143, 149-152, 230, 232, 252, 18n, 26n, 28n, 79n, 99n, 126n, 157n, 196n, 220n, 227n, 247n
focusing 23, 85, 115, 1147
folktale (*nthano*) 41f, 59, 69, 86, 94, 135, 221, 94n, 172n, 174n
frame(s), filler-frame 117, 122, 101n, 155n, 176n, 188n
front-shift 122f
function(s) 8, 14f, 21, 26f, 32, 42-43, 59, 65f, 84, 87f, 97, 102f, 107f, 117, 129, 131, 134, 138, 142, 232, 238, 239,

303

299, 14n, 26n-28n, 32n, 41n-43n, 67n, 84n, 94n, 99n, 102n, 111n, 112n, 117n, 138n, 151n, 156n, 174n, 180n, 214n, 221n, 236n
gahena 30, 98, 106, 122, 139, 146, 163, 178, 207, 261f, 268, 285f, 294
gospel 11, 16, 23f, 33, 37f, 40, 51, 56, 59, 64f, 72, 74, 89, 102, 105, 110f, 124, 126, 132, 135, 178, 191, 205, 231, 237, 239, 247, 248, 250, 252, 297, 298, 15n, 23n, 59n, 63n, 65n, 70n, 79n, 207n, 222n, 247n
Holy Spirit 21f, 38, 63, 64f, 72, 158, 184, 212, 244, 18n, 29n, 226n
homiletics, homiletical 6, 9, 13, 15, 17, 20, 33, 62, 66, 71-73, 76, 82f, 93, 104, 106-108, 118, 121, 130, 140, 226f, 230-232, 237, 239, 298, 299, 24n, 26n, 29n, 30n, 32n, 63n, 65n, 81n, 99n, 124n, 130n, 140n, 232n-235n
homily 71, 233, 148n, 149n, 233n
honorific 131, 189, 195, 169n, 92n, 202n
humor, humorous 42, 108, 138, 103n, 108n, 170n, 179n, 180n, 188n, 192n, 196n, 204n, 218n,
hymn(s) 95f, 134f, 146, 175, 216, 53n
hyperbole (exaggeration) 42, 108, 125, 154, 164, 173, 175, 181, 205
hypothetical 57, 131f, 143, 146f, 155, 188, 210, 132n, 162n, 1152n, 163n, 170n, 178n
ideophone(s) 90, 111, 121, 155, 159-161, 163f, 170, 174-177, 181, 190-194, 196-200, 205, 209, 211, 216, 219f, 222, 224, 235, 82n, 114n, 155n
idiom(s), idiomatic, idiomacity 6, 14, 81, 103, 122-129, 149, 159-162, 178, 207, 217, 225, 234, 236, 13n, 25n, 125n, 162n, 168n, 182n, 191n, 196n,

201n, 204n, 217n, 236n
imagery 56, 109f, 122, 127, 147, 32n, 82n, 114n, 124n, 126n, 148n, 168n, 170n, 224n
imagination, imaginative, imaginary 49, 54f, 74, 84, 86, 90, 102f, 110f, 127, 225f, 232, 29n, 52n, 94n, 124n, 170n, 171n, 173n, 177n, 194n
imperative(s) 36, 74, 77, 121f, 142, 228, 58n, 183n, 236n
implicit, implied 23, 45-47, 73, 77, 129, 144, 151, 17n, 32n, 192n, 202n
inductive, induction 6f, 13, 31, 34-37, 39, 44, 48, 50-62, 67-83, 93f, 98, 105, 130, 138, 140-144, 148-149, 226f, 230, 232-235, 297, 39n, 48n, 50n, 53n, 61n, 63n, 65n, 67n, 72n, 76n, 83n, 140n, 144n, 183n
inductive-relational 15, 88, 102, 142, 149, 225, 235, 238
instruction (initiation) 41, 52, 69, 14n, 91n
intensification, intensive, intensified 14, 72, 81, 93, 100f, 106, 115, 121-124, 149, 225, 121n, 144n, 148n
interaction, interactive 14, 19, 40, 43, 49, 73, 74, 95, 130, 132, 134, 143, 148, 225, 238, 12n, 17n, 19n, 28n, 30n, 83n, 130n, 173n, 190n
interjection 122f
interrogative(s) 131f, 23n, 132n
intertextuality, intertextual 94, 118, 119
intratextuality, intratextual 118
intonation 99, 101, 104, 129, 151, 99n, 101n, 119n, 162n, 172n, 179n, 196n, 218n
intuition 34, 50, 73
inventio (invention, topical selection) 26, 31-33, 17n, 28n
irony, ironic 103f, 106, 108, 112, 120, 125, 159, 175, 177, 200, 215, 230,

169n
Jerome 228, 23n, 24n, 32n, 99n, 124n, 235n
Judicial 29f, 30, 52, 170, 30n, 31n, 170n
juxtapose, juxtaposition 83, 121, 91n, 174n
key term(s) 149, 168, 195n
laugh, laughter 43, 106, 109, 112, 136f, 155, 157, 161, 164, 168, 173-175, 180, 181, 188-192, 199, 200, 203, 204f, 210, 218, 222f, 104n, 108n, 155n
loanword(s) 96, 123, 125, 154, 201
logos 27-29, 34, 70, 81, 88f, 97, 100, 102, 108, 120, 122, 126, 130, 142, 149, 225f, 232, 28n, 95n
logical argument 13, 28, 35, 38, 49, 51, 75, 141, 226, 144n
magic 19, 21, 23, 42, 98, 228, 241, 244f, 249f, 155n, 180n
Malawi, Malawian 2-4, 8-14, 18, 80, 89, 114, 125, 144, 179, 241, 246f, 251, 296-298, 12n, 15n, 16n, 18n-20n, 22n-25n, 42n, 43n, 81n-83n, 111n, 134n, 165n, 185n, 191n, 194n, 194n, 199n, 213n, 221n, 228n
medium (of message transmission) 44, 63, 107, 225, 235, 236, 27n, 32n, 120n, 236n
memorable 34, 89, 11, 120, 126, 137, 236
memoria (memory) 31f
metaphor, metaphoric 20, 42, 44, 49, 56, 74, 91, 97, 111, 123, 125-127, 142, 155, 159, 161, 165, 188, 59n, 111n, 118n, 169n, 175n
metonym, metonymic 125, 142, 154, 155, 157f, 161f, 165, 169, 176, 178, 203, 222, 165n, 201n, 212n, 223n
model 6, 15, 39, 40, 42, 62, 69, 72-74, 105, 126, 140, 230, 232, 239,
18n, 3n, 31n, 41n, 67n, 72n, 76n, 130n, 235n
motivation 65, 86, 107, 120, 143, 231, 74n, 194n
move(s), movement 8, 20, 31, 33f, 37, 45, 49, 51, 55, 60, 69-71, 85, 87, 1102, 112, 117, 118, 124, 132, 134, 141-143, 159, 161, 166, 172, 178, 182, 194, 225, 230, 245, 27n, 28n, 29n, 33n, 43n, 58n, 59n, 65n, 72n, 79n, 81n, 87n, 103n, 114n, 133n, 157n, 182n, 210n, 227n, 233n
music, musical 74, 126, 133-135, 236, 245, 101n
mystery 58, 179
mystical powers 85, 92
narrative 6, 14, 35, 40f, 43, 54-56, 59, 61, 77, 81, 83-88, 94, 102, 105, 111, 116, 121, 130, 134, 145, 147, 149, 225f, 296, 17n, 32n, 53n, 83n, 84, 87n, 99n, 144n, 194n, 224n, 227n, 237n
narrative preference 6, 14, 81, 83, 149
non-verbal 52, 94, 96, 232, 33n, 82n, 104n, 114n, 134n
nyau 21, 97, 112, 97n, 180n
oral-aural 28, 33, 40, 44, 59, 61, 225, 232, 235, 76n, 79n, 120n
oral tradition 6, 39, 40f, 44, 54, 56, 62, 69, 94, 120, 148, 238
order 26f, 29, 33, 37f, 42, 44f, 49, 53f, 56f, 59, 61, 63, 68, 71, 74, 76-78, 81-83, 87, 89, 94, 97, 99, 106, 111, 114, 121, 129, 136, 139, 143, 149f, 154, 188, 211, 232f, 234f, 238, 253, 12n, 20n, 23n, 27n, 76n, 83n, 99n, 130n, 140n, 155n, 176n, 179n, 187n, 195n, 210n, 213n
outline 32f, 66f, 71-73, 75f, 78f, 130, 141f, 227, 251, 79n, 149n
parable(s) 41, 86, 127, 300, 86n
paradigmatic 15, 82, 117, 141, 144, 83n, 101n

305

paralinguistic (devices) 99, 129
parallelism(s) 32n, 82n, 99n, 117n, 133n
paraphrase 86, 95, 125, 142, 154, 164, 217
participatory preaching 6, 37, 39
pathos 6, 26-29, 32, 34, 70, 81, 85, 87, 89, 100, 102, 104, 107f, 111, 122f, 126, 130f, 134, 142, 149, 225f, 232, 28n, 29n, 101n, 171n, 201n, 205n
pattern(s), patterning 47-49, 51, 53, 69, 80, 101, 129, 296, 16n, 119n, 133n, 144n, 155n, 162n, 176n, 179n
pause 31, 99f, 101, 129, 133f, 151, 191, 119n, 172n
peak (high point) 55, 78, 100, 121
performance, performative 32, 41, 43, 59, 106, 116, 130, 138, 148, 151, 226, 238f, 298, 14n, 32n, 81n, 99n, 112n, 144n, 151n
personal exemplification 6, 14, 81, 88, 93, 149, 225
personalize, personalization 18, 91f, 94, 11, 82n
personification 125, 161-163, 165, 162n
persuasion 26f, 63, 226, 297, 14n, 26n-28n, 33n, 148n
phatic 138
phonological 14, 33, 99-101, 111, 116, 121, 129, 151, 253, 99n, 167n, 178n
plot 42f, 54f, 72, 154, 194, 195, 212, 186, 194
power encounter 18
pragmatic 14, 46, 99f, 108, 142f, 227, 230, 14n, 26n, 144n
preaching (popular) 10, 13, 118, 25f, 32, 94, 98, 237, 17n32n, 76n, 99n, 236n
prefix(es) 102, 121, 178, 186, 218

problem 22, 37f, 49, 57f, 61, 66, 68f, 72, 74, 76f, 85, 87, 90, 106, 109, 114f, 146, 148, 154, 164f, 226, 228, 229, 234, 237, 238, 27n, 61n, 91n, 114n, 118n, 167n, 178n
progression 34, 45, 49, 53, 89, 105, 141, 143f, 230, 297, 133n, 148n, 210n
pronoun, pronominal 46, 90, 121-123, 189f, 28n, 82n, 152n, 157n, 164n, 170n, 186n, 219n
pronunciatio (oral delivery) 6, 26, 31, 32, 84, 151, 225
prayer(s) 21, 41, 52, 64, 66, 104, 118, 131, 134-136, 145, 166, 169, 184, 203, 183n
proof 32f, 35, 54, 94, 140, 141, 147, 162, 14n, 28n, 65n, 95n, 141n, 168n, 215n
proverb(s) 25, 34, 40, 56, 69, 77, 95, 164, 297, 16n, 165n, 174n, 227n
pun, punning 102, 24n, 165n
puzzle(s) 57, 58, 61, 67, 132, 199, 53n
quotation(s) 54, 59, 50n, 119n162n
radio 53, 151, 227, 236, 299, 14n, 32n, 99n, 117n 120n, 236n
rate (of speaking) 101, 101n
realism, realistic 54, 91, 103, 110, 251, 171n, 173n, 196n, 198n, 203n
recycle, recycling 71, 141, 143, 299, 183n, 209n
refrain(s) 169n
reinforce, reinforcement 13, 35f, 58, 73f, 89, 93, 99, 107, 126, 130, 135, 138, 225, 232, 28n, 67n, 99n, 165n, 194n
reiteration 6, 14, 81, 107, 115-118, 120, 122, 143, 149, 225, 101n, 117n, 144n, 201n
relevance 26, 61f, 73, 102, 126f, 227, 231, 239, 296, 42n, 140n, 231n
repetition 43, 116, 118, 22-123, 125, 151, 297, 81n, 82n, 116, 117n, 133n,

306

148n, 149n, 169n, 179n, 201n, 209n
response (audience) 12, 19, 43, 58, 60, 84, 90, 93, 131-134, 204, 218, 28n, 55n, 65n, 67n, 81n, 104n, 133n, 134n, 155n, 169n, 190n, 209n
retell, retelling 84-86, 114, 120, 145, 147,.84n, 194n
revival, revivalistic 1, 3, 6, 8, 13-15, 17, 22, 29, 33, 73, 81, 89, 92-94, 96-98, 105, 115, 126, 130, 140f, 149, 159, 190, 225-227, 229, 236, 246, 252, 12n, 18n, 19n, 23n, 32n, 81n, 99n, 101n, 114n, 133n, 134n, 152n, 156n, 167n, 183n, 229n, 235n
rhetoric 6, 12, 15, 17, 26, 28, 31-33, 79, 124, 126, 140, 143, 225, 253, 296-298, 13n, 17n, 18n, 24n, 26n-34n, 81n, 99n, 100n, 117n, 124n, 130n, 234n, 235n,
rhetorical question(s) 43, 46, 90, 106, 123, 131, 99n, 155n, 206n
rhetorical strategies 13, 17, 33
rhythm 100f, 298, 24n, 33n, 81n, 99n-101n, 133n, 201n
riddle(s) 40, 43, 58, 69, 95, 53n
role(s) 14, 40, 43, 55, 84, 90, 96, 115, 141, 231, 238, 249, 299, 19n, 29n, 33n, 65, 81n, 101n, 196n, 239n
role-playing 90, 81n
Satan 19-21, 30, 84, 87-90, 92, 95, 97f, 106, 112, 128, 134, 137, 139, 145, 158f, 164, 184, 227, 250f, 257, 261, 272, 20n, 91n, 114n, 250n
Scripture text(s) 24, 44, 65, 111, 156, 231, 118n
Semantic 31, 117, 148, 151, 121n, 142n, 152n, 167n, 192n, 194n
sense(s), sensations 12, 40, 44, 49, 54, 56f, 70, 72, 74f, 86, 92, 95, 106, 109-111, 113, 116f, 129, 140f, 144, 149, 204f, 233, 248, 251, 253, 14n, 17n, 27n, 30n, 103n, 114n, 124n,
158n, 167n-169n, 178n, 186n, 204n
significance 15, 33, 44, 56, 96, 117, 120, 122, 142, 144, 149, 230, 231, 233, 97n, 101n, 144n, 192n, 204n, 236n, 239n
simile 56, 111, 125, 126
song(s) 8, 41, 43, 60, 63, 69, 95, 116, 134f, 138, 161, 179, 180, 297, 17n, 53n, 101n, 111n
sorcery 19, 21, 23, 98, 155, 176, 207, 220, 228, 299, 19n, 155n, 170n, 180n
speech act(s) 151n
spontaneity, spontaneous 38, 43, 60, 90, 104, 133, 225, 134n
story 11, 16, 30, 35, 39, 41-43, 54-57, 60, 61, 69, 83-86, 88, 100, 110f, 115, 117, 137f, 142, 144, 201, 229, 249, 251, 26n, 37n, 41n, 43n, 65n, 81n, 84n, 94n, 96n, 124n, 169n, 172n, 199n, 205n, 212n, 221n, 233n
storytelling 83, 111, 41n,
stress 29, 71, 73, 75, 78, 92, 99f, 122, 125, 151, 251, 17nn, 22n, 48n, 142n, 169n-170n, 179n, 229n
structure 39, 43, 66, 82, 84, 98, 100, 102, 126, 226, 230-231, 28n, 32n, 87n, 133n, 149n, 172n
style, stylistic 1, 3, 9f, 12f, 15, 17, 26f, 30-33, 36, 39, 42f, 46, 48f, 51, 54, 60, 68, 70, 73-75, 79, 81-83, 88, 90, 99f, 102, 104, 107, 110, 114, 116, 118, 124, 125, 133, 142, 149, 206, 225, 227, 230-232, 234f, 239, 297, 299, 14n, 19n, 23n, 24n, 26n, 28n, 31n-33n, 41n, 43n, 53n, 82n-84n, 94n, 99n-101n, 102n, 112n, 116n, 117n, 121n, 124n, 125n, 132n, 133n, 138n, 151n, 155n, 167n, 172n, 201n, 217n, 221n, 226n, 235n, 236n, 239n
stylistic feature(s) (techniques) 13, 15, 31, 116, 23n, 82n, 101n, 155n, 167n
supernatural 43, 52, 54, 98

suspense, suspenseful 43, 54, 58, 105
synecdoche 125, 166, 217
synonymy, synonymous 117, 117n
syntagmatic 141f, 144, 83n
syntax, syntactic 100, 116f, 121-123, 141
tempo 99, 121, 151
testimony 7, 11, 16, 23, 38, 74, 185, 207, 240, 19n, 189n, 206n
thematic image 103
theme 34, 42, 45-47, 49, 53-55, 60, 66-68, 70
theme (-and-parts) 67, 76
topics (*topoi*) 20, 22, 42, 78, 144, 17n, 118n, 20n
tradition(s), traditional 6, 13-15, 18f, 27f, 34, 36, 39-44, 48, 51, 53f, 56, 59, 61f, 69, 81, 84-89, 92-98, 102, 111f, 115, 120, 127, 130, 134f, 138, 140, 145, 148, 149, 179, 225f, 228, 230, 238-240, 245, 299, 12n, 17n-20n, 2n, 41n, 48n, 65n, 81n, 89n, 97n, 100n, 104n, 121n, 134n, 140n, 170n, 172n, 179n, 183n, 211, 227n, 232n
transcription 15, 149f, 253, 12n, 151n, 190n
translation 4, 11f, 15, 29, 125, 129, 149, 151, 234, 253, 296, 298-300, 12n, 13n, 17n, 20n, 56n, 89n, 118n, 125n, 151n, 155n, 167n, 185n, 196n, 201n, 217n, 231n, 235n
TransWorld Radio 12, 18, 14n, 236n
vision(s) 16, 64, 92f, 140, 177, 235, 242, 245, 247, 251, 31n, 63n, 99n, 177n, 209n, 215n
vocabulary 32, 236
vocal modulation 33n, 162n
vocative(s) 90, 121-123, 166n, 174n
volume 99, 101, 121f, 33n, 232n
Warning 99, 103, 107f, 118, 136, 147, 165, 168, 182, 194, 245, 14n, 22n, 101n, 118n, 168n
weep, weeping 86, 106, 123, 174, 206f
wisdom 34f, 40, 42, 56, 64, 94-97, 167, 185, 199-202, 210, 243, 247, 251, 297, 37n, 41n, 183n
witchcraft 19, 21, 23, 98, 115, 122, 127f, 139, 170f, 176, 179-182, 220, 228, 241, 245, 249, 299, 19n, 103n, 170n, 179n, 182n, 250n
Word of God 35, 38, 47, 63, 68, 74, 88, 94, 97, 130, 137 153, 155, 167, 169, 185, 205, 216, 222f, 247, 249-251, 296, 299, 16n, 19n, 28n-31n, 55n, 65n, 82n, 84n, 89n, 96n
wordplay(s) 24, 236

www.ingramcontent.com/pod-product-compliance
Lightning Source LLC
Chambersburg PA
CBHW061430300426
44114CB00014B/1617